Developments in French Politics 3

Developments titles available from Palgrave Macmillan

Alistair Cole, Patrick Le Galès and Jonah Levy (eds)
DEVELOPMENTS IN FRENCH POLITICS 3

Maria Green Cowles and Desmond Dinan (eds)
DEVELOPMENTS IN THE EUROPEAN UNION 2

Patrick Dunleavy, Andrew Gamble, Richard Heffernan and
Gillian Peele (eds)
DEVELOPMENTS IN BRITISH POLITICS 7

Paul Heywood, Erik Jones and Martin Rhodes (eds)
DEVELOPMENTS IN WEST EUROPEAN POLITICS 2

Stephen Padgett, William E. Paterson and Gordon Smith (eds)
DEVELOPMENTS IN GERMAN POLITICS 3*

Gillian Peele, Christopher Bailey, Bruce Cain and B. Guy Peters (eds)
DEVELOPMENTS IN AMERICAN POLITICS 4

Stephen White, Judy Batt and Paul Lewis (eds)
DEVELOPMENTS IN CENTRAL AND EAST EUROPEAN
POLITICS 3*

Stephen White, Richard Sakwa and Zvi Gitelman (eds)
DEVELOPMENTS IN RUSSIAN POLITICS 6*

Of related interest

Ian Holliday, Andrew Gamble and Geraint Parry (eds)
FUNDAMENTALS IN BRITISH POLITICS

If you have any comments or suggestions regarding the above or
other possible *Developments* titles, please write to Steven Kennedy,
Palgrave Macmillan, Houndmills, Basingstoke RG21 6XS, UK or
e-mail s.kennedy@palgrave.com

---

* Rights World excluding North America

Developments in French Politics 3

edited by

Alistair Cole

Patrick Le Galès

and

Jonah Levy

This book is designed as a direct replacement text for *Development in French Politics 2*
edited by Alain Guyomarch, Howard Machin, Peter A. Hall and Jack Hayward (2001)

This edition first published 2005 by
PALGRAVE MACMILLAN
Houndmills, Basingstoke, Hampshire RG21 6XS and
175 Fifth Avenue, New York, N.Y. 10010
Companies and representatives throughout the world

PALGRAVE MACMILLAN is the global academic imprint of the Palgrave
Macmillan division of St. Martin's Press LLC and of Palgrave Macmillan Ltd.
Macmillan® is a registered trademark in the United States, United Kingdom
and other countries. Palgrave is a registered trademark in the European
Union and other countries.

ISBN-13: 978-1-4039-4179-4   hardback
ISBN-10: 1-4039-4179-3   hardback
ISBN-13: 978-1-4039-4180-0   paperback
ISBN-10: 1-4039-4180-7   paperback

This book is printed on paper suitable for recycling and made from fully
managed and sustained forest sources.

A catalogue record for this book is available from the British Library.

Library of Congress Cataloging-in-Publication Data

Developments in French politics 3 / edited by Alistair Cole, Patrick Le Galès, and
Jonah Levy.
     p. cm.
   Includes bibliographical references and index.
   ISBN 1-4039-4179-3 (cloth) – ISBN 1-4039-4180-7 (pbk.)
   1. France–Politics and government–1995- 2. France–Social policy–1995- 3.
France–Foreign relations–1995- I. Title: Developments in French politics three.
II. Cole, Alistair, 1959- III. Le Galès, Patrick IV. Levy, Jonah D.

JN2594.2D482 2005
320.944'09045–dc22   2005043747

10   9   8   7   6   5   4   3   2   1
14 13 12 11 10 09 08 07 06 05

Printed in China

Contents

List of Tables and Figures

Tables

Figures

List of Abbreviations

AFSOUTH	NATO Southern Command Forces
ANEF	Association Nationale d'Etudes Féministes (National Association of Feminist Studies)
ASS	Allocation de Solidarité Spécifique (Soladarity Allowance)
ATTAC	Anti-Globalization Organization
AVFT	Association des Violence Faites contre les Femmes au Travail (Association against Violence against Women at Work)
CADAC	Coalition des Associations pour le Droit de l'Avortement et de la Contraception (Coalition of Associations in favour of the Right to Abortion and Contraception)
CAP	Common Agricultural Policy
CATI	Telephone Survey
CECOP	Electoral Panel
CEDAW	Convention for the Elimination of Discrimination Against Women
CERES	Centre de Recherches et d'Etudes Socialistes (Centre for Socialist Research and Studies)
CES	Conseil Economique et Social (Economic and Social Council)
CEVIPOF	Centre d'Etudes de la Vie Politique Française (Centre for the Study of French Political Life)
CFDT	Confédération Française Démocratique du Travail (French Democratic Labour Confederation)
CFSP	Common Foreign and Security Policy
CGT	Confédération Générale du Travail (General Labour Confederation)
CIDSP	Electoral Panel
CMU	Couverture Maladie Universelle (Universal Illness Cover)
CNAL	Commission Nationale de l'Action Laïque (National Committee for Lay Action)
CNAM	Caisse Nationale de l'Assurance Maladie (National Health Insurance Council)
CNCDH	Commission Nationale Consultative de Droits de l'Homme (National Consultative Commission on the Rights of Man)
CNDF	Collectif National des Droits des Femmes (National Committee for the Rights of Women)
CNE	Commission Nationale d'Evaluation (National Evaluation Commission)

CNOSF	Comité National Olympique et Sportif Français (French National Olympic Sports Committee)
CNPF	Conseil National du Patronat Français (National Council of Franch Employers)
CODAC	Commission for Access to Equality
COREPER	Comité des Représentants Permanents (Committee of Permanent Representatives)
CPNT	Chasse, Pêche, Nature et Tradition (Hunting, Fishing, Nature, Tradition)
CSA	Survey Institute
DARES	Direction de l'Animation de la Recherche, des Etudes et de Statistiques (Research and Statistics Division)
DDA	Direction Départementale de l'Agriculture (Agriculture Ministry's Field Service)
DDASS	Direction Départementale des Affaires Sociales et Sanitaires (Social and Health Affairs Ministry's Field Service)
DDE	Direction Départementale d'Equipment (Infrastructure Ministry's Field Service)
DEP	Direction des Etudes et de Prévision (Education Ministry's Research and Forecasting Division)
DESCO	Direction de l'Enseignement Scolaire (Education Ministry's Schools Division)
DGSE	Direction Génerale de la Sécurité Extérieure (foreign intelligence agency)
DIWAN	Breton – Medium Schools Association
DL	Démocratie Libérale (Liberal Democrary)
DLC	Droite Libérale et Chrétienne (Liberal and Christian Right)
DRM	Direction du Renseignement Militaire (Military Intelligence)
EADS	European Aeronautic Defence and Space
ECB	European Central Bank
EC	European Commission
EDF	Electricité de France
EDSI	European Defence and Security Identity
EMS	European Monetary System
EMU	European Monetary Union
ENA	Ecole Nationale d'Administration (National Administration School)
ENVEFF	Enquête Nationale sur les Violences Envers les Femmes en France (National Survey into Violence against Women in France)
EIRO	European Industrial Relations Observatory
EPCI	Établissements Publics de Cooperation Intercommunal (Intercommunal Organizations)

ERASMUS	EU-funded Student Exchange Scheme
ERDF	European Regional Development Fund
EU	European Union
EUROMEFOR	Force Maritime Européenne (European Maritime Force)
EUROFOR	Euroforce Opérationelle Rapide (European Integrated Force Structures for Air, Land and Sea)
FEN	Fédération de l'Éducation Nationale (National Education Federation)
FN	Front National
FNPE	Fédération Nationale des Parents d'Elèves (Federation of School Parents)
FO	Force Ouvrière (Workers' Force)
FSU	Fédération des Syndicats Unifiés (Unified Trade Union Federation)
FRS	Forum des Républicains Sociaux (Forum of Social Republicans)
GATT	General Agreement on Trades and Tariffs
GDP	Gross Domestic Product
GMO	Genetically Modified Organism
HCI	Haut Conseil à l'Intégration (High Council for Integration)
IMF	International Monetary Fund
ISF	Impôt de Solidarité sur la Fortune (Solidarity Wealth Tax)
INSEE	Institut National de la Statistique et des Études Economiques (National Institute for Statistics and Economic Research)
IPSOS	Survey Institute
IUT	Institut Universitaire de Technologie (University Technology Institute)
JHA	Justice and Home Affairs
LCR	Ligue Communiste Révolutionnaire (Revolutionary Communist League)
LDH	Ligue des Droits de l'Homme (League for the Rights of Man)
LMD	Licence–Mastère–Doctorat (Bachelors–Masters–Doctorate)
LO	Lutte Ouvrière (Workers' Struggle)
LOLF	Loi Organique du 1er Août 2001 Relative aux Lois de Finance (Organic Law of 2001 Setting Out a New Budgetary Procedure)
MDC	Mouvement des Citoyens (Citizens' Movement)
MEDF	Mouvement des Entreprises de France (French Employers' Association)
MEP	Member of the European Parliament
MPF	Mouvement pour la France (Movement for France)

MNR	Mouvement National Républicain (National Republican Movement)
MRAP	Anti-Racist Organization
MRC	Mouvement Républicain et Citoyen (Citizens' Republican Movement)
MSF	Médecins sans Frontières (Doctors without Borders)
NATO (OTAN)	North Atlantic Treaty Organization
NIMBY	'Not in My Back Yard'
NPM	New Public Management
NSM	New Social Movement
OECD (OCDE)	Organisation for Economic and Co-operation and Development?
PACA	Provence–Alpes–Côtes d'Azur
PARE	Plan d'Aide au Retour à l'Emploi (Welfare to Work Scheme)
PCF	Parti Communiste français (French Communist Party)
PEJ	Programme Emploi Jeunes (Youth Employment Plan)
PERP	Plan d'Epargne Retraite Populaire (Popular Savings and Retirement Plan)
PRDF	Plan Regional du Développement et de Formation des Jeunes (Regional Youth Training Plans)
PS	Parti Socialiste (Socialist Party)
PTA	Rarent–Teacher Association
RMI	Revenu Minimum d'Insertion (Minimal Income Programme)
RP	Permanent Representation
RPF	Rassemblement pour la France (Rally for France)
RPR	Rassemblement pour la République (Rally for the Republic)
SCALP	Anti-Racist Group
SCGI	Secrétariat Général du Comité Interministeriel pour les Questions de Coopération Economique Européenne (General Office for Co-ordinating Ministerial Policies towards the European Union)
SMEs	Small and Medium-Sized Enterprises
SMIC	Salaire Minimum (Minimum Wage)
SNES	Syndicat National des Enseignants Secondaires (Secondary Teachers' Union)
SOFRES	Survey Institute
SOS-Racisme	Anti-Racist Group
SUD	Trade Union
TRACE	Youth Employment and Training Programme
UDF	Union pour la Démocratie Française (Union for French Democracy)

UFCS	Union Féminine Civique et Sociale (Women's Civic and Social Union)
UFR	Unité de Formation et de la Recherche (University Department)
UMP	Union pour une Majorité Présidentielle (since 2002 Union pour une Majorité Populaire) (Union for a Popular Majority)
UNAPEL	Union Nationale des Associations de Parents d'élèves de l'Enseignement Libre (National Union of 'Free' School Parents Associations)
UNR	Union pour la Nouvelle République (Union for the New Republic)
UNSA	Union National des Syndicats Autonomes (National Association of Autonomous Unions)
WMDs	Weapons of Mass Destruction
ZEPs	Zones d'Education Prioritaire (Priority Education Zone)
ZUPs	Zone Urbune Prioritaire (Urban Priority Zone)

Notes on the Contributors

Andrew Appleton is Associate Professor in the Department of Political Science at Washington State University, US. He has published widely on new social movements and political parties in France and is co-editor (with Robert Elgie) of the journal *French Politics*.

Alistair Cole is Professor of European Politics in the School of European Studies at Cardiff University. He has published extensively on France and Comparative European politics and policy. His most recent book is *French Politics and Society* (London: Prentice-Hall, 2005, 2nd edition) He is preparing a monograph entitled *Governing and Governance in France* to be published by Cambridge University Press in 2008.

Sophie Duchesne is a CNRS research fellow based at the CEVIPOF, Institute of Political Studies, Paris. She is also currently at the Maison Française and the Department of Politics and International Relations, Oxford. She has published widely on issues of citizenship and identity in France and Europe, themes she develops notably in her monograph *Citoyenneté à la française* (Paris: Presses de Sciences Po, 1997).

Robert Elgie is Professor of Politics in the School of Law and Government at Dublin City University, Ireland. He has published extensively in the field of French and comparative politics. His most recent book is *Political Institutions in Contemporary France* (Oxford: OUP, 2003). He is co-editor (with Andrew Appleton) of the journal *French Politics*.

Jocelyn Evans is Senior Lecturer in Politics at the European Studies Research Institute, University of Salford. He has published extensively in the area of political parties and electoral behaviour within (and beyond) France. His most recent book is *Voters and Voting: an Introduction* (London: Sage, 2004).

Virginie Guiraudon is a Marie Curie Professor at the European University Institute, Florence and a CNRS Research Fellow at the CERAPS, University of Lille 2. She has published widely in the area of immigration politics and policies, with recent articles in *West European Politics* (2004) and the *Journal of European Public Policy* (2003).

Florence Haegel is CNRS Director of Research at the CEVIPOF in the Institute of Political Studies, Paris. She is the author of numerous publications on French political parties, with recent articles appearing in the *Revue Française de Science Politique* (2002) and *French Politics* (2004).

John Keiger is Professor of International History and Director of the European Studies Research Institute at the University of Salford. He has published widely in the field of the history of French foreign policy. Recent works include his monograph on *France and the World since 1870* (Oxford: OUP, 2001).

Andrew Knapp is Senior Lecturer in French Studies at the University of Reading. Amongst his numerous books on French politics are (with Vincent Wright) *The Government and Politics of France* (London: Routledge, 2001, 4th edition) and *Parties and Party Systems* (Palgrave: 2004).

Patrick Le Galès is CNRS Director of Research at the CEVIPOF and Professor of Politics and Sociology at the Institute of Political Studies, Paris. He has published extensively in French and English in the field of governance and public policy. His most recent works include the edited book (with Pierre Lascoumes as co-editor) *Gouverner par les Instruments* (Paris: Presses de Sciences Po, 2005) and the monograph *European Cities* (Oxford, OUP, 2002)

Jonah Levy is Professor of European Politics in the Department of Political Science at the University of California – Berkeley, USA. He has published widely in the field of French and comparative economic and welfare policy. Amongst his numerous works are the monograph on *Tocqueville's Revenge: State, Society and Economy in Contemporary France* (Cambridge, MA: Harvard University Press)

Nonna Mayer is CNRS Director of Research at the CEVIPOF in the Institute of Political Studies, Paris. She has published extensively on political parties (especially the Front National), and on elections and electoral behaviour in France. Recent works include *Ces Français qui votent Le Pen* (Paris: Flammarion, 2002) and the edited collection (with Bruno Cautrès) *Le nouveau désordre électoral. Les leçons du 21 avril 2002* (Paris: Presses de Sciences Po, 2004).

Amy Mazur is Professor in the Department of Political Science at Washington State University. Her books include: *Comparative State Feminism* (Sage, 1995) (editor, with Dorothy McBride); *Gender Bias and the State: Symbolic Reform at Work in Fifth Republic France* (Pittsburgh University Press, 1995) and *Theorizing Feminist Policy* (Oxford, OUP, 2002). She has also published articles in leading journals such as *Political Research Quarterly*, *West European Politics* and the *European Journal of Political Research*.

Andy Smith is FNSP Senior Research Fellow at the Institute of Political Studies in Bordeaux. He has published extensively in the field of comparative public policy and Europeanization. His most recent books are the monograph on *Le Gouvernement de l'Union européenne* (Paris: LGDJ, 2004) and (with Claude Sorbets) *Le leadership politique et le territoire: les cadres d'analyse et de débat* (Rennes: Presses Universitaires de Rennes, 2003).

Lille
NORD-PAS-DE-CALAIS

HAUTE-
NORMANDIE
Amiens
PICARDIE

Rouen
Reims
Metz
ALSACE

Caen
LORRAINE

BASSE-NORMANDIE
Paris
Strasbourg

ILE DE FRANCE
CHAMPAGNE
ARDENNE

BRETAGNE
Rennes

PAYS DE LA LOIRE
Orleans
Besançon

Nantes
CENTRE
Dijon

BOURGOGNE
FRANCHE-COMTE

Poitiers

POITOU-CHARENTES
Limoges
Clermont-
Lyone

LIMOUSIN
Ferrand
RHONE-ALPES

Bordeaux
AUVERGNE

AQUITAINE

MIDI-PYRENEES
Montpellier

Toulouse
LANGUEDOC-ROUSSILLON
PROVENCE-ALPES-COTE D'AZUR

Marseilles

CORSE

Ajaccio

⊚   Regional prefecture

——   Regional boundaries

Map 1   France: regions and main towns

Chapter 1

Introduction: The Shifting Politics of the Fifth Republic

JONAH LEVY, ALISTAIR COLE AND PATRICK LE GALÈS

On 21 April 2002, France experienced a political earthquake. Instead of the widely expected run-off between Gaullist President Jacques Chirac and Socialist Prime Minister Lionel Jospin, the first round of presidential balloting placed the Far-Right, xenophobic leader of the National Front, Jean-Marie Le Pen, in second position. With this shocking development, Jospin was evicted from the presidential run-off, Chirac was assured a triumphant re-election, and observers of French politics were left to try to make sense of it all.

It would be easy to dismiss the events of 21 April as a fluke, the political equivalent of a perfect storm. Leftist voters deserted Jospin on the first round of presidential voting (or didn't vote at all) because pollsters and pundits had given no indication that Jospin was in jeopardy. Had Leftist supporters known that Jospin risked failing to qualify for the run-off against Chirac, they would have voted for him. Similarly, had the French Left contented itself with two Trotskyist candidates for president instead of three, or had the former Socialist, Jean-Pierre Chevènement, not thrown his hat in the ring as well, Jospin would have almost certainly outpolled Le Pen.

The fact remains that France's historic political families were each challenged on 21st April: Communists, Socialists, Gaullists, Liberals, Christian Democrats, even Greens. None of their candidates performed as well as expected, and many electors were dissatisfied with all of the mainstream choices. The strong performance of the Far-Left and Far-Right candidates, the high abstention rate, and the general dispersion of votes to candidates not generally considered to be genuine presidential contenders (such as St Josse, Chevènement and the Trotskyists) were all part of this trend. Chirac and Jospin, the anticipated second-round contenders, obtained barely one third of the votes and one quarter of the registered electors between them.

The 21 April balloting was not a bolt from the blue. Rather, it was the continuation of five long-standing trends in French voting behaviour.

1

Several of these trends are discussed at greater length in the chapters by Haegel, Knapp, and Evans and Mayer in this volume. The first electoral trend is a repudiation of incumbent governments. If the initial twenty years of the Fifth Republic were marked by uninterrupted conservative governance, since 1981, the outgoing prime minister has been defeated in seven consecutive national elections (1981 presidential and legislative, 1986 legislative, 1988 presidential and legislative, 1993 legislative, 1995 presidential, 1997 legislative, 2002 presidential and legislative). Jospin's ouster was certainly in line with recent history.

The second electoral trend is the decline of the *quadrille bipolaire*, the four main political parties – Gaullists and UDF (Union pour la Démocratie française) on the right; PS (Parti Socialiste) and PCF (Parti Communiste française) on the left – that have governed France for nearly 50 years. Whereas the *quadrille bipolaire* captured almost 94 per cent of the vote in 1981, by 2002, its share had slipped to just 65 per cent. A third, related trend has been the multiplication of small parties – from Trotskyists and Greens on the left to xenophobes and conservative Catholics on the Right – as French voters search for alternatives to the political mainstream. This fragmentation of the party system culminated in the 2002 presidential election, when 16 candidates vied for France's highest office. The 2002 election also confirmed a fourth trend, the growing indifference of the French electorate, as abstention reached its highest level ever for a presidential campaign, 28.7 per cent, an increase of nearly 7 per cent over the 1995 election.

The fifth trend, the most notorious no doubt, has been the breakthrough and persistence of a Far-Right, xenophobic political movement, of dubious democratic principles – the *Front National* of Jean-Marie Le Pen. The FN first burst onto the French political scene in 1983. Since then, despite internal quarrels and external condemnations, Le Pen's movement has remained a fixture of the French political landscape, receiving a steady 10 to 15 per cent of the vote in election after election. In recent years, the FN has been especially successful in courting the 'losers' of modernization and economic adjustment, who feel abandoned by the mainstream parties, including their erstwhile defenders on the left. The FN has become the number one party among the growing French underclass of vulnerable blue-collar workers and the unemployed. In the second round of the 2002 presidential election, industrial workers (33 per cent) gave Le Pen more support than any other socio-professional group, highlighting the popular bases of the Le Pen electorate and the degree of working-class alienation from the Republic. If Le Pen's 16.86 per cent of vote on 21 April 2002 represented a personal best, however, it was not significantly beyond what the party has polled in a number of elections.

Taken together, these five electoral trends – rejection of incumbents, decline of the *quadrille bipolaire*, party fragmentation, increasing abstention and the persistence of a powerful radical Right – attest to a growing disjuncture between France's governing parties and the electorate. There has been significant erosion of party identification and of party capacity to mobilize voters to support official party candidates. The April 2002 election was an extreme manifestation of French electoral trends, but not a departure from them.

Voter discontent in France, as in many European countries, has been fuelled by poor economic performance. Unemployment has ranged from 8.5 to 13 per cent over the past decade, and the figure is considerably higher among youths, those with limited education and ethnic minorities. But the roots of voter malaise run deeper than the economic indicators. French politics has long revolved around a statist Republican model. Over the past twenty years, however, essential parts of this model have been eroded and repudiated. The problem is that no clear alternative has emerged in the place of the traditional model. As a result, French politics often appears rudderless, lacking a coherent discourse and direction. It is not that the French refuse to change, but rather that the change is halting, hidden, inconsistent and poorly articulated. In this climate, French voters feel disoriented, upset or abandoned, and the April 2002 election was a clear expression of their wrath.

The French republican model: a political construction

As Serge Berstein (1999) demonstrates, French Republicanism is a plural object. Different versions of Republicanism have been in the ascendancy at distinct stages of French history: conservative Republicanism, progressive Republicanism, bourgeois Republicanism. When we consider French Republicanism, we are necessarily constructing an abstraction. The revolutionary Republicanism of the Jacobins during the French Revolution had little in common with the conservative Republicanism of the founding fathers of the Third Republic. During the Third and Fourth Republics, Republicanism was defined primarily in terms of parliamentary sovereignty. During the Fifth Republic it has become synonymous in political terms with would-be providential leaders in the office of president.

We must also distinguish between Republicanism as an overt political project and as a more diffuse societal norm. Debates since the 1980s have revolved around Republicanism in France as a political construction. The rise of Left-Republicanism (of the Chevènement variety) coincided with the decline in Socialist discourse of breaking with capitalism following the 1983 economic U-turn. Political Republicanism of the Left and the Right was defeated in the 2002 electoral series, but there remains a strong constituency disoriented by the failure of the traditional Left. There is also an underlying strand of French pragmatism. Rather opportunistic political practices can be cloaked in the gabarit of Republicanism. So well has the

Fifth Republic assimilated Republicanism that we tend now to forget that the creation of the Fifth Republic in 1958 challenged the traditional French Republican model in several important respects. By introducing a strong presidency, it ignored the Republican fear of strong leaders. By placing formal limitations upon parliamentary sovereignty, the 1958 Constitution consigned the revolutionary doctrine of the sovereign assembly to the dustbin of history.

In this introductory chapter, we use the phrase 'Republican model' as shorthand for a set of practices and beliefs that draw their inspiration from a combination of the ethos of the Third Republic, the Jacobin, nationalist spirit of the French Revolution, and the philosophy of Charles de Gaulle. The Republican ideology, which is analysed in the concluding chapter by Duchesne, has four main elements. The first is an unmediated relationship between the citizen and the state. In the Republican conception, all citizens are created equal and are members of a national political community. They owe their allegiance to the nation as a whole, rather than to ethnic or interest groups. From the Republican perspective, intermediary associations are bearers of particularistic agendas and pose a threat to national identity and cohesion. This spirit is exemplified by the Revolution's Le Chapelier Laws of 1791 that banned most intermediary associations. This belief has militated against the development of identity-based movements. The lesbian and gay movement, the women's movement, even environmental groups have all found it more difficult to operate in France than elsewhere. This universalist concept of citizenship also explains the desire by French elites to assimilate minority ethnic groups into mainstream French culture. Equality is a formal principle of the French Republican tradition, rather than a substantive outcome. Underpinning the Republican model is an ideal of formal equality, rather than equity, of equality of opportunity, rather than equality of outcomes. In practice, the French Republic has been more pragmatic and accommodating. There has been a long tradition of imposing formal rules, but accepting exceptions to rules. While formal rules stress uniformity, exceptions to rules have allowed a state-centric polity to adapt to territorial, social and religious pressures.

The second dimension of the Republican model is enlightenment through education in secular public schools. The Third Republic established a free, universal, public educational system as a way of combating the influence of the Catholic Church, a key supporter of the anti-democratic camp. Free public education would offer opportunities for upward social mobility, but more importantly, would liberate the minds of French citizens from clerical domination. Public schools are also the primary vehicle for transmitting French values and culture to successive generations. If the French political community is open to all, regardless of ethnicity or origin, central to becoming 'French' is socialization into French values through a secular, uniform, public school system. While public schools are seen to embody Republican citizenship, ever since the Debré law of 1959, there has been a *de facto* compromise between Church and State. Church schools now 'contract' with the state, and their staff are on the public payroll.

A third element of the Republican model is the belief in a special vocation for France on the international stage. Beginning with the French Revolution, the French have seen themselves as the bearers of universal values, notably democracy and the rights of man, and have sought to export these values and other aspects of French culture the world over. France is no ordinary country, but rather the repository of unique genius and eternal principles. It is the duty of every politician – a duty embraced most enthusiastically by de Gaulle – to spread the French cultural *patrimoine* and uphold French political principles, even if these actions cause conflicts with France's allies, such as the United States.

The fourth, related element of the Republican model is a 'strong', activist state. The state is seen as the bearer of the general will, over and above the partial wills of interest groups and local authorities. The Republican ideal concentrates power in the central state, and the state's missions are more than a match for its capacities. Critical state responsibilities include: modernizing the economy; educating the population, transmitting French norms and culture to successive generations and children of immigrants; providing opportunities for social mobility; transcending class conflict and assuring social cohesion; and projecting French values and influence throughout the world. As the Republic was for long a fragile edifice, menaced by counter-revolution and clerical reaction, universalism developed a defensive character. Equality was interpreted as uniformity, to be safeguarded by an interventionist state that had the duty to enforce written rules.

Challenges to the republican model

The Gaullist version of the Republican model is an ideal-type. It reached its apogee under the Gaullist regime in the 1960s. The Fifth Republic concentrated power in the presidency, and de Gaulle wielded this power aggressively to modernize France at home and expand its influence abroad. Since the late 1960s, however, a number of developments have conspired to weaken and, in some cases, overturn critical components of the Gaullist Republican model. De Gaulle himself fell victim to the first development, expressed through the near-revolution of May 1968 – a French society that has become more sophisticated, active, open and heterogeneous, hence less willing to embrace a uniform, top–down approach to politics and policy. A second development, a series of decentralization reforms, has expanded the opportunities for diverse local communities to pursue their own direction, thereby fragmenting the previously uniform policy-making system.

Other challenges to the Republican model have emerged from outside France's borders. European integration has shifted key powers from Paris to Brussels and from states to markets. Globalization has narrowed the economic leverage and autonomy of French technocrats. And the end of the Cold War has expanded German influence within Europe and American influence beyond, threatening to marginalize France as an international player. Taken together, these developments have made the French state considerably less able to pursue the Republican project both because its powers are more circumscribed and because its values are more contested. Europeanization and globalization appear to challenge many traditional French public policy preferences. They go against the grain of *une certaine idée de la France*, the belief in the universal mission of French civilization, as the European construction becomes a melting pot of European cultural influences, rather than a mirror to reflect French grandeur or a policy space to regulate world capitalism.

Developments in French politics cannot be studied in isolation from economic and social trends. So it is with the crisis of the Republican model. Since 1980 the Republican model has appeared increasingly unable to deliver on its core promise of rising living standards and upward social mobility. French social scientists point to the growing problems of French society: surging inequality and poverty (over 5 million people below the poverty line); stubbornly high unemployment (still around 10 per cent); the lack of innovation and investment in higher education and research; a shortage of job opportunities for young people; growing crime, fear, and insecurity; the difficult integration of immigrant populations, particularly North Africans (including the so-called 'second generation' born in France); pressures on public services and the incapacity to negotiate changes; the marginalization of the working class, isolated in the grim housing projects of the suburbs, far away from services and collective infrastructures. Other observers are more optimistic. They emphasize the relatively successful adaptation of the French economy to globalization, a high level of social protection and quality of life, decentralization reforms that have provided more flexibility within the once-centralized political system, and a revival of associational activity.

Both perspectives are partially correct. They reveal the tensions at play within French society. The middle classes and white-collar workers have fared relatively well since 1980, increasing both earnings and leisure time. By contrast, production workers and lower-level service employees, who still represent the backbone of the French social structure, have struggled. *La France d'en-bas* faces more uncertainty in the labour market (expansion of flexible, part-time working contracts), diminished retirement pensions and health benefits, growing difficulties finding decent housing, and not much hope of their children climbing the social ladder. Even the spread of educational opportunities has failed to translate to social and economic advancement. Although 62 per cent of the current generation now reaches the *baccalauréat*, i.e. the final high school exam before university level, the impact on social mobility has been modest, at best. One of the most enduring problems of French society has been the reproduction of social inequalities through the educational system, as the children of the upper-middle classes continue to dominate the most sought-after educational positions in the *grandes écoles*. The combination of a stratified educational system and diminished job prospects for low-skilled workers means that the social escalator has slowed or stalled for large segments of the French population. Although the language of class has vanished, there are indicators of the remaking of a large employees/working class group, which is losing ground in relative – and sometimes absolute – terms.

These simmering social problems are particularly crucial to analysing the resistance to change within French society. The increased flexibility of the labour market and accompanying economic insecurity have generated considerable stress and alienation. French society has become more competitive, hence the crystallization of conflicts around the social security system, pensions and public services. These conflicts reveal not just the conservatism of some public-sector trade unions, but also a growing sense of insecurity and distrust of elite strategies among large swathes of the French population. The demand for protection by the state is related to this sentiment. Public spending in France exceeds 50 per cent of GDP, a level comparable to that of Nordic European countries, and some 10 percentage points higher than the British figure.

The chapters in this volume examine the difficult transformation of France's Republican model, against a backdrop of growing social anxiety and uncertainty, focusing on developments under the Chirac presidency. French authorities have made significant changes, especially in areas where international pressures are felt most intensely, such as economic policy and foreign affairs. That said, faced with an anxious and antagonized population, ready to protest both through the ballot box and in the streets, successive governments have proceeded with great caution, and policy reversals have been quite common. Moreover, dismantling the old order has proven easier than creating the new. French authorities have often balked at incorporating new ideas that challenge traditional Republican understandings. They have also hesitated to move towards a new kind of politics – a politics marked by negotiation, consultation and cooperation with independent centres of power (local governments, European agencies, interest groups, new social movements), as opposed to unilateral state imposition.

Adapting the Republican model

The years since 1980 have seen three significant adjustments in French politics. The first is the adaptation of policy to a changed international environment. As the chapter on economic policy by Levy shows, French authorities have responded to heightened international competition by jettisoning a dysfunctional, *dirigiste*, industrial policy model. At the same time, they have created new policies, notably in the social and labour market arenas, to help smooth the movement toward a more market-based political economy. Although this 'social anesthesia' strategy has proven expensive, and further economic and social reforms are needed, France's economy has become modern, competitive and export-oriented.

The chapter by Keiger shows that France's foreign and defence policy has likewise adapted to a changed international environment. In the postwar period, France's military strategy was oriented toward resisting a possible Soviet invasion through a mass conscription army and, if necessary, nuclear weapons (the *force de frappe*). With the end of the Cold War, these military assets were devalued, and France found itself lacking the capacity to respond to new threats from terrorists, rogue states and ethnic groups, including within Europe itself. In response, the Chirac administration eliminated compulsory military service, shifting to a professional army, and scaled back the *force de frappe*, redirecting resources into more sophisticated military technology. Chirac has also sought to move away from de Gaulle's unilateralist tradition, expanding military cooperation with European allies and flirting with reintegration into the military command of NATO.

The second important shift in French politics has been the modernization of the state. The chapter by Le Galès describes a series of reforms designed to enhance the efficiency and coordination of the French state, most notably the 2001 overhaul of the budget procedure, the *Loi Organique relative aux Lois de Finance* (LOLF). In addition, state authorities have sought to bolster the capacities of local governments and to design processes for managing a more fragmented political environment. The new Article 1 of the French constitution, which declares that 'The organization of the Republic is decentralized', epitomizes the change.

The chapter by Cole tells a similar tale of state modernization, focusing on the domain of education policy. French authorities have invested massively in upgrading the educational opportunities and skills of the population. In 1984, the government announced the goal of increasing the percentage of students taking the *baccalauréat* exam from 34 per cent to 80 per cent; the figure today is approaching 70 per cent. The number of students enrolled in some kind of post-secondary education or training has also doubled, reaching roughly 50 per cent. Alongside this expansion of the educational system, French officials have sought to streamline the functioning of the traditionally hyper-centralized and bureaucratized ministry of education. The number of central divisions has been reduced; responsibilities have been shifted downward, giving localities and individual schools more autonomy; and expectations have been made explicit through management by objectives and widespread contracting, thereby facilitating accountability. As in the case of decentralization, education policy has been marked by efforts to move from top–down state control to more light-handed forms of coordination, and a key component of effective steering is the ability to work with autonomous local actors, who bring significant financial and administrative resources to the table.

The chapters by Elgie and Knapp touch on another critical dimension of state modernization, the operation of the dual executive system, that is of a political system in which the president and prime minister share power. The dual executive was devised by the founders of the Fifth Republic to strengthen the president, who possesses the power to dissolve parliament and call new elections, whereas parliament can only sanction the prime minister. The prime minister was expected to serve as a kind of buffer, keeping the president above the fray of day-to-day policy-making. The dual executive functioned as intended as long as the Gaullists dominated the political system. Once the electoral context tightened in the 1970s, however, the dual executive evolved into a dual threat to the government. With parliamentary and presidential elections usually held in different years, there were essentially twice as many opportunities to change the government as there were under a pure parliamentary system: either by electing a parliament hostile to the president, which would produce cohabitation, with leadership passing to the prime minister, or by electing a president hostile to the parliament, which would induce the president to dissolve parliament and appeal to the electorate for a majority to support him. The result of frequent, high-stakes elections – particularly in an era in which incumbents have been defeated regularly – has been to shorten the time horizons of French governments. Fearing for their electoral lives, French governments have often shied away from controversial reforms. French authorities finally addressed the dual executive/dual election problem in 2000, via a constitutional reform that shortened the president's term from seven years to five years, the same duration as the parliamentary mandate. By aligning the two electoral cycles, these constitutional changes have given French governments the luxury of time. Because both the presidential and parliamentary elections were held in 2002, the second Chirac administration was the first government since 1980 to confront a clear, five-year horizon without having to face national elections. Thanks to the alignment of presidential and parliamentary mandates, such clear horizons will become the norm, rather than the exception.

Knapp's chapter describes another dimension of state modernization – the spread of judicial review and accountability. Once-insular state authorities must now conform to the rule of law. Their legislation is subject to review by the constitutional council, a procedure that has become more frequent since a 1974 reform enabled 60 deputies or senators to refer constitutional questions to the council. The Constitutional Council has struck down laws on both nationalization and privatization; in 2004, it compelled the government to revisit its reform of the regional electoral laws. State authorities are also being held accountable on a personal level. The ability of governments to stymie judicial inquiries has clearly declined, and corruption scandals have led to the ouster and, in some cases, jail terms for a number of cabinet ministers, the mayors of Lyon, Nice and Grenoble, and former prime minister and RPR leader, Alain Juppé. It is true that many powerful figures, notably President Chirac, have escaped trial, but it is equally clear that age of impunity for the French ruling class is over.

The third new development in French politics has been a somewhat more open attitude towards the needs of disadvantaged groups, notably immigrants and women. Traditionally, group-based claims have been viewed with disfavour under the Republican ethos, as fomenting ethnic particularism and threatening the principle of equal treatment of all citizens. In the case of immigrants, government reluctance has been bolstered by the fear of losing votes to the *Front National*. Yet, as Guiraudon describes in her chapter, French authorities have found a way round these constraints through a 'politics of stealth' that buries integration policies within territorial policies. Government policies to assist disadvantaged urban areas (*politique de la ville*) or educational communities (ZEPs) have provided significant benefits to immigrants, who are heavily over-represented in these communities. Likewise, youth employment measures (such as the *emplois-jeunes* programme introduced by the Jospin Government) have enrolled large numbers of disadvantaged immigrants and French-born children of immigrants.

Changes in policies toward a second disadvantaged group, women, have been even more dramatic, as Mazur's chapter relates, especially in recent years. The list of recent reforms includes: the easing of access to abortion services, with minors no longer needing permission from their parents and with the elimination of a pre-abortion counselling requirement; expanded corporate obligations to report on female representation within the workforce; the creation of a parental leave for fathers, designed to increase male involvement in child-rearing; a new law against sexual harassment in the workplace; and a law and constitutional amendment to promote 'parity', that is greater female representation, in elected offices at both the national and local levels. Gender equality remains elusive in a polity marked by a traditional, Latin, Catholic culture and by Republican reluctance to acknowledge group differences. Still, the proliferation of legislative reforms has led Mazur to suggest that France has experienced a 'sea change in the way gender equality issues are discussed and addressed in public policy'.

These various dimensions add up to substantive change. Though the rules stress formal equality, in practice the case for equity has been made increasingly strongly. French pragmatism counterbalances the Republican rhetoric. In his chapter, Cole evokes the role of positive discrimination in education and urban policy. Targeting resources to the most unfavourable neighbourhoods is an important feature of the ZEP programme, the *contrats de villes*, and the social cohesion programme made public in June

2004 by Raffarin's Minister of Social Affairs, Jean-Louis Borloo. These cross-cutting issues have been very important for integrating minority communities.

The limits of reform

France has clearly experienced fundamental, far-ranging change. Yet this change has been primarily negative. In a number of areas, French authorities have been quite effective at dismantling the old, but have very little sense of how to construct the new. As a result, policy lacks an anchor or clear direction. At times, French authorities seem to be moving towards a new kind of politics, more pluralistic and partnership-based, while on other occasions they appear to be trying to resurrect elements of the traditional Republican model. The result is policies that are confusing and contradictory, leaving French citizens without a sense of where their leaders are taking them.

The economic and social reforms described in the chapter by Levy offer a good illustration of the confusion and hesitation among French policymakers. The *dirigiste* model has been repudiated, and the Anglo-American neoliberal model is rejected, but two negatives do not make a positive. Thus, France finds itself in a kind of economic halfway house. French authorities seem to have enacted just enough liberalizing reform to spread insecurity among the working (or would-be working) population, yet not enough reform to fully revitalize business and relaunch job creation. French companies, especially small- and medium-sized enterprises (SMEs), complain of burdensome regulations and taxes that make it difficult to expand and hire. At the same time, French authorities have provided just enough social protection to weigh down the balance sheets and hiring decisions of employers, but not enough to make citizens feel genuinely protected. The problem of social exclusion continues to grow, especially among minorities and those with limited education. Moreover, a cash-strapped French state appears increasingly unable to respond to the cries of pain from society's losers: the long-term unemployed, marginalized youths and the residents of the troubled *banlieues*.

Keiger's analysis of French military and foreign policy notes a similar confusion and disorientation. Officially, France is moving from a mass conscription army and the *force de frappe* to a rapidly deployable, high-tech, professional army. Yet France has not kept up with the latest military technologies, which appear increasingly unaffordable for a medium-sized country. The Chirac administration initially sought a rapprochement with the United States, including rejoining the NATO military command, but with the second Gulf War, appears to have returned to a more critical perspective (admittedly, aided by the blunders and boorish behaviour of the Bush administration). Thus, it is unclear what kind of relationship France seeks with the world's only superpower. Finally, France has long championed a common European military and foreign policy, yet its heavy-handed efforts to impose a common opposition to the Iraq War and disdainful treatment of accession countries – famously told by Chirac that they had 'missed an opportunity to keep quiet' when they voiced support for invasion – has left Europe more divided than ever on foreign policy. Fundamentally, Keiger notes, France appears to have lost its sense of mission in the world. French foreign policy has shifted from championing universal French values to resisting US hegemony and defending particularistic values. The affirmation of a 'French alternative' has given way to the defence of 'French exceptionalism'.

The lack of a positive vision or roadmap for where France should be going is perhaps most striking in Smith's chapter on the Europeanization of French politics. Smith notes that a range of policies is increasingly determined in Brussels. Yet French political discourse continues to operate as if the French state were making policy unilaterally. To the extent that France has a European agenda, it is a negative one of resisting further integration. The Chirac administration openly flouted its refusal to adhere to the European Stability Pact, and France is regularly among the laggards in translating EU directives into national law.

This pattern of halfway, halting and contradictory reform applies not just to specific *policies*, but also to the character of French *governance*. On the one hand, French authorities acknowledge that the state can no longer do everything. On the other hand, they remain exceedingly reluctant to share power with autonomous actors and, in many instances, undercut the very partners whom they claim to need. France's stance toward Europe – pro-European in theory, recalcitrant in practice – is but one example. Another is centre–periphery relations. As the chapter by Le Galès reveals, the Jacobin model of state domination has been broken. Decentralization reforms, the creation of autonomous, democratically elected local institutions, mean that Paris can no longer dictate to the provinces. That said, Paris is not always the ally of the provinces. Promising initiatives, such as the 1999 Chevènement law that greatly improved intercommunal cooperation, co-exist with predatory practices, such as efforts to offload the state's fiscal and labour problems on local governments through the transfer of unfunded mandates. Such predatory practices are especially prevalent in education, as Cole describes. In education, Paris has devolved the construction and maintenance of schools – extracting as much funding as possible from the localities – while jealously guarding control over curriculum and staffing. Overall, Le Galès characterizes the process of decentralization as 'messy' and incoherent, and state authorities do not seem to know what they really want.

State authorities also remain reluctant to share power with voluntary associations. As the chapter by Appleton relates, the French are joining organizations in record numbers. There has been a proliferation of associations and new social movements speaking to critical issues, from globalization, to the environment, to social exclusion. Yet these organizations tend to operate in the political wilderness, unconnected to French policy-makers. French civil society has advanced more than state authorities are willing or able to recognize.

State ambivalence is no less pronounced with regard to traditional associations, such as employers and trade unions. In the past decade, a number of European countries in Western Europe have reformed their labour markets and systems of social protection through processes of tripartite negotiation, a strategy sometimes called 'competitive corporatism' (Rhodes, 2001). As Levy describes, France appeared to be developing such an approach under the employer-initiated *refondation sociale*. Despite some initial successes, notably a reform of the unemployment system, the *refondation sociale* ultimately stalled. On the Left, the Jospin government opposed what it saw as a Right-wing agenda and threat to state authority, while on the right, the Chirac government (supported by the employers) privileged a strategy of legislation over *consultation* as the best means to achieve its objectives. In the process, an opportunity to invest in a new partnership and a new kind of politics was missed.

State authorities are also having difficulty adapting to a more pluralistic and heterogeneous society. As Duchesne, Guiraudon and Mazur show, the myth of Republican equality has presented a formidable obstacle to policies designed to help those who are substantively disadvantaged. In the case of women, according to Mazur, that obstacle seems to be finally breaking down, as a number of reforms have been enacted in the past few years. The treatment of immigrants is more ambiguous. Governments have enacted some social and labour-market policies to help immigrants and their children, but Guiraudon notes that these reforms have occurred only through a 'politics of stealth' that hides the true intention of state policy. Moreover, alongside these concessions, state and local authorities have been extremely resistant to any public displays of faith by France's sizeable Muslim community: blocking the construction of mosques; not recognizing Islamic religious institutions until quite recently; and most importantly, passing a law barring the wearing of 'ostentatious religious symbols' in public schools, a reform clearly aimed at headscarves worn by Muslim girls. As Duchesne observes, the headscarf affair attests to an enduring resistance to pluralism, where diversity is seen as threatening Republican egalitarianism and equality is confused with uniformity.

Much the same could be said of opposition to greater autonomy and diversity among French universities. As Cole relates, the French educational establishment – teachers, unions and Ministry of Education functionaries – has balked at reforms that would allow universities greater latitude in setting standards for admission and curriculum. From a Republican perspective, such reforms would undermine the cherished principles of uniform, equal education for all French citizens. Once again, Republican egalitarianism trumps pluralism.

The lack of openness of the French political system to the voices of voluntary associations and new social movements is especially visible in the party arena. The chapter by Haegel demonstrates that one of the major reasons for the proliferation of new political parties is that the established parties have failed to address emerging issues in French society. New issues or cleavages have generated new political parties, as opposed to adjustments among existing political parties. Opposition to immigration begat the *Front National* and later Bruno Mégret's *Mouvement National Républicain* (MNR). Resistance to European integration and concerns about national sovereignty fuelled Chevènement's *Mouvement des Citoyens* (MDC), later renamed the *Mouvement Républicain et Citoyen* (MRC), Philippe de Villier's *Mouvement pour la France* (MPF), Charles Pasqua's *Rassemblement pour la France* (RPF), and Jean Saint-Josse's *Chasse Pêche, Nature et Tradition* (CPNT). These issues also provided an opening for the FN and for long-marginal Trotskyist parties. Debates about the uses of nature spawned the formation of several green parties on the Left and Saint-Josse's CNPT on the right. Finally, the battle between individual autonomy and traditional, Catholic morality underpinned the emergence of the Greens on the Left and de Villier's MPF, Christine Boutin's *Forum des Républicains Sociaux* (FRS), and Charles Millon's *Droite Libérale et Chrétienne* (DLC) on the Right. Millon's movement originated equally from the question of how to respond to the FN, when Millon negotiated an alliance to secure his position as president of the Rhône-Alpes region. Whatever the virtues of the particular positions taken by these new political parties – and many of them are contestable – it is clear that the established political parties have failed to convince the electorate that they are responding to emerging concerns and challenges.

Responding to rejection

French politics in the new millennium is characterized by a shift beyond the original framework established by the Gaullist regime for the Fifth Republic. The original French Republican model is undergoing serious revisions, but French elites have not been entirely honest about these changes. Although large firms have successfully reorganized to become competitive on global markets, though industrial SMEs are becoming innovative and dynamic, and though the governance of the economy took a liberal turn in the 1980s, the French political debate seems to ignore these changes. The hidden secret of the French state, i.e. that it has lost some of its capacity to control the economy, remained unspoken. When then-Prime Minister Jospin acknowledged on television that the state could not do everything and that firms had their own logic, he was stigmatized as a traitor to the Republican state and to the Left.

The same is true for Europe. On the one hand, French elites present themselves as the leading 'motor of Europe' with Germany at a time when, first, France has been losing ground in terms of influence within the EU Commission and Parliament, and secondly, the French political debate seems to be isolated from the EU. Except during the referendum on the Maastricht Treaty in 1992, and at times during European elections, French politics has not taken notice of the impact of accelerated EU integration. French political leaders kept instrumentalizing the EU to make reforms in France, while blaming the EU for all unfortunate consequences. French members of the European Parliament remained well known for their lack of interest, and French political parties scarcely notice what is going on in Strasbourg or Brussels, even among their own appointees.

In other words, French politics has been for a decade or so characterized by a remarkable level of schizophrenia. France has become significantly more open, but politics has epitomized the fear of change and the temptation to remain closed to external forces: immigrants, large firms, foreign culture, EU laws, etc. On the one hand, France has become Europeanized and internationalized. Interest groups, mayors and organizations have developed horizontal and vertical transnational networks. EU norms and rules are increasingly structuring public policy. On the other hand, politics remains shaped by classic oppositions, and public and elite opinion massively support preserving or expanding the role of the state, increasing welfare expenditures, and maintaining public services unchanged – in short, pretending that nothing has really changed in French politics and policy-making.

The same schizophrenia applies to globalization (Berger, 2001). Over the last ten years, France has run steady trade surpluses. The country has been very successful in attracting foreign investment (second to Britain within the EU), which has played a major role in modernizing some sectors of the economy and supporting the development of regional economies. State *dirigisme* has been more or less abolished. Nevertheless politicians and citizens still blame globalization for destroying French jobs. They speak as if all roads lead to Paris, and the role of the state is to keep the French economy free of foreign influence.

France has been subjected to intense pressures for change since the late 1970s. As a leading European nation with a particular state tradition and historical legacy, endogenous and exogenous pressures have challenged the traditional French model at least as much as in any comparable country. French politics and public policy-making has become far less introspective. Still, there is much evidence of French resistance to unwelcome external ideas, such as 'neoliberalism'. There are also deep obstacles to reform from entrenched domestic interests, as illustrated during the Jospin government by the difficulty in implementing policy reforms in the education or fiscal administrations. The referential frames of public service and equality remain very potent barriers to domestic political change.

Each European nation has interpreted pressures in accordance with its own traditions, but these traditions have gradually been reinterpreted to take account of new realities. In the case of France, the distance travelled is far, especially in macro-economic policy. The highly distinctive nature of the original model has made the ideological effort of legitimation more difficult. As Schmidt (1997) argues, there has been a failure to develop an accompanying discourse to legitimize changes. French authorities have been forced to rely on discursive tools developed at various pivotal points in French history (equality and the general will from the French Revolution, *laicité* from the clerical–Republican conflicts of the nineteenth century, modernization from the period of postwar social and economic reconstruction). None of these has equipped French governments particularly well to respond to the challenges of the third millennium.

The 21 April 2002 ballot was a slap in the face, a rejection of the French political establishment, including the eventual winner of the election, Jacques Chirac. Chirac's score of 19.88 per cent was the lowest of any incumbent president, not to mention any Gaullist presidential candidate, in the history of the Fifth Republic. What is more, the French electorate continues to punish incumbents. In 2004, the Right was trounced in both regional and European Parliament elections.

The rejection of the political establishment cannot be reduced to policy mishaps or the personal inadequacies of Chirac and Jospin. Rather, it reflects a more fundamental crisis. The statist, Jacobin, uniform, Republican model is breaking apart. Yet French politicians remain unsure what to insert in its place. The result is a halting and contradictory movement without a coherent narrative – a messy combination of three steps forward, two steps backward, and quite a few steps in no particular direction at all.

There are signs that France may be gradually moving towards a different kind of politics. Within the realm of policies, transnational norms, EU ones in particular, are starting to modify the classic Republican model. In politics, a new generation of leaders is appearing, breaking the classic mould of the Fifth Republic. On the Right, beyond Chirac, the Gaullist tradition is disappearing. Valéry Giscard d'Estaing, once a promising young politician in the early 1960s and president between 1974 and 1981, is at last retiring (after drafting the EU constitution). Jacques Chirac, the president, who also started his career in the 1960s, is now 72 and nearing the end of his political career. The new strong man of the Right, Nicolas Sarkozy, now chairman of the UMP (Union pour une Majorité Presidentielle), the main Centre-Right party, does not look back to the past and the grand role of France. Sarkozy looks instead towards the US, Spain and the UK, not Germany. He brings in new ideas about the role of the market, religion, multiculturalism, and law and order. On the Left, the Communist party is being effectively supplanted by the Greens as the second party behind the Socialists. Socialist leaders are now escaping the legacy of Mitterrand, opponent of de Gaulle in the 1960s and president from 1981 to 1995. After the retirement of Jospin and the decreasing influence of Fabius (both started as Mitterrand protégés in the early 1970s), the new Socialist leader François Hollande is closer to the legacy of Jacques Delors, and more European.

Responding effectively to the rejection of April 2002 will require not just new political faces, however, but new developments in French politics. Four political needs stand out. The first is a set of policies, probably negotiated with the social partners, to lay the foundation for renewed economic growth and social integration. The second is a coherent vision for where France is going: the kind of market economy that it is building, its strategy for Europe, its relationship with the United States, its place for immigrants and their children, its approach to changing norms and social values. The third requirement is openness to the increasing diversity and maturity of French society, in which the kinds of recent efforts to address the problems of women described by Mazur become the rule, rather than the exception. Fourth and finally, France will need a new kind of politics – a politics that treats the French as adults, that draws on the ideas and initiatives of society, and that shares power with societal and local actors, both established and new. How well France moves along these four dimensions will determine whether 21 April 2002 goes down in history as a salutary warning to French elites, the springboard for successful adaptation, or a missed opportunity and foretaste of far worse things to come.

Chapter 2

Parties and Organizations

FLORENCE HAEGEL

One major recent study of the French party system concludes that France is a 'disconnected democracy' (Knapp, 2004). The virtual absence of mass organizations and the influence of *notables* have become routine observations in the study of French parties. Essential political functions such as mobilization, interest aggregation, the organization of political competition, feedback, public management and political recruitment are poorly performed within the French system. The extent to which parties penetrate society, or their weakness on the ground is notorious. We will address these issues of party functionality in the second half of this chapter. We begin, however, with an overview of the structure of the French party system, focusing upon its recent evolution in the light of the 2002 electoral series. The debate about structure captures one important dimension of the study of French parties as gauged by the importance of the literature. The first part of this chapter examines recent transformations in the structure of the party system, focusing on interpreting the party splits that occurred prior to 2002 and the power struggles within the Left and the Right since 2002. In the second part, we assess the level of penetration French parties have in society by examining party ties among the electorate and the level and forms of party attachment. Our aim, as well as surveying current developments in French parties, is to contribute to broader academic debates about parties and the party system in France.

The structure of the French party system

A number of specialists have referred to the French party system as a bipolar multiparty system with two dominant parties, one of the Left and one of the Right (Evans, 2003; Knapp, 2004). This appreciation needs to be placed in historical context, as we can observe a number of distinct stages in the evolution of the party system in the Fifth Republic. The structure of the party system has been influenced by distinct phases of French history. Following the confusion and uncertainty surrounding the establishment and consolidation of the Fifth Republic, the French party system gradually adapted to the Fifth Republic's institutions. Bipolar coalition formation was strongly influenced by the combined effects of two-ballot majority voting and the presidentialization of the system of government. Political variables were also important: the party system was rationalized under the impetus of the powerful Gaullist party and the reaction of existing players to Gaullist ascendancy. The emergence of the Gaullist UNR (*Union pour la Nouvelle République*) as a federating force of the French Right in the 1960s forced the parties of the non-Gaullist Centre and the Left to react in order to survive. Valéry Giscard d'Estaing's election as president in 1974 signalled the end of Gaullist hegemony. From 1974 to 1981, the centre of gravity within the Right-wing coalition shifted away from the Gaullists. Developments on the Left in some ways paralleled those on the Right. The decade of the 1970s was primarily important for rebalancing the French Left. The once dominant Communist Party was brought down to size by Mitterrand's Socialist Party, which established its lasting ascendancy in 1981.

The 1978 election is usually presented as representing the highpoint of bipolar multipartism in the Fifth Republic. The structure of the party system in 1978 was that of a bipolar quadrille (*quadrille bipolaire*). Four parties of roughly equal political strength divided voter preferences evenly between Left and Right coalitions. These parties were the French Communist Party (*Parti Communiste Français*: PCF) and Socialist Party (*Parti Socialiste*: PS) on the left, the Rally for the Republic (*Rassemblement pour la République*: the RPR) and Union for French Democracy (*Union pour la Démocratie Française*: UDF) on the right (Table 2.1).

Since the mid-1980s, the neat symmetry of the party system in 1978 has given way to a more complex and asymmetrical pattern. There has been an increase in the number and a change in the nature of parties and the issues processed through the political system. The bipolar contours of the French party system have also been challenged by the emergence of new political issues, such as those of immigration, security and the environment. The *quadrille bipolaire* has been undermined by a set of interrelated developments that have occasioned a new debate on the structure of the party system in France. The Socialist Party established its lasting ascendancy on the Left in 1981. Even during the dark days of 1993, the PS was the central party within the Left and is very likely to remain so. In the 1980s, the French system also saw the emergence of new parties, the Greens (*les Verts*) and the National Front (*Front National*: FN). These two new parties, each representing specific issues (environmental and immigration issues respectively) and organized along the libertarian/authoritarian cleavage, put bipolarization under strain, challenging the Left/Right cleavage and defying established alliances. The Greens nevertheless joined a Left-wing coalition in 1995, while on the Right, despite some resistance and a few localized exceptions, the official line of rejecting any alliance with the FN was upheld.

Table 2.1   *The party system before 1995*

Party	Creation date	Creation context	Creation type	Ideological position
PCF	1920	Tours Congress Association with the Communist International	Socialist movement split: the majority becomes communist	Communist Left
PS	1971	Epinay Congress Reform undertaken after losing the 1969 presidential election	Reform of the SFIO (founded in 1905) by merging Left-wing clubs and organizations	Socialist Left
Verts	1984	Perspective of European elections	Merger of environmentalist movements	Libertarian/ environmentalist
RPR	1976	Context of strong competition on the Right marked by Jacques Chirac resigning as Valéry Giscard d'Estaing's Prime Minister	Transformation of the UDR	Gaullist Right
UDF	1978	Legislative elections, support for President Giscard d'Estaing	Confederation of non-Gaullist Right-wing organizations	Non-Gaullist Right
FN	1972	Perspective of 1973 legislative elections	Merger of Extreme Right movements	Extreme Right

Key:

▨ Bipolar quadrille that prevailed in the late 1970s

☐ Parties emerging on the election scene in the 1980s

We will now present an account of party fragmentation prior to 2002, bringing to light the factors explaining this process, before focusing our attention on the party system since 2002.

The logic of party fragmentation

At the end of the 1990s, the French party system underwent a series of splits (Table 2.2). In this section, we will briefly describe these splits, and gauge to what extent party fragmentation was due to ideological divisions (as argued by the party realignment hypothesis). We will then take a look at the

Table 2.2 *Party fragmentation prior to 2002*

New parties	Creation date	Context	Creation type	Ideological position
MDC/MRC J.-P. Chevènement	1993	Gulf War Maastricht Treaty	Internal creation Split within a current of the PS	Republican Left: Defence of the nation state
MPF P. de Villiers	1994	European election	Internal creation Split of the UDF	Conservative Right Moral order/ Catholic base, sovereignism
RPF C.Pasqua P. de Villiers	1999	European election	Internal creation Merger of the MPF and C. Pasqua's followers (withdrawal from the RPR)	Conservative Right Sovereignism
The right/ DLC C.Millon	1998	Election of regional council presidents (FN support in the Rhône-Alpes)	Internal creation Split of the UDF	Conservative Right Moral order/ Catholic base
DL A. Madelin	1998	Consequence of the regional elections, debate over an alliance with the FN	Internal creation Split of a component of the UDF	Liberal Right
FRS C. Boutin	2002	Presidential election	Internal creation Split of the UDF	Conservative Right Moral order/ Catholic base
MNR B. Mégret	1999	European election	Internal creation Split of the FN	Extreme Right
CPNT J. Saint Josse	1989	European Commission action against French hunting legislation 1989 European elections	External creation Split within the network of hunting associations	Defence of rural way of life, anti-European

institutional and organizational factors that must be taken into account in any explanation of party divisions.

The transformation of factions into parties was one of main developments of the 1990s. On the left, the internal faction within the PS known first under the CERES label, then as *Socialisme et République*, headed by Jean-Pierre Chevènement, struck out on its own with the creation of the

Citizens' Movement (*Mouvement des Citoyens*: MDC) in December 1993. The MDC was later re-christened the Citizens and Republican Movement (*Mouvement Républicain et Citoyen*: MRC). On the Right, splits occurred in succession. In 1994, the Movement for France (*Mouvement Pour la France*: MPF) was created by Philippe de Villiers, a former UDF deputy. This organization joined forces with Charles Pasqua, former interior minister under Jacques Chirac and Edouard Balladur, who had assumed a voice, then an exit rationale with respect to the RPR. Together they formed a 'sovereignist' slate embodying the defence of national unity in the 1999 European elections. After their success (this slate garnered 13.1 per cent of the vote, causing an upset on the Right by pulling ahead of the official Right-wing list), they formed the Rally for France (*Rassemblement pour la France*: RPF). Following the 1998 regional elections and former UDF member Charles Millon's decision to accept FN support in order to keep the Rhône-Alpes region, he founded The Right (*La Droite*), a new organization which in 1999 became the Liberal and Christian Right (*Droite Libérale et Chrétienne*: DLC). Still on the right, the Republican Party (*Parti Républicain*: PR) the liberal-leaning main component of the UDF, in turn struck out on its own to form the Liberal Democratic Movement (Démocratie Libérale: DL). The UDF, once a confederation of parties, became the new UDF under the leadership of François Bayrou. It was rebuilt on the bases of its Christian democrat wing but primarily gave itself a centrist label. Last, in the Catholic and social right current, Christine Boutin (former UDF) founded the Forum of Social Republicans (*Forum des Républicains Sociaux*: FRS) so she could run in the 2002 presidential election. The split of the extreme right and the creation in January 1999 of the National Republican Movement (*Mouvement National Républicain*: MNR) by Bruno Mégret, former right-hand man of Jean-Marie Le Pen, is part of the same logic of fragmentation. Another new organization also emerged on the electoral scene called Hunting, Fishing, Nature and Tradition (*Chasse, Pêche, Nature et Tradition*: CPNT), founded in 1989 out of a hunters' protest against European directives and environmentalist associations (Traïni, 2003). The first success at the polls for the CNPT came in the 1998 regional elections and the 1999 European elections, its candidate making a respectable showing as well in the 2002 presidential election.

The party realignment hypothesis holds that these parties reflect new ideological divides. We will argue that party realignment is not enough to explain the phenomenon of fragmentation and that institutional and organizational factors must also be taken into account. There is no perfect overlap of political parties and ideological divisions. By describing the various splits and defections, however, clues emerge that allow us to identify the ideological lines of fracture at work. The first cleavage pertains to the issue of Europe. With the rise of the MDC, MPF, RPF and CPNT, a series of Eurosceptical organizations took a stand to reaffirm the primacy of the nation-state. With the exception of the MDC, the existence of the other three parties (to a lesser extent the CPNT, since it drew activists from both Right-wing and Left-wing parties) can only be understood by taking into account the fact that the French Right officially took a pro-European stance. Tensions were especially acute within the former RPR, where a pro-European stance was imposed by the leadership, in contradiction with the position of a wide swathe of the membership.

The second cleavage brings into play the moral order/permissiveness dimension and, through it, adhesion to traditional Catholic values. Philippe de Villiers' MPF is particularly well-established in the conservative and Catholic Vendée region. Charles Millon's *Droite Libérale et Chrétienne* is closely linked to the most traditional of Catholic circles and associations, as is the organization started by Christine Boutin. The creation of these parties is an unquestionable affirmation of a religious cleavage displaying a Catholic reaction to changing positions with regard to moral and ethical questions (such as homosexual rights, family values, or the inclusion of Christian values in the future European constitution). The third important cleavage is expressed with regard to environmental issues and the uses of nature. This cleavage highlights the significance of the urban/rural fracture. It is particularly well illustrated by the founding of the CPNT, defending the rural way of life and associated customs against an environmentalist movement that has developed primarily in an urban setting.

However, even if the party splits that occurred prior to 2002 do reflect social and ideological tensions seeking a voice through party action, the French party system clearly has trouble translating social and ideological cleavages into real party differences. This difficulty can be seen in the lack of structure and short lifespan of these small organizations. But it also arises from the lack of fit between party lines and social and ideological antagonisms. A quantitative analysis of the social and ideological profiles of sympathizers of the various French parties conducted in 2002 (Chiche, Haegel and Tiberj, 2002) thus showed that sociological and ideological differences did indeed exist within both the Left and the Right, but they were not faithfully reflected in the existing party organizations. In any event, ideological differences are not enough to justify party fragmentation in the two camps. In other words, an interpretation of party fragmentation must bring into play other explanatory factors as well as ideological ones. In particular, we emphasize the importance of explanations that are both institutional (the rules of the game) and organizational (the new rules for party financing), as well as explanations that focus upon competition within each party.

One institutional factor is, of course, the presidential structure of opportunities and the political careerism pursued by parties and party politicians (Duhamel and Grunberg, 2001). In the French party system, running for president is a way for minor politicians to assert themselves and gain an audience. Moreover, party rules for selecting presidential candidates sometimes condemn a challenger within a party to make a tactical withdrawal and to stand under a different ticket. The inversion of the election calendar in 2002 (the presidential election held prior to legislative election) forced parties to field a presidential candidate if they hoped to exist – even in legislative elections. This is why, in the 2002 presidential election, sixteen candidates were in the running, standing for established or newly founded parties.

As regards institutional factors, the issue of party financing also comes into play. The multiparty system is too well established in France to explain the French propensity for creating new parties solely by the financial advantage provided by the new public financing law passed in 1988, all the more so since party creations or splits generally occur in the context of secondary elections held by proportional representation, which are not eligible for public financing (mainly European elections). Nevertheless, financial objectives do enter into account in new organizations that decide to field candidates in the legislative elections in an attempt to become a player in the very heart of the French party system. In fact, at the same time legislation was passed putting a cap on campaign spending and setting conditions for reimbursing expenditure, the law of 1988 set up a system of public financing. Originally, public aid was attributed proportionally to parliamentary representation. At first it substantiated the cartelization hypothesis, holding that party competition is reduced through agreements reached between dominant parties and favoured established parties by making it difficult for new groups or small groups to emerge. The legislation was subsequently changed (in 1990 and 1995) in an attempt to reach a delicate balance between protecting small parties and avoiding dispersion or undue public financial support for overly territorialized or opportunistic pseudo-parties. Today the public allocation to parties is divided into two equal parts: half is distributed according to votes garnered in the first ballot of legislative elections; the other half is distributed according to the number of deputies. Fielding a candidate in the legislative elections thus becomes a means of raising funds. For instance, since the funding scheme of the CPNT, made particularly opaque by the semi-public status of large hunting associations, has been under investigation, this movement's leaders have decided to strengthen their involvement in legislative elections to take advantage of the public allocations they are now entitled to by law. The effect of the French model of public financing on the cartelization of the system is therefore debatable.

Organizational factors related to the competition within each party are also relevant to explain party fragmentation. For instance, the choice of Jean-Pierre Chevènement, previously leader of a faction within the Socialist Party, to form his own party can be explained in part by the gradual marginalization of his group within the PS (Verrier, 1999). Similarly, the repeated splits the UDF underwent in the late 1990s can only be understood with reference to the organizational changes that affected the confederation during this period. Last, the split of the extreme right in 1999 also reflects an organizational rationale. True, strategic considerations (the issue of an alliance with the Right) were at the crux of the MNR breakaway, but in fact ideological differences between the FN and the MNR are scarcely visible and the mass walkout was due to the autocratic ways of the FN, characterized by Jean-Marie Le Pen's control over party careers and the predominance of a patriarchal and familial party model and the thwarting of individual ambitions that flow from it.

The 2002 reform put to the test

Following the shock of Jean-Marie Le Pen's qualifying to run in the second ballot of the 2002 presidential election, the logic of party fragmentation was reversed. The 2002 legislative elections marked a reaffirmation of bipolarization and the existence of two dominant parties, the PS and the newly founded Union for a Presidential Majority (*Union pour une Majorité Présidentielle*: UMP). This domination was expressed not only in the parliamentary sphere but is also evident from a financial standpoint: only the PS and the UMP emerged from the 2002 electoral series without a serious deficit. PS domination was affirmed in the 2004 regional and European elections, even though these elections were held according to a partially proportional representation system, and the network of alliances (PCF, PS, *Verts*) on the whole remained intact. The Trotskyite organizations, Workers Struggle (*Lutte Ouvrière*: LO) and the Revolutionary Communist League (*Ligue Communiste Révolutionnaire*: LCR), which achieved remarkable scores in the first ballot of the 2002 presidential, stayed away from this coalition and opted for joint LO LCR slates in the regional and European elections. These parties are anti-system parties in Sartori's sense, in other words parties that exclude themselves from parliamentary and government coalitions (Sartori, 1976).

Even if the idea of grouping the left into a single party, discussed when the UMP was created in 2002, no longer seems on the agenda given the dismal example shown on the Right, the question of organizing the plural forces of the Left remains relevant. There has been some convergence of the sociological and ideological universes of the three leading Left-wing governmental parties (PCF, PS and Greens) (Boy *et al.*, 2003). For their membership, these parties all draw from the same pool, mainly public sector employees. According to surveys conducted in 1998, public sector employees (representing 30 per cent of the French working population) made up 70 per cent of PCF members, 59 per cent of PS members and 70 per cent of the membership of the Greens. The other point of convergence among members of the plural Left parties is the fact that it is an ageing population. The evolution is particularly striking among the Greens, who are generally thought to be in the younger age brackets: from 1989 to 1999 their average age rose from 39 to 47. The generational issue points to a weakness in left-wing governmental parties that leaves a window open for competing organizations. Moreover, both from an electoral and an activist standpoint, the renewal of the Trotskyite LCR largely drew on the mobilization of a young population (students and employees).

Last, converging trends within the Left also result from a transformation of the Greens. The shedding of the isolationist strategy and the choice of an alliance with the PS and their participation in government from 1997 to 2002 deeply affected the Greens, since these changes came along with a doubling of party membership. This increase not only raised questions of internal organization, particularly salient for the Greens, but also modified the makeup of the organization. Half the members joined a party rooted on the Left that had opted for a classic strategy of electoral alliance and of winning positions in parliament and the government. These members, who generally approved this strategy, were positioned in 1999 more on the Left than members in 1989, and their specificity as regards environmental issues was diluted. They are less likely to belong to environmental associations and today are less concerned than before with environmental issues and more in tune with social issues.

The situation is newer and more uncertain still on the Right due to the founding of the UMP (Haegel 2002; 2004). The UMP was created following the first ballot of the 2002 presidential election by merger of the RPR, DL and a segment of the UDF, to which a number of Right-wing associations and clubs added their support. Several individual memberships came from splinter parties. Another segment of the UDF, minus a number of elected officials and headed by François Bayrou, rejected the merger and asserted its autonomy. The creation of the UMP as a single unified party in November 2002 was truly a reformation marked by a change of name (it was relabelled *Union pour une Majorité Populaire*) and involving a new form of legitimation: the clearly asserted European orientation once and for all supplanted the reference to Gaullism. Despite obvious ex-RPR

Table 2.3   *The electoral balance of power in the 2002 and 2004 elections*

	LO/LCR	PCF	PS	Verts	UDF	UMP	FN
1st ballot 2002 presidential	10.1	3.4	15.8	5.3	6.9	19.4	17.2
1st ballot 2002 legislatives	2.8	5.1	24.3	4.5	4.7	32.2	11.4
2004 Europeans	2.5	5.2	28.9	7.4	11.9	16.6	9.8

Note: Regional outcomes are not presented as the variety of the party offer depending on the region, particularly on the Left, makes it extremely difficult to establish statistics on a national level.

domination in terms of membership, organization and leadership, it also brought with it a shift in the distribution of power. It has been weakened both by the conviction of its president, Alain Juppé, in a trial over the Paris City Hall's financing of jobs benefiting the ex-RPR and by defeats at the polls. It has failed in its ambition of unifying the entire Right, the UDF's electoral resilience foiling this plan. In the 2004 regional elections, in the 16 regions in which the UDF and the UMP ran against one another, the UDF won 11.9 per cent, the UMP, 23.3 per cent. In the European elections, the UDF took 11.95 per cent of the vote, the UMP 16.6 per cent, and sovereignist lists 7.3 per cent. But great caution must be used in assessing the balance of power between the two Right-wing groups (Sauger, 2004). The regional and European elections have two specific features. These elections do not rely primarily on a local foothold and thus on a network of elected officials. As intermediary elections, they are an ideal opportunity to express a protest vote, giving voters the chance to choose challenger parties within their own camp. It must not be forgotten that the UDF lost a number of its local seats due to internal splits. Whereas it has always been the epitome of a party of notables organized around a network of local officials, today it has been reduced to a small parliamentary group made up of some thirty deputies who are younger and less well established locally than other parliamentary groups. They make up the core of the party's structure and provide the pool of regional or European slate leaders, added to which are personalities who are not professional politicians: such as company heads and journalists. UDF deputies were for the most part elected in the 2002 legislative elections because the UMP did not field any candidates against them. The real battle of strength between UMP and UDF will come in the 2007 legislative elections. The UDF's strategy is a presidential one, but such a choice remains risky, as illustrated by the fact that the UDF did not manage to beat the UMP in either the 2004 regional or European elections.

We thus conclude that the pattern of party fragmentation that affected the party system in France in the late 1990s was due at least as much to institutional and organizational factors as to ideological ones. The tendency for the party system to fragment would appear to have been reversed in the 2002 legislative elections. This might only be temporary. Looking to the future, one can imagine various possible scenarios depending upon party strategies, the role of events (such as the referendum on the European con-stitution), competition within parties and the operation of the institutional and organizational incentives we alluded to above.

Party linkage and penetration

In the second part of this chapter, we address the issue of party linkage in France. We start by acknowledging the historical and structural weakness of French parties in terms of social integration. We observe also the loosening of party ties in western democracies as a whole. In order to capture and contextualize these related phenomena, we ask a number of related questions. In a complex and shifting multiparty system such as that of France, can parties be used as relevant political cues? Do they stimulate any form of attachment? Do they frame the vote? Our analysis will partially bear out the party de-alignment hypothesis, in that it will confirm a weakening of parties as loci of socialization and agents of voter mobilization. It will nevertheless emphasize the cognitive cue functions that parties perform and in particular the persistence, even the strengthening of polarization. With regard to the level and form of party attachment, the changes have not been that significant. However, like other European parties, French organizations have undertaken to democratize their operation and have thus strengthened party roles in political recruitment.

Party closeness and rejection

The structuring element of the political system and the vector through which individual political identification occurs in France is that of the Left–Right cleavage. The sense of closeness to a political party is also important. In its original formulation, the notion of party identification, forged in the context of the US two-party system, constituted an essential aspect of political socialization as well as a means of marking the political chessboard and simplifying voter choices. Imported into a country such as France, it naturally does not have the same meaning. In a multiparty system in which several parties co-exist, often change names, split or form alliances under different labels, parties do not play the same role as in less complex and more stable systems.

In a recent survey, Chiche, Haegel and Tiberj (2004) set out to measure the evolution of French citizens' ties to political parties by using several indicators in a mass survey. We can draw a number of main conclusions from this survey. In response to the first question ('which party to you feel closest to or the least remote from?'), French parties seem to have maintained their significance. More and more people manage to name the party they feel closest to, or the least remote from. In 1988, 17 per cent of respondents declined to answer the question or declared that they did not feel close to any party; those holding this view were 11 per cent in 1995, and the figure dropped to 6.5 per cent in 2002. More and more French people are able to identify the parties to which they feel close (Tiberj, 2004).

We can also measure change according to other indicators. The intensity of party attachment is one well-established indicator. In response to the question: 'would you say you felt close, fairly close, not very close or not at all close to a political party?, we note a clear decrease in the intensity of party ties. As is the case in most European countries (Dalton, McAllister and Wattenberg, 2002), France has undergone a drop in the intensity of party attachment. From 1988 to 2002, the number of people stating they were close or fairly close to a party dropped from 40 per cent to 32 per cent (−8 points) whereas people declaring they were 'not very close, or not at all close' rose significantly from 57 to 68 per cent (+11 points). This decline basically follows a generational trend. Young people − including those who declare an interest in politics − are much more distant from parties than their elders. The politicization of young people in France today occurs mainly on the fringe of party structures. From this perspective, French parties have trouble playing their role as a locus of political socialization.

The third indicator used in the Chiche, Haegel and Tiberj survey is that of naming parties for which the respondent would not vote for under any circumstances. Indeed, party attachment is not taken to mean solely a positive tie based on membership. It is also construed as a negative attachment, implying rejection of a party and identification of an opponent. Sartori (1976) described the French party system as a polarized multiparty system organized around a negative pole historically constituted by the PCF. What is the situation today, when communism is on the decline and party antagonisms seem to have softened with the convergence of political platforms and the succession of periods of power-sharing? There is actually little evidence of a reduction in party antagonism. The proportion of those rejecting voting for a party under any circumstances has actually increased. Moreover, this rejection cannot be simply likened to an overall disaffection for all political organizations. It is a politicized and polarized rejection, based on identifying an opponent party, and it rises with interest in politics and degree of party attachment. This evolution (Table 2.3) largely reflects a phenomenon of asymmetrical polarization around the FN (rejected by 81 per cent of the voters) on one side and the extreme Left (rejected by 55 per cent of them). It is obvious that this trend, measured in the wake of the 2002 presidential election, partly reflects a contextual effect related to the intense anti-Le Pen mobilization. There is a strong polarization for or (especially) against the FN, particularly important for the political socialization of the younger generations. If the FN is easily the most rejected party, a number of other parties were also rejected in 2002 by large proportions of the electorate. This rejection was aimed even at organizations that thus far had occupied the most central positions, such as the Greens and the UDF. The Greens probably paid for their abandoning of their 'neither right nor left' position and incurred hostility from the CNPT. For its part, the UDF may have paid for its assertion of a centrist identity. The only notable exception is the PCF, the sole organization whose level of rejection has regressed, its decline bringing about a gradual decrease of anti-communism in public opinion.

The last indicator we used measures the match between party attachment and vote in the 1988 and 2002 presidential elections. To measure this, among the respondents declaring they felt close to a party, we simply took

Table 2.4   *Changes in the type of parties rejected*

	1988	2002	Evolution
Extreme Left parties	50.5	55	+4.5
PCF	52	42	−10
PS	12	17	+5
Envi/Verts	10.5	26	+15.5
UDF	12	20.5	+7.5
RPR	21	21	–
FN	70	81	+11

Source: PEF/CEVIPOF Survey 2002, post-presidential wave 2
(% of respondents rejecting the following parties (multiple answers possible)).

those who voted for the candidate nominated by this party. Working with a population of sympathizers, one would expect this match to be fairly close. Between 1988 and 2002, we noted a sharp decrease (−18 points) in this indicator. During the 1988 presidential poll, 75 per cent of sympathizers declared to have cast their vote for the candidate fielded by the party they claimed affinity for. In 1995, 72 per cent of them were in this category. In 2002, the proportion dropped to 57 per cent. This evolution reflects the specific nature of the 2002 presidential election, which featured a large number of candidacies and a scattering of votes, especially on the Left. In addition, it provides a good illustration of the difficulty parties have of fulfilling their voter mobilization role. Not only are they having more and more trouble getting people to vote, as attests the increase in abstention rate, but they also have trouble getting their sympathizers to vote for the presidential candidates they field.

These findings enable us to establish a diagnosis of the evolution of party attachment in France. In terms of the ties with voters, parties have weakened, as can be seen in the drop in intensity of the attachment they inspire, their marginalization in the political socialization of young people and the trouble they have mobilizing voters. But, although French parties do not generate strong relations of loyalty or fidelity, they partly fulfil their role as cognitive tools for French voters in that they remain markers in a particularly complex party system and enable the public to rank their preferences and, especially, to identify their opponents.

The role of members

The role of political party members can be measured in different ways. Studies have typically focused either upon the rate of party membership, or the role members are given within parties. Measurement of membership rate is the most commonly used gauge, and, in the case of France, it has long since been established that party membership is particularly low. On the scale of Europe, French parties are known for their low membership rate: depending on the estimates it makes up 1.57 per cent (Mair and van Biezen, 2001) or 1 per cent (Andolfatto *et al.*, 2001) of the electorate, ranking France among the lowest of European countries in this respect. Using all the required caution given the lack of transparency in this area, we can roughly estimate that only the PCF, the PS and the UMP have over 100,000 members. The other organizations have a much lower rate, about 10,000 for the Greens and probably the same for the UDF and the FN, both parties being weakened by splits. Among the consequences of the mobilization resulting from the shock of 21 April 2002 (the first ballot of the presidential election in which Jean-Marie Le Pen qualified), there was an upswing in party membership. Many of these new cardholders did not pay their annual dues the following years, however, illustrating the high turnover affecting party membership. From the standpoint of party involvement, the situation has not altered in the past years, in any case if we reason in terms of level. Political parties are largely parties of notables. From a strictly quantitative standpoint, in fact, if we take into account the fragmentation of territorial administrative divisions, and therefore the multiplication of local elected offices, the presence of local officials in parties proves to be pivotal, even if a portion of these officeholders in the smallest communes do not belong to any party. And the role of the major elected officials in French party organizations, maintained by the practice of multiple officeholding – including, historically, in organizations such as the PS that demonstrated a wariness towards them (Lefebvre, 2004) – is quite obvious.

Following Max Weber, party membership can also be considered as a social relationship. In France, the forms of involvement in intermediary structures have always been weak. A change has nevertheless occurred in regard to membership in voluntary associations: in this area the French have caught up with their European neighbours, whereas they still lag behind in terms of party involvement. How can the relation between these two forms of involvement be analysed? The overlapping membership of parties and associations in activists' careers remains constant. Multiple membership is a widespread phenomenon on both the Left and the Right, but there are also bridges from one structure to another. Associations are either abeyance structures for disappointed former party members (for instance the *Ligue des Droits de l'Homme* for PS activists), or else springboards eventually leading to party membership (the case for various organizations in defence of the homeless, immigrants, the unemployed and anti-globalization movements with respect to joining the LCR). From this standpoint, the forms taken by the decline of the PCF are particularly significant (Lavabre and Platone, 2003). Historically, the PCF was an exception in terms of the size of its membership and its capacity for social and political integration and support. Research conducted in France on political parties has mainly focused on analysing the Communist Party model, thus making it the standard by which to measure the deficit of other organizations. Today, the decline of communism has affected the traditional shape of the PCF that had helped cause the spread of this party model (Mischi, 2003). In this party, which for a long time provided the archetypal figure of the activist, members and occasionally sympathizers have supplanted it. The change can also be seen in the discarding of the cell as the traditional communist grassroots structure in favour of neighbourhood networks. In this way, party boundaries have become more permeable, and, communist slates have ever greater numbers of candidates who are not party members. At the local level, the ebb of communism leaves traces of the social networks around which the Communist Party established itself. These networks are today often being reduced to festive associations and senior citizens' clubs that are more and more disconnected from the party.

In the case of France, emphasizing the connections between associations and party networks does not imply disregarding the State, given the importance of government-related associational structures, particularly those supported by local governments. The overlapping of parties and the government, brought to light by the cartelization theory, is not at all a new phenomenon in France. At the local level, it can be seen in the overlapping of party and municipal networks, whereas at the top, senior civil servants, particularly graduates of the National Administration School (*Ecole Nationale d'Administration*: ENA), usually make up the core of the party elite. However, in French politics the weight of personalities such as Nicolas Sarkozy in the UMP, Bertrand Delanoë in the PS or François Bayrou in the UDF, who were not educated at the ENA and who have led careers that have been highly focused on the party, might indicate a reversal of this trend.

A final means of assessing the role of members is to consider the role they are given within the party. In this regard, the changes that have affected French parties (Faucher-King and Treille, 2003; Olivier, 2003) are similar to those that have occurred in most European parties even if they are less momentous. Since the late 1990s, in nearly all parties there has been an increase in membership consultations, Right-wing parties being considerably further behind than Left-wing parties in this regard. European parties are tending to converge in their organizational forms. The increase in the power of party members is noteworthy in the selection process for legislative and presidential election candidates, and in the nomination of party officeholders, especially the leader (Dolez and Laurent, 2000). Consequently, if we consider members' capacity to take part in the process of political recruitment, we are obliged to qualify the theory that French parties are on the decline. Parties exercise more and more direct control over candidate selection, particularly as regards presidential candidates. The case of the UMP deserves particular attention. Two years after it was founded, no provision has been made in party regulations over the selection of the presidential candidate. Paradoxically, the president's own party seems the least presidentialized in that, as an institution, it still has no rules governing this process. This anomaly stems in part from cultural resistance (the tradition being for the president to have a direct link to the people that does not go through the party) and in part from institutional factors (the fact that Jacques Chirac occupies the presidency). It is kept alive by political considerations, namely the threat of competition from Nicolas Sarkozy for Chirac supporters.

In contrast, the influence of party members on party platforms is very weak. Party platforms are elaborated by bodies that largely lie outside member control or are only loosely connected to the official party structure. The building of Jospin's platform in 2002 provides a particularly striking illustration of the entanglement of networks (party factions, ministerial offices, experts) and the blurring of responsibilities. But the recent trend seems to be towards a rehabilitation of parties in defining campaign issues. There are a number of recent illustrations of this, such as the decisions made in the spring of 2004 in the PS national bureau to promote gay marriage; the organization of a referendum of PS members on the European constitution; or the UMP national council vote refusing Turkey's joining the EU. The problem confronting the two dominant parties in French politics is certainly to liven up the internal debate but also to organize an institutional voice for plurality. True, the organizational cultures of the two parties do differ considerably. The PS was historically built around competing factions, even if it has officially taken a certain distance from this type of functioning. The UMP officially promoted this type of organization in its statutes but has trouble deciding to put it into practice. The UMP is torn between the culture of the plebiscite (for former RPR members) and that of the informal agreement (for former DL and UDF members). UMP factions based on previous party allegiances (RPR, UDF, DL) are very obvious in the new 'unified' party, based on clubs, foundations and newsletters. Organizational networks interweave or overlay ideological tendencies and the campaign networks of potential presidential candidates.

Since 1995, a number of changes have affected the French party system. In structural terms, a high degree of instability characterized the late 1990s, as illustrated by the number of party splits, particularly on the Right. This lack of stability points up the cleavages at work in the French party system (over Europe, the role of the nation-state, a religious cleavage over moral issues, a rural/urban cleavage over issues of the use of nature), but it also attests to the difficulty the party system has in addressing these social and ideological antagonisms. In terms of penetration, the process of party de-alignment has continued. It is marked by the erosion of parties as loci of socialization for new generations and as agents of voter mobilization and the ongoing weakness of party membership in France. In some respects, however, there has been a strengthening of parties in the political system. Their institutional importance has grown, through public financing and the legislation on parity. The control exercised by parties on the process of political recruitment has also increased. Finally, the preservation, even increase, of a form of party polarization combined with the affirmation of a dominant party on the Left and on the Right still helps to structure the French polity.

Chapter 3

Electorates, New Cleavages and Social Structures

JOCELYN EVANS AND NONNA MAYER

That advanced post-industrial democracies have been subject to massive social change in the postwar period is a given of the sociological and political science literature (Dalton, Flanagan and Beck, 1984; Franklin, Mackie and Valen, 1992). Indeed, the emphasis that the latter discipline in particular places on the link between social structure and electoral behaviour can obscure the undoubtedly greater importance that such changes have had on the quotidian as well as on mass politics. The fundamental restructuring of Western economies towards service economies, away from traditional industrially oriented infrastructures; the associated expansion of education in secondary and tertiary levels; social mobility among new white-collar classes bridging the traditional opposition of 'lower' and 'middle' class; geographic mobility, as the foci of economic activity have migrated from industrial heartlands to tertiary sector business-parks – these new patterns of sociological strata have engendered large-scale changes in lifestyles which, while not necessarily apparent at the micro-level to the individuals themselves, are nonetheless undeniable at the macro-level.

In these respects, France is no different from any other European democracy. The shifts in social structure that have transformed French society since the Socialist Left's capture of power in 1981 are as striking as they are normal. The INSEE research institute has reported that the blue-collar class now only accounts for 27 per cent of the working population, rather than more than a third as in the 1980s and 40 per cent in 1975. Farmers, despite France's relatively late industrialization, have nonetheless declined to just below 3 per cent of the population. More broadly, the self-employed in a nation renowned for its small shops and businesses now only account for less than 15 per cent. The salaried middle classes have become the hegemonic occupational stratum in the economic market, and concomitantly the two elements associated with the French bourgeoisie – house-ownership and *patrimoine* (capital assets beyond income, such as shares and securities) – have also grown. White-collar employees make up almost a third of the workforce. In education, 70 per cent of young people finished secondary school diplomas in 2001, as opposed to 35 per cent in

35

1985 – and 38 per cent went on to complete a higher education course, as opposed to 17 per cent in 1985.

Of course, there has been a flipside to this socio-economic transformation. Mass unemployment has become a feature of the economic landscape in France which, whilst now lower than the atrophy years of the early and mid-1990s, still accounts for around 10 per cent of the active population. Unsurprisingly, the key cohort hit by such changes are precisely the youngsters without the educational threshold required by a service economy, and unable to insert themselves in the semi- and unskilled sectors which provided Fordist employment for their parents and grandparents. Most importantly – and the crux of this chapter – those remaining employed in the blue-collar stratum also apparently experience a feeling of marginalization, given that their voting behaviour has changed fundamentally, moving many of them from their traditional home on the Left to their new home on the Extreme Right.

This chapter, then, will consider precisely this phenomenon – how the changes in social structure have been reflected in French voting patterns since 1981. The data used in this chapter are drawn from the 1988 and 1995 CEVIPOF national election surveys and the 2002 CEVIPOF–CIDSP–CECOP French electoral Panel (Cautrès and Mayer, 2004). It consists of three samples representative of registered French voters ($N = 4032$, 4078 and 4017), using post-presidential election surveys, quota sampling, face-to-face interviews in 1988 and 1995, and a telephone survey (CATI) in 2002. We will argue that, if social structure has changed, then it is likely that voting will reflect these changes. We will aim to dispel the myth that in France, as elsewhere, electoral behaviour no longer follows social lines, and show that realignment, rather than de-alignment, is taking place (Clark, Lipset and Rempel, 1993; Hout, Brooks and Manza, 1993). To the extent that mass politics is precisely a reflection of the underlying structures in society, we would expect sociological patterns still to pertain, but not in the same format as before. Furthermore, perhaps sociologists have previously placed too much store in the clear dichotomy of social cleavages, particularly in the Marxist dyad (Evans, 1999).

Social structure and electoral behaviour in France

Socio-political structure and the anchoring of the electorate to French parties is well rehearsed in the literature (Michelat and Simon, 1977a; Boy and Mayer, 2000; Evans, 2004a), but it is useful to give a brief overview of the patterns in order to found the analysis which follows. In France, unlike Nordic countries but in keeping with other Catholic nations, Left and Right have been essentially synonymous with two fundamental cleavages: class and religion (Lipset and Rokkan, 1967). The class cleavage is common to a greater or lesser extent to all industrialized European democracies, and saw the working class voting for the Left (Communist or Socialist) and the middle class voting for the Right. However, as is sometimes overlooked despite being emphasized in sociological analyses of voting behaviour, religion was traditionally a stronger indicator of likely vote, at least in terms of choice between Left or Right bloc (Lijphart, 1978), with Catholic voters the most likely to support the Right, and secular voters most drawn by the anti-clerical Left. Thus, the Left in France has always seen support from the secular middle-class liberals, and in particular those engaged in the teaching profession, whilst the Right has received support from the Catholic working class.

Of course, religion and class both have had a nuanced empirical relationship to Left and Right. For instance, religious practice has been an important sub-setting factor in the secular/Catholic divide: those practising their religion have been more likely to vote for the Right, with non-practising and lapsed Catholics closer to the secular group. Similarly, composite measures of class, including level of *patrimoine* on the Right and union membership on the Left, as well as actual occupation, have given stronger or weaker levels of voting for Left parties. Indeed, in the 1978 election, it was precisely those voters with some *patrimoine* who might otherwise have voted Left who continued to vote Right out of fear of proposed Socialist taxes on such assets, and consequently helped delay the accession of the Socialist Party to power by another three years (Capdevielle, 1981).

The composition of class and religion being composite and consequently mutable, it would be wrong to think that such sociological indicators should be unalterable edifices in relation to voting behaviour across time. First, the class divisions were never simply a question of the Manichean worker/owner division promoted by Marxists, and included the sector of employment – public/private/self-employed – to boot. Thus, when the social changes highlighted in the introduction produce a much transformed socio-political foundation to electoral behaviour, simply to highlight a decline, say, in Marxist class voting provides no proof whatsoever of a decline in class voting *per se*.

Secondly, it is clear that social divisions such as class and religion are not the only determinants of electoral behaviour: political issues, the state of the economy, the incumbent government's credibility and political 'events' such as scandals, wars and the like, all play a role – and, crucially, have always played a role – in determining the eventual outcome of an election (Evans, 2004b). Indeed, it is these latter short-term determinants which principally motivate the electoral volatility allowing incumbents to be ousted (*sortir les sortants*) and oppositions to win. This, then, is precisely the strength of the social structural determinants. To the extent that their evolution can be measured, they provide an excellent baseline of the electorate's 'normal vote' (Converse, 1966).

Thirdly, from the supply side, the picture becomes more complicated across time. In 1981, after the first alternation of power under the Fifth Republic, the two-bloc, four-party system seemed to herald a new stabilization and moderation of the French party system (Bartolini, 1984). On the Left, the moderate Socialist Party dominated government with a minor and at the time centripetal Communist Party as its junior partner. On the Right, the UDF and the Gaullist RPR vied for dominance of the bloc, but both were moderate and oriented towards the Centre voter. The reasons for the rapid decline in this stability are numerous, but certainly one fundamental reason of relevance to this chapter was the appearance of new parties on the Left and the Right – the Greens and the *Front National* respectively – and, more recently, the strengthening of the Trotskyite Left (Evans, 2003).

Looking at Table 3.1, the change in the party system is clear. From a virtual electoral monopoly in 1981, the mainstream Left and Right blocs have dropped from almost 94 per cent of the vote to just over 65 per cent in 2002. The clearest loser has been the Left, which has seen its vote drop by almost half in the two decades since its first presidential victory. From the perspective of traditional electoral theory, what stands out is the almost identical rise in the Extreme Right's vote. Clearly, some of the Left vote has transferred to the Trotskyite Left – at least in the most recent elections – and to a much lesser extent to the Greens who, despite their New Left status, have at the national level remained a party with an essentially closed pool of voters. But, given that the mainstream Right only loses 11.4 per cent of its vote share, almost as many votes again need to be found from the Left to account for the Extreme Right success. If we stick rigidly with basic class and religious definitions of bloc voting, we can never hope to reconcile this long journey from Left to Extreme Right. One potential explanation is to introduce voter attitudes and issue-stances into the equation, to explain FN ideological appeal to workers (Perrineau, 1997; Evans, 2000; Mayer, 2002). But this does not mean that sociological explanations are impotent. To what extent, then, can the processes of social realignment account for this aggregate shift?

Table 3.1   *Presidential elections results in France, Fifth Republic, 1st ballot*

%	1981	1988	1995	2002	1981–2002
Trotskyite Left	2.3	2.4	5.3	10.4	+8.1
Left	44.4	42.9	31.9	27.2	−17.2
Green	3.9	3.8	3.3	5.3	+1.4
Right	49.3	36.4	44.4	37.9	−11.4
Extreme Right	–	14.4	15.3	19.2	+19.2

Source: CEVIPOF electoral data base.

The embourgeoisement of the Left

As a first indication, the composition of mainstream Left vote by occupation demonstrates the bias in the shifts which have occurred. Table 3.2 sets out the Left vote by proportion of occupational strata from the parliamentary elections of 1978 until the 2002 presidential contest. Given that the table indicates the intra-group proportion rather than the relative electoral weight of each, the change in size of each occupational class is irrelevant. We can see that, whilst there has been an overall decline in the Left vote among all classes, the biggest decline has been among those groups which historically would have been most closely associated with the Left: clerks and blue-collar workers. Starkly, the latter group have dropped from over two-thirds of their number voting Left to less than one half. The secular liberal group of salaried professionals and middle class executives has remained relatively stable, as have the salaried middle class. Bearing in mind the absolute increase in size of these groups in the post-industrial economy, then, it is clear that the Left's contemporary electoral interests lie increasingly in the middle class, even though the traditional working-class sectors of the electorate still represent more than half of the French eligible voters.

The clearest indication of this shift appears in the Alford index. This indicator, calculated as the proportion of working-class votes for the Left, minus non-working-class votes for the Left, can be interpreted as an

Table 3.2 *Vote for the Left by occupation*

Occupation (%)	Parl. 1978	Pres. 1988	Pres. 1995	Pres. 2002	Evolution 1978–2002
Farmer	26	29	20	18	−8
Industrialist, shopkeeper, artisan	31	32	19	20	−11
Executive, salaried professional	45	41	46	43	−2
Salaried middle class	57	48	45	50	−7
Clerk	54	52	38	39	−15
Worker	70	63	49	43	−27
N	53 (3867)	49 (3091)	41 (3149)	43 (2826)	−10
Alford index*	23	18	11	0	

Source: Post-electoral surveys CEVIPOF 1978, 1988, 1995; post-electoral survey CEVIPOF–CIDSP–CRAPS 1997; French electoral panel 2002, wave 2, weighted.
Note: Proportion of working-class votes for the Left minus non-working-class votes or the Left.

indicator of relative class voting – the higher the figure, the higher the level of class voting, as determined by the intra-party proportion of each. Using this simple indicator, the score for the Left is now zero – there is no evidence of class voting. Contrast this with the situation in 1978 when the proportion of the working-class vote for the Left was 23 per cent higher than the proportion of non-working-class voters. Part of this radical finding derives from the interpretation of what 'class voting' actually means. Is it more important to look at the balance of working-class and non-working-class votes within the Left electorate, or instead at the proportion of votes from within each class? The Alford index is simplistic inasmuch as it groups voters into only two class categories. Later in this analysis, we will use a more robust means of looking at relative class strengths in voting behaviour. However, at the very least, this does indicate that there has been a substantial realignment in the content of Left voting, from a social structural point of view.

This finding is additionally confirmed if we look at the Left vote by type of employment. Table 3.3 subdivides the active population into their employment sectors – public and private wage-earners, and the self-employed. The self-employed, as would be expected from an economic sector principally composed of the middle class and petty bourgeoisie, as well as concentrated in smaller conurbations characterized by higher levels of religiosity, are in a minority to support the Left. Apparently in 2002, however, they have no more reason *not* to vote for the Left than in 1978 – only a 7 per cent decline. As a group particularly hostile to the Left for economic reasons, and specifically the fear of collectivization which has gradually driven the independent economic classes to the Right since the end of the nineteenth century in France (Mayer, 1986), this fear has evidently not grown significantly – nor has there been any lessening of the distance, however.

Amongst wage-earners, the overall decline is similar to the self-employed – around a quarter of the group. But on categorizing this

Table 3.3   *Vote for the Left by type of employment*

Status (%)	1978	1988	1995	2002
Self-employed	28	30	22	21
Wage earners	60	54	44	44
	+32	+24	+22	+23
Wage earners in private sector	58	52	40	39
Wage earners in public sector	64	58	52	51
	+6	+6	+12	+12

Source: Post-electoral surveys CEVIPOF 1978, 1988, 1995; post-electoral survey CEVIPOF–CIDSP–CRAPS 1997; French electoral panel 2002, wave 2, weighted.

between public-sector and private-sector wage-earners, a large disparity is revealed. The decline in private-sector wage-earners has been much steeper than among their public counterparts. The Left is still the absolute majority choice for the public sector, but nowhere near for the private. Historically, the Left's ties to the public sector in Jacobin state-centralized France has always been very strong, and this relationship is still present. Thus there is still evidence of the secular Left, characterized perhaps most strongly by teachers. Who has decamped, and to where, in the private sector, however? Is it the working class, previously represented by the Left in industrialized capitalism?

Looking at Table 3.4, the evidence suggests that it is. The upper section of the table depicts the percentage of valid working-class votes in the Left, the Right and the Extreme Right camps for the three presidential elections since 1988. In aggregate terms, the Right's vote among workers has increased significantly since 1988 – unsurprising, perhaps, given the victory of the Left candidate François Mitterrand in that year – but almost as many of the working-class votes have gone to the Extreme Right as to the mainstream. Given that the Extreme Right vote is around half the size of its mainstream counterpart (see Table 3.1), it is clear that the former now represents a party which disproportionately represents the workers, if we look at intra-party proportions, rather than intra-class proportions.

Moreover, looking at the lower section, which takes the percentage from registered voters, we can see then that the Left has lost votes among workers in almost equal proportions to the mainstream Right, the Extreme Right and to abstention. Indeed, in 2002 more workers abstained than

Table 3.4 *Working-class votes*

% Valid votes	Pres. 1988	Pres. 1995	Pres. 2002	
Left	63	49	43	−20
Right	20	31	31	+11
Extreme Right	17	21	26	+9
% registered voters	Pres. 1988	Pres. 1995	Pres. 2002	
Abstention	26	20	31	+5
Left	47	39	29	−18
Right	15	24	22	+7
Extreme Right	12	17	18	+6

Source: Post-electoral surveys carried out by CEVIPOF 1978, 1988, 1995; post-electoral survey CEVIPOF–CIDSP–CRAPS 1997; French electoral panel 2002, wave 2, weighted.

voted for their traditional party candidates. We can contrast this with the 1997 parliamentary elections, however, where 52 per cent of the working-class vote went to the victorious Left, and the 2004 regional elections, where 48 per cent went that way. Little wonder, then, that the principal Left-wing candidate, Lionel Jospin, failed to reach the second round of the elections in 2002.

Goodbye workers, hello ...?

These findings suggest that the working class has become less strongly attached to its traditional representatives, and the reasons for this are clear if we return once more to the social structural shifts with which we introduced this chapter. Given its increasingly marginalized position in the economic structure, and the simultaneous growth of mass unemployment in the 1980s and 1990s, the working class has more than ever wanted to rely upon the classical welfare interventionist policies of Marxist obedience. More than in other European countries, not least due to the tradition of economic interventionism among all parties on the French spectrum, the French Left has to a large degree held on to such instruments *in principle* as part of its ideology. However, as the Socialist governments of the 1980s had already found, *in practice* the use of a strong welfare state as a cushion for economic falls is financially untenable, as well as economically unviable from the point of effectiveness, and increasingly at odds with European Union regulations of state support (for a detailed analysis of the break between blue-collar workers and the French Left, see Rey, 2004; Michelat and Simon, 2004).

In essence, the working class no longer feels protected by the party which is expected to protect its *chasse gardée*, and consequently often turns to other parties which promise to do so – the FN for instance, for whom national economic preference and rejection of supranational interference has proved a lucrative policy position. Today Le Pen directs his appeal explicitly at the blue-collar workforce: 'Miners, metal-workers, men and women of the working class in industries ruined by Maastricht's Euro-globalization (*l'euromondialisme*)' (*National Hebdo*, 25 April–3 May 2002, authors' translation). A party which in the 1980s was promoting a free-market liberalism to make Thatcher and Reagan blush has adapted to the social structural logic which puts 'modernization losers' rather than 'international Euro-citizens' in its political camp.

As a result, there is increasing identification with the FN and its leader: in the 2002 elections, the most stable electorate, i.e. the one which voted consistently for the party in 1997 and its presidential candidate in 2002, was by far and away the FN. Conversely to the short-term 'protest' vote so often used to characterize Extreme Right support, there is some evidence here of a stable, 'normalized' FN vote developing among certain sections of the electorate. The Left's inability to address its traditional voters' concerns has seemingly pushed part of its electorate away for the duration.

Such a lack of economic manoeuvrability on the part of the Left has been exacerbated by its increased appeal on socio-cultural issues characteristic of the New Left agenda. In their separate works on the post-materialist value change of Inglehart's Silent Revolution (1977), whereby younger cohorts of economically and socially stable voters are more mobilized by quality-of-life and universalist issues rather than by traditional economic concerns, Herbert Kitschelt (1995) and Piero Ignazi (1992) allude to the adoption of such issues by Left-wing parties, especially those blackmailed into doing so by New Left parties such as the Greens, and the backlash against such views among the working classes, still with very strong materialist concerns, who now find these views represented by the Extreme Right – the Silent Counter-Revolution.

From the perspective of the Left, however, such a strategy makes sound social-structural sense, even if this alienates certain sections of the electorate. Given the growth of the new middle class in the service-oriented economy, and given that this growing class is precisely where such universalist concerns are more likely to be found, a Left bloc which wishes to win power will want to focus precisely here rather than on the numerically declining and economically difficult-to-satisfy blue-collar class. This also illustrates the limits of a purely sociological analysis, however. As we noted above, in some elections, such as the 1997 parliamentary ballot and the recent 2004 regional elections, the Left did manage to win back many, or even a majority, of the workers. Yet, we have also seen the growing identification of part of the same group with the Extreme Right camp. The prodigal workers who returned in 1997 and 2004 are consequently more likely to be found among the abstainers who outstripped all other candidates in 2002. By definition, we need an additional criterion to delineate between 'Extreme Right' workers, 'Left' workers and 'oscillating' workers – and it seems evident that this is to be found in the attitudinal arrays alluded to previously.

Rather than look at the working class, then, if we focus on elements more traditionally associated with Right vote, namely religion/religious practice and *patrimoine*, but look at the Left electorate, we would expect to see a lessening of the divide between Left and Right on these. Table 3.5 looks at religious practice among the Left electorate between 1978 and 2002. The results are striking: despite a secular trend away from Catholicism in France as in all other Catholic countries, the Left sees an overall increase in the proclivity of the strongest Catholic section of the electorate to vote for it, and an overall decline in the non-practising and secular sections. More specifically, the practising Catholics' vote increases (although not mono-tonically) by 4 per cent, whereas the secular group – traditionally a mainstay of Left support – drops by 24 per cent. Given that the number of practising Catholics in France is in decline, the slight increase in percentage terms will represent a static or slightly declining level of support in absolute

Table 3.5   *Vote for the Left by religious practice*

Catholic religious practice	1978	1988	1995	2002
Regular	18	25	17	22
Irregular	38	39	29	29
Non-practising	61	53	42	42
Other religion	54	53	44	50
No religion	86	78	66	62
	+68	+53	+49	+40

terms. Thus, even if the most religious are slightly more likely to vote for the Left, the Left is unlikely to find itself now more influenced by the sacred than the profane. More important is the decline in the irreligious categories, and once again the likely destination of these voters is abstention and the Extreme, the FN increasingly becoming a party of the lapsed and atheists.

Table 3.6 looks at the *patrimoine* effect on Left vote. Here we can see a similar dynamic: the traditional Left group (0 or 1 assets) falls sharply away, whilst the asset-rich group increases slightly. Our interpretation here, however, is substantively different to our interpretation of the religiosity dynamic. Given that the number of individuals in France with assets will have increased, given rising affluence and an expansion of private share-ownership in the late 1980s and 1990s, the 3 per cent increase will represent a substantial absolute increase. Consequently, whilst the low-asset group again depicts the departure of the working-class sector of the Left, the arrival of upper-salariat Left-wingers can be seen in the rise of the 3–6 assets category.

Given these figures, it is clear many of the fundamental voter exchanges miss out the mainstream Right, moving from the Left directly to the Extreme Right. The Left remains a secular force, although it has apparently

Table 3.6   *Vote for the Left by number of assets**

Assets	1988	1995	2002
0–1	62	48	48
2	53	42	43
3–6	32	33	35
	−30	−15	−13

Note: * assets: ownership of house, country house, business/lands/ trade, real estate, securities, saving account.

lost much of its secular strength across the same bridge; the religious sections of the population remain in the Right camp, but increasingly the mainstream Right is losing its middle classes to the Left. We noted at the beginning that the middle-class and secular social liberals had always voted strongly for the Left. However, growing secularization and a social liberalization in French society mean that an increasing number of the bourgeoisie find themselves ideologically more proximate to the Left than to the Right.

Old cleavages, new cleavages, other cleavages

The dynamics we have highlighted so far coincide quite comfortably with changes which we have seen in France's social structure and political supply. There are fundamental divisions between the self-employed, even more firmly implanted on the Right since the free-market liberal developments of the late 1980s and 1990s, and employees, with the upper salariat associated with the Left, and offsetting the decampment to the Extreme

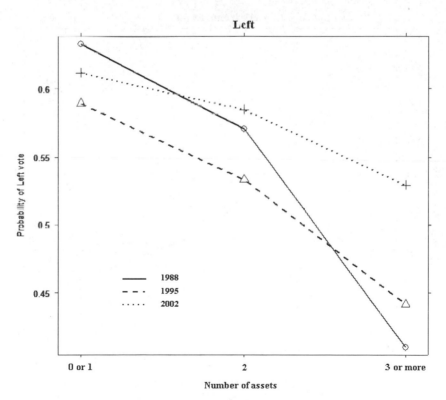

Figure 3.1 *Fitted probability of Left vote over Moderate Right vote by number of assets*

Right and abstention of the working class. Secondly, there is a division between private sector and public sector, with the latter more strongly rooted on the Left.

Yet essentially these are just disjointed elements to the social-structural whole. It would be informative to know what the relative strengths of each indicator are, as compared to each other and to other potential sources of political change – gender and age, for instance. We know that men are on average more likely to vote for the Extreme Right, but has this changed at all across time? What about the commonly received idea that the young are the most likely to vote for the FN and Jean-Marie Le Pen?

The only way to look at this information is using a multivariate statistical model, in this case – because we are interested in looking at the differences between Left, Moderate Right and Extreme Right electorates as groups – logistic regression. Unfortunately, even for the statistically minded, coefficients generated by a logistic regression are notoriously unhelpful to interpret, and given we want to look at the relative differences between three electoral groups and over a period of time (1988 to 2002),

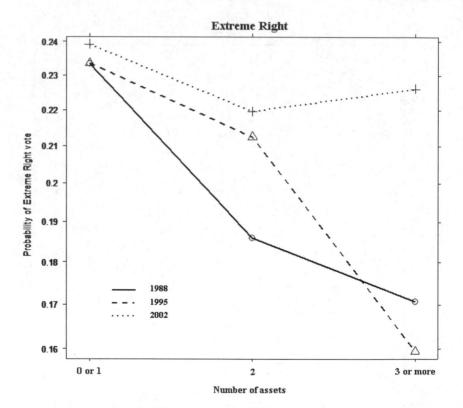

Figure 3.2   *Fitted probability of Extreme Right vote over Moderate Right vote by number of assets*

the actual coefficients will be numerous, and potentially confusing as a result. Instead, rather than provide the statistical model, we can plot the results on a series of graphs, known as 'fitted probability' graphs, that will let us look at the patterns for each electorate in each time period. Simply, the graphs chart the probability calculated from the statistical model of an individual with a certain characteristic – e.g. regularly practising Catholic; male; or public-sector employee – voting for a party of the Left or for the Extreme Right, as compared with voting for the Moderate Right, and holding all other characteristics to their mean. We can then get a sense of the relative likelihood of a certain social characteristic resulting in a vote for one of the blocs, plus how that compares with other social characteristics. It requires no statistical knowledge *per se*, simply the ability to compare across graphs.

Figures 3.1 and 3.2 show the probabilities of Left vote and Extreme Right vote, respectively, according to levels of assets. Other effects – age, gender, employment status, education and religion – are all held to their mean. The effects on Left vote remain relatively constant across time: the lower

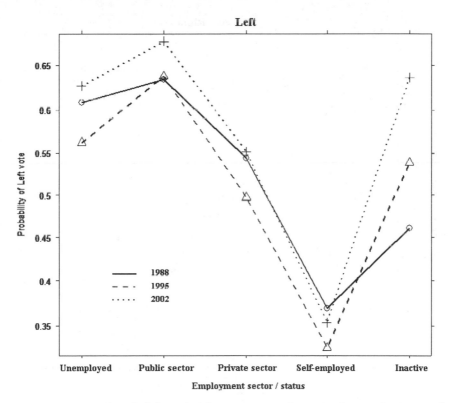

Figure 3.3   *Fitted probability of Left vote over Moderate Right vote by sector of employment/employment status*

the number of assets, the greater the likelihood of voting Left. The strength of the relationship does change, however. In 2002, the line is much less shallow than in 1988 or 1995, indicating a decreased effect of assets on separating between Left and Moderate Right. If we look at Figure 3.2 – the probability of Extreme Right vote over Moderate Right vote – we see a similar situation. The likelihood of a vote for Le Pen among the lowest asset group remains almost identical, between 23 and 24 per cent. At the other end, for the 3 or more assets group, the probability of a vote for the Extreme Right in 1988 and 1995 was lower (although only around 7 to 8 per cent lower). The two big changes occur, first, in the increase in likelihood of the middle-asset group to vote Extreme Right after 1988 and secondly – and most noticeably – the climb in the 3 or more group asset in 2002. Essentially, in the most recent election, number of assets provides no differentiation in the probability of an Extreme Right vote over the Moderate Right. Looking now at the sector of employment and employment status, a number of points stand out. For the Left, the constancy of the unemployed and the public sector is striking – across 14 years,

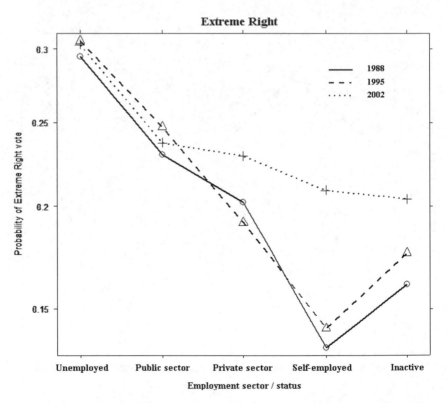

Figure 3.4   *Fitted probability of Extreme Right vote over Moderate Right vote by sector of employment/employment status*

public-sector workers on average have been absolutely predictable in their (high) probability of voting for the Socialists and their allies. Conversely, the self-employed have been consistently unlikely to do so – they have remained implanted on the Right. The private sector occupies the critical middle-ground around 50 per cent, with an increase from 50 to 55 per cent probability of a Left vote.

In many ways, the Extreme Right picture is very similar to the Left. For instance, overall the Extreme Right has traditionally been more likely to get unemployed and public-sector votes than it has to get private-sector or self-employed votes (although obviously it is in a minority even in these cases, below 50 per cent). Yet by 2002, this has changed – the private sector become almost as likely to vote Extreme Right as the public sector. Thus, if a public/private sector cleavage is to be identified, it certainly separates Left from Moderate Right (and always has done), but it decreasingly separates the Extreme Right from the Moderate Right. Lastly, the self-employed are increasingly likely to vote Le Pen, although given the disparate size of the vote share, they are still more likely to vote for the Moderate Right.

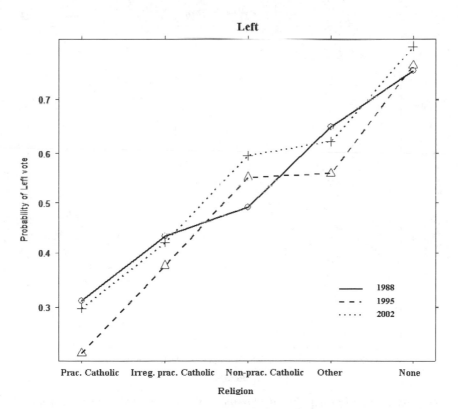

Figure 3.5   *Fitted probability of Left vote over Moderate Right vote by religion*

Turning now to religion, it is clear that the religious divide between Left and Right is as strong and consistent as ever. Looking first at the scale for the Left graph, this represents the largest disparity in probabilities, from a probability of between 20 and 30 per cent of a vote for practising Catholics to a consistent probability of about 75 per cent for the secular. Thus, whilst the proportions of the French electorate in each religious group may be changing, the overall level of cleavage voting remains consistent. The picture for the Extreme Right is rather less stable. They do consistently well among the secular voters, and relatively consistently badly among practising Catholics, with a sharp fall in 1995. But among the irregular and lapsed Catholics, there is a dramatic increase in the former in 2002 and the latter already in 1995. To look at the FN's religious profile as 'secularization' is thus misleading, given the secular component has always been strong. It is among the Catholic group that support for the Extreme Right has developed, but mainly among those who do not go to church anymore.

Lastly, we turn to a cleavage which has received increasing levels of attention in recent years, both in France and abroad (Grunberg and

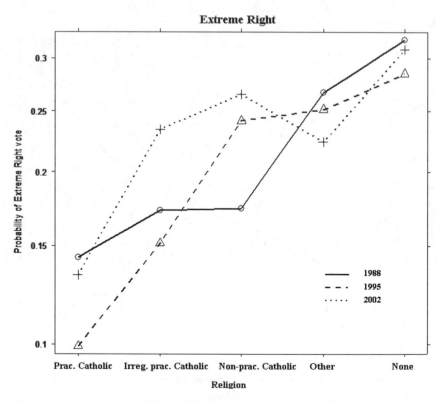

Figure 3.6   *Fitted probability of Extreme Right vote over Moderate Right vote by religion*

Schweisguth, 1997; Manza and Brooks, 1999). In France, the key contemporary development has been the view that an education cleavage is increasingly dividing the FN and Le Pen's electorate from the other parties. Looking at the two education graphs, this hypothesis certainly receives some support. From the Left's point of view, there is an increase in educational level among its voters evident from 1995. For instance, in 1988, the Bac +2 university graduates and postgraduate groups were more likely to vote Moderate Right than Left. By 2002, however, both groups were more likely to vote Left than Moderate Right, although the level of voting among the most uneducated group also increases, particularly over 1995. For the Extreme Right, the two least educated groups were the ones with the highest likelihood of support for Le Pen. Since 1988, however, support has plummeted for the highest education group (although it has remained fairly stable for the university graduates). The steepness of the 2002 line indicates that there is an increasing division between Moderate and Extreme Right. Combining these two findings then, it is true that the Left is no longer recruiting predominantly among the lesser educated, but that the Extreme Right is increasingly getting their support.

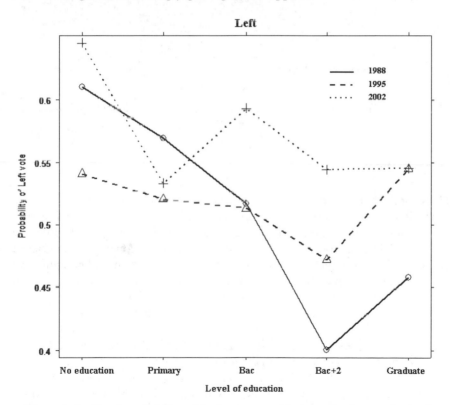

Figure 3.7 *Fitted probability of Left vote over Moderate Right vote by level of education*

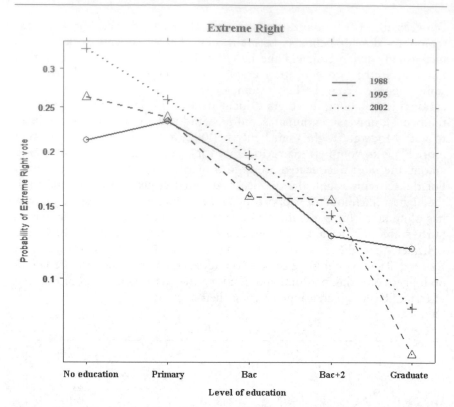

Figure 3.8   *Fitted probability of Extreme Right vote over Moderate Right vote by level of education*

Conclusion

It is somewhat comforting, from a social science perspective at least, to see that France has witnessed elements of change in its social structure, together with points of stability, and that these for the most part coincide comfortably with voter–party alignments. Societies are meant to experience gradual shifts in their composition, rather than overnight realignment, and the emphasis given to both 'political destabilization' and 'new' elements to politics, such as issues, personalities and the media, push us to expect to see more change than is actually there. It is evident that society has changed since 1980 – but equally it would be astounding if the effects of, for instance, religious practice, which have been crucial in democratic politics for the past century, had disappeared in this short space of time.

Of course, they have not. There have been shifts in the social bases to electoral alignment, but there is no convincing evidence that this foundation is crumbling, simply flexible. In only one case is there a shift which has occurred with relative speed – *patrimoine* – and in this case, the reasons

are fairly evident. Assets are economic elements which are easily manipu-
lable, for example via the expansion of share-ownership, facilitation of
house-purchasing and the like. To the extent that precisely these changes
were initiated over the period studied here by Right and Left governments
means that short-term changes could occur. It is not that the relationship
between assets and vote has experienced an axis-shift, but rather that it is
now fairly irrelevant.

Rather than use *patrimoine* and sector, we could have looked at class
using a more nuanced scheme, for instance the Goldthorpe schema of
class categories. Instead of the brutal delineation between working class
and non-working class which the Alford index relies on, this scheme looks
at income, hierarchy, promotion-structure, responsibility and a host of
other work-related indicators to construct its multi-category classification.
But, in fact, it is precisely these elements which our use of service sector and
education tap anyway – who tells you what to do? Who do you tell what to
do? Are you in an educated, career-oriented post or a precarious routine
position? If such elements define class, then clearly class is still as relevant in
France as it was in any other period.

It would be remiss to conclude without mentioning other potential
cleavages which may be emerging in French society. There is an obvious
gender gap, for instance when it comes to supporting the Extreme Right
(Sineau, 2004). The younger generations are developing a different relation
to politics, with at the same time the lowest level of electoral turnout and
the highest support for protest and non-conventional means of participation. The debate around the 'Islamic scarf', and the international context
(September 11, the Iraq War, the Middle East conflict), could foster ethnic
cleavages, particularly with the 'second generation' of Franco-Maghrebins
asserting their identity as Arabs and Muslims. Additionally, the European
Union process stirs pro- and anti- feelings which contribute to the making
of political identity, inward or outward-looking, parochially attached to the
FN 'put the French first' or cosmopolitan and universalistic. But for the
moment at least, these cleavages combine with the present social and
religious cleavages, rather than replacing them (Cautrès and Mayer, 2004).

Chapter 4

Associational Life in Contemporary France

ANDREW APPLETON

'The average French person loves the idea of France, but hates all other French people', General de Gaulle once famously observed. What prompted this somewhat dour observation must be left to the imagination, although it is no doubt not unconnected to his frequent sense of the ingratitude of the French population towards himself. Nonetheless, amusing as it is, the epithet touches upon one of the predominant strains in French political life since the Revolution of 1789, the notion that society is a field of combat and that contention and conflict are an enduring part of the political process.

Nowhere is this more evident than in the associational life of the French polity, both past and present. Paradoxes abound. In arguably the first modern national state, freedom of association was recognized early on as being an inseparable component of citizenship. Yet the French were comparatively slow to exercise that right as part of the organized process of politics. By contrast, mass demonstrations and protest quickly became an integral part of the post-revolutionary political culture of the nation. The powerful institutional role accorded to associations, ranging from trade unions to sports groups, is not in doubt; yet the numbers of French who participated in those associations was traditionally rather lower than in either Great Britain or Germany. And where mass mobilization has had the most impact, it has often been outside the institutions of the state; indeed, it has often been directly aimed at the institutions of the state.

This chapter seeks to highlight and evaluate the major changes that have taken place in associational life in France in recent years. The primary interest for those who study associations and social movements in France is to determine whether the age of the contentious French has drawn to a close and if new forms of political participation and civic engagement have begun to supersede the old paradigms of *immobilisme* and popular protest. We turn first to the historical roots of the French system.

The historical context

The right to organize and participate in free associations was one of the early (ephemeral) conquests of the French Revolution, formally recognized by the Constituent Assembly on 21 August 1790. However, the more enduring and well-known body of legislation from this era was the *loi Le Chapelier*, enacted in July 1791, which prohibited any gathering or organization of artisans and workers along corporate or syndical lines. Under the Empire, the penal code was modified to prohibit gatherings of more than twenty people, and the provisions of Article 291 were stiffened in April 1834. Thus were laid the foundations of what Pierre Rosanvallon has called the 'anti-associational state' in France, and a tension established between the concepts of freedom of association and the mediation of interests, on the one hand, and those of direct democracy and republicanism, on the other hand. In an emerging political culture whose tenor was vastly more dictated by Rousseau than Montesquieu, equality of citizenship and the freedom bestowed by the state could not in any way co-exist with or be subsumed into the manifestation of partial interests.

This is not to say that no civic organizations existed, nor that the French did not participate in numbers in such associations. However, the forced depoliticization of the world of voluntary associations that took place meant that such organizations became largely connected to either sanctioned institutions or groups that were not considered threatening to the political order. In practice, this signified (largely) the Church and women, and often a combination of the two. Charitable organizations were widespread, and constituted an arena in which women could conduct social relations and form networks of action, albeit non-political in character.

In the second half of the nineteenth century, the French working class began to organize into trade unions. Labour organizations were repressed under the Second Empire until the liberalization of 1864, and ambiguously tolerated thereafter. Formal legal sanction was granted in 1884 under the Waldeck–Rousseau government. By the mid-1890s, four principal tendencies had become rooted in the universe of trade unionism in France; anarcho-syndicalism, revolutionary Marxism, reformism and Catholic corporatism. In 1895, the representatives of the first three agreed to federate at the Congress of Limoges and the *Confédération Générale du Travail* (CGT) was born.

The right to freely associate was finally granted at the beginning of the twentieth century, recognized by the law passed on 1 July 1901, once again under the stewardship of Waldeck–Rousseau. Other than the recognition of the right to freedom of association, the law prescribed the conditions under which associations may take on a juridical character (i.e. be recognized as such by the state). The effect was dramatic and instantaneous. Along with the explosion of labour organizations that had been taking place in the previous two decades, new organizations, clubs, associations and even newspapers sprang up. Public meetings, rallies, protests, and strikes became commonplace (Tilly, 1986).

Having recently celebrated its centenary, the *Loi Waldeck–Rousseau de 1901* (referred to by most French people as the *loi 1901*) remains the framework within which associational life thrives in modern France. It has survived modifications (such as those limiting the rights of foreigners introduced in 1939) and outright challenges (such as the attempt to give the State the power to prevent associations from legal registration proposed in 1971), and remains essentially intact in its original form. The centrality of the law to contemporary French political life and culture can be gauged by the fact that the government created a commission in 1999 to organize the centenary celebrations; it sponsored a general assembly (*assises générales*) of voluntary and civic associations, conducted a series of opinion polls and commissioned several studies of the law.

The institutional context

The rapid growth of trade unions and social movements in the *belle époque* of associational life in France was quickly accompanied by another of the enduring features of the political culture of associational life in France, the presence of ideological conflict. Indeed, some have seen in this pattern the exemplar of a 'Latin confrontational model' of trade unionism. Unions, social movements and even civic associations have been linked fairly consistently to political parties and/or political families and as such have become a key channel for the representation of political interests. However, the State has been highly interventionist and domineering; from the 'commanding heights' of the national economy to the most far-flung reaches of the periphery, representatives of the State have structured public policy, political action and discourse. In this model, the sectional or partial interests of groups have been treated by the technocratic class with distrust and disdain, unless organized into neocorporatist structures where the state guided with a firm hand. Given the necessity for generally weak and divided groups to accommodate with the state, political protest has been characteristically spontaneous and uncontrolled, bringing the state into confrontation with 'the street'. The exemplar remains the outburst of demonstrations in 1968, where both the government and the trade union movement found themselves unprepared for and outflanked by an unprecedented popular mobilization that almost succeeded in toppling the institutions of the Fifth Republic. A more recent example that will be returned to below was the wave of strikes and demonstrations in late 1995 that have to some extent galvanized the social movement universe in contemporary France.

In practice, the relationship between the state and economic interest groups has been more complex and interdependent than suggested by the

'Latin confrontational model'. The fact that levels of formal participation in both union and non-union groups in France have been lower than in other European countries may be a bit misleading. Through a wide system of consultation and, frequently, interorganizational competition in specialized elections, large numbers of the French population actually participate in the process of interest-group articulation even if they are not formally members of the aforesaid groups. The state, historically depicted as centralized and monolithic, has provided institutional access points to unions, groups and associations through a vast array of councils, commissions and committees. In 1971, the number of such consultative organs was estimated at 500 councils, 1200 commissions and 3,000 committees; a recent government estimate put the total number at 20,000, including 645 national councils. While many of these bodies deal with industrial, commercial or agricultural issues, large numbers are devoted to various aspects of social and environmental policy. Membership is most often composed of (political) representatives of the government, (administrative) members of the bureaucracy and (elected or appointed) members of associations. The decentralization of the State has only accelerated the growth of such bodies, it seems, as the consultative process has deepened at the local level.

The most visible such council is the Economic and Social Council (*Conseil Economique et Social*). Lynchpin of the Gaullist vision of a political process of *concertation*, the CES today is composed of 231 members. Of these, 69 come from trade unions, 65 from employers and professional associations, 19 from mutual associations and 10 from family organizations. The other 68 members are appointed by the government, with slots being reserved for civil servants, representatives of housing and savings cooperatives, and those who have distinguished themselves in the social, scientific or cultural domain. In short, the CES is designed to capture the full panoply of organized interests in the French economy and society. While it has no actual decisional power, the CES is endowed with the capacity to review relevant domestic legislation and report to the government; the government can also request the advice of the CES on new proposed legislation.

In the area of labour relations, most disputes and arbitrations are handled through the system of elected labour tribunals (*conseils de prud'hommes*). An institution that dates back to 1806, the labour tribunals constitute the backbone of the application of all laws governing the workplace in France today. The main provisions of the current regime date back to 1907 when, contrary to more general practice, women were rendered eligible both to vote and stand for office. The governing principle of the tribunals was to accord bipartite representation to employers and workers (trade unions) in equal numbers. Decisions of the tribunals would be binding on all parties. Care was taken in modifications to the 1907 legislation to ensure that the control of each section of the tribunal (*les conseils de prud'hommes* are organized into five sections) would alternate between employers and workers. The modern system of elections to the tribunals was instigated in 1979, and since then, six elections have taken place.

Since the inception of elections in two 'colleges' (workers and employers) in 1979, participation has fallen rather steadily. In the first such election, fully 66 per cent of the eligible electorate participated. By 1992, that figure had fallen to just 40 per cent; five years later, only 34.4 per cent of the eligible electorate cast their votes in the prudhommal elections. An all-time low was reached in the latest round in 2002, with just 32.6 per cent of workers and 26.6 per cent of employers turning out to vote. Despite this constant decline in voting and electoral participation, the actual competences of the *conseils de prud'hommes* are significant, including conflicts over wages, bonuses, lay-offs and holidays.

Many French groups and associations are subsidized by the State. In the case of trade unions, subsidies often take the form of the payment of salaries of public employees, who are employed full-time as union officials or support staff. This financial aid has taken place irrespective of the ideology of either government or union; there is little evidence that unions have been any less confrontational towards the State as a result of receiving public money. In the case of civic associations, the subsidization of groups by the state is routine. Indeed, this practice has been an integral part of local political life in France (and has not always operated on the correct side of the law). Anyone who has visited a town hall in France cannot fail to notice the number of associations that have official, often financial, backing from the mayor's office.

Non-economic interest groups

Outside the economic arena, the French state's relationship to interest groups has been more top–down in nature. Take, for example, the arena of sports. Today, according to surveys, more French people participate in sporting groups than any other kind of association. As in many other countries, there is a national committee that oversees all Olympic and international sports, the *Comité National Olympique et Sportif Français* (CNOSF). Unlike many other countries, this organization (which was founded in 1908) has specific powers and a competence accorded to it by law (the current version was revised in 1984). The CNOSF is given the legal authority to regulate and oversee all chartered Olympic sports, and to participate in the decision-making forums for sports policy as the privileged interlocutor of the state. Much of the history and culture of interest groups in France is reflected in Article 2, section 8 of the statutes of the CNOSF which charge it with 'working to develop harmonious and cooperative relations with the State' while at the same time exhorting it to 'preserve its autonomy and resist all forms of pressure, including those of a political nature'. In reality, the CNOSF is better viewed as a para-public organization, which serves as the vehicle for the integration of autonomous and specialized interests into the larger, collective interest so implicit in the Rousseauvian and Jacobin tradition.

This model is replicated in other policy areas. For example, women's associations, such as the *Union Féminine Civique et Sociale* (UFCS, created in 1925), were recognized as 'partners of the state' and given the same kind of privileged status as the CNOSF enjoys. However, the role conferred upon these associations was not to 'advance women's interests'; after all, in the Jacobin model, how could any citizen have a partial interest that differed from the collective norm? Rather, these associations were seen as being the intermediary between women and the State and affording the former a voice in the elaboration of the collective interest. For women in France, this meant primarily state-sponsored natalism and the elevation of motherhood to the status of collective need. Thus, the relative vitality of women's associations from the 1920s until the 1970s conspired to preserve the exclusion of women from the public and economic realms, the very late recognition of reproductive rights and legalization of contraception, and a host of legal restrictions upon the freedom of women to exercise independent activity (i.e. hold an individual bank account). Only when autonomous and independent movements emerged in the 1970s did the state begin to respond to women as a group with specific interests, albeit hesitantly.

Religious organizations also work closely with the state. The separation of Church and State was cemented in France in 1905, although certain key issues (such as public subsidies for religious schools) remain unresolved even to this day and are liable to excite great passions. Yet the Catholic Church, along with its panoply of charitable associations, is perhaps better viewed as one of the main pillars of traditional interest group activity in France through the twentieth century. Despite declining patterns of church attendance in the latter part of the century, the Church has had a hand in organizing and mobilizing groups that range from unions to cultural groups. One of the largest is the *Union Nationale des Associations de Parents d'Elèves de l'Enseignement Libre* (UNAPEL), which has mobilized parents with children in private (predominantly Catholic schools) to defend public subsidies for private education. Survey data show that the French do not participate today in religious associations as frequently as their British or German counterparts; however, this gap may mask the relationships between a multiplicity of organizations in different domains that have traditional ties to the Church or to Catholicism more broadly writ, and yet which may not be thought of by participants in those organizations as being primarily religious in nature.

Whether it be sports, religion, women, education or culture the pattern of traditional interest groups in France cannot be thought of in terms of the Madisonian pluralist model, nor is it adequately described by the model of neocorporatism. Associations and groups exist and have done so since the law of 1901; however, the notion of a partial interest is one that has been firmly rejected by the State, and traditional institutions have served less to present a diverse array of such interests for consideration in the policy-making process than to serve as the vehicle for the integration of groups into the republican, Jacobin mould. Under such conditions, it made little sense to think of such groups as being autonomous from the State; nor was it useful to think about the organization of interests in France as emanating from civil society. Where interests have been organized into groups, the latter have been integrated into the political institutions and culture of France only with suspicion and under the strict tutelage of the State.

Sources of change

In recent years, three sets of changes have begun to move France away from the state-dominated, top–down model of interest representation. The first is the crisis of the French state. The combination of globalization, European integration and economic liberalization has squeezed the fiscal resources of the French state. State authorities are less able to buy the loyalties of voluntary associations; indeed, increasingly, they are seeking to tap the financial and administrative resources of these associations, who then demand policy concessions, in return. The French state has also lost status and authority. Its perceived policy failures, along with the spread of a more generalized distrust of public institutions, have led the French public to challenge state solutions and mobilize in favour of alternatives.

A second challenge to the French model of State–interest group relationships comes from the resurgence of social movements (and, possibly, trade unions). The renewal of social movement activity has challenged the perception of such movements as either marginal or irrelevant, or both. By definition operating outside the confines of State institutions, social movements in France have ebbed and flowed over the course of the twentieth century. Not to be confused with anomic political protest, most observers have characterized so-called New Social Movements (those born in the 1960s and after) in France as weak, compared to other advanced industrial democracies. But in recent years, France has witnessed an extra-ordinary upsurge of grassroots, often localized, but sometimes globalized, social movement activity. Less wedded to traditional ideological cleavages in French society, more ecumenical in nature, less overtly confrontational and more strategic in orientation, this new wave of social movement activity challenges the fundamentals of the model of *concertation*, and has many of the characteristics of Madisonian pluralism. Observers such as Touraine have even seen in the phenomenon a transformation of citizenship, a renunciation of the Republican (Jacobin) model (see Waters, 1998).

A third important change has been the flourishing of French interest groups. Although perhaps not a nation of joiners, the French have been adhering to associations on an unprecedented scale. French associational life has become more vibrant, with citizens often belonging to multiple organizations. Taken together, these three developments – the crisis of the State, the emergence of new social movements and the increase in interest group participation – mean that a less affluent and legitimate State confronts a more organized and mobilized society, possessing considerable expertise and resources. As a result, the character of French policy-making has begun to shift, albeit hesitantly.

Social movements

Social movements in France have traditionally been portrayed as relatively weak and ephemeral. One of the old maxims about French politics holds that the periods of greatest social mobilization have taken place outside organized movements and in a relatively spontaneous (some would suggest anomic) fashion. Indeed, France has often been used as the exemplar of a polity with low levels of social movement activity, against which to compare and explain higher levels of mobilization in other countries. However, recent events suggest that New Social Movement (NSM) activity in France is comparatively vigorous, and that social activism is on the upsurge. Recent studies have suggested that this new wave of social activism is more oriented towards individual or sub-group interests than in previous eras (Duyvendak, 1995).

The so called first wave of NSM activity in France occurred in the years following 1968, and is closely connected (both as cause and consequence) with the renewal of the Left and the consolidation of the non-communist movements. Protest activities encompassed demands for women's rights, regionalism, ecology and anti-nuclearism, although the latter two were undeniably less present in France than in other countries such Germany and the Netherlands. Elsewhere, I have argued that the primary limiting factor on social movements during this period was, paradoxically, the very same recomposition of the Left (Appleton, 2000). In the foment following the earthquake of 1968, the movements were quickly and easily subsumed into the larger political project of the Left, and this led to an apparent diminution of their activity in the second half of the 1970s. As Sidney Tarrow has observed, the impact of NSMs during this period upon the policy process was surprisingly low (Tarrow, 1994).

NSM activity witnessed a resurgence in the 1980s, largely structured around the anti-racism movement. The burst to prominence of the xenophobic *Front National* (FN) was countered by an explosion of groups espousing anti-racism; many of the early movements were formed by those of immigrant descent. However, these local and grassroots organizations were supplanted in the public eye by the anti-racist group *SOS-Racisme* and its highly media-savvy spokesperson, Harlem Désir. Although other national anti-racist groups such as *Ras l'Front* and SCALP existed, along with more traditional organizations like MRAP, *SOS-Racisme* gained the support of the Socialist government (both political and, it was rumoured, financial), and it provided the springboard for a new generation of entrants into the Socialist party.

Anti-racism activism gradually gave way to a broader movement concerned with the status of immigrants in all walks of French society and, in particular, those without official papers or up-to-date documents *(les sans papiers)*. Cooperation among older groups such as the *Ligue des Droits de l'Homme* (LDH) and *Terre de l'Homme* with the newer organizations born in the anti-racism struggle gave rise to a broad-based mobilization that became known as the solidarity movement. In conjunction with internationalist associations such as Amnesty International and even *Médecins sans Frontières* (MSF), the solidarity movement formed a broad front that by the 1990s was highly visible in everyday life in France. The concerns of the movement extended beyond just immigrants, and came to include the unemployed and those in precarious social and economic circumstances. Its activity surged again in the winter of 1997–8, and can be seen as a challenge to the predominant role that trade unions have played in the provision of assistance to the unemployed, both statutorily and organizationally.

Along with this new wave of social movement activity came advocacy groups. Some of the more visible and active organizations were those working on behalf of AIDS research and victims. This concern was magnified in France by the tainted blood scandal of the 1980s, when public hospitals continued to take blood donations and give transfusions, even while evidence was mounting at the ministerial level that AIDS transmission could occur. The scandal had the effect of removing the issue from the sub-group status to which it had been relegated in the United States for so long. Groups such as *Aides* attempted to push the issue to the forefront of the policy agenda. Initial rejection of them as interlocutors by the government only served to fuse the movement with more radical gay rights groups such as Act Up, and the movement began to achieve widespread visibility in the public eye.

Whereas the women's rights activism of the early 1970s (see Duchen, 1986) had largely subsided, partly through co-optation by the left and partly through internal divisions, the issue of parity provided a rallying cry in the 1990s. The failure of women to penetrate the political arena and the disillusionment with the Socialist party in the 1980s led to the call for legislation to ensure political, social and economic equality between men and women. Analysts have seen in the parity movement not just a demand for access to political office, but a new conception of citizenship and a new form of democracy (e.g. Baudino, 2003). The term 'parity' was able to appeal to both the women's movement that espoused an equality of difference and the feminist movement with its insistence upon the equality of rights, and the fusion enabled women's organizations to transcend many of the traditional rivalries that had hindered their policy impact. Public opinion responded most favourably to the demands for parity, and the success of the movement was crowned by the passage of the Parity Law in May 2000. Although the effects of the law have been somewhat mitigated, the parity movement was one of the most successful examples of grassroots social activism in contemporary France.

While the environmental movement in France had a lower level of participation and achieved a lower level of public visibility in the first two decades of NSM activity than in other countries, it has begun to see an upsurge in public consciousness and support since then. The movement was late to organize into political parties, and the impact of those parties was limited by interparty rivalries and the electoral system. Nonetheless, the decentralization of the French state was a particular boon for the environmental movement, as environmental advocates have been able to slowly but steadily penetrate the political system at the grassroots level, and now constitute a significant set of actors at the local and regional levels. Some observers have seen a particular model of success in localized, grassroots environmental campaigns in France that continue the protest tradition of Larzac in the 1970s (Alland, 1994). Local protests, whether against a dam, a tunnel or a new industrial plant, have achieved noteworthy results, and constitute a new and often unremarked dynamism in the ecology movement in France. Much of this activism can be seen as emanating from the NIMBY (Not In My Back Yard) phenomenon that has been much analysed in the United States. Most recently, the issue of GMOs (genetically modified organisms) provided the stage for a groundswell of opposition from all sectors of French society, and this has connected many grassroots environmental activists to the anti-globalization movement (Whiteside, 2003).

The latter is perhaps the most interesting NSM in France today, in that it has (a) succeeded in co-opting and interweaving many of the issues discussed above into its discourse, and (b) taken on a peculiarly emblematic status in France. Born in the wake of the strike movement of 1995 and the rejection of neoliberalism as a policy imperative, the main anti-globalization organization, ATTAC, has succeeded in forging a hybrid discourse that marries social mobilization with calls for state interventionism. French intellectuals have rallied to the cause, and indeed people such as Alain Touraine have argued that this is the new *causis belli* for the public intellectual. The face of José Bové has become familiar worldwide, and the self-described goat-herder from the Auvergne can lay claim to speak for a particular audience. Issues such as GMOs, fast food, and gastronomy have been coupled with analyses of the power of global financial markets to produce a potent response to the discourse of globalism and neoliberalism. The centrepiece of ATTAC's programme is the Tobin Tax, which would tax speculative profits from financial transactions to finance local development and, presumably, to reduce local inequalities.

The emergence of ATTAC as the exemplar of the transformation of social movements in modern France serves to open a discussion of the evolution of the relationship between such movements and the State. As we have seen, traditional associations were either recognized and patronized by the state as privileged interlocutors or excluded from the policy process. In the era of new social movements, the French state remained, it has often been argued, exclusionary and it initially regarded NSMs as another form of protest emanating from the street. But many of the political and social causes championed by these movements – anti-racism, environmentalism, women's rights and anti-globalization – have remained undeniably popular and, little by little, there have been responses from the State. Let us examine these for a moment.

Despite the ubiquity of media coverage of ATTAC, the movement claims only about 30,000 members – perhaps high by historical French standards, but not exactly overwhelming when placed in comparative perspective. Internally, ATTAC is more fragmented than often acknowledged and less well-organized than it has claimed to be. But the success of ATTAC in defining popular discourse on globalization and neo-liberalism is uncontested. With about two-thirds of the adult population expressing scepticism over globalization in opinion polls, as many as 43 per cent say that their views have been significantly shaped by the anti-globalization movement (see Uggla, 2003). Even more revealing, 71 per cent of those polled in 2001 expressed support for the centrepiece of ATTAC's manifesto, the Tobin Tax. These numbers may explain the attempt by the leadership of political parties from all sides to develop a dialogue with ATTAC and other groups (backing for ATTAC reflected in these poll data is consistent among supporters of all political parties except the FN). As many as one third of the deputies in the National Assembly are members of the organization, and ATTAC is able to call upon a reservoir of support in the legislative arena. In 2001, Lionel Jospin publicly endorsed the Tobin Tax, only to be quickly emulated by Jacques Chirac. In January 2002, six government ministers accompanied the French delegation to the World Social Forum in Porto Allegre; three ministers from the Raffarin government attended in 2003. That same year, the European Social Forum (the regional successor to the World Social Forum at Porto Allegre) was held in Paris, and some 60,000 people attended. Prime Minister Raffarin welcomed the delegates with 'warmth and generosity', while the Elysée announced the creation of a commission to study the feasibility of the Tobin Tax.

Indeed, so eager were elected officials and members of political parties to join ATTAC or embrace its themes that their actions provoked a deep debate (and almost a schism) within the movement. Given the perception that the French state has so often succeeded in co-opting grassroots movements, those behind ATTAC wanted to ensure that the autonomy of the organization would be guaranteed. The movement published a statement of principles in 2001, in which it promised not to engage in talks or negotiations with political parties, but to hold all dialogues 'in the open with the citizens'. Members are now prohibited from using their status as a factor in political campaigns. National leaders of the organization are prohibited from standing for election. Finally, ATTAC made a commitment to relate to people and parties across the political spectrum, with the exception of the extreme Right (Uggla, 2003).

Much has been written about the growth of what in Europe is called 'governance', a term that has less familiarity to an American audience. Trials of new forms of governance have taken place in many European countries – Denmark, the United Kingdom, the Netherlands and Germany, to name but the more prominent cases. In France, such experiments have taken place to date in two high-profile policy domains, genetically modified organisms (GMOs) and nuclear power. 'Citizen commissions' brought together scientific and technical experts with ordinary citizens, and the social dimension has been included in the policy-making process as an integral part of making what had hitherto been considered strictly technical decisions. Although these flirtations with co-decision have been relatively restricted thus far, they have been non-trivial in their impact and have recast the relations between State institutions and civil society in these precise arenas.

Patterns of participation

The traditional view of France has been that membership in unions and voluntary associations has been comparatively low; social movement activity has been mostly dominated by upsurges in mobilization at various points, and has tended to recede fairly quickly thereafter. So what are the patterns of participation of the French in associative life in the first years of the new millennium?

Looking at membership in trade unions, the portrayal of union membership in France as being both low and in decline is confirmed. According to the OECD data shown, France exhibits the lowest rate of union density among the largest countries, although the reported data for France end in 1995 (OECD, 1995: the OECD data are available from the OECD website, *Labour Market Statistics* series: www.oecd.org). If we are to rely on membership figures provided by the unions themselves, a slightly different trend emerges over the last decade; the CGT claims a 4.5 per cent increase in membership between 1993 and 2003, while the CFDT reports a massive 44.5 per cent increase. Although these numbers are no doubt somewhat unreliable, they do confirm the perception of most observers that union activity has been waxing in the wake of the 1995 strike wave and the 1997–8 Solidarity movement.

The European Industrial Relations Observatory (EIRO), analysing the reported increases that have taken place in union membership in several countries since the early 1990s, suggests that much of the increase can be attributed to women. Comprehensive data are not available for the French case, although the CFDT reported that the proportion of women in its ranks grew from 36 per cent in 1993 to 44 per cent in 2003. If this is indeed correct (and once again, caution must be exercised in using figures given by the unions themselves), it would mean that of the 222,120 new members, 169,040 were women: i.e. approximately five women have joined the CFDT for every three men. These findings would concord with two sets of observations that have been made: one by those who saw, in the strikes of 1995 and particularly in the solidarity movement of 1997–8, signs of a new, gendered type of union activism, and the second by those who have observed the recent demands for inclusion of women and women's issues into unions in countries other than France.

Turning to associational life, it has been noted that while the number of members of associations may have been historically lower in France than in some other countries, the number of associations themselves has been comparatively higher (Wilson, 1987). It is impossible to give an exact figure for the total number of active associations registered under the 1901 law, but it has been estimated that new associations are being created today at

Table 4.1   *Membership in associations, 2000*

Membership in associations		
Yes, several associations	15	
Yes, one association	22	} 37
No	63	
No response	–	
Total	100	

Source: The CSA Survey into associations can be found at: http://www.csa-tmo.fr/fra/dataset/data2K/opi200001109d.htm.

Table 4.2   *Number of associations to which the respondent belongs*

One	59
Two	19
Three	13
Four	3
Five	3
Six or more	2
No response	1
Total	100

Source: CSA Survey.

the rate of about 20,000 per year. According to the *Institut National de la Statistique et des Etudes Economiques* (INSEE), in 2002, 49 per cent of men and 40 per cent of women were members of associations. The largest two categories of associations, in terms of membership, were those representing *le troisième age* and sporting organizations.

These figures can be contrasted with survey data available from the CSA and the World Values Survey. To celebrate the centenary of the *loi Waldeck–Rousseau de 1901*, the government commissioned a survey of attitudes towards and participation in associations. Tables 4.1 and 4.2 give, respectively, the figures for those who reported that they participate in associations, and the number of associations to which these people belonged. Over one third of French adults declared in this survey that they belonged to one or more associations, and of those, two in five had multiple memberships. Nonetheless, the data from the World Values Survey systematically place France as less participatory than either Britain or Germany (in 1990) in a range of selected kinds of organizations, from sporting associations to charities. While these data are now over a decade old, it is worth noting that there was no change in the placement of France in the 1990 sample compared to that conducted in 1981.

The INSEE data reveal some interesting and familiar patterns relating to gender. While men are more slightly likely to join associations than women, almost all of this gap is accounted for by an over-representation of men in sporting associations, groups of retirees from particular firms, and trade unions. In most other kinds of associations, whether cultural, religious, PTAs or the elderly, women form the larger group. However, when it comes to distinguishing between simple members and those who hold administrative or executive responsibilities, 60 per cent of the positions are held by men, irrespective of whether they are majoritarian in the association as a whole.

Table 4.3 *Participation rates in selected associations, 1990*

Type of association	France	Britain	Germany
Environmental	3.1	6.2	4.7
Political party	3.1	5.8	7.5
Religious	6.7	16.4	16.6
Sports	16.2	17.9	21.7
Arts	6.4	10.3	12.0
Charitable	7.4	8.8	7.5
Professional	5.6	11.1	9.1
Other	6.0	7.9	9.5

Source: World Values Survey available for download at: http://www.worldvalues survey.org.

Overall, the French seem to have a fairly positive view of associations: 95 per cent of those asked in the CSA study declared that they had either a very or fairly positive view of associations; 84 per cent agreed with the statement, 'Citizens can make themselves better heard in society through the intermediary of associations.' Two-thirds agreed with the sentiment that, 'Without associations, there can be no social cohesion', and a similar figure thought that the 'the state does not give sufficient aid to associations'; 58 percent wanted to see more associations in France. However, these positive views were slightly mitigated by the perception of nearly four-fifths of the sample that, 'Associations often play the role that the state ought to play', and of three out of five respondents that, 'Many people use associations for personal ends.'

Nonetheless, the view that emerges from this statistical portrait of union and associational life in France today is that economic and social activism is in a period of renewal and revitalization. Although there is as yet no evidence that the French have surpassed their European neighbours in terms of such activism, there are significant signs, both at the organizational and the individual level, that the landscape of associational life in France is changing. Despite the venerable age of the legal framework that dictates the conditions of economic and social activism in France, patterns of participation themselves are modern and widely visible across the towns and regions of the country.

Conclusion

This survey of associational life in France shows that there are some significant changes taking place. Europeanization, globalization and political modernization are all having an impact at both the political cultural and the institutional level. In recent years, issues such as the wearing of Islamic headscarves in schools have challenged the model of Republican universalism and integration that have underpinned the relationship between the individual and the State since the days of the Revolution. While neo-liberalism as a credo may not be as overtly espoused in France as in Britain or the United States, it has not been without impact in the political arena. All of this points to a nascent willingness to think of the individual in terms more familiar to Locke or Madison than Rousseau; interest groups then become admissible as the aggregation of individual self-interest.

It is in this light that the new patterns of grassroots social activism and participation in associational life are quite discordant with the traditional view of associational life in France. Some wish to see this either as a new turn in French society or as constituting a new form of citizenship. While this may be an apt description of some of the more militant NSMs, such as the gay rights or the anti-racism movements, it does not adequately capture the full panoply of activisms (including the anti-abortion movement, 'new age' religious movements, the defence of techno-parties, etc.), nor does it take into account less politicized ones, such as participation in sports or cultural associations. Groups and group life are an integral part of modern France and, as such, have contributed to a sense of pluralism that has not always been the foremost characteristic of the French polity.

How deep will these changes go? The experiments in citizen co-decision in the fields of nuclear power and the environment may be one indication that the institutions of the State themselves are adapting to this new reality. The increasing diversity of the French political class may be another; the penetration of this universe by ATTAC is a good example of the kind of interest-group impact upon the policy process more familiar to an American audience than in the traditional French variant of corporatism. Of course, less easy to predict will be the influence that these changes may exert upon the corollary of the 'strong statist' model, the propensity of the French to take to the streets in protest. Farmers do not seem less willing to use direct action tactics to protest ongoing attempts to reform agricultural subsidies, and the anti-globalization movement has spawned many episodes of confrontation (most famously, the highly mediatized dismantling of a McDonalds in the southwest of France). Nonetheless, the old corporatist ways are under threat, and a new vitality of associational life is the defining characteristic of civil society in contemporary France.

Chapter 5

The Political Executive

ROBERT ELGIE

The Fifth Republic has a dual executive. That is to say, the 1958 Constitution gave powers to both the president and the prime minister. In so doing, it helped to create the potential for tension within the dual executive. At the beginning of the Fifth Republic, this tension was resolved in favour of the President. The first President of the Fifth Republic, General Charles de Gaulle, was a towering figure who took responsibility for making the most important decisions in key policy areas. In so doing, he created the popular expectation of presidential leadership in France and de Gaulle's successors tried to imitate the General and emulate his achievements. Even so, the Constitution of the Fifth Republic is such that presidential leadership can only occur indirectly through the Prime Minister and, during periods of what is known as 'cohabitation', leadership responsibilities have shifted to the head of government. Whether presidential or prime ministerial, executive leadership has always been difficult to achieve because of the many structural and political divisions both within the dual executive and between members of the dual executive and the wider core executive. Indeed, executive leadership is perhaps even more difficult to exercise now than ever before because of the wider context in which the core executive operates, particularly the impact of Europeanization and globalization on the decision-making process. Nonetheless, presidents maintain the potential to set the political agenda. Moreover, a supportive parliamentary majority means that the prime minister has the capacity to pass reforms in particular areas. What is more, as President Jacques Chirac's response to the American plans to invade Iraq showed, when the domestic political and wider external circumstances are right the president has the opportunity to exercise leadership in foreign affairs as well.

There are four parts to this chapter. The first part sketches leadership traditions in France. The second part sets out the structure of the contemporary French dual executive. The third part places the president and prime minister in the context of the wider core executive, examining their relationship with ministers and administrative organizations. The fourth part considers the core executive in a wider context still, looking at the impact on executive leadership of more general domestic and international factors. There is a brief conclusion.

Leadership traditions in France and the collapse of the Fourth Republic

Prior to 1958, there were two separate leadership traditions in France: a tradition of personal leadership and a tradition of parliamentary leadership. These traditions were mutually exclusive and each was based on a very different perception of how the political and social system should be governed. In 1946, the Fourth Republic was founded on the principle of parliamentary leadership. However, the inherent instability of the regime meant that there were calls for a return to a more personalized style of leadership when the system collapsed in 1958. These calls were consistent with Charles de Gaulle's vision of the political system and the Constitution of the Fifth Republic increased the powers of the President and downgraded the role of parliament.

The tradition of personal leadership in France dates back to pre-revolutionary times. This period was marked by a strong, or absolute, monarchy. The King had ultimate and virtually unchecked responsibility. The 1789 Revolution brought about the end of the absolute monarchy, but not the end of the tradition of personal leadership. During the revolutionary period itself, Robespierre established himself as a powerful figure, albeit for a short period. At the beginning of the nineteenth century, Napoléon Bonaparte emerged as an autocratic figure, crowning himself as Emperor and legitimizing his rule by recourse to plebiscites. During the rest of the nineteenth century, the monarchy was restored on a number of occasions and in 1852 Louis Napoléon Bonaparte re-established the French Empire and governed in a manner similar to his uncle previously. The Third Republic marked the end of both the monarchy and Bonapartism, but not the end of personal leadership. In the early years of the Republic, President MacMahon seemed to want to return to a more authoritarian form of leadership. Moreover, with the collapse of the Third Republic in 1940 executive power was vested in Marshal Philippe Pétain as head of the French State. The so-called Vichy regime supported the Nazis and began to install a fascist regime that lasted until the Liberation of Paris in 1944.

All told, there has been a strong tradition of personal leadership in France. This tradition is often associated with undemocratic, populist, authoritarian, self-serving figures. All the same, the myth of personal leadership was, and to an extent remains, very powerful. To some, the French are inherently ungovernable. Therefore, the only way to ensure the unity of the national territory and the integrity of the political, economic and social system is to allow stong personal leadership. Indeed, such leadership, it has been argued, is a prerequisite for French grandeur. According to this line of argument, the only way that France can maintain its supposedly rightful position as a world leader is for the country to be governed by a single, strong figure who can make decisions that are in the national interest. The idea that a strong leader will promote the national interest is particularly important. This is because even though personal leadership has been associated with fascism and the authoritarian right generally, there is also a sense in which it transcends ideological and party political boundaries and has an appeal to French people more broadly.

The tradition of parliamentary leadership emerged during the revolutionary period. The Revolution was a direct response to the absolute concentration of power in the monarchy and was founded on the principle of representative government. In the end, the lofty principles of the revolutionary period were betrayed and the system was unable to establish a long-standing set of democratic institutions. Even so, the principle of rule by the people through a parliament composed of elected representatives was firmly established as one of the basic ideological elements of the French system. In particular, it came to be a constitutive principle of the French Left and, particularly, the revolutionary Left.

The collapse of the Vichy regime in 1944 meant that the Right was discredited. It also meant that calls for anything that sounded even remotely like a return to personal leadership were bound to fall on deaf ears. As a result, the new regime, the Fourth Republic, was founded on the principle of parliamentary leadership. The powers given to the parliament were extensive, while the executive was weak. The head of state, the President of the Republic, was merely a figurehead. What is more, the head of government had little authority. The mixture of a fragmented party system and a proportional electoral system meant that coalition governments were the norm and were constantly faced with the threat of parliamentary defeat. As a result, 'instead of the leader of a united team, almost every premier had to be a broker between rivals over whom he had little control' (Williams, 1964, p. 195). In total, there were 25 heads of government in 12 years and one government survived for just a couple of days.

In the end, the war in Algeria proved too much for the institutions of the Fourth Republic to bear. The system collapsed and Charles de Gaulle was invited to return to power. Previously, he had been the leader of the postwar provisional government in 1944, but he had resigned after less than two years because of his opposition to the Left's plans for the institutions of the Fourth Republic. With the regime now in crisis, de Gaulle was prepared to return to power on condition that a new Constitution be drafted and one that, on this occasion, he would be in a position to craft. At the time, there were fears on the Left that de Gaulle would try to restore the authoritarian and undemocratic form of personal leadership. He did not. However, he did ensure that the Constitution of the Fifth Republic decreased the powers of parliament and increased the powers of the executive. At the heart of the new Constitution was now a dual executive in which both the president and the prime minister have considerable constitutional powers. Thus, the Fifth Republic created an executive-centred regime, but one in which there is an inherent tension between the two elements of the dual executive and where power can, on occasions, shift from the president to the prime minister.

The dual executive

The 1958 Constitution gives day-to-day policy responsibilities to the prime minister. For example, Article 20 states that the government decides and directs the policy of the nation, that it has the administration and the armed forces at its disposal and that it is accountable to the lower house of parliament, the National Assembly. Article 21 states that the prime minister is in general charge of the government's work and is personally responsible for national defence and the implementation of laws. Article 8 states that the prime minister has the right to propose the names of government ministers to the president. Articles 34–50 indicate that the prime minister is responsible for the government's business in parliament and outlines the considerable powers that the government now enjoys over parliament. So, for example, the prime minister fields questions to the government in the National Assembly once a week. By contrast, the president is forbidden from even entering the parliamentary chamber. He may only have a message read out there (Article 18) and this happens very infrequently. All told, the prime minister is placed at the head of a government which dominates the National Assembly and which is charged with the day-to-day realization and implementation of public policy.

That said, the 1958 Constitution also provides the basis for presidential leadership. For example, the president is responsible for negotiating and ratifying international treaties (Article 52). This means that the president is involved in foreign policy-making. In addition, the president is the head of the armed forces (Article 15). In some countries, this title is purely honorific. After all, in Britain the Queen is commander-in-chief of the armed forces, but her position is merely symbolic. In France, the same does not apply. Even though Article 21 states that the prime minister is responsible for national defence, the president's finger is on the nuclear button and the president heads the main defence policy-making committees. For example, it was President Chirac personally who decided in 1995 that France should resume nuclear testing in the South Pacific. Overall, the president is in charge of 'high' politics, meaning France's position in the European and world order. More than that, the president also has a more general influence. The president appoints the prime minister (Article 8). As we shall see, if the political conditions are right, this means that the person appointed may be someone who is unswervingly loyal and/or politically junior to the president, thus giving the head of state an indirect influence over the system as a whole by way of the head of government. Moreover, Article 8 states that the prime minister proposes the names of government ministers to the president, but it also states that the president appoints ministers. So, the president has the power to decide whether or not to accept the prime minister's suggestions. In practice, this has meant that ministers have often been thought of as presidential nominees rather than people chosen by the prime minister personally. The Minister for Foreign Affairs from 2002 to 2004 was a case in point. Prior to his appointment, Minister Dominique de Villepin had been the most senior adviser to President Chirac. Consequently, during de Villepin's time at the Quai d'Orsay – the home of the French Foreign Ministry – Chirac knew that he could rely on the minister's complete loyalty. Finally, Article 9 states that the president chairs the meetings of the Council of Ministers, the French equivalent of the British Cabinet. This means that the president is intimately involved in the weekly meetings of the government's most senior representatives, usually determining what is and is not discussed.

In these ways, the 1958 Constitution provided the basis of France's new-found system of executive leadership. However, it was the 1962 constitutional reform establishing the direct election of the president that created the system we know today. In 1958 Charles de Gaulle was elected president by a wide-ranging electoral college mainly comprising representatives of local government. Yet de Gaulle believed that it was important for the president to be able to speak on behalf of the French people as a whole. In order to do so, he believed that the president needed a direct link with the people. In 1958 it had been impossible to create this link because it would have meant giving the vote to electors in Algeria, which was then an integral part of the French territory. In 1962, when Algeria had gained independence, a reform of the electoral system was possible. Consequently, following an assassination attempt on his life, de Gaulle proposed a constitutional amendment. The reform was passed in a referendum and the first direct election of the president took place in 1965 with de Gaulle winning a clear victory.

The 1962 reform was fundamental because it meant that the presidential election is now the centre-piece of the political process. At the election candidates put forward a programme outlining what they stand for and what policies they will introduce if elected. For example, at the 2002 election Jacques Chirac's re-election programme was a 24-page document called 'My commitment for France' (*http://perso.wanadoo.fr/rpr.infos.27/ 00000005.htm*). A key element of this document was a 'zero-tolerance' law-and-order policy. Other measures included the promise of tax cuts over five years and a reform of the system of local government. What is important about this programme is that, following Chirac's re-election, the policies in it became the priorities of the incoming government and newly appointed Prime Minister Jean-Pierre Raffarin. In fact, the appointment of Raffarin tells us a great deal about how the French dual executive usually works. The prime minister was personally chosen by the president. Raffarin was a senator and president of the Regional Council of Poitou-Charentes, but he was not one of the most senior political figures on the right. However, he had become a loyal supporter of Chirac and the two shared a number of ideas about how to reform the system, including a commitment to a greater decentralization of political powers. When he was appointed Raffarin made it clear that his task was to implement the president's policies. For example, in his investiture speech to the National Assembly the prime minister outlined the policies of his new government. He stated that these policies were founded on the principle of 'humanism' and then he went on to say: 'In bringing about this new French human-ism, we will be fulfilling the President's promise to the French people. This is our binding contract' (*http://www.premier-ministre.gouv.fr/en/ p.cfm?ref= 34983*). In this way, even though President Chirac did not play a direct role in the detailed formulation and implementation of government policy after the 2002 presidential election, he could be sure that the policies being pursued by the prime minister were the ones that he had proposed at the election.

That said, the presidential election is a necessary but not a sufficient condition for presidential leadership. As the Raffarin example demon-strates, the president's influence over the system is exercised indirectly via the prime minister. However, the prime minister is accountable to the National Assembly and most legislation must be passed through parlia-ment. As a result, even though the government has powers to control parliament, if a majority in the Assembly is actively opposed to the prime minister, then policies will not be passed and the prime minister will be dismissed. Ultimately, then, presidential leadership is founded on the presence of a supportive majority in the National Assembly. Following the 2002 parliamentary election, the President's party, the UMP, won more than 60 per cent of Assembly seats. So, Chirac was able to appoint Raffarin as his loyal lieutenant. However, when an election has returned a majority opposed to the president, then the head of state has been obliged to appoint an opponent as prime minister. This is known as 'cohabita-tion' and it describes the situation where there is a president from one party/coalition and a prime minister from an opposing party/coalition. There have been three periods of 'cohabitation' since 1958: 1986–88, when François Mitterrand, the Socialist President, was opposed to Jacques Chirac, who was then the Gaullist Prime Minister; 1993–95, when Mitter-rand was opposed to another Gaullist Prime Minister Edouard Balladur; and 1997–2002, when Chirac, this time as President, was opposed to the Socialist Prime Minister Lionel Jospin.

During 'cohabitation' the decision-making process within the executive exhibits a very different dynamic. In defence and foreign affairs the president maintains an influence, but the prime minister tries to be more active than normal albeit usually with little success. For example, Chirac was the first foreign leader to visit the United States and meet President Bush after the 9/11 attacks. This was a highly symbolic meeting and it is noteworthy that it was the President and not the Prime Minister who attended. Equally, the President was instrumental in the international efforts to restore peace in Kosovo during the 1999 crisis. So, the Constitution allows the president to maintain the image of being a world leader. For their part' 'cohabitation' prime ministers have often tried to influence foreign policy, but with a limited degree of success. For example, in 1998 Prime Minister Jospin made a highly publicised visit to the US which included a high-level meeting with President Clinton. However, when Jospin visited the Middle East in 2000 the outcome was not so positive. At a press conference during the visit Jospin spoke about Palestinian terrorists. In so doing, he was perceived to have upset the supposedly balanced French position on the Arab–Israeli conflict. Whether or not he did so is open to debate. However, the Prime Minister's words were received badly by the Palestinians and his car was attacked as he tried to leave an engagement at the University of Bir Zeit. More humiliatingly politically, President Chirac summoned him to come to the Elysée for a ticking-off immediately on his return to France. The Prime Minister refused to do so, but by that time the political damage had been done. The Prime Minister's attempts to appear like a leading world statesperson had badly backfired and his reputation was tarnished.

In domestic affairs, the situation is different. By virtue of Articles 20 and 21 of the Constitution the prime minister is now able to formulate and implement policies of his/her own. By contrast, the president, now lacking the support of the prime minister and the parliamentary majority, becomes a figurehead. The 1997–2002 period is illuminating in this regard. Prime Minister Jospin was able to pass a series of reforms to which President Chirac was opposed. These included the introduction of the 35-hour working week, the so-called 'parity' reform that tried to ensure 50/50 representation of men/women in representative institutions, an increase in public sector recruitment to help young people gain employment, and a reform of political institutions in Corsica. Indeed, in his first few days in office, the new Prime Minister was able to reinforce the social chapter of the Amsterdam Treaty, something that President Chirac had been unwilling to do previously. For his part, President Chirac was largely impotent to influence the course of domestic policy. For example, in February 2001 the President refused to allow the government's bill on the future of Corsica to be placed on the agenda of the Council of Ministers. However, he did agree to do so only a week later. Thus, his power was more symbolic than substantive. More specifically, what power the president does have in this area is negative rather than positive, that is to say, the president can propose and implement very little. However, the president can delay or even prevent the prime minister from passing certain reforms. For example, President Chirac was able in effect to veto a constitutional amendment that would have altered the structure and powers of the judiciary. This was undoubtedly an irritation for Prime Minister Jospin, but it did not compromise the government's overall policy programme.

In general terms, then, the prime minister seems to have most to gain from 'cohabitation'. However, power has come at a price (Lewis-Beck and Nadeau, 2003). Periods of 'cohabitation' have always preceded a presidential election, but the 'cohabitation' prime minister has never won that election. Chirac lost to Mitterrand in 1988; Balladur lost to Chirac in 1995; and Jospin lost to Chirac in 2002. While many factors contribute to electoral defeat and victory, 'cohabitation' seems to have played a part in each case. For example, at the 2002 election presidential candidate Lionel Jospin was judged on his economic record as Prime Minister over the previous five years. For many people, the record was poor, or at least not good enough, and Jospin was punished. For his part, Jacques Chirac, who had been mostly a figurehead President for five years, was able to win support by promising what he would do if he was returned to office. So, at the first ballot of the election people sanctioned Jospin's past performance and supported, albeit fairly unenthusiastically, the programme that Chirac proposed for the future. Paradoxically, therefore, 'cohabitation' made Chirac appear to be the challenger, whereas Jospin was the unfortunate incumbent.

Overall, the experience of the Raffarin and Jospin premierships are poles apart. The former is a loyal supporter of the President, while the latter was an avowed opponent. Between these two extremes, there have been other types of presidential/prime ministerial relations. Even outside periods of 'cohabitation', the relationship between the president and the prime minister has sometimes been more conflictual. For example, in 1974 Valéry Giscard d'Estaing, a Liberal, was elected President with the support of the Right-Wing Gaullists. In return, Giscard appointed the leader of the Gaullists, who was none other than Jacques Chirac even then, as Prime Minister. The two parties and the two people did not see eye-to-eye. Chirac accused Giscard of trying to undermine his position as head of government and he resigned in protest after just two years in office. Similarly, in 1988 President Mitterrand appointed a fellow Socialist but long-time rival, Michel Rocard, as Prime Minister. Again, this was mainly as a reward for the fact that Rocard had loyally supported Mitterrand's 1988 re-election campaign. However, in office the two did not get on and Rocard often found it difficult to win the President's support when he was trying to deal with government ministers. This last example is doubly instructive. It tells us something about the potentially tense relations that can occur between president and prime minister as a function of France's dual executive structure. In addition, it also indicates that the two main members of the executive have to deal with the wider core executive, notably government ministers and the administration generally. It is to this aspect of the core executive that we now turn.

The wider core executive

The president and prime minister stand at the apex of a wider governmental and administrative structure. The two key elements of this structure are government ministers and civil servants. The opportunity for executive leadership depends at least in part on the relationship between the dual executive and this wider core executive. Specifically, the members of the dual executive, and particularly the prime minister as the head of government, face the problem of ensuring joined-up government, meaning the capacity of the government and administration to act as a coherent and purposive unit. For political and structural reasons the wider core executive in France is very disjointed. There are formal and informal mechanisms that help to increase the unity of the system, but the president and, particularly, the prime minister often find that the wider core executive can be very difficult to manage, never mind direct.

The structure of the government has an important bearing on the process of executive leadership because the prime minister has to manage an inherently divided system. For example, one of the first and sometimes most difficult tasks of any new government is to decide the so-called '*décrets d'attribution*' of each minister and, particularly, junior minister. These decrees set out the domain within which each minister can legally act. They are the source of a brief but often intense period of interministerial rivalry as each minister tries to maximize his/her sphere of competence at the expense of colleagues. However, this brief period of rivalry is symptomatic of a more institutionalized competition within the government generally. Political careers are determined at least in part by whether or not ministers are seen to be successful at their job. Therefore, even though all ministers are part of a government that is collectively responsible to the National Assembly, inevitably they compete against each other. One way in which this competition manifests itself is through the budgetary process. Ministers want to maximize their share of a scarce resource: government money. So, if the Minister for Industry requires funds to finance a pet project and prove that s/he has political clout, then it can only be at the expense of another project in another ministry. This situation encourages ministers to scheme against each other and, sometimes, to criticise each other more or less openly. More than that, individual ministries are often made up of more than one junior ministry. For example, after the March 2004 reshuffle the Ministry for Employment, Labour and Social Cohesion comprised five junior ministries: Labour Relations; the Fight against Vulnerability and Exclusion; the Professional Development of Young People; Housing; and Integration and Equality of Opportunity. The creation of such a large ministry was a sign that the government wanted to prioritize social affairs. All the same, it also institutionalized competition for scarce financial resources within the ministry.

Ministerial divisions of this sort are compounded by the structure of the permanent administration. The central administration in France is highly compartmentalized, meaning that it is made up of many separate and, once again, competing units. All French ministries consist of a number of administrative units called 'directions'. For example, in 2004 the Ministry of Culture and Communication comprised seven separate directions: General Administration; Architecture and Heritage; National Archives; Development of the Media; Books and Reading; Music, Dance, Theatre and Festivals; and Museums. Despite being in the same ministry, each direction has its own interests and priorities. Moreover, there is no overarching official in the department. So, the Minister of Culture has to deal with seven different senior directors, the name for the head of a direction, each of whom wishes to promote the interests of his/her own direction first and foremost. Indeed, administrative divisions do not end there. Directions are divided into sub-directions – seven in the case of the aforementioned direction of Architecture and Heritage alone. In turn, sub-directions are divided into bureaux. In addition, there are myriad stand-alone organizations within ministries: delegations, centres, administrative, scientific, commercial and educational public bodies, and so on. In addition, there are field organizations, or deconcentrated services, that operate across the national territory. The net result is that ministries are very divided organizations.

The structural divisions within the government are overlaid by a set of political divisions. For example, governments can be divided on ideological grounds. This is particularly true for coalition governments. In the 1997–2002 government there were various disputes between the main coalition partners. For example, reform of the public sector and the administration would have been more extensive if the Communist party had not been in government. As it was, Prime Minister Jospin had to take account of his coalition partner's priorities. Ideological divisions are not confined to coalition governments. In the early days of the 2004 Raffarin government there were sharp disagreements between the Finance Minister, Nicholas Sarkozy, and the Minister for Employment, Labour and Social Cohesion, Jean-Louis Borloo. Both are members of the UMP party, but Sarkozy is a Liberal, which, in addition to his role as Finance Minister, means that he has a general tendency to promote a less extensive role for the state in general and, hence, limit government spending. By contrast, Borloo believes that the State should play an active role to ensure social justice. This means greater financial support by the State. In the early days of the new government, there was open competition between the two. More generally, in any government some ministers are more influential than others. There may be senior party figures whose views the prime minister cannot ignore. For example, during the 1997–2002 government the Minister for Social Affairs, Martine Aubry, took personal responsibility for the passage of the

35-hour working week laws. In so doing, she came into conflict with other ministers, notably then Finance Minister Dominique Strauss-Kahn. In this case, the Prime Minister fully supported the Aubry reforms, but there is no doubt that Aubry's senior status within the Socialist party and the government hierarchy helped the eventual passage of the reforms.

At times, ministers can even seem to challenge the very position of the prime minister. This is particularly true if the prime minister is politically damaged. In the 1991–92 government of Edith Cresson, the Finance Minister, Pierre Bérégovoy, was able to impose his priorities on the government at the expense of the Prime Minister whose opinion poll ratings were so low that she soon lacked any authority. The position of Jean-Pierre Raffarin immediately after the 2004 regional elections was quite similar. The right's performance was so poor at these elections that the head of government's position was weakened. At the same time, though, the prime minister's ability to manage political priorities successfully may also be compromised if ministers are weak. This situation sometimes occurs when ministers are drawn from 'civil society', or outside politics. A case in point was Francis Mer, a businessman who was appointed as Finance Minister at the Prime Minister's request in the 2002–04 Raffarin government. He had little party political experience and the fact that he lacked explicit presidential support meant that he had little political authority. As a result, he found it difficult to impose his views on government colleagues. Indeed, the same was true for the academic, Luc Ferry, who was the Education Minister during the same government. Both ministers were highly talented, but the inability to control their respective departmental briefs weakened the position of the Prime Minister and ultimately the government as a whole. In the end, both ministers were replaced at the 2004 reshuffle.

These structural and political divisions do not mean that joined-up government is impossible but they do reinforce the need for governmental coordination (Hayward and Wright, 2002). Ministers have to manage the divisions within their own departments. They are assisted in this regard by a set of personal advisers who are collectively known as the '*cabinet*'. Each minister has a *cabinet* of between 7 and 12 people. They look after the minister's political career, writing speeches and providing policy advice. In addition, they play a key role liaising with the permanent administration and coordinating the work of the department. More generally, the prime minister has to manage the government as a whole. To this end, the prime minister also has his/her set of personal advisers. There are usually about 40–50 people in the prime minister's *cabinet*. Generally speaking, there is one *cabinet* member for each government department. This person follows the work of his/her assigned ministry and provides policy advice. At the top of the *cabinet* structure is the head of the prime minister's personal staff, or *directeur de cabinet*, who coordinates the work of the *cabinet* as whole and who has an overview of the government's work generally. These staff resources help the prime minister to coordinate the system, although Raffarin was criticised for the choice of his first *directeur de cabinet*, Pierre Steinmetz, who seemed unable to ensure that ministerial advisers abided by the Prime Minister's decisions. In this role as chief coordinator, the prime minister is sometimes helped and sometimes abetted by the president's personal staff, which is called the General Secretariat of the Presidency. The organization of the president's personal staff is similar to the prime minister's *cabinet*. The relationship between the two teams mirrors the relationship between the president and prime minister. At times, they work in tandem. On other occasions, they seem to be in competition with each other. In the most extreme case, during periods of 'cohabitation' regular contact is only allowed at the highest level between the prime minister's *directeur de cabinet* and the head of the president's staff, the General Secretary of the Presidency (Schrameck, 2001). In addition to these political staffs, there are also various overarching administrative units. Most notably, the General Secretariat of the Government is the French equivalent of the British Cabinet Office, providing advice on matters of law and taking care of the administrative aspect of the government's work, including the preparation of weekly meetings of the Council of Ministers, the name for the French Cabinet. In addition, a separate institution, the SGCI, coordinates the government's work as it relates to the formulation and implementation of law at the EU level.

Helped by these organizations, one of the prime minister's main functions is to arbitrate between the conflicting demands of the different ministers. Again, the budgetary process is instructive in this regard. Much of this process takes the form of bilateral relations between the finance and budget ministers on the one hand, and spending ministers on the other. Many issues are resolved during the course of protracted negotiations between the two sets of actors. Each year, though, some issues will be impossible to resolve. A minister will demand money that the Finance Ministry is unwilling to give. In these cases, the prime minister arbitrates. This places the prime minister in a potentially powerful position. The head of government is in a position to determine the government's priorities. That said, the prime minister's ability in this regard is limited. Most notably, as we have seen, outside 'cohabitation' the prime minister's priorities have to be consistent with the President's and in arbitration meetings the president's advisers will emphasize this point if the need arises. More than that, in some cases the president may intervene more directly in the arbitration process. For example, a strongly placed minister may be unwilling to accept the arbitration of the prime minister, especially if the head of government's authority has been weakened. In these cases, the president may be required to make the final decision either formally or informally.

Ultimately, the political success of the president and, particularly, the prime minister depends on the ability to ensure joined-up government within the wider core executive. Structural and political divisions make this an extremely difficult task. The president can offset these difficulties somewhat by adopting a position above the fray and focusing on world events. But there are limits. For example, Chirac was heavily criticised for not doing enough when the government failed to prevent the hundreds of deaths that occurred during the heatwave in the summer of 2003. Whatever the president's ability to concentrate on foreign policy, the prime minister has no such luxury. The head of government's performance is determined as a function of the public's perception of the state of the economy, how safe people felt on the streets and in their homes, and how well they feel France is performing generally. In recent times, a rash of books have argued that France is in decline (e.g. Bavarez, 2003). Certainly, recent prime ministers have found that their lot is not always a happy one. Alain Juppé had a poor record and his government was kicked out of office in 1997. Lionel Jospin governed for five years only to find that he came third at the 2002 presidential election behind the leader of the Extreme Right, Jean-Marie Le Pen. Jean-Pierre Raffarin found that his honeymoon period was very short and his party fared disastrously at the 2004 regional elections, weakening his political authority. These examples illustrate the difficulties associated with running the country. They are partly a function of the problems with managing the wider core executive. They are also partly the result of the wider context within which political leaders operate.

The core executive in a wider context

There is an increasing mismatch between the promises presidential candidates make at elections and their ability to keep these promises in office. This trend was illustrated first and perhaps most starkly in 1981. President Mitterrand was elected on a very reformist programme. In fairness, many reforms were passed, but many were not. Moreover, in March 1983 the government had to embark on a complete economic policy U-turn. Since this time, presidential programmes have tended to be somewhat less ambitious. Even so, they still contain the prospect of a brighter future. For example, Chirac's 2002 programme began with the following statement: 'Before us ... there are undreamed of possibilities ... to take France forward for the well-being, the blossoming, the happiness of every French woman and every French man' (*http://perso.wanadoo.fr/rpr.infos.27/00000005.htm*). There is little doubt that voters are now more cynical than before and that they take the claims made in presidential programmes with a pinch of salt, if they read them at all. However, there is also no doubt that presidential elections still create the expectation of change and change for the better. Arguably, though, such change is more difficult to bring about than ever before. In particular, the dual executive faces more constraints at home than was previously the case and more challenges internationally. Thus, presidents, and particularly prime ministers, sometimes seem doomed to failure. Even so, when the circumstances are right there is still the opportunity to show leadership as the French attitude to the US–UK invasion of Iraq demonstrated.

For many years there was a strong *étatiste*, or state-centred, approach to policy-making in France. For example, there was a *dirigiste* system of state-led economic intervention; there was a highly developed system of economic and social planning; and the state promoted and supported a policy of national industrial champions and costly high-tech projects. These policies, and many others, were underpinned by a wide-ranging set of state institutions whose organization and powers provided the dual executive with key decision-making powers. These institutions included public enterprises (*entreprises publiques*); quasi-public organizations (*établissements publics*); as well as individual institutions, such as the Bank of France and the state-controlled investment organization, the Caisse des Dépôts et des Consignations. In recent times, this system has been reformed. Compared with countries like Australia, New Zealand and the UK, the degree of reform might be considered relatively modest (Pollitt and Bouckaert, 2000, p. 231). However, in the French context the extent of reform has been significant. For instance, both Left and Right-wing governments have privatized public enterprises; quasi-public organizations have been transformed into public–private partnerships; decision-making powers have been transferred from government ministries to independent administrative authorities; and institutions such as the Bank of France have been granted operational independence. In short, the French state still comprises thousands of institutions that continue to carry out an almost bewildering variety of tasks. Hence, there is a continuing need for joined-up government. All the same, over the last decade or so the state has been divested of many of its most important responsibilities.

In addition to these domestic changes, France has been affected by international challenges. Indeed, some of the aforementioned domestic changes have been brought about by such challenges. In particular, France, like other European countries, has been affected by Europeanization and globalization. At the European level interest rate decisions are now taken by the European Central Bank; agriculture policy is determined in Brussels not Paris; decisions about company mergers and acquisitions have to be approved by the European Commission; member-state governments are forbidden from subsidizing ailing state companies and industries; and so on. In the international arena, French economic growth is at least partly a function of economic demand in the US; American foreign policy in the Middle East helps to determine oil prices, which in turn impact on inflation, debt and growth rates in France; French companies are in competition with huge multinational private companies, meaning that to survive they have to be given the opportunity to form strategic alliances with foreign partners and privatization is often a necessary condition of any such strategy; and so forth. All told, while decision-makers in France were never free from external pressures, these pressures now manifest themselves in ways that are often much more immediate and, sometimes, much more dramatic than was previously the case.

These domestic and international changes have had a profound impact on the decision-making capacity of the dual executive. For example, during the 2002 presidential election campaign Jacques Chirac made a pledge to reduce the level of income tax by a third over five years, including a 5 per cent cut in the first year of his term of office. This latter pledge was met and Prime Minister Raffarin reiterated his commitment to fulfilling the more general promise on a number of occasions. However, this campaign promise has huge cost implications and the government has been wrestling with how to deal with them ever since. Given the current very modest levels of economic growth, in order to keep this promise the government will need to reduce public spending, increase the size of the public debt, or raise taxes elsewhere. However, it is notoriously difficult to reduce public spending. Upwards of 90 per cent of public money is pre-committed from one year to the next in the form of multi-year spending programmes, public sector salaries, investment and ongoing costs. By the same token, the terms of the European Union's Stability and Growth Pact mean that France's budget deficit cannot go above 3 per cent of Gross Domestic Product. France's deficit already exceeds that figure. So, even though the French government, along with the German government which faces similar problems, has attempted to make the application of the rules of Stability and Growth Pact less stringent, there is in effect very little room for manoeuvre in that regard. As a result, the only way that the President's promise can be met is if other taxes are raised to compensate for the loss of income resulting from the reduction in come tax. This seems to be what the government is doing. In particular, it has been accused of transferring the responsibility for certain issues from central government to local government. The effect may be that people pay less in national income tax, but more in local taxation. In this case, the President may be able to claim that he has kept his promise to reduce income tax, but he may have done so by having to raise taxes elsewhere. This is not necessarily what the public expected, so there is the potential for disillusionment and cynicism.

Faced with the problems of managing the wider core executive and with the constraints imposed upon the core executive by the wider domestic and international context, it would be tempting to conclude that French political leaders are now powerless. This is not the case. Reforms are possible. Indeed, in the period from 1 October to 18 December 2003 no fewer than 10 laws and 16 international treaties were passed. What is more, governments can pass significant reforms. For example, the flagship reforms of the Jospin government, including the 35-hour working week and the parity reform, were specific initiatives that introduced major aspects of social change and that flowed directly from the election of a new government. They would not have happened otherwise. By the same token, while there is an ongoing debate about how they should be funded, the decentralization reforms passed by the Raffarin government in 2003–04 have the potential to make a big difference to the balance of power between central and local government. In this case, the decentralization reform figured prominently in the President's campaign programme and was one of Chirac's priorities when he was returned to office. It was also one of his loyal Prime Minister's policy priorities (Raffarin, 2002, pp. 144–8). There were few ministerial objections in principle and it was supported by the parliamentary majority. What is more, there were few European or wider international issues at stake. The decentralization reform was a purely French affair.

In foreign affairs, too, leadership may be possible. President Chirac's controversial stance in the run-up to the American-led invasion of Iraq is instructive in this regard. Like many other people, Chirac did not believe the claims that Iraq had ready-to-go weapons of mass destruction and that it was actively supporting Al Qaeda activity. More than that, even if time and time again over the course of his political career, and he was Prime Minister as far back as 1974, Chirac has flip-flopped on foreign and domestic policy, his Gaullist roots are very deep. In terms of foreign policy, what this means is that he believes France should be a major world power and, more importantly, one that is separate from the world's other superpower(s). When the US and the USSR were fighting the Cold War, France often tried to steer a third way between them and upset the Americans in so doing. Now there is only one superpower, France is keen to lead or at least be part of a block of countries that can provide an alternative to the US point of view. Even so, Chirac's political beliefs do not explain why he was so outspokenly opposed to the US's plans. Here, the answer lies in domestic politics. After the 2002 elections, Chirac's party, the UMP, controlled all the main institutions of state – both houses of parliament, much of local government, the Constitutional Council, the higher reaches of the civil service, and so on. Thus, there was very little opposition to the President. Moreover, public opinion was massively opposed to the war, so Chirac was on safe ground. The combination of all these factors allowed Chirac to adopt a much firmer stance than he might have been able to do so at another time. It is true that over the years France has been a more consistent supporter of the 'Arab' position than many other countries (*la politique arabe*). Indeed, when President Mitterrand was elected in 1981 he was criticised at home for being too close to the American line in his support for Israel. It is also true that France has a long history of good relations with Iraq. The deal to build the Isis and Osirak nuclear reactors was signed in 1975 when Chirac was Prime Minister and, more recently, France was heavily involved in the exploitation of Iraq's oil fields. Even so, economic self-interest alone does not explain Chirac's anti-American position. If it did, then France would have been just as outspoken on similar issues before now and consistently so. After all, up to this time, France has had a habit of making a diplomatic nuisance of itself and then coming back into line at the last minute. The Iraq issue was different. Chirac's opposition to the war in Iraq was motivated by the failure to be convinced of the need for swift action against the country, by a long-standing Gaullist attitude towards a particular type of foreign policy and by the knowledge that he had almost complete freedom to pursue this policy at home. This combination of factors allowed to him adopt a stand against the invasion of Iraq and led to him being reviled in the US as the rat-faced leader of the 'axis of weasel'. Whether or not Chirac was right to do so is another matter. The point being made is that presidents, while constrained, can exercise foreign policy leadership when the conditions are right.

In fact, foreign policy is the domain in which the difference between the president and prime minister is most stark. In his first two years in office Prime Minister Raffarin made no significant foreign policy contribution. This was the President's 'reserved domain'. Even during 'cohabitation', as we have seen, when Prime Minister Jospin tried to outline his thoughts about the Arab–Israeli issue, he was publicly humiliated. In short, prime ministers do not have the popular authority or the constitutional legitimacy to influence foreign policy. In stark contrast, presidents can use foreign policy as a resource. Indeed, this point applies perhaps most notably when their domestic stock is falling. Here, the most dramatic example concerns François Mitterrand. In 1984, when the socialists where doing badly in the opinion polls after three years in office, he engaged with Europe. More than that, he became a key actor in the negotiation of the Single European Act and then the Maastricht Treaty. In so doing, he shaped the course of European integration. At the same time, he also helped to restore his flagging authority within France. What this example shows is that while foreign and international events may sometimes limit the decision-making capacity of the French executive, at other times the link between foreign and domestic policy can be used to the advantage of the president.

Conclusion

The 1958 Constitution established a dual executive in which both the president and prime minister have considerable powers. However, for much of the Fifth Republic the president has been the dominant actor. Indeed, following his re-election as President in 2002 Jacques Chirac appointed a loyal Prime Minister Jean-Pierre Raffarin to implement his programme and establish the policy agenda. Even so, events during the Fifth Republic have shown that leadership responsibilities can pass from the president to the prime minister. From 1997 to 2002 Prime Minister Jospin was fully responsible for domestic policy-making and was able to introduce major policy reforms. Whoever is in overall charge of policy-making, the key actors within the French dual executive still have to ensure joined-up government within the context of the wider core executive. Moreover, they also have to react to events and developments within the broader domestic and international context. At times, these factors serve to limit the leadership capacities of the president and prime minister. Certainly, successive presidents and prime ministers have found it very hard to keep true to their campaign commitments. On other occasions, though, events help to strengthen the position of executive actors. This is particularly true for presidents and foreign policy. The French look to the president to promote France on the world stage. Presidents look to the world stage to strengthen their own reputation among the French. In this regard, President Chirac, like his predecessor, François Mitterrand, before him, has been very successful.

Chapter 6

Prometheus (Re-)Bound? The Fifth Republic and Checks on Executive Power

ANDREW KNAPP

Many constitutions in democratic states were drawn up to restrain and limit executive power. That of the French Fifth Republic, more unusually, was written to extend it. The main loser of the 1958 Constitution was the legislature, viewed by de Gaulle and his followers as the extravagant and divisive forum of the old 'régime of parties' they derided. The winners were two: the President, and the Prime Minister and government. The President was given significant new powers – to take discretionary powers in an (exceptional) state of emergency (Article 16), to call a referendum (Article 11), to dissolve parliament (Article 12). He also enjoyed a much higher political profile, thanks first to the general authority entrusted him by the Constitution's Article 5, second because he was de Gaulle, and third because the constitutional reform of October 1962 – a veritable 'second foundation' of the régime – ensured that the General's successor (and indeed de Gaulle himself, in 1965) would be directly elected.

The prime minister and government, for their part, benefited from a detailed battery of constitutional provisions designed to strengthen their hand in relation to parliament. Though still responsible to its lower house, the National Assembly, the government enjoyed, among other things, priority for its bills on the parliamentary agenda (Article 48); the right to compel parliament to vote on the government version of any bill, including only those amendments it favoured (Article 44); and the right to declare any bill a question of confidence, requiring the Deputies in Parliament either to accept the bill or to vote a censure motion against the government by an absolute majority (Article 49.3). The duration of parliamentary sittings was limited, and the detail of legislation was reserved to government decrees, not parliamentary laws (Article 34), and even primary legislation could be delegated, on a temporary basis, to the government (Article 38). Deputies could no longer propose extra spending or lower taxes. Parliamentary committees, meanwhile, were rendered large, unwieldy, unspecialized and ineffective, their numbers being limited to six (Article 43). The most aggressive form of parliamentary questioning of the executive, the *inter-pellation*, was ended by the National Assembly's new standing orders.

These constitutional safeguards were reinforced, quite unexpectedly, by the emergence of a coherent Gaullist-led parliamentary majority from the elections of 1962. The Senate, it is true, retained the constitutional power to block constitutional reforms or legislation concerning itself; de Gaulle, however, overrode that, quite unconstitutionally, by proposing the referendums of 1962 and 1969 directly to the people, over the head of the Senate. Small wonder, then, that de Gaulle and his successors were viewed as the most powerful chiefs of any Western democratic executive. Securely elected for an exceptionally long term (the *septennat*, or seven-year mandate, two years longer than that of parliament), the French president could both appoint and (effectively, though not constitutionally) remove the prime minister and government, who in turn could discipline at will the parliamentary majority to which they were notionally responsible, and which, in any case, soon adopted a more or less servile mode of behaviour.

That state of affairs no longer prevails. Heroic presidential leadership, delivered regularly by de Gaulle, has been in short supply under his (supposedly Gaullist) successor Jacques Chirac, elected in 1995. Indeed, the title of one recent study ('The Fifth Republic: Birth and Death': Donégani and Sadoun, 1998) suggests, not just that the Constitution works differently, but that France has undergone régime change. This is exaggerated but not fanciful. Early analyses of the strength of the Fifth Republic presidency tended to stress its structural bases (the president's constitutional powers, the legitimacy procured by direct election for a seven-year term) at the expense of the contingent ones (the control of a presidential party, the support of a parliamentary majority, and presidential popularity). The tendency of presidents to stress the former and to downplay, if not to conceal, the latter, encouraged this. But a constitution, as de Gaulle remarked in 1964, is a state of mind and a habit of behaviour as well as institutions – 'un esprit, des institutions, et une pratique'. Since 1962 the Fifth Republic's institutions have mutated as a result of both deliberate change – most obviously constitutional amendments – and less formal transformations to their spirit and their workings, as dormant checks and balances have leapt into operation while once-formidable weapons of presidential power have been blunted or worse. Moreover, the EU, though shaped by France at least as much as by any other member-state, both constrains and reinforces the power of France's executive, and especially of the president. Finally, the French public, both as voters and as activists, have been less ready in recent years to accept the leadership of the political executive than at the outset of the Republic. All of these developments have made such leadership harder to exercise. None has made it impossible.

Traditional institutional accounts identify the legislature and the judiciary as the main constraints on executive power. Each was considered weak under the early Fifth Republic; each has regained some degree of assertiveness since. We now consider whether the French parliament and France's judicial and quasi-judicial actors have forced French governments to be more accountable.

The French parliament

'The French Parliament, once one of the strongest in Europe, has become one of the weakest' (Williams, 1969). We have noted the formidable array of constitutional mechanisms designed precisely to minimize parliament's powers. They were reinforced in the regime's early years by the emergence of coherent majorities, by the often-cavalier attitude of governments towards the legislature, and by the reflection of this in the supine attitude of many parliamentarians.

Institutional accounts of parliaments often focus on two essential functions. The first is legislation. 'Transformative' assemblies actually draft and make laws, or at the very least are free to amend government bills very substantially. The second is scrutiny. 'Debating' assemblies aim to hold the executive to account, both in committee and in plenary sessions. Some legislatures (like the US Congress) may do both, while others focus more on the legislative function (like the German Bundestag) or on scrutiny of the executive (like the British House of Commons). The French National Assembly did little of either in the early years of the Republic. It has done more more recently. The legislative function was reinforced by a constitutional amendment of 1995 that reserved one sitting a month to parliamentary business rather than the government's agenda, allowing greater scope for private members' bills. Of the 98 laws promulgated in the 2002–2003 session of parliament, 17 originated, at least formally, with individual deputies or senators. Many were of relatively minor importance (referring to safety in swimming pools or driving under the influence of drugs); some were almost certainly planted by government. But this was a stronger parliamentary record than in the early years. The right to amend was similarly reinforced, though this was more through the changed behaviour of deputies than by formal institutional means. The watershed year in this respect was 1981: conservative opposition deputies seeking to obstruct the new Left-wing government began to propose industrial quantities of legislative amendments. The number tabled in the Assembly, in particular, grew exponentially, and has remained high ever since. In 2002–2003, admittedly a record year in which the Left-wing opposition did its best to obstruct the Raffarin government's welfare reforms, nearly 32,500 amendments were tabled – over 25,000 of them by opposition deputies. This was over three times more than in the whole of the 1968–73 Assembly. Although many were merely obstructive and only 3,266 of them – one in ten – were passed, this was still nearly two-thirds of the whole 1968–73 period – and 420 of the successful amendments had been put down by the Left-wing opposition.

A further opportunity for parliamentarians to affect legislation was offered by the 1974 constitutional amendment allowing 60 deputies or 60 senators to refer a bill to the Constitutional Council. This, along with the Constitutional Council's more general role, is discussed below.

The record on questions – central to the scrutiny function – is comparable. In the 1968–73 Assembly, the government's response rate for 'oral questions without debate', the commonest form of parliamentary questioning, was barely 25 per cent. More recently, however, changes to Assembly rules under the 1995 constitutional amendment and in particular the institution of a regular question time *à l'anglaise*, have transformed this desultory performance. In 2002–03, a total of 771 questions to the government, or about 80 per cent of the total number tabled, received answers over some 64 sittings; of these, roughly a third were put down by the opposition. The number of written questions answered in the same period was over 16,000, of which 5,000 came from the opposition. Finally, the proliferation of parliamentary committees of inquiry, such as the committee on the prison system set up in 2000, has indicated a greater willingness to engage in more than merely formal scrutiny of the executive.

Despite this substantial quantitative change, France's parliament lacks the centrality it enjoyed under previous regimes. The non-specialized nature of committees, and the ever-present possibility that the government may use its prerogatives under Articles 44 or 49.3, limit the scope of most amendments. The research resources of parliamentarians, though much improved since 1958, remain limited. With most deputies holding important local government responsibilities, absenteeism is common; fewer than 150 deputies, for example, were present at most of the debates in June–July 2003 on the government's important pensions reform project. Similarly, while ministers take parliamentary questions more seriously than their predecessors of the 1960s, parliament is seldom the place where political reputations are made or broken. Ministers and party leaders risk far more at the hands of judges than they do at the rostrum of the Assembly, and are readier to use the media to raise their political profile than to establish a standing as skilled parliamentary debaters. And, crucially, while the prime minister appears regularly to answer questions, the president, under Article 18 of the Constitution, communicates with parliament only by messages.

To view 'parliament' as a check on the executive is to imply an intrinsically adversarial relationship that does not really exist. For the two are linked by party. This was perhaps unclear at the outset of the Republic. De Gaulle's initial conception of the presidency was of a figure above the partisan fray, whose main political resource would be his direct links with the nation. This myth has persisted: all French presidents have relinquished their party posts before even campaigning for the top office. It has been belied, however, by the behaviour of de Gaulle and his successors. From the legislative election campaign of 1962, the General gave his public support to the Gaullist party, the Union for the New Republic (*Union pour la Nouvelle République*: UNR), which, with its Giscardian allies, won the first stable majority in French republican history. Since then, the French parliament has represented, as in other democracies, an arena of conflict between the executive's partisans and its opponents. Because of that, the extent of parliamentary constraint on executive power will vary, to some degree, with the National Assembly's party composition.

Of the six configurations set out in Table 6.1, the first two are the most benign for the president and government. They may, under these circumstances, face disaffection and grumbling among their own parliamentarians. They may even have to give way on some secondary issues. In November 2004, for example, the Raffarin government dropped plans for a new law to give homosexuals better legal protection against discrimination owing to opposition from within the ruling conservative party in parliament, the UMP. But on larger issues, the command of an absolute parliamentary majority, or at least a clearly dominant position in the majority coalition, ensures that executives need fear little serious obstruction. Constitutional weapons under Articles 44 and 49.3 are seldom required, though they may be used to speed the passage of a bill. Scenario no. 3 occurred during the Giscard presidency, when his Centre and

Table 6.1   *Presidents and parliamentary majorities since 1958*

President and period	Parliamentary majority
de Gaulle 1968–69; Pompidou 1969–73; Mitterrand 1981–86; Chirac 2002	Overall National Assembly majority for president's party (but other parties still in majority coalition)
de Gaulle 1962–68; Pompidou 1973–74; Chirac 1995–97	Overall majority for president's coalition: president's party the 'majority of the majority'
Giscard 1974–81	Overall majority for president's coalition: president's party the 'minority of the majority'
Mitterrand 1988–93	President's coalition a few seats short of absolute majority
de Gaulle 1958–62	No overall majority: president's party strongest in Assembly
Mitterrand 1986–88, 1993–95; Chirac 1997–2002	Overall majority opposed to the president, leading to 'cohabitation'

Centre-Right groupings, federated in 1978 into the Union for French Democracy (*Union pour la Démocratie Française*: UDF), were outnumbered in the Assembly by the increasingly fractious Gaullists under Chirac's leadership. Despite initial reluctance, Giscard was increasingly driven to use the constitutional disciplines, especially in the latter part of the presidency, on bills as basic as the annual budget. Under scenarios 4 and 5, we see governments remaining in office without an overall majority, and using the full means offered by the constitution in order to do so. Of the 329 times that the procedure of the *vote bloqué* (Article 44) was used between 1958 and 2003, a total of 122, or over a third, occurred in just ten years: 23 in 1958–1962, 17 between 1967 and 1968 (when the government's majority was wafer-thin), and 82 between 1988 and 1993. More striking still, of 81 times the government engaged its responsiblity on a bill under Article 49.3, fully 48, well over half, occurred in the same ten years: 7 in 1958–1962; 3 between 1967 and 1968; and 38 between 1988 and 1993.

The most radical transformation, however, occurs when the National Assembly majority opposes the president, as under Scenario 6. The end of each of François Mitterrand's presidential terms saw a Right-wing majority elected – small but sufficient in 1986, overwhelming in 1993. Chirac had to cohabit with a Left-wing majority for five whole years after his botched dissolution of 1997. Under these conditions, 'the executive', which under scenarios 1 to 5 could be viewed as a single, if composite, entity, divides into two opposed camps. In scenario 6, the prime minister, no longer either a loyal presidential supporter or a leading politician from the presidential coalition, is instead a choice imposed on the president by circumstance. He is the *de facto* leader of the National Assembly majority, and as such is hostile to the president, the case for Chirac in 1986, Balladur (a choice delegated by Chirac) in 1993 and Jospin in 1997. Whereas the prime minister under scenarios 1 to 5 depends for his survival on presidential goodwill (both de Gaulle and Giscard even required their prime ministers to supply undated letters of resignation on their appointment) and heads a government approved by the president to carry out presidential policies, the prime minister under 'cohabitation' remains unmovable as long as he retains the Assembly's backing, selects his own ministers and, at least in domestic matters, is the nation's chief policy-maker.

The prime minister under cohabitation is rather more constrained than a president under 'normal' conditions. True, the prime minister retains control of the constitutional armoury of provisions designed to manage an undisciplined parliament outlined at the start of this chapter. He may also appear as a 'locomotive' for his party or even for the whole majority. But he invariably faces rivals within his own camp for the prize of the presidency, while himself lacking the legitimacy of direct election. These tensions, while not necessarily resulting in parliamentary indiscipline, render the task of party and coalition management steadily more difficult as the presidential election approaches. It is significant that while each of these prime ministers has run for president at the end of the period of cohabitation, each has been defeated. The possibility of cohabitation recurring has been much reduced by the constitutional change of 2000 reducing the presidential term from seven years to five. Any future cohabitation would require either the French voters to choose opposed sides at two elections, presidential and parliamentary, a few weeks apart, or for the synchronization to be broken by a dissolution or a presidential resignation or death. These eventualities are unlikely, but far from impossible.

The early, dismissive verdicts on the French parliament should therefore be qualified (Camby and Servent, 2004). Institutional changes, more assertive parliamentarians, and less predictable majorities have made it a significant force. At the same time, however, governments do retain the essential, Draconian, powers granted them by the Constitution, and have repeatedly shown their willingness to use them, even against supportive majorities. In addition, France's parliament suffers from common European disabilities. The technicality of much legislation restricts the scope for a truly 'transformative' legislature, as does the fact that the framework for some of it is now European. And the media have taken over part of parliament's scrutiny function. These tendencies encourage parliamentarians to look first to constituency interests, thus further diminishing their role as legislators. On the other hand, the most important new power given to parliamentarians is effectively the power to refer legislative disputes for judicial arbitration.

The judiciary and quasi-judicial actors

Of the three branches of government in France, the judiciary has traditionally been a poor relation. The revolutionaries of 1791 expressly curtailed its right of interpretation, while the first Napoleon placed the appointment and advancement of judges firmly under the executive's control. More recently, the judiciary has suffered from chronic underfunding. That has not prevented an increasing judicial assertiveness in the course of the Fifth Republic.

Not one, but three distinct types of judicial body constrain France's executive: the administrative courts headed by the Council of State (*Conseil d'Etat*), the Constitutional Council, and the ordinary criminal judiciary. First, the Council of State, set up by Napoleon in 1799, has two long-established roles. It judges the use and abuse of administrative activity (and in some cases vindicates individual complainants over specific administrative acts). The Council also advises the government on legal matters. The Constitution of 1958 specifies that the Council of State must be consulted on the legality of all government bills, all proposed delegated legislation and decrees, and all European Union acts having a legislative character in France. Its opinions – which the government is not bound to follow, but which it cannot, in practice, systematically ignore – cover both the constitutionality of the proposed legislation and its consistency with existing statute law. A parallel Napoleonic creation is the Court of Accounts (*Cour des Comptes*), which undertakes selective annual audits of government accounts (while regional chambers of accounts do the same at sub-national level), and publishes an annual report. This details the really major instances of financial waste in France's public sector, though such remonstrances are not backed by any obligation on government to act in accordance with any recommendations given.

The second judicial, or quasi-judicial, constraint on the executive is the Constitutional Council (*Conseil Constitutionnel*), an innovation of the Fifth Republic. Like the US Supreme Court, the Constitutional Council is the supreme jurisdiction for the verification of the constitutionality of legislation, as well as for disputes arising from presidential elections. Unlike the Supreme Court, however, it is entirely distinct from the main body of the judiciary. Its nine members, three appointed by each of the 'three presidents' (of the Republic, of the National Assembly and of the Senate) for a non-renewable term of nine years, do not have to be judges by profession. And they can only rule on the constitutionality of bills referred between the definitive parliamentary votes and final promulgation – not, as in the United States, on any law, old or new, passed up to them through the judicial system. Moreover, under the 1958 Constitution, only the prime minister and the three presidents had the right to refer bills. That confirmed the purpose de Gaulle had had in mind for the Council: not to limit the freedoms of the executive, but to limit the possibilities of parliament passing legislation outside its newly restrictive remit set out in Article 34.

The Constitutional Council changed its own role on 16 July 1971, when after twelve years of quietism it struck down a law that would have required prior prefectoral approval to register an association – a break with 70 years of liberal treatment of citizen associations. The long-term implications of the decision were far-reaching because the Council justified it by reference, not to the main body of the constitutional text, but to its preamble, which in turn refers back to the 1789 Declaration of the Rights of Man and the Citizen. The effect of recognizing these para-constitutional texts as having the same force as the constitution itself was therefore to incorporate, at a stroke, a Bill of Rights into the constitution, vastly extending the range of grounds on which the Council could question the constitutionality of a law. The Council's range of activities was further extended, three years later, by the constitutional amendment of 1974 extending the right of referral to the Council to include either 60 deputies or 60 senators. Attacked by the then Left-wing opposition as a *réformette*, the 1974 amendment was nevertheless speedily taken up by France's parliamentarians as a tool of opposition. The Right-wing opposition used referral against the Left's nationalization law in 1981; the Left in turn referred the privatization law of 1986. In the 1997–2002 parliament, 61 laws (out of a total of 261 voted) were referred, 46 of them by parliamentarians; this number included almost all the most important texts.

Many referrals, moreover, are at least partially successful: while the Constitutional Council seldom strikes down a whole law, it frequently refuses one or more articles, requires amendments, or stipulates a particular interpretation of a text as a condition of its being constitutionally acceptable. The 1981 nationalization legislation, for example, became constitutional once amended to provide what the Council viewed as sufficient compensation for shareholders; five years later, another Council decision warned that the state must be paid at the full market rate for the sell-off of firms it owned. Right-wing immigration legislation was struck down in both 1980 and 1993. The most significant recent reverse for a government occurred in 2004, when major changes to the law governing regional elections were ruled unconstitutional on a technicality; the government, which had intended a minimum qualifying vote of 10 per cent of registered voters at the first round to be required for any list of candidates to stand at the second, was obliged to settle for 10 per cent cent of votes cast, a considerably lower threshold. Perhaps more important than any individual decision by the Constitutional Council, however, has been the resulting effect of anticipation. All important bills are drafted in the expectation that they will be referred by the opposition. Thus, for example, when the 1986–88 Chirac government undertook a massive redistricting of France's parliamentary constituencies, the Interior Minister's highly developed instinct of partisan advantage was restrained by the certainty that the bill would have to pass the Constitutional Council's scrutiny.

The amendment of 1974 represents the most important new formal limitation by a branch of the judiciary on executive power (for it is the executive that drafts most major legislation) since the Constitution came into force in 1958. Nevertheless, the limitation is itself limited, in two ways. First, the Constitutional Council only exercises *a priori* control over laws referred to it by the president or by legislators, not *a posteriori* control over laws referred up through the judicial system. Secondly, the Council's decisions can be overridden with relative ease by amending the Constitution, a procedure that requires the vote of an identical text by each chamber of parliament, followed either by a joint sitting of both (a congress), at which a three-fifths majority is required, or by a popular referendum. All but one of the amendments since 1962 have been passed by the congress procedure; France being a unitary state, no further confirmation is needed at sub-national level. Thus the Constitutional Council's opposition to the Balladur government's 1993 immigration legislation was overturned by amendment. And indeed, when it declared the unconstitutionality of the Maastricht Treaty in 1992, and then of the European Constitutional Treaty in 2004, the Council was issuing an invitation to amend the Constitution of the Fifth Republic rather than trying to obstruct the passage of the treaties.

The third branch of the judiciary that has limited the powers of the executive is represented by France's criminal courts. For most of the first thirty years of the Fifth Republic (1958–1988), they remained in a position, in relation to politicians, as supine as that of the pre-1971 Constitutional Council. Widespread rumours of the corrupt funding of politicians and, especially, of parties went ignored by the judges. This was partly due to a tenacious convention, underpinned by a tacit agreement between parties, that kept all but the most brazen political corruption beyond the limits of judicial (or indeed press) investigation. It also resulted from the Justice Ministry's continuing right to appoint, promote, and transfer state prosecutors and to direct their work on particular files. Only the immunity of examining magistrates (as opposed to prosecutors) from removal limited this powerful combination of taboo and patronage that kept politicians in a charmed circle for over three decades.

The breakdown of this conspiracy of silence dates from the years 1989–91. It had multiple causes: the determination of a police inspector, Antoine Gaudino, and an examining magistrate, Thierry Jean-Pierre, to pursue the nationwide system of illegal finance that funded the PS, and to keep the media fully informed of their activities; the hesitancy of a Justice Minister, Pierre Arpaillange, to use the full weight of his hierarchical authority against Jean-Pierre and other politically embarrassing judges; the willingness of a group of UDF deputies, led by Philippe de Villiers, to press Arpaillange's successor Henri Nallet on the corruption issue at parliamentary questions, despite the advice of the UDF group leadership; the decision by Prime Minister Michel Rocard to attempt a 'fresh start', admitting that parties, including his own, had been illegally funded and legislating, in 1990, to provide official public finance for the future and to cover the activities of the past with an amnesty (Favier and Martin-Rolland, vol. III, 1996, pp. 307–333). Rocard's efforts to draw a line on a consensual basis were reinforced, under the Right, by two constitutional amendments. One reinforced the representation of judges in the High Council of the Judiciary, the body constitutionally responsible for disciplinary sanctions against judges, with an entitlement to be consulted over appointments. The other created a Court of Justice of the Republic, composed of deputies, senators and judges from the Court of Cassation, with the purpose of judging ministers for crimes committed in office. The Court of Justice of the Republic has been used once only, in 1999, to try ministers involved in the distribution of HIV contaminated blood in the 1980s: in an inconclusive verdict, it found one of the three accused guilty but imposed no penalty.

None of these measures succeeded in drawing a line under the corruption issue. On the contrary, the French became more convinced than ever that politicians were 'generally corrupt', while the 1990s saw a form of guerrilla warfare develop between the judiciary and governments of both colours. Examining magistrates, in particular, pursued inquiries against politicians of all parties. Politicians, and especially justice ministers, were always tempted to use their powers of appointment and transfer to warn off or wear down inconvenient magistrates. Jacques Toubon, Justice Minister from 1995 to 1997, famously appointed his own chief of staff to the key post of public prosecutor for Paris; he was also reported to have sent a helicopter to the Himalayas in an unsuccessful bid to recall a loyal magistrate from a mountain holiday to take charge of a case that was running out of control. Loyal public prosecutors were important because they in turn could use their powers to assign cases to trusted colleagues, or to slice cases into discrete components dispersed between different jurisdictions and hard to knit into a coherent whole. Independent-minded magistrates, on the other hand, regularly leaked to the media rather than have their inquiries completely buried (Charon and Furet, 2000).

By 2004 the process had, if not ceased, at least reached a point of precarious equilibrium. Parties, by then, had had to publish more or less plausible accounts for some fifteen years – an obligation from which they had previously been immune. And the judges had several major scalps to their credit. No fewer than three ministers, Michel Roussin, Gérard Longuet and Alain Carignon, resigned from the Balladur government (1993–95) after being placed under investigation, under a (recently established) informal convention that any minister so embarrassed should leave the government. Carignon was later imprisoned for a year for having used proceeds from the privatization of water distribution of the city of Grenoble, where he was mayor, for his own political campaigning. Under the Raffarin government (2002) the convention was upheld, forcing the resignation of Pierre Bédier, Minister for Prisons. Investigations into corruption at the Paris Town Hall, where Chirac was mayor from 1977 till 1995, revealed an impressive mix of ballot-stuffing, clientelism in housing allocations, rigged tenders for major municipal contracts, and payment of (RPR) party workers out of the municipal payroll. The last finding led to the conviction of Alain Juppé, who had been assistant-mayor in charge of the capital's finances as well as secretary-general of the RPR from 1988 to 1995, before being prime minister from 1995 to 1997, and head of Chirac's new party, the UMP, from 2002 to 2004. Juppé's sentence, a suspended prison term linked to a ten-year ban on holding elective office (reduced on appeal to one year), led him to leave politics, at least temporarily. Meanwhile an investigation into the activities of Elf-Aquitaine revealed how the state-owned oil company had been used as a channel for illicit finance for all parties; part of this inquiry had caused the resignation of the president of the Constitutional Council, Roland Dumas, former foreign minister and a close friend of Mitterrand (Wolfreys, 2001). Mitterrand's name was also much evoked in the trial that opened in November 2004 and concerned the numerous illegal bugging activities undertaken from the Elysée Palace during his presidency. That illicit activities so close to the summit of the French state should come to trial in this way would have been unthinkable as late as the 1980s.

Of the three main branches of the judiciary named at the beginning of this section, therefore, one, the administrative courts and especially the Council of State, has played a reasonably constant and independent, albeit discreet, role in constraining government since the early years of the Fifth Republic. The other two, the Constitutional Council and the ordinary judiciary, have greatly increased their activity and independence. The executive is bound to ensure the constitutionality of all new legislation to the best of its ability, in the full expectation that any text may be referred by the opposition. The impact of activism among the ordinary judiciary is more complex. By comparison with northern or Anglo-Saxon countries, France remains tolerant of its rulers' peccadilloes. The most recent, if minor, illustration, has the been the regularity with which senior ministers' cars have been caught speeding in the middle of a nationwide road safety campaign without their suffering any significant consequences. At the very top, a dossier comparable to the file on Chirac's stewardship of the Paris Town Hall would probably have forced the resignation of a British prime minister, and provoked a serious movement for his impeachment in the United States. Partly for this reason, France ranked eleventh among the EU15 countries in Transparency International's 2004 survey of perceptions of corruption – behind all other member-states except Spain, Portugal, Greece and Italy. Judicial activism has not transformed France into Finland. It has, however, brought political parties at least partially within the orbit of the law, and it has imposed a political obligation on parties and governments not to keep politicians accused of serious misdemeanours in the front rank.

Public opinion, president and party

France's executive, like that of any democratic government, is more or less constrained by public opinion. Bold initiatives and calculated risks come easier to popular presidents and governments than to those that have lost the confidence of voters, especially in the run-up to an election.

The French have voted often under the Fifth Republic. Thanks to the lack of synchronization between the seven-year presidential term and the five-year parliamentary mandate, eighteen of the years between 1958 and 2004 – over one in three – saw a presidential election, a parliamentary election, or both. Another six saw European elections, and another four referendums. Municipal or regional elections were held in a further six years, bringing the total to 34. If cantonal elections – held across only half the country at a time, and generally viewed as the least important – are also counted, France has seen only seven truly election-free years since 1958. Although the synchronization of presidential and parliamentary terms from 2002 should lend somewhat greater stability to the system, with president and majority normally able to expect a clear five years in office, the overall effect of a more or less permanent election campaign has so far been undiminished by the reform. Moreover, French presidents, unlike their American counterparts, are not limited to two terms. All, with the exceptions of de Gaulle after 1965 and Mitterrand after 1988, have expected to run for re-election. With the partial exception of Mitterrand between 1988 and 1993, the phenomenon of a second-term American president, nearing the constitutional end of his mandate and seeking a place in history, has no French equivalent.

More than most nations, the French are addicted to opinion polls. The popularity of president, prime minister, government, parties and leading politicians is surveyed on a monthly basis by three or four polling institutes in France. Regular surveys also cover views of France's politicians generally. They show, with some consistency, a growing mistrust of politicians since the 1980s. This mistrust is confirmed by election results: since 1981, the French have generally used their votes to punish those in power.

The poll indices indicating declining trust in politics are widespread. An average of 62 per cent of respondents, across seventeen SOFRES polls run between 1990 and 2003, said that politicians 'didn't care what people like us think'. Fifty-nine per cent, over fifteen polls in the same period, considered that politicians were 'generally corrupt'. Before 1981, 40 per cent or fewer had given the same answer to these questions. When asked to declare their feelings about politics, an average of 59 per cent of respondents, across eleven polls between 1993 and 2003, expressed 'mistrust', twice as many as mentioned 'hope' (29 per cent); 'disgust' was mentioned by 19 per cent, and 'enthusiasm' by just 1 per cent (Teinturier, 2004). As Table 6.2 shows, views of individual presidents have taken a similarly gloomy turn. Since 1978, SOFRES has asked poll respondents to express either 'trust' or 'lack of trust' for the president. Over Giscard's last three years, the number expressing trust in the president outnumbered his detractors by 10.53 points on average. Mitterrand, though deeply unpopular in the middle of his first term, recovered sufficiently by 1988 to secure

Table 6.2   *Presidential popularity, 1978–2004*

President	Popularity index
Valéry Giscard d'Estaing (1978–81)	10.53
Mitterrand (1981–88)	5.96
Mitterrand (1988–95)	−1.48
Chirac (1995–2002)	−1.35
Chirac (2002–2004)	−8.55

Source: SOFRES monthly polls (averages of per cent 'trust' minus per cent 'lack of trust' for each month).

re-election; in his second term, on the other hand, his ratings turned negative in the summer of 1991 and never recovered. Chirac's ratings in his first term show a sharp decline followed by recovery during his cohabitation with Jospin; within a year of his re-election in 2002, on the other hand, they had already declined to historically low levels.

The electoral impact of this public disenchantment has been very clear. For the first two decades of the Fifth Republic, every parliamentary election (in 1962, 1967, 1968, 1973 and 1978) confirmed the existing majority in power. From 1981, every parliamentary election (1981, 1986, 1988, 1993, 1997 and 2002) has led to a change of majority. Turnout has also suffered. At no parliamentary election since 1986 have two-thirds of the registered electorate cast a valid vote; in 1978, admittedly a record year, valid votes had been cast by over 81 per cent of the electorate. Presidential elections tell a similar story, if at a rather higher level: whereas valid votes cast had been close to or above 80 per cent of the electorate from 1965 to 1988, the level fell below 70 per cent for the first time in 2002. And voters have been increasingly tempted by extremes of the Right (chiefly the Front National) and the Left (one of the two main Trotskyist groupings on offer). Indeed, at the first round of the 2002 presidential elections, fewer than half the registered voters (45.8 per cent) turned out and voted for a candidate of the mainstream parties of Left or Right; the rest abstained, spoilt their ballots or supported candidates of the extremes (Knapp, 2004, p. 346).

These developments have important implications for presidential leadership. De Gaulle's initial conception of the presidency rested on the president's capacity to appeal over the heads of quarrelsome and selfish parties directly to the electorate: hence Articles 11 and 12 of the 1958 constitution, allowing the president to call a referendum on institutional issues and to dissolve the National Assembly without countersignature. Dissolution served on two occasions, in 1962 and 1968, to resolve a political crisis, and on two more to provide President Mitterrand with a parliamentary majority, at his election in 1981 and re-election in 1988. The referendum was used to great effect by de Gaulle to build a consensus over Algerian self-determination and independence in 1961 and 1962, and to introduce direct presidential elections in 1962.

Both powers, however, have come to appear as boomerangs rather than presidential trump cards. This was true in the first instance of the referendum (Table 6.3). The 1962 vote on direct presidential elections, though it gave a convincing result by most standards, nearly led de Gaulle to resign because less than half the registered electorate voted yes. Seven years later, a narrow but clear defeat over senate and regional reforms provoked his departure. Since 1969, while all referendums have been carried, no proposal has won the backing of even 35 per cent of registered voters. The referendum on the Maastricht Treaty came within half a million votes of destroying Mitterrand's European policy. That of 2000, given minimal backing by Chirac, mobilized barely a quarter of French

Table 6.3 *Referendums under the Fifth Republic*

Date	Issue	Yes as % valid votes	Yes as % registered voters
28 Sept. 1958	Fifth Republic Constitution	82.6	65.9
8 Jan. 1961	Algerian self-determination	75.0	53.7
April 1962	Algerian independence	90.8	64.8
28 Oct. 1962	Direct election of president	62.3	46.7
27 April 1969	Senate and regional reforms	47.6	37.1
23 April 1972	EEC enlargement	68.3	31.7
6 Nov. 1988	New Caledonia	80.0	26.0
20 Sept. 1992	Treaty on European Union	51.0	34.4
24 Sept. 2000	5-year presidential term	73.2	18.6

voters on both sides. The 2003 proposals on a new statute for Corsica was rejected by 51 per cent of voters on the island. Although a constitutional reform of 1995 allowed referendums on social and economic issues or public services as well as institutions, no such consultations have so far been held. The referendum may still be used, as it is likely to be in 2005 over the European constitution, as a means to resolve controversial but cross-cutting issues. But it has lost its effectiveness as a tool of heroic presidential leadership. The insistence of Mitterrand and Chirac that the results of 'their' referendums should not be seen as affecting their position as presidents contrasts with de Gaulle's repeated stress on precisely such a link.

The same is broadly true of dissolution. The president of France is, as Olivier Duhamel remarks, the only head of a democratic executive to be able to call new parliamentary elections and stay in office if he loses (Duhamel, 1999). Nevertheless, the ruling conservative coalition's defeat in 1997 after Chirac's dissolution of parliament was rightly blamed by his own camp on the president. Moreover, it established that French voters, unlike their British counterparts, mistrust dissolutions effected for the convenience of the executive. Again, therefore, while dissolution may be used in the future (though the five-year presidential term makes it less probable than before), it is unlikely to be viewed as a very effective tool of presidential leadership.

If public opinion can constrain French political leadership, so too can mobilized social movements. The French public has often forced governments to change course by striking and demonstrating, or threatening to. De Gaulle, for instance, was in many ways a casualty of the May 1968 disturbances; his referendum of April 1969 was an unsuccessful attempt to rebuild the broken lines of communication with the French voters. The

Chirac presidency offers a number of contemporary examples. In 1995, a social security reform, aimed at limiting the use of doctors by the French and at ending the very favourable pension arrangements of several groups of key public service workers, was substantially withdrawn after France's public service workers launched the biggest strike wave since May 1968. In 2000, the attempt by the Jospin government to reform the notoriously inefficient workings of the Finance Ministry was withdrawn after the ministry's personnel threatened to hold up tax collection. In 2003, a package including pension and university reforms presented by the Raffarin government was scaled down after nationwide strikes and demonstrations. In resisting successive reform plans, public service workers, unionized or not, were able to take a leading role thanks to their capacity to paralyse the country by blocking vital public services, especially transport. Yet their success, and the failure of governments, was due in no small measure to the public's view of them. In December 1995, for example, a narrow but clear majority of French poll respondents expressed support for strikes even as they moved into their third damaging week, and blamed the government, not the strikers, for the dispute (Duhamel and Méchet, 1996). Some were public service workers themselves; many more feared that if the pensions of these groups were downgraded, they would be next; still more identified the strikers' cause with a more general notion of public service, to which they were attached, or simply mistrusted the politicians attempting the reforms. The contrast is striking with the ability of the Thatcher governments in Britain to isolate and defeat one group of public service workers after another.

Conclusion

Within a year of arriving in power, with as yet no overall majority in the National Assembly, de Gaulle was capable of imposing a fierce austerity programme on the French. Aimed at curbing inflation and budget deficits, it included rises in taxes and charges for public services, and cuts in such politically sensitive areas of spending as veterans' pensions. He went on successfully to mobilize a growing consensus in favour of Algerian self-government, and then independence, in order to face down an *Algérie française* lobby prepared to use armed revolt, terrorism and assassination attempts on the president to get its way. The post 2002 Raffarin government, by contrast, enjoyed comfortable majorities in the National Assembly and Senate, as well as the support of a president elected, at the run-off ballot, by over four voters in five; yet it was incapable of more than timid structural reforms to France's generous pension and healthcare systems, despite a public-sector deficit exceeding 4 per cent, and debt in excess of 63 per cent of GDP in 2003, by which time French budgets had been in deficit for every one of the previous thirty years.

This contrast suggests a weakening in France of executive leadership generally and presidential leadership in particular. Institutional change in France has gone some way to balance the very considerable power vested in the executive at the outset of the Fifth Republic. The rights of parliament have been widened, with new provisions for questions and for referral of bills to the Constitutional Council; these powers have been actively used, as has the right of amendment. The phenomenon of cohabitation has breached the unity of the executive on three occasions, and served as a reminder of the government's dependence on a parliamentary majority. The Constitutional Council itself has been more demanding in its assessment of bills, enlarging the domain of constitutionality by reference to the Declaration of the Rights of Man and the Citizen; the judiciary has become more active in its pursuit of crooked politicians. Meanwhile, Europe has acted as a constraint on policy-makers, in ways that are developed in the next chapter.

Societal constraints weigh heavily upon French governments. Our chapter highlighted the hostility to the political world of a large section of French public opinion. The evidence of opinion polls, the rise of abstention and spoilt ballots, the audience enjoyed by extreme parties of Left and (especially) Right, and the frequency of defeats for governing parties all point towards an electorate that is reluctant to be mobilized for a large-scale political project. This is hardly an exclusively French condition: something like it has been observed in recent years in almost every developed capitalist democracy. Nevertheless, the fact that the re-election of an incumbent parliamentary majority, a common enough event in most democracies, should have escaped the French in six successive elections suggests that the phenomenon is more marked in France than elsewhere. While the institutional and societal checks and balances we have discussed in this chapter are healthy additions to the 'Republican monarchy' as conceived by de Gaulle, the apparent inability of French governments of any stripe to retain public confidence for very long is not. France's decision-makers face stiff challenges in the years that lie ahead, in the fields of employment, economic management and education to name a few. Rising to these challenges will demand a level of mobilization and consent unknown to French politics in nearly two decades.

Chapter 7

The Europeanization of the French State

ANDY SMITH

Chapter Six discussed the importance of domestic checks on the operation of executive power in the French Fifth Republic. A growing wealth of empirical research has also convincingly shown that European integration is now a pervasive influence upon the way the agents of the French state think and act. In this chapter we focus on the impact of Europeanization upon the operation of the French State. We will argue that it has become difficult to make and implement any form of public intervention in France without reference to EU law and public policy. Of course, this change is not necessarily recognized by all the actors themselves, many of whom understandably are still attempting to fight a rearguard action to maintain at least some semblance of state power. Neither is the degree of overlap between the French state and the EU recognized by most media commentators, let alone the general public. Brought up to believe in the myth of a strong central state, journalists and citizens alike have had great difficulty in adapting to a more complex set of institutional arrangements within which the locus of power is constantly shifting over time and according to issue area.

Rather than simply regret the gap between the results of social science and the way most French policy-makers and beneficiaries see their state, this chapter seeks to present the 'Europeanization' it has undergone from two angles: the organization of French public authority (section 1) and the way representatives of these bodies now make public policy (section 2). In order to grasp the mechanisms and extent of change observed, with Radaelli we define Europeanization to mean 'a set of processes through which the EU political, social and economic dynamics become part of the logic of domestic discourse, identities, political structures and public policies' (Radaelli 2001, p. 113). While charting the modifications of these logics wrought by France's membership of the EU, two cross-cutting themes will be introduced in each section. The first concerns the highly sectorized nature of the French state. Specialists of France have consistently underlined the function-linked cleavages which fragment this country's public authority (Suleiman, 1974). It will be shown here that their engagement in the EU has caused most actors within the French state to accentuate this form of fragmentation and the problems of policy coordination it entails.

The second theme developed in the chapter is how little the Europeanization of the French state has been accompanied by a shift in the mindsets and practices of politicians. Be they ministers, MPs, MEPs or sub-national authority leaders, virtually all French politicians call for deeper involvement in EU decision-making. However, they have taken relatively few steps towards integrating the consequences of this ambition into their discourse and practices in a systematic and durable way. As will be shown, the explanation of this contradiction lies not only in the behaviour of the politicans themselves, but also in a set of unintended consequences which stem from how the Europeanization of the French state has progressively become institutionalized.

Europeanized French administrations

Under the tumultuous Fourth Republic, French governments came and went but the administrative structure of the state remained largely the same. A similar general comment can be made about the Europeanization of this structure: many significant changes have taken place but this basic structure has been largely untouched. Chiefly because of the strength of administrative *corps* within the civil service, the weakness of party cohesion and a paucity of interministerial bodies, divisions between ministries remain as strong as ever. Instead, one needs to look for evidence of EU-wrought change in the French state from two alternative angles. The first is through examining the actors responsible for formulating national positions within functional ministries. The second is by looking closely at their colleagues within the 'coordinating' bodies which ostensibly defend these standpoints in Brussels.

The guardians of sectoral priorities: function-specific ministries

Contrary to popular belief, the French president and prime minister are not the key decision-makers behind the policy positions defended in the name of their country within EU institutions. Nor has this role been devolved to the level of Foreign or European Affairs ministers. In reality, such a 'heroic' vision of European politics only has any credence during the final stages of treaty revisons. The rest of the time, as in any other member-state, national positions are instead essentially drawn up on the basis of reactions to an EU-level agenda by function-specific ministries. For this reason it is important to underline two important variables which determine to what extent a ministry has become Europeanized.

The first concerns the degree of involvement of individual civil servants in EU management and regulatory committees. Both the European Commission and the Council of Ministers do not operate in a vacuum but closely associate national officials in the preparation and implementation of EU legislation. In the case of the Commission, this association usually takes the form of advisory groups and committees which take 'low level' decisions on questions such as the details of agricultural price support or fishing quotas. In the case of the Council, most preparatory work on draft directives and regulations takes place within 'working groups' that are made up of 'national experts' from each state capital and/or agents from each country's Permanent Representation in Brussels (Fouilleux, de Maillard and Smith, 2002). In either or both of these contexts, officials from most French ministries now spend considerable amounts of their working week actually in the Belgian capital, preparing to go there or reporting on what they have just taken part in. The intensity of this work varies over time and between policy areas. Nonetheless, as even issue areas such as policing or defence procurement serve to highlight, French ministries simply cannot ignore the importance of the EU as a, and often *the*, major locus for public decision-making.

The second variable which can explain the pace and extent of a ministry's Europeanization is its own internal organization. In the 1960s, 1970s and early 1980s, many ministries began reorganizing themselves to adapt to the growing importance of the then European Community by setting up specialized 'European Units'. Charged with liaising directly with France's Permanent Representation in Brussels and the European Commission, these units initially played the role of a 'letter box'. They redispatched missives 'from Europe' to more specialized services, but also collated opinions from these services in order to draw up ministerial positions on each issue. Some ministries, such as the Ministry of Justice, continue to centralize contacts with the EU in this way. However, since the 1987 Single Market Act, the sheer volume of draft and enacted EU legislation has meant that in most ministries responsibility for this work is now distributed throughout each administration and there is much less pressure to centralize information flows through one single unit. Indeed, direct contacts between specialized national civil servants and their counterparts in the Commission are often the cause of short-circuited hierarchies and administrative fragmentation.

Of course, there are many different reasons which explain why some parts of the French civil service have become more Europeanized than others. The timing of EU legislative expansion – particularly around the relaunch of the single market (1986-1992) – provides one means of answering this question. The type of policy instrument – regulatory, distributive or redistributive – may provide another. But, as a recent study of the Infrastructure Ministry shows (Prudhomme-Leblanc, 2002), only ongoing and future sociologies of each administration's adaptation to 'Europe' will provide us with more clues to this puzzle for intersectoral comparison.

What is more certain is that the involvement of French civil servants in EU policy-making and implementation has in nearly all cases reinforced their primary loyalty to their own ministry. The first reason for this is that the highly sectoral nature of EU policy-making tends strongly to oblige all national administrations to take on this logic. A second explanation is that unlike in the British civil service, within Parisian-based ministries there is very little commitment to a single national administration. French civil servants are trained and their careers are made within individual ministries. Consequently, EU issues are looked at primarily from the angle of such organizations without even paying lip service to the notion, currently so in vogue in Britain, of 'joined-up government'. Finally, the low level of involvement of the French Parliament in EU policy-making provides a third explanation for the sectorized nature of most ministerial involvement (Rozenberg, 2004). Although recent debates about the draft EU Constitution appear to have put the weakness of parliamentary input upon the political agenda, until now there has been little pressure from the legislature upon ministries to construct coherent intersectoral policy positions.

The synthesizers of France's European policies: the SGCI and the permanent representation

An additional explanation of the sectoral organization of French ministries as regards the EU comes from a more unlikely source: the composition and structure of the very bodies designed to overcome interministerial fragmentation and foster the production of single and coherent French national positions, the *Secrétariat Général pour du Comité Interministeriel pour les Questions de Coopération Economique européenne* (SGCI) and the French Permanent Representation (RP) to the EU. Contrary to what is often written about these bodies (Lequesne, 1993; Guyomarch, 2000, 124; Menon, 2001), and although they have most certainly become unavoidable parts of French and EU decision-making process, the SGCI and the RP are not highly efficient in overcoming intersectoral differences. Rather they provide battlegrounds for continuing inter-, and sometimes intra-, ministerial turf wars.

Attached to the prime minister, since the 1970s the SGCI has become an integral part of the way the French state develops its standpoints on European issues. This is most apparent whenever the European Council of Ministers is called upon to react to draft directives and regulations proposed by the Commission and, in the case of Justice and Home Affairs, by individual national governments. Although one ministry is almost invariably named as lead department (*chef de file*) when organizing the French reaction to such proposals (e.g. the Ministry of Agriculture for legislation on farming), many other ministries also seek to have an input into this process. Indeed, frequent clashes arise. For instance, in 2002–3 draft EU legislation that sought to harmonize prison sentences for the peddling of 'soft' drugs has divided officials from the Ministry of the Interior and the Ministry of Justice. The official purpose of the SGCI is to provide an arena for these interministerial confrontations as well as a set of 'neutral' officials whose job is to mediate conflicts and work out acceptable 'national' positions. In some policy areas this form of interministerial coordination does indeed lead to producing French standpoints which do appear coherent. However, given that the SGCI is staffed much less by career diplomats who have no sectoral axe to grind and much more by specialized civil servants seconded from functional ministries (Eymeri, 2002), coherence and harmony are often not the end result. Consequently officials are sent to the SGCI as watchdogs to protect the interests of their ministry and/or their *corps*. Issues therefore continue to be 'owned' by the most powerful ministry in each policy area, thus minimizing the impact of administrations, such as the Ministry of the Environment, which might seek to introduce questions on the negative externalities of purely sectoral approaches to public intervention.

This 'sectorization' of the French state's involvement in the EU is partly a result of the fragmentation of EU policy making within negotiating arenas in Brussels. In France's case, however, this trend is further exacerbated by the internal structure of this country's Permanent Representation to the EU. Like the SGCI, the RP is ostensibly an organization designed to coordinate the formulation and defence of French national positions within the EU's institutions in general and the Council of Ministers in particular. As research has repeatedly underlined (Lequesne, 1993; Lewis, 1998), this mediating is carried out in two main ways. First, officials from the RP (RPs) are well placed to find out about draft legislation as early as possible, discover the likely reaction of other national governments and convey this information to the SGCI and individual ministries back in Paris. Second, RPs accompany ministerial civil servants during negotiations in Council working groups, the Committee of Permanent Representatives (*Comité des Réprésentants Permanents*: COREPER) and the Council itself. During both these activities, RPs are supposed to position themselves as policy generalists commited to negotiating intergovernmental and inter-institutional compromises in an essentially diplomatic style. Given that most of these officials were trained and have built their careers within individual ministries, however, many of them frequently act less like diplomats and more like specialized representatives of function-driven administrations. This trait may mean that the RPs contribute specialized knowedge to often very complex and detailed negotiations. But it also tends to put another nail in the coffin of coherent and coordinated policy both at the level of the EU and of the French state.

It would be misleading if one were to leave the reader with the impression that the reorganization of France's public authorities that has taken place in response to deepened European integration has only produced dissension and contradictory policies. In areas where the central thrust of EU policy has been coherent (e.g. the completion of the single market), a relatively consistent line has been worked out within the French state. Indeed, an elite within this entity has worked intensely to make the 'neoliberal watershed' experienced throughout Western Europe produce radical effects in France (Jobert, 1994). However, even this ideology-fuelled process of liberalization has taken place in a context where public debate and the involvement of politicians have not been encouraged. Apart from the weak involvement of parliamentarians mentioned above, it is important to take into account the fluctuating role of ministers themselves in making French policy on Europe. Often seeing themselves as 'occasional visitors to Brussels' rather than politicians working in the heart of the government of the EU, the lack of involvement of major national political figures in EU decision-making is frequently criticised by senior civil servants. Research has yet to tackle this subject other than by identifying a clear trend in which French politicians try to influence EU decisions by working solely 'at the top' on the Commission president and commissioners (Joana and Smith, 2002). This elitist and largely covert form of engagement by French ministers with the rest of the EU seems likely to be one of the reasons why they still find it so difficult to incite public interest in European politics.

The Europeanization of French public policies?

If, as has just been shown, French administrations are now very much parts of the government of the EU, it is important to underline that the French state still makes a range of national or 'domestic' policies. However, it is just as important to grasp the extent to which these forms of public interventon are made within a political space that is heavily structured by EU law, policies and institutionalized practices. Indeed, by looking more closely at the French actors who have made policy in different sectors and at different times since 1965, one can better understand the varying depth of European integration within France.

This intersectoral and intertemporal comparison will be tackled here with the additional aim of countering the legal positivist argument that the Europeanization of national policy is determined by the way policy competences are defined in EU treaties (Constantinho and Dony, 1995). According to such a view, 'common' EU policies produce the deepest forms of Europeanization, 'shared' policies produce less, and issue areas where state sovereignty is 'untouched' give rise to virtually none at all. By focusing upon the way the French state has intervened since the 1960s in eight policy areas with very different treaty provisions, this section refutes such a simplistic view of Europeanization. Instead this section shows that the depth of Europeanization is dependent upon how actors engage with and 'use' (Jacquet and Woll, 2004) European integration. Consequently it will also be shown that this process is neither linear nor inexorable.

'Common' policies, uncommon Europeanizations: agriculture, competition, telecommunications and monetary union

Formally speaking, the category of 'common' EU policies encompasses issue areas which are structured by a comprehensive set of EU law and procedures that apply automatically throughout the member-states. In other words, not only are existing legal and procedural provisions implemented by national administrations but it is expected that the latter will simply enact any new directives and regulations which emanate from the EU's decision-making process. By looking at how two long-standing (Agriculture and Competition) and one relatively new (telecommunications and Monetary Union) common policies have taken root and produced their respective effects in France, the density of European law and procedures will indeed be highlighted. However, it will also be shown that this density has not removed all leeway for domestic policy (Hayward and Wright, 2002). Neither has there been anything 'automatic' about its application to the French economy and society.

Agriculture

In this case, the Common Agricultural Policy (CAP) has undisputedly and indelibly marked French public intervention in this sector since its inception in 1962 (Servolin, 1989; Fouilleux, 2003). Consuming more than 45 per cent of the EU budget, the CAP still represents the most comprehensive set of norms and procedures which are supposed to apply throughout the member-states. These have caused and mirrored a wide range of changes in the way the French state has sought to regulate farming and food production. Indeed, agriculture is certainly one of the first sectors in this country to have become Europeanized. However, a combination of globalized politics, policy reform and changes in centre–periphery relations have meant that since the early 1990s the CAP now has less of a stranglehold on French actors than it did over the previous three decades.

When revisiting the beginnings of the CAP one is reminded just how much French politicians, civil servants and interest groups participated in inventing this policy. In the late 1950s, 25 per cent of France's workforce were still on the land, a figure that was defined by various French elites as negative for both the efficient production of food and the emergence of a stronger industrial base. Brought together under the banner of 'modernization' (Muller, 1984), these elites called for changes in public support to agriculture that would provide incentives for the intensification of farming and discourage 'inefficient' producers from remaining in the countryside. Here the creation of the European Community was seen as an opportunity to open up new tariff-free markets for French produce, set up an EC-wide system of subsidies which would increase agricultural production, and avoid passing its cost directly on to the urban consumer. By participating vigorously in devising the CAP, French actors were able to ensure that their interests were protected and enhanced. More precisely, these practioners made propositions which favoured French farmers in a number of key sub-sectors (cereals, milk, beef, wine) and, by getting them adopted by the EC Council of Ministers, managed to lock this advantageous position into European law.

Of course, the rise of French and European agricultural production and productivity levels of the period 1960-1980 cannot solely be ascribed to the incentive structure provided by the CAP. During this period, technological advances (fertilizers, pesticides, animal husbandry), mechanization and increased farm sizes all contributed strongly to a trend which also saw the percentage of the French workforce in agriculture reduced to around 5%. However, the guaranteed prices and export subsidies offered by the CAP not only encouraged agricultural intensification but came to dominate the politics of farming at both French and European levels. For more than twenty years (1960–80), this politics was essentially reduced to a highly sectoral debate over the optimum level of price support. Played out in and around the annual meetings of the Council of Agricultural Ministers which set these prices, within France the importance given to these debates also marginalized alternative, less sectoral visions of farming which had become concerned both by the overproduction supported by the CAP and its negative effects on the environment and on land use. In addition, the exclusive focus upon price support contributed to reducing the involvement of MPs in the politics of agriculture to virtually zero.

Put succinctly, from the late 1950s to the early 1990s, the Europeanization of French agricultural policy reached its zenith and became virtually all-encompassing. Since then, however, reforms of the CAP and other political developments have both changed this policy and given new autonomy to French actors for devising alternative means of intervening in this sector. In the late 1980s, pressure for CAP reform built up from a combination of the GATT world trade negotiations, criticism internal to the EC of the budget for price support and calls for more environmentally and food quality 'friendly' policies. Since 1990, these forces for change have led to drastic reductions in subsidized prices paid to farmers for agricultural commodities and to exporters selling these goods in third countries (Fouilleux, 2003). The CAP is still in place but it now increasingly provides direct income supplements to farmers in disadvantaged areas rather than EU-wide sums of money in order to 'correct' price fluctuations. This policy change has in turn created a political space within which the French national, regional and county (*département*) levels of government now intervene more in the name of rural development than in that of agriculture *per se* (Le Pape and Smith, 1999). More precisely, these public authorities are authorized either to top up EU funding or set up their own initiatives in order to realize a range of policy objectives such as keeping young farmers on the land, protecting the environment and encouraging the growth of niche markets for products like free-range chicken or *foie gras*. All these attempts to re-regulate agriculture still have to conform to EU rules on both agriculture and competition. However, despite continuing resistance to CAP reform, it now seems reasonable to conclude that in France a certain 'de-Europeanization' of agricultural policy has recently taken place.

Competition policy

Although the legal basis for a European-wide competition policy was clearly set out in the Treaty of Rome, it is only since the end of the 1980s that these articles of law have been enacted in any systematic way. Closely linked to the internal market programme launched in 1985, European competition law has subsequently been well and truly activated. Given the interventionist nature of the French state, in particular its industrial policies in favour of 'national champions' such as Thomson (electronics) or Bull (computers), both 'sides' of EU competition policy – the outlawing of state aids and the control of oligopolistic mergers – have consistently caused conflict in this issue area. Initially, the reaction of French industrial, administrative and political actors was limited to provoking showdowns in the college of commissioners. More precisely, because the college is the sole arbiter over competition cases and every commissioner has a vote, French members of this entity were expected to orchestrate case-by-case resistance to Commission activism in banning state aids and mergers likely to lead to unfair competition. This trend continued throughout the 1990s, particularly over the bailing out of the Crédit Lyonnais bank by the French state.

Notwithstanding the continued importance given by French elites to this highly political form of intervention in the college, more deep-seated changes in this country's approaches to competition policy have nevertheless occurred because of the EU's changed approach to this issue area. Since the mid-to-late 1980s, the state's own competition watchdog The Competition Council (*le Conseil de la Concurrence*) – has grown from being an advisory into a decision-making body. In so doing, the Europeanization of French competition policy has largely been taken charge of by actors within the national administration itself. Secondly, senior managers of French industries have become increasingly aware of the economic risks they would be taking in simply ignoring the constraints of EU competition law and policy. Of course, as the Raffarin government's attempt to save Alstom in 2003–4 testifies, this does not mean that French public and private actors do not continue to try and bulldoze their way past the college of commissioners. In most cases, however, the combined weight of other national governments, competing firms and the Commission mean that their chances of success are severely limited.

Telecommunications

As part of the drive to complete the 'internal market' of the EU, since the late 1980s this crucially important sector has progressively become the subject of a common set of laws and decision-making procedures. As in many other sectors, this process has been based upon the deregulation of national policies and 're-regulation' at the level of the EU (Majone, 1995). The extent of the changes undergone in the telecommunications sector are all the more remarkable given that until 1980 it was totally dominated by national monopolies staffed by civil servants and largely financed by the public purse. In the French case, this monopoly took the form of a single national operator (*France Télécom*) working in collusion with a range of national equipment manufacturers (Thomson, *Alcatel*) and in close cooperation with the Ministry of Communication (Cohen, 1992; Brénac, 1994). During the 1980s, this set of actors began a drive to modernize the French telephone system using a range of new technologies that were beginning to come on stream at that time. In 1988, *France Télécom* became separated from the French Post Office thus giving its management more freedom to make decisions on key subjects like capitalization and pricing. But privatization of this company took place in only 1996, the state continues to retain around 40 per cent of its shares and many of its employees remain civil servants.

Notwithstanding these limits placed upon the deregulation of the French telecommunications sector, its liberalization has been encouraged and extended by a parallel process involving the creation of an EU policy in this issue area (Sandholtz, 1998; Rivaud, 2001). As of 1986, the European Commission became much more active in promoting a common approach to the regulation of this sector and, the following year, formalized their propositions in a major consultation paper. Heavily influenced and bolstered by a more general 'white paper' on the completion of the single market, this paper advocated the re-regulation of telecommunications at the level of the EU by 1998. Without going into the detail of the several series of negotiations that subsequently took place, this policy goal has been largely achieved. Consequently the French state has given up much of its right unilaterally to regulate this sector. However, this does not mean that a form of totalizing Europeanization has taken place. EU telecommunications law is certainly very detailed and sets out how free competition between all European operators is to be regulated. Nevertheless, national regulatory bodies still have considerable discretion in implementing EU law, a discretion which specialists of this sector underline they do not hesitate to use (Thatcher, 2001). Formally speaking, such regulators are independent of the French state. In reality they are far from immune to political pressure and cannot afford to totally ignore the policy priorities and choices of the government of the day.

Monetary union

Ratified in 1992, the Maastricht Treaty mapped out a series of stages which, over the following ten years, were to lead to the replacement of national currencies by the euro. If successive French governments were vocal supporters of this policy, they and other actors in France have had to cope with its two sets of medium- and long-term political effects. The first of these effects of monetary union was institutional: La Banque de France had to be made independent of the state and then progressively become linked into the new European Central Bank (ECB). This process has significantly changed the links between the French administration and the world of finance in this country. Although it would be illusory to claim that there is now no contact between the Ministry of Finance and the revamped Banque de France, the level of interdependence between the two is much lower than ever before. In addition, France's commercial banks have also changed their logics of individual and collective action.

The second political effect of monetary union has been the impact upon national budgets and policies of having to respect a number of precise statistical targets. From the early 1990s onwards, these 'convergence criteria' (inflation rates, interest rates, budget deficits) began to bite hard upon the freedom of French governments to set both tax rates and expenditure levels. In 1997, these criteria were toughened by a 'Stability and Growth Pact' signed by all the heads of government of the euro zone. Indeed, the 'politics of austerity' that has marked French government over the last ten to twelve years can in many ways be directly attributed to monetary union. For this reason a whole host of sectoral policy reforms (e.g. arms procurement) can in part be traced back to the commitments made in Maastricht. The majority of French policy and political elites has not resisted these constraints either because they want the EU to develop its own 'economic government' and/or they have been in favour of the neoliberal reforms that budgetary austerity made it more easy to legitimate. Nevertheless, as the Raffarin government's non-respect of the convergence criteria in 2003 and 2004 underlines, a fundamental tension continues to exist between a euro 'run' by a federally structured ECB and a European Council of Finance Ministers which certain French politicians would like still to be dominated by the logic of intergovernmentalist bargaining.

In summary, agriculture, competiton, telecommunications and monetary union provide four clearcut examples of where EU 'common' policies have had massive impact upon the action capacity of the French state. As has repeatedly been stressed, however, European authorities by no means find themselves in a position of hegemony in any of these policy areas. Indeed, studying the multi-level implementation of common policies provides valuable insights into both the contemporary nature of the French state and how the EU as a whole is governed through sectoral configurations which intensely associate 'European' and national actors.

'Shared' policies, unshared Europeanizations: regional development and the environment

A second category of EU policy formalized in the treaties concerns issue areas where European level law and intervention is supposed to complement national and sub-national actions by respecting the principle of 'subsidiarity'. The implicit expectation in this provision is that such policies will produce relatively shallow forms of Europeanization which leave state sovereignty largely untouched and instead bring about forms of peaceful co-existence between EU, national and local actors. By looking at the political effects of EU involvement in regional development and the protection of the environment, it will be shown that if there is certainly co-existence in these policy areas it is usually anything but peaceful. Indeed, rather than providing a solution to inter-institutional conflict, subsidiarity is better conceptualized as a term around which powering and disempowering takes place. Ultimately, the politics of subsidiarity (Faure, 1997) provides clues for understanding the fluctuations in the degree of Europeanization that has taken place in the two policy areas examined here.

Regional development

This form of intervention first became part of the EC's armoury of policy instruments in 1975 and took the form of a European Regional Development Fund (ERDF). Initially adopted in order to compensate the British and Italian governments for the unbalanced nature of the EC budget due to the CAP, the ERDF began life as a series of grants from the Commission to national administrations to fund individual development projects such as roads and bridges (Anderson, 1990). By 1988, however, both the political meaning of this policy and the mechanisms for delivering it underwent radical change. In a context marked by the relaunch of the Single Market but also the adhesion of Spain and Portugal, the fund was reframed as part of the EC's commitment to 'social and economic cohesion'. This broad commitment to correcting the spatial consequences of liberalization led in turn to the association of the ERDF with two other 'structural funds' (the European Social Fund and the Agricultural Guidance Fund), the doubling of their combined budget and a new implementation strategy based upon 'partnerships' between the Commission, national governments and individual regions. More precisely, from 1988 onwards European regional development policy has operated through five- or six-yearly intergovernmental deals on the size and distribution of its overall budget, the negotiation of development 'plans' for each eligible region and constant battles over the interpretation of EU rules governing the permissible use of the structural funds.

In the French case, these funds have undoubtedly stimulated and accelerated a number of signficant changes in the way regional development is tackled in this country but also, more fundamentally, in the balance of power between national, regional and local actors. First introduced in the mid- to late 1980s at a time when decentralization began to take effect (see Chapter 8), the reformed structural funds provided regional and local actors with additional finance but also a set of new policy norms (partnership, programming, subsidiarity, evaluation) which they had to come to terms with (Smith, 1995). In interpreting these norms, new relationships between local actors, national administrations and representatives of the Commission had to be worked out in each region. In some, such as Britanny, relatively harmonious partnerships between state prefectures, regional councils and department-level authorities (*Conseils généraux*) were concocted. However, in many others, such as Rhône-Alpes, implementing the structural funds has produced a battleground for regional–national and regional–local relations. In short, applying the subsidiarity principle in this issue area has given rise to very different configurations of hierarchy.

Notwithstanding these differences in the distribution of power, it is also clear that over time the EU's regional development policy has given rise to different levels of substantial policy change. From the 1988 reform until the mid-1990s, in nearly all French regions adapting traditional methods of encouraging spatial developement to fit with the EU's rules led to a number of significant changes. In particular the pluri-annual planning of development objectives and funding mechanisms frequently led to more detailed negotiations between the different public authorities and societal actors (for example chambers of commerce) involved. Pushed strongly by the Commission, the obligation to evaluate these programmes *ex ante*, at mid point and *ex post* also led to more systematized forms of governing regional development. Since the end of the 1990s, however, the political effects of the structural funds upon French centre–periphery relations appear to have progressively weakened. In the context of Eastern enlargement, many French local actors consider that they have less and less to gain from engaging in the EU's regional development policy. They have also learnt that EU rules in this field are extremely general and can often be interpreted to suit locally set priorities. As overworked Commission officials intervene less and less in countries like France, sub-national actors thus appear to have largely taken over EU regional development policy. Optimists in the Commission see this trend as a fine example of successful Europeanization. More sanguine observers see the lack of policy change and direction this trend often entails as an example of an increasingly shallow form of European government (Faure and Smith, 1998).

Environment policy
EU policy designed to protect and enhance the environment provides a second example of a 'shared' issue area where Europeanization has certainly taken place but where the deepening of this trend in France is open to question. The EC first began making law in the name of the environment in the early 1970s but its formal competence to intervene in such matters stems from only the 1987 Single Market Act. As the threats of pollution have increased and been mediatized, since then protecting the environment has become a more established part of global, European, national and local political agendas. Partly for this reason but especially because of increased Commission activism in this field, EU environmental law

underwent considerable and rapid expansion until the early 1990s. Since then, however, the number of EU laws adopted in this field has slowed considerably and its constraining effects have steadily weakened.

Despite this overall trend, in the case of France one must first stress how much the initial growth of EU law has given rise to a wide range of rules and procedures which have modified the way actors in this country approach environmental protection. As in other 'Southern' European countries, protecting 'nature' by placing constraints upon industry, farming and the general public was definitely not a priority for the French state before EU legislation forced it to change its ways. However, as long ago as 1995, a report by the Council of State considered that as much as 90 per cent of French environmental legislation stemmed from the obligation to implement EU law (Sicard, 1995). As in other member-states, this form of Europeanization has therefore obliged the French state to intervene in different ways in order to respect EU-set minimum standards on air and water quality, car exhausts, rubbish disposal, etc.

Notwithstanding these Europeanization-driven policy innovations, there continues to be strong resistance to fully incorporating the effect and meaning of EU legislation into French measures for protecting the environment. Resistance to conforming with environmental directives has become stronger since the early 1990s. A good example of French resistance is that of the European Commission's attempts to encourage the proactive protection of flora and fauna through establishing a European-wide system of protected habitats. Often known as the 'Natura 2000' Directive, the transposition of this legislation into French law and administrative practice is fiercely contested by a group of hunting, farming and forestry lobbies. Often aided and abetted by field officials from the Ministry of Agriculture and Forestries, in many regions this opposition has effectively blocked implementation of the EU Directive (Traïni, 2003). In so doing many national MPs have been enrolled in a campaign which seeks to interpret the subsidiarity principle in such a way that the EU would have no say in 'telling regions how to protect their environment'.

Another example of French resistance to a European directive is provided by France's reluctance to apply 'the polluter pays' principle. Although this principle is now formally present in a wide range of EU directives, in France its application is resisted strongly by representatives of both farming and industry. Whilst it is not surprising that French economic actors strive to minimize the effects of EU legislation upon their activities, the relative silence of the French state and politicians on such matters merits deeper analysis. Rather than offer culturalist explanations of their lack of enthusiasm for environmental protection, it is more important to understand the flexible character of much EU law in this area and how, as in the case of regional development, in practice subsidiarity so often means that the most powerful actors ultimately end up getting their way.

In both these issue areas, if considerable Europeanization of the French state has certainly taken place, it is important not to overstate the order of change this has entailed. The adoption of EU law does not automatically imply the modification of national policies and political practices. Only institutionalized forms of negotiation, norms and sanctions cause deep levels of change, something which 'shared' EU policies appear unable to do consistently and in any durable fashion.

'No EU policy' but Europeanization nonetheless: internal and external security

A final category of EU law concerns issue areas where formally the EU has little or no competence to intervene at all and 'should' instead intervene solely upon the instructions of national governments which only decide to act amongst themselves on the basis of unanimity voting. Consequently in these policy areas one would expect there to be virtually no Europeanization of national political practices. In reality, as will be shown through the examples of internal and external security, at least in France neither is it possible to argue that the EU does not intervene in such 'no go areas' nor that no modifications of national norms and behaviour have taken place. Instead, it will be stressed how Europeanization can both occur 'without the European Union' (Irondelle, 2002) and how this 'bottom–up' process can eventually lead to the invention and growth of EU legislation.

Internal security

Since the events of 11 September 2001, international cooperation between police forces and other agents involved in controlling borders has undoubtedly increased. If one looks more closely at this subject, however, in the case of Western Europe this form of transgovernmental cooperation had already been steadily increasing since the rise of terrorism in the 1970s (Bigo, 1996). At the beginning of the following decade, a number of actors began to stress that when abolishing border controls for the trading of goods, changes would also have to be brought in for freeing up, but nevertheless controlling, the movement of people. In 1985 an agreement on this point was signed at Schengen between the governments of France, West Germany and the Benelux countries. Since that time this agreement has come into force, steadily been integrated into the EU treaties and, directly and indirectly, led to considerable Europeanization of three policy areas – immigration, policing and judicial cooperation- commonly linked together as 'Justice and Home Affairs' (JHA). Although the Council continues to vote under rules of unanimity for most of these matters, in the French case not only has considerable policy change been sparked throughout this issue area, but successive French governments have argued for even deeper EU involvement in these matters.

External security

If this 'normalization' of internal security as a European public problem can therefore clearly be seen in France, most commentators consider that such a trend is much less advanced in the case of external security (Menon, 2002). Repeated differences of opinion between the French and British governments, particularly over the Iraq war, clearly highlight that foreign policies in Europe are still frequently unsynchronized and that the EU as a whole has difficulty adopting common standpoints. However, focusing uniquely upon a few ultimately isolated results of European cooperation on foreign affairs and defence policy leads too many writers on this subject to completely ignore the density of consultation and common actions which currently take place at the European level and thereby heavily involve representatives from states such as France.

In the case of formulating common positions on international events, the EU has, at least in purely quantitative terms, a relatively good track record. Such cooperation has in fact existed for three decades and given rise to a set of rules and procedures which now produce, literally on a daily basis, both diplomatic-style declarations and more concrete actions such as sanctions or humanitarian aid (Smith, 1998). Although still jealous of its independence, the French Foreign ministry has been and is very much part and parcel of this process (Buchet de Neuilly, 2001). A second related set of external security issues concerns cooperation between European armed forces and arms industries. Engaged in many joint peace-keeping operations, armies in Europe, and the French army in particular, now have a much better understanding of each other. Although major differences remain, a model of the professionalized soldier has emerged and had considerable impact, for example upon the ending of conscription in France (Irondelle, 2002). European cooperation over arms procurement is more structured and has had more concrete outputs despite taking an essentially intergovernmental form that has sidelined the European Commission. In existence since the 1960s, cooperation over arms production and procurement has recently been redesigned and relaunched in order to lock national governments into a set of binding agreements (Joana and Smith, 2004). As one of the major producers of arms in Europe, France's position in favour of this change is deeply significant in terms of both industrial and defence policy.

Conclusion

Of course, analysis of the Europeanization of each of these sectors could, and probably should, be pushed much further. For the purposes of this chapter, however, the preceding analysis at least allows one to compare the trajectories of Europeanization across sectors, understand why the depth of this process varies so widely and grasp the idea that there is nothing

Table 7.1 *Trajectories of the Europeanization of the French state*

Sector	Europeanization	De-Europeanization
Agriculture	1958–92	1992 >
Competition	1989 >	
Telecommunications	1987 >	
Monetary union	1992 >	
Regional development	1975–94	1994 >
Environment	1980–92	1992 >
Internal security	1985 >	
External security	1991 >	

inevitable or linear about European integration. The highly sectoral character of this integration has also been stressed.

As has also been shown by looking at the Europeanization of its administrations, the French state is certainly firmly embedded in the government of the European Union. Relatively little law or public policy can now be made in France without some reference to the EU's norms and procedures. Nonetheless, the vast majority of the representatives and citizens of this state still fail to recognize this transformation in the locus and form of political power. The major challenge for future research is to explain the causes and consequences of this 'gap'.

Chapter 8

Reshaping the State? Administrative and Decentralization Reforms

PATRICK LE GALÈS

Concluding a volume on *The Nation State in Question* Ikenberry wrote:

> The first half of the twentieth century belonged to strong states that could mobilize their societies for industrialization and war ... [nowadays] states need to be flexible and to work efficiently with societal groups. (Ikenberrry 2003, p. 353)

Implicit in this conclusion is a paradoxical claim: states that institutionally restrain the coercive power of government – through normative consensus and legal-constitutional rules – actually unleash the ability of government leaders to work with and through society to mobilize resources and solve problems. The power of the state 'emerges from its ability to harness the social capital and resources of the people it rules'.

Right or wrong, the argument sums up some of the most difficult challenges facing the French state. The centralized Jacobin state was able to mobilize society to fight wars, and then to modernize the economy and the country after 1945. The French statist model was seen as an exception in Europe (Dyson, 1980). However, during the late 1980s, the crisis of the hierarchical model of the French state became a central feature of academic analysis (Muller, 1998; Cohen, 1992; Rouban, 1998). The French state appeared under pressure from above (from the European Union and transnational firms) and from below (from the sub-national levels of government following the French decentralization reforms of the early 1980s).

Reshaping the French state became a major concern of French elites. The French state is struggling with contradictory challenges on various fronts: the impact of the institutionalization of Europe, the growing individualization of its citizens and their shifting loyalties, the world scale of its large firms (making the traditional *dirigiste* economic approach more difficult), the gathering forces of globalization and the entrenched support for the *service public*, this conception which associates the general interest,

122

the state, the citizen and the delivery of public services. Politicians and the representatives of the *grands corps* – the top level of the bureaucracy – are now painfully trying to learn new tricks. Reform is essential in order to gain effective control and enhance political capacity to change behaviours, to modernize the economy and society. French governors are aware of the need to adopt new policy instruments and to invent novel ways of working with increasingly autonomous groups and interests.

This chapter contributes in part to this understanding of the reshaping of the French state in parallel to Levy's chapter on economic policy, Smith on Europeanization, Keiger on defence and foreign policy or Cole on education. In this chapter we deal with the internal restructuring of the state: the administration, the political and territorial order, the instruments and the delivery of public policies. We elucidate two contradictory trends. The first of these is the erosion of the hierarchical model of the French state. There has been a decline in the importance of hierarchies and central norms, along with an ongoing rise in the significance of sub-national government. We also stress, however, the ongoing attempts to reinvent the state and to strengthen centralization mechanisms within a general context of EU institutionalization and increased market pressure. This effort at coordination implies increased interdependence between levels of government, as well as a calling into question of the traditional model of the French state as representing the general interest, embodied in particular by the *grands corps*.

The chapter contrasts the high-profile State administrative reforms enacted by the political and administrative elites to the ongoing, partly silent revolution of decentralization. Both cases illustrate the underlying theme of change within the State. There is no such thing as a classic heroic grand scheme to change the State. Neither is there a frozen State. What we observe is a rather slow, non-linear, chaotic process fuelled by competition and conflicts between powerful political actors and interest groups, themselves representing conflicting pressures driven by marketization and the process of Europeanization. As a result of these cross-cutting pressures, the French polity appears more pluralist, less State-led, less hierarchical, but also less able to organize to face, resist or adapt to market pressures and altogether a more diverse, competitive, plural, messy perhaps but also dynamic polity.

Reforming the French public administration to reduce costs and increase the steering capacity: buzzword and elusive quest

Reforming the State was essential for the Gaullist modernizing project of the Fifth Republic against what was seen as the archaism of political elites, local in particular. Nowadays, this heroic, entrepreneurial vision of State reform has given way to a belief in 'new public management (NPM)'. In the French case, NPM refers to the introduction of competition to deliver services, the fragmentation of the civil service, the multiplication of specialized agencies, the rise of auditing and tools for budget control, privatization, and the increasing role of regulation at the expense of direct State intervention. These different mechanisms and changes have been introduced in a piecemeal and partial manner. There was no such thing as a clear neoliberal turn in France of the type that led to such far-reaching reforms in the UK, New Zealand or even in the Netherlands. Rather the French case is one of ongoing experimentation and the diffusion of incremental reforms that borrow some features from the NPM toolkit. These reforms, as shown in detail by Philippe Bezès' work (2004), come under different headings, such as the reform of the State, administrative reform and the modernization of the administration.

Major confusion therefore emerges in the political debate. Opponents, and in the first place the public-sector trade unions, typically associate State reforms with the search for more cost-effectiveness, more flexibility and the imposition of the discipline of market mechanisms upon French public services by administrative and political elites who have sold out the French model to the EU and to market pressures. For better or worse, this characterization is broadly accurate and reveals the normative conflicts of the debate (Rouban 1998).

A resourceful state: The public sector in the large sense remains central in the making and organisation of France

Despite two decades of international pressure to reduce the role of the State, a first indicator to stress is the relative stability of the macro-importance of the public sector (which is an essential part of the state). The fiscal revenue of the State as a percentage of GDP was 42.1 per cent in 1980, increased in the 1990s to over 47 per cent but was down at 46.1 per cent in 2003. Total public spending in France (on the basis of OECD figures and definitions) represents 51 per cent of GDP in 2001, similar to the figure in 1985 and comparable with Nordic European countries like Denmark and Sweden, though higher than Germany and Italy (between 42 per cent and 45 per cent) and much higher than Britain (39 per cent), not to mention the USA (29 per cent).

Public spending can be divided more or less into two broad domains: nearly half, 417 billion euros in 2002, goes to social protection (pensions, health, unemployment benefit, family policy), and about the same amount goes to expenditure of the state and local authorities (261 billion euros in 2001 for the State, 128 billion euros for local authorities).

The public debt was 57.3 per cent of GDP in 2001, against 63,1 per cent in the euro zone. In 2001, France was far more indebted than the UK

(39.1 per cent) but much less than Italy (109.7 per cent). However, the decision to lower tax and the lack of control of spending under the Raffarin government appointed by President Chirac in 2002 has led to a serious increase of the deficit and the debt.

The State in France is made visible by civil servants. In line with what happened elsewhere in Europe and in order to deliver the services of the expanding welfare state (in particular education) the number of civil servants grew massively in the postwar period from about 800,000 to over 2 million. By contrast with other EU countries, however, this number has kept rising, so that there were over 2.5 million civil servants in 2003. This inflated figure includes 8,000 top civil servants, the elite of the elite. Moreover, if one adds local government staff (who have public-sector status) and those working for quasi-public-sector organizations (in energy or the health system), one reaches a total of 6 million employees within the public or the quasi-public sector. Between 25 and 30 per cent of jobs are within this sector in France. Public-sector employees are classified according to whether they work in the public health service (over 900,000 employees), for the State itself (2.5 million) or for local authorities (1.4 million). Wages paid to civil servants account for 40 per cent of State expenditure.

As elsewhere, the public sector, often a quasi-public sector, is very differentiated between the core of the State (education, hospitals, police or the Ministry of Finance), large service delivery organizations (French Electricity (EDF): The Post Office (La Poste), the national railways (Société Nationale des Chemins de Fer Français)), or the social service sector and local authorities. With the institutionalization of Europe, and increasing pressure from DG competition, market mechanisms have had to be introduced in some sectors and public-sector recruitment has had to be opened to Europeans.

The coming of age of an administrative reform policy

The reform of the State has been a constant source of preoccupation since the 1980s. A number of different reform programmes have been attempted across a range of ministries. The reform effort has been fragmented, marked by failures and slow implementation. However, Bezès convincingly argues that there is more than just the aggregation of half measures in different ministries, but an 'ongoing process of institutionalization and differentiation of administrative reform policies within the French state' (Bezès, 2004), a matrix of ideas, policy instruments and goals that have established their presence on the political agenda. During the 1990s, within leading political parties and within State elites, the view that reforming the State was essential for France's competitiveness and adaptation to Europe became dominant. This view encompassed conflicting representations about solutions and entrenched political rivalries between Left and Right. The implementation of State reform has proved difficult despite numerous policy documents and a myriad of initiatives. Beyond political conflicts and the leadership strategies followed by prime ministers, ongoing rivalries exist between the *grands corps* on the one hand (for instance the Financial Inspectorate [*Inspection des Finances*] against the Court of Accounts [*Cour des Comptes*]) and, more importantly, between ministries. The Ministry of Finance, the ministry in charge of State reform and administration, and the Ministry of the Interior all play a major in the process, in competition with each other to take the lead and impose their own ideas and people.

The reform of the State emerged as a powerful new public policy paradigm and programme in the 1980s. In the eyes of France's political and administrative elites, the State was too top-heavy. It was not cost-effective, the classic example used being that of the cost of collecting taxes: much higher in France than in most EU countries. The French state was rooted within a territorial organization inherited from the Third Republic, which laid great stress on the role of the external services of central ministries in every department. The French state model was too static, too hierarchical, mosaic-like and overly rigid in its organization.

A first set of reforms in the 1980s mainly dealt with the introduction of new policy instruments in a piecemeal way. Instruments are less controversial than major reforms. The Socialist governments (1981–86) in particular introduced new tools to manage staff in different ministries, and attempted to develop the use of contracts between ministries, local authorities and territorial policy communities (Gaudin, 1999). Contracts became a tool for improving coordination within the public sector and adding a strategic focus to the delivery of public policies. In many ways, however, and despite the profound restructuring related to the decentralization process, not much happened except in the field of economic policy.

The main legacy was that of the Rocard government. The Rocard government wholeheartedly embraced the theme of the reform and renewal of the public service. Rocard came closer than ever before to defining a French version of NPM, focused upon new methods of managing staff, new financial arrangements and the introduction of performance indicators. The 1989 programme entitled 'the Renewal of the Public Service' (*Renouveau du service public*) presented a modernist Left-wing programme of reforms negotiated with the non-communist public-sector trade unions. It was mainly based upon the introduction of flexibility and training into public-sector work practices. The Rocard programme also embraced managerial autonomy, referring to the importance of goals and contracts as tools for achieving a more autonomous and self-sufficient public service.

Much energy was spent on these programmes, which led to profound disillusionment, modest outputs and a failure to mobilize public sector employees. The incremental strategy within the 'public sector' did not deliver much in the first round. However, the Rocard reforms created a real dynamic of change. In several governmental ministries, organizations were created dedicated to changing the working practices of the administration.

The scale of the problem was publicly recognized, as was the need to undertake systematic evaluation.

The idea that there should be a large-scale rescaling of the State, piloted by State elites themselves, came out of the 1990s (Bezès, 2004). Rising costs and deficits at a time of financial constraints organized by the Maastricht Treaty, slow adaptation to EU rules and pressure from decentralized power centres combined to strengthen the consensus about the need to reform the State. There were a number of reports dedicated to this theme during the 1990s, culminating with the landmark report, *L'Etat en France, servir une nation ouverte sur le monde*, a report provided for the Right-wing Balladur government. This report directly led to the creation of an *ad hoc* committee (*Commissariat à la Réforme de l'Etat*) and then the creation of a ministry. The report was a mix of lasting Gaullist heroic reformist vision under the leadership of enlightened Europeanized civil servants, aiming at reinforcing the strategic capacity of the state together with ideas coming from the new public management doctrines: flexibility, evaluation, cost assessment in particular.

The Juppé government, appointed after Chirac's election as president in 1995, decisively took on the 'state modernization' agenda and promoted a vast reform agenda in a rather top–down fashion. Massive protests in 1995 over the pension reform and the defeat at the parliamentary elections in 1997 paved the way to a more limited and gradual approach. Many experiments and new initiatives were launched across a wide range of ministries, in the Ministry of Finance in particular. They fell far behind the ambitious reformist drive of the *Etat en France* report. Within the French state, resistance to change was made obvious through the resistance of both the administration and the trade unions. French trade unions are now very weak within the private sector but remain a force in the public sector, although they are divided. In addition to the CGT (representing the communist tradition), the reformist CFDT, and the more corporatist FO, several new trade unions have emerged, in particular SUD, which mobilizes radical militants in the public sector. The division between unions feeds competition and protest, producing strikes within the public sector together with opposition to change. Trade unions epimotize the fear of a part of French society of the decline of public services, threatened by market mechanisms which challenge one conception of equality within the French Republic. The capacity of these public-sector unions to block reforms, in a context where reducing costs is also a priority, remains strong.

The 'Plural Left' Jospin government elected in 1997 (composed of Socialists, Greens, Communists, Citizens and Radicals) benefited from popular protests against top–down state reforms. Massive reform against the will of public employees, who massively voted for the Left, was not an option. The Plural Left government did introduce a number of piecemeal changes, designed to raise the quality of service delivery, to improve the management of public services and to embed practices of evaluation. The Plural Left government was anxious to cooperate with the trade unions in any reform, as well as to change the budgetary process. Most importantly, government ministers referred to the need to develop a more strategic vision of the mission of the central state, one that went beyond the simple delivery of services.

The real innovation came not from the government but from parliament. A cross-party working group advocated a profound reshaping of the budgetary process in order to increase the strategic and political capacity of the government and improve the control of parliament. This parliamentary initiative was taken in cooperation with a Ministry of Finance (through its budget division) that was eager to introduce the reform, creating an unusual alliance of parliament and the Ministry of Finance. The key idea was to increase the effectiveness, transparency and visibility of public spending, and to strengthen the possibility of political control: that is, the ability of parliament to accept or reject new spending plans. This led to the introduction of the new law on the organization of the budget (*Loi Organique du 1er Août 2001 relative aux Lois de Finances*: LOLF) in August 2001, which marked a decisive change (Bezès, 2004). The law simplifies the presentation of the budget, changes the labels and dramatically reduces the number of divisions within the budget. It systematizes the 'real cost' approach to policies including all the costs, from personnel to equipment, associated with a policy programme. It brings with it some basic elements of managerialism which had been remarkably absent from the running of the state in France. The law makes more visible the connections between expenditure and programmes, including objectives and evaluation. Most importantly, public expenditure will be reorganized within precise programmes. Each ministry will have more freedom to manage its resources (investment, current expenditure …) within a fixed expenditure limit. These measures are supposed to increase the role of forecasting and control. The LOLF generalizes the introduction of indicators and performance measures, which had been gradually brought in here and there over the past decade. The LOLF represents a decisive shift to modernize the budget process and to enhance political control. New IT systems have been brought in to change the way to assess costs and expenditure and to collect precise indicators. The new budget law is therefore central as a coordinating mechanism within the French government, a powerful counterweight to the ever-increasing autonomy of ministries.

The timetable for implementation of this major change is five years. The new process was part-introduced in 2004, but without the new tools and indicators, creating confusion and chaos in the implementation process. Characteristically this major piece of legislation, which will have deep and ongoing consequences for the budgetary process and the making and implementation of public policies in France, was adopted over the summer, when most people are on holiday, with no or little publicity, without a public debate, or explanations given, as the result of negotiation between MPs and the Ministry of Finance.

After Chirac's triumphal re-election in 2002, the Raffarin government has once again placed emphasis on the need to reform the State and the administration. The government has, of course, learned from the failure of the Juppé government and is therefore committed to a gradual and negotiated approach to State reforms. This includes active support for the implementation of the new budgetary law, and for strengthening new tools. New policy instruments include the creation of an Observatory of the Public Administration; the introduction of performance measurement for the evaluation and wages of some civil servants; the use of EU agreements to force changes in the ownership of public corporations (the case for the electricity giant EDF, now a limited company); the partial replacement of important waves of retiring civil servants; and increased budget cuts. One notable absence has been the failure to reform the National Administration School (*Ecole Nationale d'Administration*) which selects and trains the elite of the French administration.

Prime Minister Raffarin, a committed decentralizer and former president of the Poitou-Charentes region, saw decentralization as another means of forcing through an ambitious reform of the state. Let us now consider whether, and if so in what ways, decentralization has reshaped the French state.

Decentralization and the restructuring of the territorial order

Decentralization in France signifies the transfer of powers, resources and staff from central ministries to democratically elected sub-national levels of government. The first timid moves to decentralization began in the 1960s, driven by the combined pressures of regionalist movements in Alsace and Brittany and the recognition by central State elites that administrative decentralization might be appropriate for tackling certain types of policy challenge. Decentralization gathered pace in the 1970s, supported by the economic crisis and by the failure of the State to organize full employment. Moves to political decentralization gained real momentum in the 1980s and 1990s. Decentralization remains high up the political agenda today. It appears as a dynamic process, with significant reforms passed every three or four years, fuelled by the political competition between rival levels of government to gain more resources and more autonomy. Decentralization has come to represent a massive long-term change in the organization of the French polity, and, together with Europeanization, has provoked a major restructuring of the French state. It has also introduced new problems of policy coordination. Under the influence of decentralization, France has become a more pluralistic, negotiated and territorialized democracy, one less dominated by a Parisian elite.

Cycles of reforms and the new structure of local and regional government

The point of departure was the stable system invented during the French Revolution, organized around 36,700 communes and 100 *départements* (including the four overseas departments *départements d'outre mer*), with an elected level of government. At the departmental level the state apparatus brought together the field services of the major ministries under the coordination of the prefect. Small communes and Right-wing rural interests still dominate the French second Chamber, the Senate which, under the Fifth Republic has always been controlled by Right-wing parties. This old system came under pressure because of France's late urbanization. In the last decade, medium-sized regional capitals such as Nantes, Rennes, Strasbourg, Montpellier, Toulouse, Grenoble or Nice have been booming cities, enjoying considerable economic and demographic growth. Each of these cities is far away from Paris. There has also been a shift in political power to cities.

The decentralization reforms started in the 1970s but were given renewed impetus in the 1980s with the coming to power of the Socialist President Mitterrand. Cities, metropolitan areas and regional councils are becoming more important sites for the organization of interests, for decision-making and the implementation of public policy, and for the creation of collective strategies. On the other hand, the pre-existing players – communes and *départements* – have adapted and resisted well.

Over the last decade, decentralization has been strengthened by five pieces of legislation. Each law passed has given rise to heated political debates that cut across traditional Right and Left cleavages:

- First, in 1995, the Gaullist Minister Charles Pasqua introduced the *pays* as a new level for the mobilization of local interests. The *pays* are voluntary groupings of mainly rural communes. They were intended to be a locus for territorially based projects. The *pays* were initially contested on the Left in part because of the personality of their promoter. A leading figure of the French Euro-sceptic movement, Pasqua deliberately used the classic images of rural France, small villages and towns, as the bedrocks of the Republic, eternal French symbols to be supported by the Republican State against the foreign threats such as immigrants, American capitalists or EU technocrats.
- Secondly, the Corsican question became once again a major political question during the Jospin government (1997–2002). The Matignon agreements of 2001, signed between the government and Corsican nationalist movements, envisaged granting new powers to the

Corsican assembly, including secondary legislative powers, in the hope of undermining the regular waves of bombing and killing. This controversial statute for Corsica was undermined by reactions from the Council of State, which challenged the provisions for secondary legislative powers. This innovative policy with differentiated institutions within French territories was taken on board despite the change of government. However, the failure of the 2003 referendum in Corsica to approve the new set of institutions, marked, once again, the failure of the autonomists in Corsica and the French state to find a lasting agreement. To a lesser extent, during the same years (1999–2001) the Council of State also prevented the *Diwan* network of Breton-speaking schools to be integrated within the Ministry of Education, despite the agreement with the then Minister of Education. In both cases, the controversy opposed so-called 'Republicans', attached to the classic view of the French state and its autonomy towards the EU, and decentralizers, advocating large-scale decentralization including forms of quasi-federalism.

- The Jospin government also undertook important moves towards strengthening intercommunal cooperation. No fewer than three laws were passed to this effect. The Voynet Act of 1999, on regional planning and sustainable development, principally concerned the Ministry of the Environment and Regional Policy, the main provision of the Act being a re-launch of the *pays* as structures for intercommunal collaboration in rural areas. The Chevènement Act of 1999 provided a mixture of sticks and carrots to encourage communes to cooperate in intercommunal structures in towns and (especially) cities. The Act greatly encouraged communes to pool their resources and to adopt single taxation instruments for common services. The Interior Ministry piloted the Chevènement Act. The 1999 Act gave new powers to the state's territorial representatives, the prefects, to force cooperation among communes. The 2000 Urban Renewal and Solidarity Act, piloted by the Infrastructure Ministry, followed shortly afterwards. Taken together, these three Acts revealed a desire to legitimize the territorialization of public policies. They were also highly revealing of the search for new instruments to manage and control the national territory, a major concern for State ministries that are in rivalry with each other. The three laws organize the territorialization of State strategies and promote the development of collective projects that reinforce social and spatial redistribution at different scales. These different laws are aimed in particular at fostering cooperation between local government within urban and rural areas to develop economic development strategies, planning strategy, and the management of services and utilities. These interrelated, but separate processes introduced a new form of competitive bidding. The French state agreed to provide financial incentives to create these new bodies (providing about 15 per cent extra funding). The intercommunal public corporations (établissements publics de cooperation intercommunal:

EPCI) created by these laws themselves must bid for funds from central government and they are to some extent pitted against each other.

- Fourth, at last, the democratic issue was brought into the decentralization debate. The new Neighbourhood Democracy ('Démocratie de proximité') Act of 2002 created new consultation procedures and gave more power to neighbourhood associations within urban politics.
- Finally, the Raffarin government launched its Act II of decentralization. This involved introducing changes to the constitution to recognize the rights of local authorities and to give constitutional recognition to the Regions for the first time. It also involved the transfer of 150,000 civil servants to local and regional authorities, as well as giving new powers to different levels of government. The *départements* obtained new powers in the field of roads, social assistance and waste disposal. The Regions obtained grants to firms, training, regional strategic planning and public infrastructure. All local and regional authorities were allowed to bid for experimental powers to run new services, and to reorganize their structures.

Local and regional actors have driven this process of decentralization, much more than the administrative elite in Paris or top–down processes such as Europeanization or globalization. Local and regional politicians are powerful groups within the French party system that they dominate and within the state: they have been the political driving force behind the decentralization reforms. By contrast, decentralization is not a salient issue for the population as measured by opinion polls. Major reforms have been promoted by the lobbying of powerful groups with French local and regional government. Urban mayors within the Socialist party were in the forefront of those pushing for decentralization in 1981–82. More recently, Premier Raffarin (formerly a regional president himself) lent a very attentive ear to the demands of the Right-wing presidents of the Regional Councils for the decentralization of more powers from 2002 onwards. The Left has tended to emphasize the role of cities and urban areas, and, to a lesser extent, regions and to combat *départements*, but not too much. The Right has tended to support departments and regions at the expense of cities, but not too much. The most formidable political battles take place between the rival national associations representing local government. Le Lidec (2001) has shown the importance of those groups, such as the Association of Mayors of France (*Associations des Maires de France*); the Association of Presidents of Departmental Councils (*L'Association des Présidents des Conseils Généraux*), and lately the Association of Presidents of Regional Councils (*Association des Présidents de Conseils Régionaux)* and the Association of the Mayors of Large Cities (*Association des Maires des Grandes Villes de France*). Even if recent laws have limited multiple officeholding (*cumul des mandats* is now limited to two offices; it is also now impossible to combine two positions of executive authority within local authorities), the strong link between local and political spheres remains. The large majority of French MPs hold local mandates and still gain their political influence through the consolidation of their local power. These groups are permanently engaged in never-ending battles to develop the transfers of power from the State and to prevent other levels of government from benefiting at their expense. The latest reform, the Raffarin decentralization reform, also reflected power relations in the new Right-wing party, the UMP. Although the Prime Minister managed to strengthen the role of the regions in the constitution, he could do so only by giving more resources and powers to the *départements* and by increasing the role of the Senate in local matters. Once the Socialists and their allies had massively won the regional elections in the spring of 2004 (winning 20 out of 22 regions for the first time), granting more powers to regions became much less of a priority for the Raffarin government.

The world of local and regional government comprises 500,000 elected members and 1.6 million public-sector employees (150,000 more with the new decentralization, reform comprising about 27 per cent of the French public sector). Crucially, local and regional governments are in charge of more than 70 per cent of public investment. Two levels of local government appear to have gained legitimacy and the capacity to act in recent years: the regions and largest cities.

Regions

The regions have gained considerable influence in strategic domains in spite of an initial lack of resources. Regions mainly deal with economic development, training and the building of secondary schools. The *départements* have particular power and resources in social services – the minimum income policy, support for the old – and transport (local roads). In spite of their difficult institutionalization, regions have gained credibility and legitimacy. They have been favoured by the European Union as the scale for the implementation of structural funds. Regions have been given a constitutional status; their fiscal autonomy has been reinforced. Under the Raffarin government, they have obtained a constitutional right to experiment in new domains such as those of higher education, professional training, and the management of ports, airports and roads. Already, some regions have proved very ambitious, claiming their legitimate competence in areas such as transport, a traditional dominion of the central State, on the basis of their success in development regional rail networks.

Cities

The largest cities, equipped with strong intermunicipal institutions, are the second winning level of government. At the lower level, communes mainly deal with social services, their own roads and primary schools, basic services, environment, sport and culture. The law has created a new category of intercommunal government: the EPCI, of which three different

types exist. On 1 January 1 2004, 2,461 EPCI existed, covering 82 per cent
of the population, particularly in cities. This represents a major change of
scale of local government. The communes remain, but important strategic
powers have been and will be transferred to the new level of government.
The strategic capacity, resources and autonomy of metropolitan government have been strengthened, though they have yet to be directly elected.
These new structures lack democratic legitimacy, as their members are
for the moment nominated by municipal councils (though recent reports
have advocated the direct election of the intercommunal councillors).
But they are now in charge of strategic policy domains and they control
important resources. Indeed, their competences encompass urban planning,
public transportation, infrastructure, economic development, social housing, environment protection, and waste collection and treatment. The EPCI
levy a common rate of business taxation across their constituent communes (whereas previously taxes had varied between neighbouring towns).
Finally, each EPCI finds itself with a set of compulsory responsibilities
and the obligation to choose among a list of optional competences. The
new intercommunal administrations can boast a high level of technical
expertise, able to challenge not only their departmental and regional
counterparts but also the central state's field services. In large conurbations,
the presidents of these intercommunal structures, who often happen to be
the mayor of the core commune, are becoming the powerful leaders of
genuine city governments, able to launch large projects and to mobilize
local elites and institutions around those projects. The pro-urban stance of
the Left–Green Jospin government (1997–2002) action was clear. The aim
of several acts passed by this government was to enable French cities
to build up solid integrated governments able to launch policies positioning cities in European territorial competition. The central State itself has
privileged the city level to implement some of its policies, particularly in the
sector of urban regeneration policies. The State thereby recognizes that
territory can provide policy coherence, and act as a substitute to the older
vertical integration through the direct intervention of the central State. The
elites of France's largest cities have also been able to develop a sort of
parallel diplomacy, establishing connections not only with European
institutions but also with their European counterparts in order to exchange
experience in economic development, social and cultural policies (Pinson
and Vion, 2000).

Other organizations

The world of local government also comprises myriads of other organizations (Lorrain, 1991). Some of these have a non-governmental status, such
as associations acting as quasi-services for local government, running
festive or social services. Others have a mixed status, such as the mixed
economy societies (*sociétés d'économie mixte*), private agencies with
majority public ownership, which often act as subsidiaries of, or manage

services for, local government. If some organizations are public, such as those that run social housing, others are quasi-public (for example in town-planning) or public–private agencies running services operated by private firms. Finally, a number of these organizations are clearly privately run utilities (in the areas of environment, transport or social housing).

Decentralization and the search for new mechanisms of central coordination

Pressures from local and regional politicians were identified as the main force pushing for decentralization reforms. State elites have also played a role. Although top state civil servants have not usually been key supporters of decentralization reforms, some have pushed for the 'decentralization of penury', that is the decentralization of rapidly increasing social expenditure or powers to make painful cuts. Also, rivalries between the *grands corps* (notably Ministry of Finance and *Trésoriers Inspecteurs Généraux*, Ministry of Infrastructures and *Directions Départementales de l'Equipement*, Ministry of Interior and prefects) and within ministries themselves have led some sections of the State to support decentralization in some specific ways. For Prime Minister Raffarin, decentralization has the advantage of driving the State modernization agenda forward, despite the resistance of civil servants and their trade unions. The prospect of staff transfers from the State to the Regions has produced a number of difficult social conflicts. Over the years, the mechanisms of cooperation between the centre and sub-national levels of government (the State–Region contracts [*contrats de plan*] in particular) have shown their limits. Too often, the representatives of the State in the field services have proved unable to adopt a coherent territorial strategy, or to deliver the funds promised by the State. In other words, State failures to deliver or to keep its word have fed the bottom-up demand for more decentralization.

The need to manage State reforms has, over the years, led to an increase in mechanisms for interministerial coordination at the central level (Bezès, 2001). By contrast, the lack of State coordination at the departmental or regional level is now seen as a major issue. There is an intense pressure within State external services to reinforce the strategic regional level of the State, under the leadership of the regional prefect, to coordinate more closely and effectively all State external services, not for the first time it must be said. Decentralization has led to a differential impact within State bureaucracies. It has produced increasing difficulties and problems of coordination for the State external services on the one hand, but has led to the strengthening of the Ministry of Finance and the controlling bodies at the centre on the other hand. The departmental field services of central government ministries (the DDE in the ministry of infrastructure and housing; the DDASS for the ministry of social affairs; the DDA for the

Ministry of Agriculture, even the prefects accountable to the Ministry of the Interior), now face local and regional leaders who have resources, strategies, expertise and money to invest. They often feel they represent an incoherent, impoverished state, torn between the conflicting goals of the ministries in Paris and the lack of resources, staff and increasingly legitimacy on the ground.

By contrast, both the Ministry of Finance and the Regional Chambers of Accounts (*Chambres régionales des comptes*, public organizations created by the decentralization reforms in charge of controlling local authority expenditure) have increased their capacity to control local authorities. The Regional Chambers have become powerful organizations, which have developed a real expertise in their technical and financial control of local authorities. The Regional Chambers set the parameters under which local leaders are freer to act.

After years of state retreat, the success of the 1999 Chevènement law fostering municipal cooperation has been interpreted as a 'return of the State'. Undoubtedly, the 1999 law implies that building metropolitan governments calls for strong State intervention. Yet this intervention is of a particular nature: it rests more on constitutive policies than on substantive actions. In other words, the State defines rules and procedures, roles and settings, but it does not go into details as to how exactly these shall contribute to a particular purpose: that task is left to local officials. In this respect, the 1999 law is perfectly consistent with a whole series of other laws that have seen central government define priorities and procedures to achieve these goals, with local actors being left to adopt the necessary means and concrete measures within the framework hereby defined (Duran and Thoenig, 1996). Hence, the State still has significant capacity to act, but the nature of its activity has changed. The State intervenes much less directly than before in detailed management. It has a weaker hold on what exactly goes on inside the procedures it has conceived. On the other hand, the attempt to provide the central State with more coordinating powers is the corollary of the move to greater decentralization.

Conclusion

Within the domains examined in this chapter, the French state appears to be moving from the classic model of 'hands-on policy' with direct intervention in every *département* of the Republic, to a more strategic regulatory, and possibly enabling role. This transformation is far from complete and requires further examination. Important questions about the coherence and the effectiveness of the French administration remain. One could characterize the current situation as one of 'freer local government, more rules' ... from the state or the EU. It remains to be seen if, beyond the regulatory role, France still has a strategy for the future of its territories.

A more complex picture of local government has emerged, a mosaic-like pattern resembling somehow the situation in other countries throughout Europe and very different from the previous well-organized state-view of local government: uniform, controlled by civil servants and enshrined within financial and legal constraints set by the State. France is no longer a uniform state, just a unitary state with regions and local authorities. France is now officially defined as such in the first article of the Constitution, which asserts that 'the organization of the Republic is decentralized'.

The administration, the public sector and the State remain central organizations in France. We can identify two risks in relation to the developments we have surveyed in this chapter. The first is that of state disengagement. French administrative and political elites are obviously tempted by defining a slimmer 'regulatory' state, one that would abandon important sections of the population to their fate and would undermine territorial solidarity. The level of extreme Right and extreme Left vote in recent elections suggest that this would have dangerous consequences. A second risk is that of institutional inertia: unreformed, the French state will remain too heavy and conservative, colonized by different interests, unable to deal with key social and economic issues, and losing key resources and staff. Some middle way must be found between these options.

Chapter 9

Foreign and Defence Policy: Constraints and Continuity

JOHN KEIGER

How much freedom do politicians have in determining a state's foreign and defence policies? It might be said that over the 'longue durée' very little and in the case of France even less given the burden of history. Politicians and their permanent officials are more often prisoners of a state's traditional modes of foreign and defence behaviour than sculptors of it, precisely because many of the determinants of foreign and defence policy lie outside the direct control of the State. This should be borne in mind when evaluating the degree to which President Jacques Chirac has altered the course of that policy since 1995.

Determinants of French foreign and defence policy

Historians of international relations have always maintained that the physical determinants of a state's external relations cannot be taken for granted. France's geographical position on the western tip of the continent of Europe ensures that geopolitically she is caught 'twixt Britain and Germany. Her Mediterranean outlook implicates her more closely in the 'threat from the south', where a destabilized North African rim potentially poses a serious security threat to her southern flank. More advantageously, geographical remnants of empire provide her with confetti-like possessions giving her toeholds in most areas of the globe. Demography may no longer be a determinant in the early twentieth-century crude sense of population equating to military power, but the growing multi-ethnic mix of her citizens has implications for the foreign and security policy she feels able to conduct, making a traditional pro-Arab policy difficult to modify. The economy remains a powerful conditioning agent. Ever since the 1980s, France's foreign and defence policies, with their Gaullist insistence on national independence and grandeur, have found difficulty in aligning the goal of national self-reliance with an under-performing economy. Financial stringency has played no small part recently in conditioning France's foreign and defence priorities, from nuclear strategy and defence procurement to retrenchment from Africa.

A more abstract determinant would be the Burden of History. France has a greater sense of the past than many other states and a self-conscious awareness of being different that is at the heart of French national identity and exceptionalism. This has conditioned not only her self-perception as a state (the self-styled purveyor of universalist democratic freedoms from Republican equality to the Rights of Man), but also how she is perceived by others (a champion of democracy, but also a conceited maverick). This exceptionalism has long conditioned her role as a world power. General de Gaulle made it a primary feature of French foreign and defence policy in the 1960s. His successors were borne along with the trend, either having little desire to modify it or, more often, no freedom to do so. This trend, though muted, is still intact in the post-Cold War era. But France's Cold War exceptionalism has metamorphosed from self-styled champion of smaller and underdog nations against the superpowers, to being the standard-bearer of cultural particularisms in the face of American 'hyperpower' and cultural 'hegemony'. This has to do with French national identity and how France seeks to define herself as a nation, often more by what she is not than by what she claims to be. Thus national identity has a clear impact on French foreign and security policy and helps to explain France's multi-lateralist stance in opposition to American unilateralism.

To these overarching determinants could be added another of a constitutional and political nature with a potential impact on the formulation and execution of foreign and defence policy. The tradition going back to the Third Republic of foreign and defence policy being in the President's reserved domain was brought to its zenith by the Fifth Republic's Constitution. This set of legal requirements whereby the President of the Republic defines foreign and defence policy, which is then carried out by foreign and defence ministers, has its full force when President, Prime Minister and parliamentary majority are politically one. But the Constitution does not provide for what has become a feature of French politics since 1986 – 'cohabitation' – when President and government hold differing political views and potentially different foreign and defence priorities. Thus the potential existed in the cohabitations of 1986–88, 1993–95 and 1997–2002 for politically different governments to limit a President's capacity to maintain a foreign and defence course.

Finally, the ultimate constraint on a state's foreign and defence policy is the context of the international system. That context comprises architectural and contingent elements: the former being anything from alliances, such as NATO, to international organizations like the United Nations or the European Union. Contingent elements, such as the fall of the Berlin Wall in 1989, the 1990–91 Gulf War or the 11 September 2001 attack on the United States, are 'events', as British Prime Minister Harold Macmillan once quipped, which test policy-makers and limit their freedom for manoeuvre.

Continuity of policies

It is in the nature of democratic politics that political leaders seek to carve out policies that distance them, rhetorically at least, from their opponents' period of government. The socialist François Mitterrand's presidential victory in May 1981, followed by the Left in the general elections of June, ended twenty-three years of opposition for the Left. Mitterrand was a long-standing critic of the Fifth Republic's institutions and of Gaullism. In opposition Mitterrand had countenanced nuclear decommissioning and disbanding the intelligence services. It would soon be clear, according to his former diplomatic adviser and Secretary General of the Elysée, Hubert Védrine in *Les Mondes de François Mitterrand: à l'Elysée 1981–1995*, that Mitterrand would continue the Gaullist legacy and merely attempt to modify it at the margins. By September 1983 he had reiterated Gaullist dogma on nuclear deterrence. Despite the initial rhetoric underlining differences with former President Giscard d'Estaing's policies, the realities and responsibilities of office combined with the constraints of foreign and defence interests ensured overall continuity in French policy.

Cold War comfort

Mitterrand's first presidential mandate adhered to the main tenets of Gaullist foreign and defence policy. But one year into his second term, in 1989 he had to cope with the remarkable contingency of the fall of the Berlin Wall, reunification of Germany and the velvet revolutions in Eastern and Central Europe that ended the Cold War. This was the greatest upheaval in international relations since the Cold War began in 1947. Close on its heels came the First Gulf War of 1990–91, bringing home not only the might of the only remaining superpower, but also its awesome technological superiority. The trick for any French political leader was to manoeuvre a foreign and defence policy styled for a world of two competing blocs to fit the 'new world order'.

The ending of the Cold War and German reunification forced France, more than most powers, to rethink its relations with the wider world. France had always blamed the 1945 Yalta settlement, at which it was not present, for producing the geopolitical freeze of the Cold War. In French eyes it was at Yalta that the Anglo-Americans and the Soviets decided on the division of Europe into two blocs. Yet ironically the Yalta settlement benefited France.

First, it allowed her to carve out a niche between the superpowers, enhancing her freedom for manoeuvre in international politics. General de Gaulle put this to good use during his presidency to champion Third World or small nations against the superpowers. Hence, a medium-sized power appeared to have the status of an independent force in world politics, something of no small advantage to a state wishing, for instance, to maintain a neocolonial empire. This enhanced France's great-power pretensions by a device unavailable to a similarly ranked power, Britain, given international perceptions of the latter's being in America's pocket.

Second, in pretending to be aloof from the two blocs and the Cold War, France could have its cake and eat it. It benefited from the US nuclear umbrella, yet remained on relatively good terms with the Soviet Union, giving it a privileged position in Europe and also achieving a traditional foreign policy objective of having a 'friend' at Germany's back.

Third, the division of Europe was fortuitous for dividing France's old enemy Germany, arguably the single most important issue in French foreign policy since 1870. That division satisfied a French war aim of 1918 and 1945: the dismembering of the greater German state. France achieved the long-standing objective of seeing its old enemy reduced to manageable proportions without the stigma of having brought it about itself. Not only did the Cold War perpetuate that division: it also prolonged French military occupation rights in Germany.

Fourth, the Cold War legitimized France's possession of nuclear weapons. The nuclear deterrent was held to defend the national 'sanctuary' against a Soviet attack, although the latter was never designated as a target in any of the five-year defence programme laws, until Mitterrand's presidency in the 1980s. Nuclear weapons served as a badge of great-power status as well as being an additional guarantee of security against a potentially resurgent Germany.

Fifth, the Cold War indirectly justified France's other outward sign of greatness, a permanent seat on the United Nations Security Council. While the Soviet Union was the adversary of the Western powers, it was unlikely that those powers would give up their numerical superiority of vetos amongst the 'Big Five' on the Security Council. France's permanent seat, like Britain's, was therefore guaranteed for the Cold War's duration. Moreover, Germany's divisions, lack of self-confidence and reluctance to play an international role made the European Community a Franco-German club in which France remained the dominant partner, especially on international issues.

Post-cold War transitions

With the end of the Cold War, France lost a mission without finding a role. The transition to the 'New World Order' would go beyond Mitterrand's final presidential mandate. Not surprisingly, in addressing such monumental issues Mitterrand seemed to fumble. Initially opposed to a speedy German reunification, along with British Prime Minister Margaret Thatcher, he was forced to rethink his game plan when it became clear that America, the Soviet Union and German public opinion would push the issue through with or without London and Paris. His reflex was to reach for the alternative solution France had used to neutralize German power: binding her closer with European integration. On 25 October 1989 he stated that European construction was 'the only response to the problem which confronts us'. That was the price of French acquiescence to German reunification. The resulting 1992 Maastricht Treaty committed both states to deeper European integration, notably through monetary union and a common foreign and security policy, both of which were French priorities. These measures not only bound Germany, but also Mitterrand's successor.

In the meantime, that old Gaullist chestnut of France's relation to American power dropped in Mitterrand's lap following Iraq's invasion of Kuwait on 2 August 1990. France was confronted with a dilemma. As a permanent member of the United Nations Security Council she could neither tolerate this blatant international aggression, nor dissent from the UN-mandated United States-led coalition. However, active support could jeopardize France's traditional Arab policy, discontent her 4 million Muslims, make France, as in the 1980s, a target for Islamic terrorism and undermine the Gaullist dogma of maintaining France's independence *vis-à-vis* the US. After much public havering, in which Mitterrand first suggested an embargo and then a Middle Eastern international conference, he finally engaged France in the military coalition to evict Saddam Hussein from Iraq, contributing the third largest contingent of 11,000 military personnel after the US (540,000) and UK (35,000). But France's military engagement in Iraq exposed fundamental flaws in her defence organization, equipment and financing and laid bare the unsuitability of her military capability for the post-Cold War era. Many of the serious lessons France was forced to learn from this experience are, in 2005, still not fully addressed, and will not be so until 2015 according to the 2003–2008 Military Programme Law. But sacred cows in France's defence strategy had to be slaughtered.

First was France's Cold War over-investment in nuclear defence that had dominated her defence policy since 1960, but which was quite unsuited to the post-Cold War era. Grounded in the humiliating French defeat of 1940, the nuclear deterrent was posited on a declaratory strategy warning of immediate escalation from tactical to strategic fire to deter a massive Soviet invasion force and protect the national sanctuary at all costs. For this deterrent policy to be credible France had to refuse to contemplate conventional, still less, tactical nuclear war. Characterized as the policy of *dissuasion du faible au fort* (weak to the strong), its inflexibility was inappropriate for the post-Cold War where small 'rogue' states, or 'non-state actors', were the new threat. The Gulf War demonstrated that nuclear weapons did not deter 'rogue states' and that a more appropriate posture would be deterrence of the *fort au fou* (strong to the mad). Mitterrand was conscious of the need for change, but did not tackle it during his presidency. By February 1996, President Chirac had announced the closure of the Plateau d'Albion nuclear silos and the scrapping of the French *Hades* short-range nuclear missiles by 1998, thereby reducing the triad of nuclear forces on land, sea and air to the latter two. Indeed, the post-Cold War excuse for scrapping France's land-based nuclear strike force came at a most propitious moment. Towards the end of the Cold War, France was confronted by the financial nightmare of needing to modernize and upgrade her nuclear arsenal and her conventional forces. She now had a convenient excuse to 'down-size' her nuclear force without losing face and move to a professional army. As the 1997–2002 military programme law explained, dispensing with the land-based nuclear force would reduce nuclear military expenditure from 31.4 per cent of the defence budget in 1990 to less than 20 per cent in 2002. France could now focus on more flexible air and sea capabilities, notably the four nuclear submarines with a second-strike capability, and by increasing the number of aircraft carriers by bringing into service the *Charles de Gaulle*. Particularly noteworthy, given the nuclear deterrent's traditional justification of protection of the national sanctuary, was France's stated willingness to give a more European dimension to its independent nuclear deterrent through 'concerted deterrence'.

Second, the 1990–91 Gulf War demonstrated that modern war fighting required highly mobile, 'high-tech', professional, rapid reaction forces capable of deployment in distant theatres. France's forces were geared to national defence rather than long-range force projection, despite the creation of a rapid deployment force in 1983. France had great difficulty putting together her contingent for the First Gulf War, because at the time she possessed a conscript army, most unsuited politically and by training and temperament to distant theatres of conflict. Only by stripping out conscripts from army corps – with all the delay and disorganization that ensued – was France able to participate. As a result Chirac officially announced conversion of French defence to a professional army in February 1996 with the phasing out of the sacrosanct Republican principle of military service by 2002. The 1997–2002 military programme law outlined how this would give France greater flexibility and force projection in traditional defence roles against aggression in Europe and the resolution of distant crises with up to 50,000 troops.

Third, when the French force was in theatre, it did not possess the high-tech capability of either the US or UK forces; its *Jaguar* fighters were unequipped for night vision, for example. Furthermore, for a military weaned on the Gaullist dogma of national independence, it was humiliating to rely on American satellite technology for virtually all its battlefield intelligence. As Socialist Defence Minister Pierre Joxe confessed: 'Without Allied intelligence, we were almost blind'. For decades French intelligence had long been held in poor esteem, even suspicion, by the public and political class of all political colours, underfunded and under-utilized. The Gulf War lesson was learned: the 1994 Defence White Paper called for greater resources to be devoted to intelligence, while under Chirac the 1997–2002 *loi de programmation* militaire scheduled an increase in the foreign intelligence agency (DGSE) and military intelligence (DRM) in order to help France catch up with Western agencies, especially in communications, electronic and imaging intelligence. The call was for greater development of the European collaborative military observation satellite programmes *Helios*, first launched in July 1995 and its sister radar system, *Horus*. European defence intelligence was again emphasized in the 2003–8 military programme law stressing the need for greater space observation and space telecommunications, notably through France's leading role in *Helios 2*.

Fourth, France learned that she could no longer continue with the Gaullist dogma of national procurement for military equipment. Given the sophistication of modern weapons systems, she was conscious of possessing neither the technological knowledge, nor the funds to develop and build alone. Here was an opportunity to prise open the French military–industrial complex's grip on equipment procurement, which in 1987 had successfully lobbied for the French-constructed *Rafale* fighter-aircraft in defiance of both military and political recommendations for France to join the *Eurofighter* project. Thinking was in place to reduce the State's role, to restructure and merge the national arms industry's 5,000 firms and 200,000 employees and to allow firms to strike up partnerships with European rivals. In 1996 under Chirac the merging of France's major defence manufacturers Dassault and Aerospatiale was announced for 1998 along with the privatization of Thomson. A European defence procurement system was to be developed to compete with the Americans and to equip more integrated European defence. The 1997–2002 military law predicted international cooperation agreements to rise from 16 per cent to 34 per cent of production. In June 2004, following the signing of an agreement between erstwhile rivals Dassault Aviation and the European aircraft consortium EADS (European Aeronautic Defence and Space) for the construction of unmanned military planes or drones, the French Defence Minister Mme Alliot-Marie stressed that this prefigured a European military aircraft industry.

Finally, the First Gulf War demonstrated the awesome power of the only remaining superpower, or 'hyperpower', as Hubert Védrine named it. Despite rhetoric to the contrary, under Mitterrand and Chirac, France pragmatically recognized the necessity of a closer military relationship with the United States. Having left NATO's integrated military command under de Gaulle in 1966 (though not the Alliance) to demonstrate against the United States' domination of it, Mitterrand signalled a desire to return France to the NATO fold. Gulf War lessons were not the only motive for this; European powerlessness and divisions, notably between Bonn and Paris, over a solution to the conflict in ex-Yugoslavia from 1991 to 1995 also figured. Serious disagreements with a more confident and independent Germany contrasted starkly with a closer relationship with London from the Gulf War to military action in former Yugoslavia. Britain and France, through NATO, provided the bulk of air cover from 1994 to maintain the protective 'security zone' around the Bosnian Muslims against the aggressive Serbs, as well as providing most troops for the UN interposition force on the ground. The Yugoslav episode demonstrated the European Union's inability to conduct a unified, let alone autonomous, defence policy even on its doorstep. This and growing dissatisfaction with European integration after Maastricht (a common occurrence after leaps forward in integration), as testifed by the very marginal victory for French ratification in September 1992, altered France's foreign and defence objectives *vis-à-vis* Europe and NATO.

Ironically, Mitterrand was helped by the Gaullist victory in the March 1993 general elections, which began the second cohabitation. Cohabitation until 1995 was marked by greater consensus on foreign and defence issues than in 1986–88, despite Mitterrand's weakness of illness and expiring two-term presidency. France, the erstwhile proponent of a European defence strategy independent of the United States based on a muscular and militarized version of the largely defunct Western European Union, now moved closer to the concept of a 'European pillar' of the Atlantic Alliance that she had hitherto rejected. Despite refusing officially to relinquish her policy of non-integration of the Atlantic Alliance's military command, France gingerly returned to a number of NATO committees from which she had withdrawn in the late 1960s, even rallying in January 1994 at the Brussels summit to the NATO Combined Joint Task Force. Only six months after Chirac's election to the presidency, his Foreign Minister Hervé de Charette announced in a NATO ministers' meeting in Brussels that France was reintegrating NATO's Military Committee. Only a Gaullist could carry out officially a 'strategic revolution' involving the discarding of much traditional Gaullist policy, albeit under way under the Socialist Mitterrand.

Chirac accelerates the 'strategic revolution'

When elected President in May 1995, Chirac also stressed international policy differences with his predecessor. The clearest example was his decision immediately to restart nuclear testing of France's nuclear weapon in the South Pacific, suspended by Mitterrand since 1992, when France had finally signed up to the 1968 Nuclear Non-Proliferation Treaty. Facing down a wave of international condemnation, Chirac sent out the Gaullist message that France would plough her own furrow, especially when in the 'national interest', the supreme example of which was France's defence. Yet by January 1996 testing had stopped and, by March, France, together with the USA and Britain, had signed a treaty making the South Pacific a denuclearized zone. With all the zeal of the convert, France became a passionate advocate of the Comprehensive Test Ban Treaty, which she and Britain signed in April 1996, the first nuclear states to do so. The break with the Mitterrand years was more style than substance.

Chirac, like Mitterrand, could not ignore the need to reorientate French priorities in the post-Cold War world. The adjustments Mitterrand had started were now pushed forward by the 'bulldozer' with brio, and occasionally, bad timing and blunders. Politicians are more limited in the changes than the mistakes they can make. By temperament Mitterrand and Chirac were poles apart; the former patient and manipulative; the latter brusque and risk-taking. In wishing to shunt through rapid change, Chirac would occasionally hit the buffers with a bang.

When Chirac took over in 1995, international relations appeared to be stabilizing since the turmoil of the ending of the Cold War in 1989–91. The USA, though the only superpower, was still reluctant to intervene abroad, as the Bosnian crisis revealed. Russia was pursuing its transition to a liberal economy, Europe its construction, despite the pessimism of public opinion, abetted by slow economic growth. In Asia there were renewed tensions between Pakistan and India over Kashmir. China was still in the ascendant, bolstered by remarkable economic growth, contrasting strongly with Japan's relative decline, hamstrung by a deflationary economy. South America had returned to economic growth and relative stability, but Africa was still racked by genocidal civil wars, economic meltdown and a seemingly impossible transition to democracy. Slight progress had been made in the Israeli–Palestine conflict, albeit against a backcloth of rising Islamic fundamentalism. Nuclear proliferation seemed contained following agreements with the Soviet successor states and extension of the Nuclear Non-Proliferation Treaty in 1995. Nevertheless, whereas from 1945 to 1990 the world experienced 138 wars causing 23 million deaths, the six years to 1996 saw 40 wars and 7 million dead (Gordon, 1996). In France debates abounded on the threat of globalization and loss of national identity.

One cannot be a French president, especially Gaullist, without having a precise idea of the role and place France ought to have in the world. French foreign policy's dilemma since the Second World War has been the degree of collaboration with her Allies versus national autonomy; to what extent does collaboration reinforce French power in the world and to what extent does it limit it? From 1995 Chirac embraced collaboration with NATO in the belief that this would bolster French power and interests. His stated aims, expressed through his Defence Minister Charles Millon in March 1996, were to radically reform France's armed forces, move towards a European defence and renovate the Atlantic Alliance, leading to a 'European pillar'. On a visit to Washington in February 1996 he carefully warned that the Atlantic partnership had to be more 'equal'.

The Anglo-Saxons, Europe and the world

Chirac had to work against a long-standing backdrop of French ambivalence towards the 'Anglo-Saxons' (broadly understood as the Anglo-Americans), dating back to the beginning of the twentieth century and highlighted under de Gaulle. In the post-Cold War era, despite the changed strategic configuration, France remains extremely ambivalent towards the Anglo-Saxons. Gaullist rhetoric notwithstanding, France had called for an American presence in Europe after the First and Second World Wars to bolster French security; reluctance characterized the American position. During the Cold War, France benefited from the protection of the American nuclear umbrella while professing anti-Americanism and profited from a strong Western Alliance without paying the full costs of Western discipline. Beneath the veneer of scepticism towards Washington's presence on the European continent is an old French fear, shared by other European nations, that the USA will return to isolationism, or that its geopolitical interests will restrain it from intervening on Europe's behalf. Logically then, France and Europe should organize their own security. However, given the unlikely prospect of European defence in the near term, by 1995 France was dangling the carrot of full NATO reintegration to lever reform into its organization and priorities.

From 1995 to 1997 Chirac attempted to reposition NATO's eastward strategic focus southwards to satisfy French anxieties about risks from rogue states across the Mediterranean (the so-called 'Club Mad'). In December 1995 Chirac set as a condition for reintegration that a European (read French) officer should become commander of NATO's southern command forces (AFSOUTH) based in Naples and that a new balance be established over duties and responsibilities between the USA and NATO–Europe. Optimism about a French return was demonstrated on 13 June 1996 after a North Atlantic Council meeting attended by the French Defence Minister. NATO's Secretary-General Javier Solana opened the press conference in French, something unheard of for years. The final communiqué spoke of the rapprochement with France as 'a historic event'. But the Clinton administration was reluctant to put AFSOUTH and the US Sixth Fleet in the Mediterranean under European command. Chirac attempted to bounce the Americans by prematurely declaring in early September 1996 that the USA was ready to concede to French aspirations, only to be contradicted by Clinton on 26 September. Chirac had overplayed his hand. France sank into a sulk. Enthusiasm for NATO evaporated and Paris reverted to customary rhetoric on American hegemony, resurrecting ideas of an integrated European defence. French support for US-led NATO enforcement of the November 1995 Daytona peace agreement on Bosnia weakened. Traditional reluctance to support US policy positions out of the NATO area returned, notably for the 1998 Israel–Palestine Wye Accords and UN enforcement in Iraq. On 2 December 1997 socialist Defence Minister Alain Richard described France as being 'in, but not integrated'. *Le Monde* called France's position 'à la carte cooperation with NATO'. Former Chief of the French Defence Staff General Douin insisted: 'France will not return to NATO like an errant school-boy to class' (quoted in

Keiger, 2001, p. 223). Despite this set-back France's 2003–2008 military programme law stressed that France would take a leading role in European defence, but 'in harmony with Transatlantic solidarity and the Atlantic Alliance, which remains the basis of collective defence in Europe'.

French differences with the United States, or more generally the Anglo-Saxons, are not limited to NATO. For some the USA has become the scapegoat for France's difficulty in coming to terms with globalization at the beginning of the twenty-first century. Consensus reigns over the evils of US-led 'ultra liberalism' and there is widespread support for the stand against the encroachments of Anglo-Saxon cultural norms and the debasement, or 'Coca-Cola-ization', of French, European and world values. Yet in recent years, with remarkable creative flair, France has made a foreign policy virtue out of misfortune. This subtle inflexion in de Gaulle's championing of small states against the Cold War superpowers has growth potential if France's prominent opposition to the 2003 American-led invasion of Iraq pays off. Through *l'exception française* France has become the self-styled champion of the 'cultural particularisms' of nations threatened by American 'cultural imperialism'. The decline of the French language internationally – portrayed as a victim of hegemonic English – is seen as a metaphor for the decline of France in the world. Consequently, much foreign policy effort is devoted to redressing this situation. As early as 1966 the High Committee for the French Language (*Haut Comité de la Langue Française*) was established to find new words to replace invading English terms. In 1984 an international Francophone television station, TV5, was set up and financed by France, Quebec, Wallonia and Switzerland. In February 1986 President Mitterrand created the first Francophone summit in Paris with 42 delegations. In June 1988 the Rocard government established a Minister for Francophonie to organize and promote the French language in the world. Despite there being only 120 million French speakers globally and French being only the eleventh most spoken language in the world, France invests heavily in language promotion. French teaching and cultural exchanges abroad are organized by the Education Ministry and the General Directorate for Cultural Scientific and Technical Affairs in the Foreign Ministry, absorbing about one third of the foreign affairs budget. Numerous organizations promote the French language abroad from the *Alliance Française* to the *Mission Laique Française*, so that overall some 85,000 French *agents culturels* operate abroad, of whom 28,000 are civil servants.

Official defenders of the language believe their mission justified because the French language is the vehicle for universalist principles – liberty, justice, equality and fraternity encapsulated in the Rights of Man. As the self-styled home and guardian of these values French official speeches reiterate the glorious heritage dating from the French Revolution. Given that French foreign policy is presented as the promoter of these values France's world role is legitimized. The English language threat is therefore much more than just a linguistic struggle; it strikes at the heart of France's *raison d'être* in the world. France's Minister of Culture and Francophonie declared pointedly in 1994, when preparing legislation to limit the use of English in France: 'the use of a language is not innocent. It becomes ... an instrument of domination, an agent of uniformity'. He proclaimed that the French must 'remain faithful to our culture and to the universality which is the thousand-year-old mission of France' (quoted in Keiger, 2001, p. 28). Despite struggling against the tide with myriad pieces of legislation in the 1980s and 1990s, the French were still spending nearly $1 billion annually promoting French language and culture in 1997.

France's imperial idea, which once underpinned French claims to grandeur and world status, has been repackaged to emphasize defence of cultural particularisms, not retention of territory. Asserting French cultural specificity in the face of Americanization was one of the roles assigned to the Secretary General of the international organization, *la Francophonie*, the former UN Secretary-General Boutros Boutros-Ghali (whom the Americans had rejected for a second UN mandate), on this post's creation in 1997. In the wake of French opposition to the invasion of Iraq in 2003, French cultural diplomacy may become an even more potent instrument of foreign policy.

Since the ending of the Cold War, French relations with Britain have been more positive. As so often in the two countries' history, French relations improve with Britain when they deteriorate with Germany. With a larger, physically stronger and more self-confident, reunified Germany, Paris has drawn closer to London, notwithstanding disagreements like the late 1990s 'beef crisis'. Policy differences with Germany within the European Union have multiplied over: future expenditure, Common Agricultural Policy reform, the rigours of the European Central Bank, EU enlargement, and at the end of 1999 the size of increase in Germany's MEPs in the European Parliament, to reflect Germany's greater size. France and Germany have long held differing visions of the EU's future: the latter attracted by federalism and the former attached to a strong European identity, but built on weak institutions where intergovernmentalism prevails on important issues. More novel, and perhaps serious, is where France and Germany have clashed on extra-EU issues. This was so during the Bosnian crisis, when at the end of 1991 Germany unilaterally and recklessly recognized Slovenia and Croatia, to Mitterrand's intense public annoyance. Cool relations between Chirac and German Chancellor Gerhard Schröder have not helped, unlike the cordial relations between Mitterrand and Chancellor Kohl who, as the last of the war generation of French and German political leaders, attempted to contain Franco-German differences. Although Franco-British differences over Europe are so well accepted by both parties as to be *acquis*, Europe was never constructed around a Franco-British understanding.

Whatever the rhetoric, London and Paris have a mutual interest in cooperating on foreign and defence matters. Close diplomatic and military cooperation over the Bosnia and Kosovo crises paved the way for further collaboration. In July 1993 the Franco-British Joint Commission on Nuclear Policy and Doctrine was established as a permanent forum to harmonize nuclear doctrine. In summer 1994 discussions focused on sharing the burden of nuclear deterrence through joint ballistic missile submarine patrols. In October a joint military air command was planned to support international peacekeeping and humanitarian operations. Though Franco-British differences remain over European integration, Paris and London agree on the need for closer cooperation on European defence, even if the latter believes that this should be through the medium of NATO. On nuclear defence the two states are drawing ever closer. At the annual Franco-British summit in October 1995, Chirac and Britain's Prime Minister John Major declared that they could see no situation in which the vital interests of one state could be threatened without threatening those of the other. They confirmed their aim to reinforce joint nuclear deterrence. Since 1997, under Prime Minister Tony Blair, defence relations have continued to tighten with the 1997–2002 military programme law speaking of a 'privileged partnership' with Britain. That document planned for Franco-British cooperation on armaments projects to rise between 1996 and 2002 from 2.5 to 13.9 per cent of total arms programmes. In December 1998 the Franco-British summit at St-Malo proposed a European Security and Defence Policy to coordinate effective crisis management, while its February 2004 Le Touquet successor committed the two powers to a wide range of joint actions, from defence procurement to the inter-operability of their aircraft-carrier groups. Symbolically, the 2004 annual 14 July Bastille Day celebrations saw British troops lead the military parade down the Champs Elysées to take the salute from the French president.

Where France's relations with the Anglo-Saxons have seriously clashed is over the March 2003 American-led invasion of Iraq. Following the devastating terrorist attack on the United States on 11 September 2001, with the loss of 2,800 lives, the French bound themselves morally to America's predicament, encapsulated in *Le Monde* newspaper's memorable headline the following day: 'We are all Americans.' Chirac was one of the first world leaders to tour the rubble of the Twin Towers in New York and pledge French support for America. Paris militarily supported the UN-sanctioned, American-led coalition's attack on Afghanistan to evict the fundamentalist Taleban regime, which had given succour to the organizer of the '9/11' attack, Osama bin Laden. After the Taleban's fall, American President George W. Bush, supported by British Prime Minister Tony Blair, targeted Iraqi leader Saddam Hussein's likely possession of weapons of mass destruction (WMD). France, and other states, insisted this was for United Nations weapons inspectors to determine. Frustrated at the length of time the inspectors were taking to find evidence of WMD, Britain and America pressed the UN Security Council in spring 2003 to sanction an attack on Iraq. As a permanent member of the Council with a veto, France stridently opposed such action, enlisting the support of veto-wielding Russia and Security Council member Germany to block the Anglo-American-led move. London and Washington abandoned the UN route and moved to military action.

France championed a multilateralist approach to international relations in opposition to 'Anglo-Saxon' unilateralism. Paris luxuriated in the splendour of the moral high ground, condemning the notion of pre-emptive strikes, stressing the French way of respect for international law and the will of the United Nations. Cynics suggested that Chirac seized this glorious opportunity to wipe clean some of the embarrassment of his re-election by cloaking himself in the Gaullist mantle of national independence and moral opponent of the 'Anglo-Saxons'. Whereas the American-led coalition was unpopular with world opinion, France, Russia and Germany were not. Chirac, and his flamboyant Foreign Minister Dominique de Villepin played to the gallery of world opinion, and counter-manoeuvred against a furious George Bush. But the American-dominated coalition ignored criticism, moved to spectacular military action in March 2003 and within three weeks had toppled the Iraqi president and begun an inglorious occupation of the county.

What is significant about the whole episode is that the gambler Chirac was playing a game of high stakes. First, he was taking on the United States at a moment of its considerable power. Until the occupation slid into violent attacks against the American administration in May 2003, Paris's position was distinctly unpopular with American opinion, the French being caricatured widely as 'cheese-eating surrender monkeys' and their imports boycotted. Chirac was seeking to forge an alternative position in international relations, as well as culturally, outside the American *imperium*. Had he not declared in early 1997, after his rebuff from Clinton over NATO: 'The United States has the pretension to direct everything, it wants to rule the whole world' (Keiger, 2001, p. 222)? In the short term, he again appeared to have overplayed his hand and there was some rowing back on the French position after Saddam was toppled. Second, the issue divided Europe, with Britain, Spain, Italy, Portugal, Denmark and the new accession countries of Central and Eastern Europe pitted against France, Germany and Belgium. In February 2003, at the end of a European summit, Chirac publicly criticised the accession countries for their support for the Coalition, tetchily declaring that 'they had missed an opportunity to keep quiet!' and threatening them with reaping the whirlwind when it came to ratifying their accession. Chirac was clearly, but riskily, making a play for re-establishing France, and 'the French way', as the dominant force within the European Union. Whether Chirac wins in this high-stakes game will be largely decided by the success or failure of the new 'Anglo-Saxon'-supported Iraqi regime in place since the end of June 2004.

That outcome is likely to affect France's long-standing attempts to develop a European Defence and Security Identity (EDSI). Chirac, like

Mitterrand before him, supported EDSI, though more on French terms than Europe's, with Paris defining defence and security policy for Europe rather than with Europe. The notion of 'what is good for French defence is good for European defence' was clear when Chirac down-sized French nuclear forces in 1996 and then presented them as a contribution to European security. Given France's long-standing nuclear, military and diplomatic dominance on the continent, such 'arrogance' is not surprising. However, the end of the Cold War's ramifications for everything from nuclear policy to defence industrial policy has forced France to forsake some of its independent stance for a more genuine and inclusive approach to a Common Foreign and Security Policy (CFSP), precisely because the new risks and threats cannot be dealt with by France alone. It was at France's insistence that a clause was inserted into the Maastricht Treaty establishing a CFSP with the explicit objective of framing a common defence policy. For a country once opposed in principle to the idea of integrated command structures, France is, since the mid-1990s, part of a number of European integrated force structures for air, land and sea, such as EUROFOR and EUROMARFOR, to act as Mediterranean rapid reaction forces, or the Franco-British Euro Air Group. But, as has been shown above, this does not imply the rejection of NATO as an essential element of European defence. What is significant is the approach France has adopted for Europeanizing its defence: intergovernmentalism rather than a pan-European approach. Thus a French European defence commitment has been assembled through a series of bilateral agreements with Britain (examples above) and Germany (Franco-German Defence Commission 1982, then Council 1988, Franco-German brigade 1989, Eurocorps), or multilateral accords such as with Italy, Spain and Portugal for EUROFOR and EUROMARFOR. She feels more comfortable with this intergovernmental and incremental approach to Europeanizing her defence rather than dissolving her sovereignty in a giant European defence melting pot. France's awareness of its declining influence in the EU provoked outgoing French EU trade commissioner Pascal Lamy to declare in September 2004: 'The French have to realise that Europe will be something different from a big France' (*Financial Times*, 22 September 2004).

Much of France's customary overseas intervention will, in the wake of the reorganization of French armed forces, now be carried out in cooperation with European, Allied and UN partners. French military agreements with a dozen or so African nations have all but evaporated. Her capacity to intervene alone has dwindled. Whereas in the 1980s she was able to intervene in Chad, Zaire and the Lebanon, often to shore up regimes with deplorable human rights standards, in the post-Cold War era she no longer has the appropriate military materiel, manpower or structures to do so effectively on any scale. Under the guise of UN peacekeeping or 'humanitarian interventions', France managed a few last interventions in Zaire in 1991 and Rwanda in 1994: the latter a tardy move to counter her previous support for the Francophone Hutu majority which committed the genocide of some 800,000 Anglophone Tutsis. In the early 1990s France still staked her claim to Francophone Africa by maintaining there some 8,000 troops and 1,200 military advisers, but the advent of a smaller professional army forced her in 1997 to announce a 40 per cent reduction in troop levels in Africa. Foreign Minister Hubert Védrine tetchily denied that this was a 'retreat', merely a switch to a 'smaller, more flexible and more effective force'. The Franco-British St-Malo and Le Touquet (2004) summits committed France to work with Britain on future African diplomatic and military action. Nevertheless, France remains the largest contributor to UN missions across the world. Shared action is the shape of French interventionism for the future.

Conclusion

Jacques Chirac's foreign and defence policy is essentially the continuation of his predecessor's by other means. Mitterrand initiated the thinking and changes that needed to be made to French foreign and defence policy at the end of the Cold War; Chirac accelerated their implementation.

There is a continuity in French foreign and defence policy over the last half-century that neither domestic politics nor personalities have altered in any fundamental way. Ambivalence towards the United States, aspiration to a world role and a Gaullist philosophy of national independence, albeit reduced, still characterize that continuity. There is a sense in which de Gaulle's dictum that France should continue to behave as a great power precisely because it no longer is one, lives on. In that half-century, France defined its great-power status less by physical attributes than by what it believed itself to be, and then acted out the role. The international community came to accept the personality and performance France ascribed to itself on the world stage. Centred squarely on the nation-state, France cultivated a French model based partly on what it believed it stood for, the Rights of Man, French language and culture, and partly on what it was not, the American model. With the ending of the Cold War, the spread of globalization, the growth of European integration, the decline of the nation-state, the growth of multiculturalism and the rise of American power, France is no longer clear what its role is and how it should perform it. It has begun to define itself most by what it is not, rejecting American political and cultural 'hegemony' and championing 'cultural particularisms' (albeit not to be tried at home ...). Conscious of being first and foremost a European nation, it is still wary about blending its identity into an extended European structure over which it has less and less control. How it accommodates restrictions on its sovereignty as a nation-state will condition its foreign and defence policies and, by extension, whether it can remain a world power.

Chapter 10

Immigration Politics and Policies

VIRGINIE GUIRAUDON

On 21 April 2002, with almost 17 per cent of the vote, Jean-Marie Le Pen, the leader of the Extreme-Right National Front (FN), came in second after Jacques Chirac in the first round of the French presidential election. Politicians spoke of an 'earthquake' whose aftershocks led to a massive mobilization of the Left, and in particular young people, in the streets. Demonstrators often chanted the slogan 'first, second, third generation, we are all the children of immigrants', a sentence heard for the past twenty years in mobilizations against the anti-immigrant extreme-Right and in marches led by youths of migrant origin in the mid-1980s. This moment of high salience of the immigration issue on the political agenda reminds us that immigration remains a 'public problem' in France. Exit polls revealed that concern among all voters about immigration was 18 per cent and 60 per cent among Le Pen's supporters (IPSOS, 2002). The anti-Le Pen protests also reveal that there remains a section of the electorate that can be mobilized in social movements in favour of the rights of migrants. In brief, debate on migration continues to be polarized in France as it has been since the 1980s.

France is one of the oldest lands of immigrants in Europe. It started recruiting foreign workers in the nineteenth century to remedy an early drop in fertility rates and provide a flexible labour force during the industrial revolution, and Belgians, Poles and Italians came to work in French factories. Since then, France has known two periods characterized by high levels of migration: the 1930s and the 1960s. After the war, France recruited foreign workers from Southern Europe and later saw the arrival of migrants from its former colonies in North and sub-Saharan Africa and South-East Asia. In 1973, France stopped soliciting foreign labour except for seasonal workers and high-skilled workers. Notwithstanding, new flows have since settled in France legally: the family members of foreign residents and nationals and people fleeing conflict and persecution. To this day, each year, most of the newcomers are welcomed as part of family reunification and asylum.

As Table 10.1 shows, the foreign-born population has been remarkably stable since 1980 (7.4 per cent of the total population). The last census also showed a decline in the number of foreigners residing in France

Table 10.1   *Foreigners and immigrants in France since 1975: census data*

	Foreigners (thousands)	Foreigners as part of total population (%)	Foreign-born (thousands)	Foreign-born as part of total population (%)
1975	3,442	6.5	3,887	7.4
1982	3,714	6.8	4,037	7.4
1990	3,597	6.3	4,166	7.4
1999	3,259	5.6	4,306	7.4

Source: Boëldieu and Borrel (2000) based on census data from the national statistics institute INSEE.

Table 10.2   *Stocks and flows: top sending countries*

Rank	Top countries of origin for inflows of foreigners in 2001	Top countries of origin of asylum-seekers in 2002	Top countries of origin for stocks of foreigners (1999)
1	Morocco	Turkey	Portugal
2	Algeria	Congo	Morocco
3	Turkey	Mauritania	Algeria
4	USA	Algeria	Turkey
5	China/Haiti/Sri Lanka (tied)	China	Italy

Source: OECD (2004).

since 1990: a quarter of a million left the country, the rest either died or became naturalized.

France is a multi-ethnic society in large part because of the presence of immigrants and their descendants. Less than half of the foreign-born are from Europe and the number of immigrants from North Africa has risen. Among the people who acquire French nationality each year, about 60 per cent come from Africa, 20 per cent from Asia (including Turkey) and 16 per cent from Europe.

Policies towards immigrants are often reactive and *ad hoc*, leaving it up to associations, churches and kin to help new migrants adapt to the host society and intervening only after focus events such as riots or racist arson attacks. In France, in the postwar period, the official rhetoric was that migrants would individually be turned into Frenchmen just like nineteenth-century peasants through their participation in social institutions such as schools, the army or the workplace. Access to citizenship was relatively open, especially for the second generation that automatically acquired French nationality at 18. France had specific challenges with respect to postcolonial migrants since these migrants became foreign after their countries' independence. Moreover, they were not as welcome as South Europeans.

Debates on integration started in the 1980s, when it was acknowledged that migrants had durably settled in France and were raising children. There were divisions within the Left. Some within the Socialist party questioned the assimilationist paradigm and called for a 'right to be different', echoing multicultural policies in other countries. Moreover, the 'second generation' mobilized to call for equal rights and opportunities. Meanwhile the Communist party local leaders spoke against immigration. The mainstream Right, eager to accuse the new government of being lax towards immigration, was soon overrun to its right by the National Front with its first electoral successes in 1983 and 1984. Given this crowded political space, which increased the salience of immigrant policy in the media and public opinion, there was a polarization of the debate around immigrants. By 1987, when a commission was set up to try to take the issue out of partisan politics, the mainstream Left and Right decided to reach a compromise. The Left rejected multiculturalism as too costly with respect to its Centre-Left electorate while the Right sought to temper its nationalistic positions to distinguish itself from the extreme Right. The solution was the reinvention of the French model of integration.

Official policy goals have barely changed since 1973 when France stopped recruiting foreign workers: (1) strict immigration controls; and (2) the integration of legal migrants. The number of immigrants arriving legally each year has not drastically changed since the early 1990s, with around a hundred thousand new entries. Yet, beyond this relative stability in policy goals and outcomes, there have been numerous public controversies focused on the place of immigrants in French society. Moreover, official policy goals have yet to be met: there are a number of illegal migrants known as 'sans papiers' (those without identity papers) living in precarious conditions, which shows that migration control policies have perverse effects. As to the integration of migrants and their descendants in the French melting pot, certain groups face socio-economic difficulties including high unemployment. There are also signs of increasing segregation in housing and education.

Given this context, one can construe policy developments in recent years as attempts to devise new initiatives in a polarized environment. In a nutshell, the challenge for policy-makers consists in finding solutions for populations that are socio-economically deprived and politically disenfranchised without any direct electoral benefit that could reward improving their situation. Moreover, policy instruments must be compatible with an overarching conception of the nation that does not allow for the differential treatment of ethnic groups. Given the strength of the extreme Right and the ethnocentrism of a large section of the French electorate, governments do not feel that they can claim credit for measures that improve the situation of migrants and thus must frame them as part of a more general concern for equality. Conversely, governments have sought to continue stemming new migrant flows and ignored arguments about the need for migrants in the labour market that could also remedy the French demographic decline.

In this chapter, we analyse recent developments in immigration policy and politics, focusing first on migration control and asylum, and then on integration policy. We conclude by highlighting some of the outstanding challenges that France has to resolve with respect to immigrants.

Immigration and asylum policy: a law and order approach

When a new Right-wing government came to power in 2002, it announced that it would reform the French law on the entry and stay of foreigners. This 1945 Ordinance has systematically been tampered with by every new government since 1977, a sign of the apparent partisan polarization over immigration. In fact, since the mid-1980s, both Left and Right have a tacit agreement that consists in denying entry to non-EU migrants and to make it more difficult for unwanted humanitarian migrants (family members and asylum-seekers) to come and stay. Policy is framed in security terms, with migrants designated as 'illegal', asylum-seekers as bogus and both manipulated by transnational criminal networks that orchestrate smuggling. In the absence of an organized coalition between very discreet business leaders and existing migrant communities that seem to close the door behind them, it is unclear that policy goals will change. Human rights associations and legal aid groups on their own cannot reframe a policy guided by electoral motives.

The electoral presence of the National Front since 1983 has durably influenced the attitude of mainstream parties and governmental agendas towards immigration. The Right seeks to assert its commitment to a firm 'law-and-order' stance and emphasize its capacity to control French borders to avoid being outflanked on its Right. The Left is afraid of seeming lax on migration control since it has lost part of its working-class vote, in particular young males and the unemployed, to the National Front. Moreover, over time, voter attitudes for the mainstream parties have tended to view immigration as a concern, albeit to a lesser extent than the National Front's loyal voters. Finally, it should be pointed out that local politicians and local party members from the mainstream parties have put pressure on party leaders on the immigration issue since it is at the local level, in municipal councils and regional assemblies, that the National Front has had the most influence. In sum, the National Front has directly and indirectly led successive governments to call for strict migration control policies. The reality is more complex and the goal of 'zero immigration' is a chimera:

migrants continue to arrive through legal and illegal channels and, given French constitutional guarantees, not all can be sent back.

Especially since the 1993 reform, restrictive policies have created an important number of '*sans papiers*', people who have no permits of residence and work, yet often cannot be expelled back to their home country for legal and practical reasons. Some, such as Chinese migrants working in sweat-shops, live hidden in conditions of forced labour. Foreigners who have committed criminal offences can be deported, even if they have lived in France for decades and have no family ties in their country of origin. They are referred to as '*double peine*' (double sanctions): prison and expulsion. In recent years, both the '*sans papiers*' and the '*double peine*' have mobilized through occupations and hunger strikes to draw attention to their conditions.

They have received the support of human rights organizations, extreme-Left activists but also famous movie directors and actresses and respected personalities. These movements have been partly successful. The Socialist government in power between 1997 and 2002 regularized about 75,000 of the '*sans papiers*'. The Right refused to engage in mass regularizations. Yet, the Minister of Interior agreed to tackle the '*double peine*' problem, conceding that one could not expel back to a country someone who had never lived in it since childhood because that person had sold marijuana. These examples of mobilizations underline the limits of a strict immigration policy.

Notwithstanding, there has been no effort spared to make it more difficult for undesirable foreigners to migrate to France. The main focus of the Raffarin government since 2002 has been on the restriction of asylum. In this respect, they were helped by the Schengen and European Union legal framework that called for many of the measures adopted in France in 2003. Similarly, when the government decided to organize charters to expel illegal migrants, they soon organized flights with other EU member-states in conformity with EU-level guidelines.

The insistence of French governments of the Left and Right in deterring migration is not warranted by any sudden increase in migration pressure. In fact, recent events have shown that France is a transit country on the way to other destinations. From 1999 to 2003, the makeshift Red Cross camp in the small town of Sangatte housed thousands of migrants who wanted to cross the Channel and settle in the UK or beyond in the US and Canada. Sangatte was a reminder that today's migrants are ready to take risks to escape countries that give them no perspective. For the French government, it was only a diplomatic conundrum as the Blair government in the United Kingdom, encouraged by the tabloid and local press, accused the French of not guarding their borders to prevent people from leaving.

French migration policy remains restrictive and official discourse repeatedly calls for the fight against illegal migration. In this context, public opinion often believe that *immigrés* are not welcome. This makes the integration of immigrants more difficult.

Integration policy and the fight against racial and ethnic discrimination

In 1991, the High Council for Integration (HCI), a consultative body in charge of making recommendations to the government regarding migrants, was born and gave an official definition of the goals of integration:

> Integration consists in encouraging the active participation in all spheres of society of all the men and women that are destined to live durably on our soil by accepting truthfully that cultural specificities may endure yet by stressing resemblance and convergence towards equal rights and duties, so as to insure social cohesion.

The definition tries to strike a precarious balance between the tolerance of difference and the need for cohesion. In practice, it legitimizes assimilationism in a new guise, rather than multiculturalism. As outlined in HCI reports and official government statements, the basic tenets of the French model of integration are the following:

- *It is up to individuals to 'integrate'*
  Group rights and the public recognition of difference is therefore not on the agenda. In fact, the target of integration policy is vague: no groups are identified except the periphrastic 'men and women destined to live durably on our land'. 'Cultural specificities' are best expressed in the private realm.
- *The apex of the integration process is the acquisition of French nationality.*
  Access to citizenship should be relatively open through a variety of procedures and constitutes a right for the 'second generation'. Conversely, reforms that de-link nationality and citizenship, such as the extension of local voting and eligibility rights for (non-EU) foreigners, are not recommended.
- *Integration is inextricably linked to the notion of equality.*
  Active policies should aim at ensuring equal chances and conditions for all members of society.

In practice, it is difficult to reconcile these principles. For instance, to be coherent with the principle that one only recognizes individuals rather than groups, equalizing conditions between migrant populations and the rest of the population precludes ethnic monitoring and makes 'positive discrimination' difficult to justify, since both instruments require the identification and targeting of groups. As we discuss below, policies have sought to circumvent this dilemma.

There is also an inherent political problem in the model of integration: the political enfranchisement of migrants comes last in the process. There is reason to believe that this greatly diminishes the influence of migrant groups on the political parties and, more generally, on policies that could help ensure their socio-economic emancipation. Furthermore, the fact that many migrants are politically excluded cannot be disconnected from their feeling of social exclusion and being 'second-class'. A greater *political* integration of ethnic minorities would create a new balance of power in policy-making. As it stands, political parties are more concerned with the anti-immigrant vote. Furthermore, in this context, governmental actions towards immigrants resemble a politics of stealth in which one seeks to make it difficult to trace the actual beneficiaries of public policies.

Studies on migrants and their children, especially the first and only large-scale 1995 survey that interviewed almost 8,900 immigrants and 2,500 young adults with one parent born abroad (Tribalat, 1995), underline that many indicators suggest migrant-origin populations are adopting the way of life of French natives, from eating habits to fertility rates. This copycat behaviour implies that migrants are 'assimilated' into French society. Still, a significant proportion of the migrant populations that belong to specific ethnic groups suffer from socio-economic disadvantage, live in unsafe derelict areas and have few job prospects.

Migrant communities are not spread out throughout the French territory and economy. In fact, over a third of the immigrant population lives in Paris and its surrounding suburbs. Two-thirds live in large cities, especially in former industrial bastions in the north, the Alps, eastern and southeastern France, and only 3 per cent live in rural municipalities (Boëldieu and Borrel, 2000). Within cities and regions, migrants are highly concentrated in certain neighbourhoods and high-rise housing developments. Postwar migrants settled in industrial cities to work in factories. By 2000, two-thirds of the foreign workers worked in services that are also situated in urban centres. Since migrants and their children tend to be overrepresented in socio-professional categories with modest incomes and among the unemployed, it is not surprising that they live in neighbourhoods that provide low rents either in subsidized public housing or in the private market. Yet, there are perverse effects to the fact that certain migrant communities are concentrated in city districts that have accumulated social problems such as urban decay and crime since the 1970s with industrial restructuring and the advent of permanent high unemployment. The more affluent move out or take their children out of the local public schools, employers avoid hiring residents from certain known housing projects: this in the end reinforces phenomena of segregation and discrimination.

If one looks at the situation of the foreign-born and their descendants with regard to employment, according to the 1999 census 24.1 per cent of the foreign active population was unemployed and 22 per cent of foreign-born workers were also unemployed, well above the national average of 13 per cent, which stems from the level of qualification of foreign workers and their overrepresentation in industrial sectors exposed to unfavourable global competition (Glaude and Borrel, 2002). Yet, beyond these aggregate numbers, the situation needs to be nuanced. There are significant differences among migrant groups. The percentage of men of Maghreb origin in the 16–29-year-old age group who were not employed was between 34 per cent and 45 per cent in 1990 (20 per cent–25 per cent for women) above the national average but also well above the percentage of unemployed youths of South European origin. In other words, although, as a whole, children of immigrants have better career prospects than their parents due to their access to education and training, differences on the basis of the origin of their parents persist, which suggests different resources (such as interpersonal relations, social codes or cultural capital) that are useful in getting a job and employers' attitudes towards the hiring of migrant-origin workers. Youths of Algerian origin are more likely to be unemployed and less likely to find a job again than others with the same qualifications and social background and they are also much more dissatisfied with their situation (Silberman, 2002).

The migrant groups that face difficulties and experience discrimination are the same ones that French respondents to attitudinal surveys identify as most likely to experience racism and that they most dislike. Since 1989, the National Consultative Commission on Human Rights has commissioned an opinion poll to measure racism, xenophobia and anti-Semitism. Its annual reports make clear that the French public dislikes North Africans most and is aware that these populations are the most stigmatized. This is a constant, whereas the polls show important fluctuations in the number of persons polled who think that there are too many foreigners in France: 51 per cent in 2002, an electoral year that saw the National Front do well, 41 per cent the following year (CNCDH, 2004). In 2002, racist violence primarily concerned Arabs: 81 per cent of all violent racist acts recorded by the police (CNCDH, 2004).

The political challenge is thus to improve the situation of ethnic minorities while not drawing attention to it since there is little voter support for these groups.

Affirmative action à la française: giving more to those who have less

Given the French model of integration, key policies since 1990 have focused on improving the situation of migrant communities without targeting them as such. Instead, migrants and their descendants benefit from public programmes because of their socio-economic characteristics rather than their belonging to a particular ethnic group.

This is the case of *politique de la ville* (urban renewal policy) launched in 1990 to fight social exclusion and 'give more to those who have less'. Certain neighbourhoods (*quartiers* or *cités*) in city centres and suburbs (*banlieues*) that confront socio-economic problems tend to be immigrant neighbourhoods. It is reflected in public and popular discourse: migrant-origin youths are referred to as 'youths from the projects' or 'suburban youths' and vice versa. This has had political consequences with respect to the construction of the migration issue. Policies towards migrant populations in the 1990s have essentially been targeted at urban renewal with policies targeted at certain areas. Yet, these policies have been enacted in a difficult electoral context with little clout for migrant populations that can only vote if they are naturalized and local politicians who are more interested in catering to the remaining voting middle class in their district.

A territorial approach to redistribution was adopted, exempting ever-smaller urban 'zones' from taxes or using other incentives to create jobs for the young people residing there. On paper, migrants and their descendants were not targeted but because many lived in the neighbourhoods that were, they did benefit in disproportionate numbers from these spatially defined policies. The state also financed local initiatives whose objectives included social inclusion through 'contracts' with municipalities. For instance, between 1994 and 2000 over a hundred contracts were signed between central state agencies and local authorities (Espinasse and Laporte, 1999). The type of actions undertaken with the financial backing of the central state included after-school aid for pupils, female migrant empowerment and the prevention of juvenile delinquency. This decentralized territorial approach meant that street-level bureaucrats could locally gear policy instruments to improve the situation of certain groups, without the central government's direct involvement.

In education policy, for a high school to qualify as a 'priority education zone' (ZEPs) and thus obtain a better budget and smaller classes, the high number of foreigners living in the area is an argument along with others such as unemployment rates. Another example is the sponsorship programme set up in 1993 as part of employment policy. At first, the policy had no well-defined public. The children of migrants did benefit from the measure in large numbers. In 1997, out of the 13,500 youths who participated in the programme, 35 per cent were 'youths of migrant-origin' (Aubert, 1999). The measures to diminish youth unemployment under the Jospin government after 1997 applied the same logic (programme TRACE, 'emplois-jeunes').

Yet, the Jospin government also acknowledged that this was not enough and tried to tackle an issue that had been long overlooked: discrimination in employment and in the provision of goods and services.

Reframing integration as the fight against discrimination: 1997–2002

The change of government in 1997 with the victory of the Left in the legislative elections offered policy actors inside and outside the government an opportunity to present policy initiatives in a domain that seemed to have run out of steam.

The government decided to make 'the fight against discrimination' a priority and claimed it was the only way to ensure equal opportunities for all. In fact, this focus on discrimination could generate bipartisan support since the first leader to draw attention to the issue was Right-wing Alain Juppé. One of his close advisers had been the *rapporteur* of a High Council of Integration report, headed by Centre-Right wise woman Simone Weil, that had called for the creation of an agency in charge of fighting discrimination on the model of the British Commission for Racial Equality (HCI, 1998). The Right had perhaps realized then that it was in their interest to woo migrant-origin voters who had been disappointed with the Left.

While compatible with the French attachment to equality, the shift in focus from 'integration' to 'anti-discrimination' resulted in a very different conception of the 'problem'. As Didier Fassin has argued, the source of the problem shifts responsibility from the migrant to the host society (Fassin, 2002). The integration model implies that it is up to immigrants to integrate and their failure to do so displays some social defect. Yet, with anti-discrimination policies, French institutions and individuals are responsible for the migrants' situation. French societal institutions have to change so as to get rid of French society's attitude towards people with different 'origins', who suffer independently of citizenship status and regardless of their social class. No longer acting *in favour of* integration but fighting *against* discrimination, public authorities needed to develop a new policy toolbox.

The Left government turned out to be quite prudent. The Ministry of Social Affairs created a Group of Experts (*Groupe d'Etudes et de Lutte Contre les Discriminations*) and consulted the social partners. It also set up a hotline (dial 114) to receive complaints. The Minister of Interior set up regional bureau where people who felt they had been discriminated against could come to seek advice.

EU developments turned out to speed up change. In the 1997 Amsterdam Treaty, Article 13 called for measures to combat discrimination on a number of grounds, including race and ethnicity. During the first months of 2000, there was an acceleration of negotiations at EU-level based on Article 13. On 3 February, a coalition government was formed in Austria with the extreme-Right party of Jorg Haïder receiving six of ten full ministerial posts. At an informal meeting of the Ministers for Employment and Social Affairs in Lisbon the following week, the French minister Martine Aubry was the most vocal in calling for quarantining the new Austrian government. To match word with deed, she issued a joint position paper calling for the swift adoption of the Commission's anti-discrimination proposals. One of the directives was aimed at combating racial and ethnic discrimination in a wide range of areas (employment, training and education, the provision of services including housing) and was swiftly adopted in June 2000. The French initial position made sense given the need for the Left government clearly to state its condemnation of an extreme Right that was also very strong in France. Yet, the end product (Council Directive 2000/43/CE of 29 June 2000) was an EU legally binding law that required substantive change in the French case (Geddes and Guiraudon, 2004).

Ultimately, the European Union justified reforms for the cautious domestic Socialist government: they could invoke 'Brussels' in the face of opposition. In November 2001, parliament examined the transposition of the directive on race discrimination. On the one hand, parliamentarians added grounds for discrimination not mentioned in the directive including the person's name and residential address, thereby displaying a will to appropriate EU legislation in a way relevant to the French situation on the ground. On the other, they refused to fully implement the provisions on indirect discrimination, i.e. the fact that apparently neutral laws and practices disadvantage specific ethnic and racial groups. They introduced the concept in French labour law, yet without authorizing the collection of statistics on the socio-economic characteristics of the ethnic and racial groups that could help prove in court that they were victims of indirect discrimination (Calvès, 2002).

In spite of a precautious government, by 2002, part of the edifice necessary for fighting the discrimination for ethnic and racial minorities when they looked for a job, an apartment or simply wanted to enter a night-club was in place. Next, we examine developments since a new government of the Right came to power in 2002 to identify continuity and change in policy goals and instruments.

Return of the old model? 2002–2005

As stated in the introduction, the 2002 presidential elections shook political life in France. President Chirac was re-elected on 2 May, with over 80 per cent of the voters thanks to the mobilization of the Left at the polls. The President swore that he felt responsible for fighting the intolerant ideas of Le Pen and the National Front and his government spoke of 'the spirit of May' as a commitment to guaranteeing the nation against xeno-phobic tendencies. The government included a young woman with North African roots as Secretary of State of Sustainable Development as a token of its good faith and as a means of appealing to the '*beur* vote' (second-generation voters of Arab origin).

In fact, there was both change and continuity in governmental action. Discrimination is still on the agenda yet a return to the assimilationist model that suspects migrants are responsible for integration is also quite clear. Regarding discrimination, the government confirmed in 2004 that 'an independent administrative authority for equality and the fight against all forms of discrimination' will be set up. This is the crucial element of the

2000 EU race directive that the French had not complied with thus far. Yet, while the Prime Minister acknowledges that immigrants' children 'feel they are second-class citizens because their name is an obstacle on the job market, because their address is a turn-off for employers', the problem with focusing on discrimination is that it gives 'the French a bad conscience and penalizes them' (Raffarin, 2003). He has suggested that the Commission focus on 'best practices' – a common word in eurospeak – and give out labels and prizes to firms and social actors that do not discriminate. This declaration is in line with the High Council of Integration nominated in 2002 and headed by Chirac's loyal supporter Blandine Kriegel. In her first report, she called for a break with 'the logic of guilt and discrimination', preferring the logic of 'positive mobilization' in favour of integration (HCI, 2004).

Still, since 2002, there have been debates on 'positive discrimination', i.e. measures that give extra help to minorities. One stems from an initiative by the Paris Institute of Political Studies that welcomed a very small quota of students from ZEPs (Education Priority Zones) alongside its competitive entrance exam that recruits 'white' and bourgeois youths. The other controversy arose when Interior Minister Sarkozy declared that there needed to be more visible members of 'deserving immigrants' among top civil servants and that he wanted to nominate a 'préfet musulman' (a Muslim head of the *départements* administration). In his words, 'there are, among immigrants, those who are meant to integrate and those that will not be accepted' (Zappi, 2003). After having passed a tough law on immigration and asylum, he was showing a softer side when he nominated Algerian-born Aïssa Dermouche prefect in 2004.

The Minister of Social Affairs presented in 2002 an initiative called 'the integration contract' for newcomers, a formula that the Dutch had put into place in 1994 inspired by the French model of integration. The contract highlights the rights and duties of incoming migrants during a half-day workshop where they are presented with a film on French society and briefed with respect to Republican principles. The idea is that they should learn the French language and embrace French values to allow them to work and not be dependent on the French welfare state.

The future of immigrant policy seems to echo the past. Immigrants are again suspected of not wanting to assimilate and only a handful are celebrated as 'deserving'.

The integration of cultural minorities: the risks of political procrastination

With immigration from Africa and Asia, new faiths have become part of the French religious landscape. With ethnic diversity came religious diversity.

Although figures available are only rough estimates based on the main religion in the migrants' country of origin, Islam, for instance, is considered to be the second religion in France in terms of potential affiliates (3.7 million according to demographer Michèle Tribalat in *L'Express*, 4 December 2003). Although the French Constitution protects the right to religious practice, the accommodation of religious expression in the public sphere has been at the centre of repeated political controversies for at least since 1990. In the fall of 1989 and again in the fall of 2003, media headlines, intellectual energies, dinner conversations and politicians' speeches narrowed in on the fact that some schoolgirls wore a veil in a public high school. Perhaps more than any other issue, the public display of the Islamic faith has exemplified the reluctance and/or inability of the French state and society to manage the cultural difference that comes with immigration.

Although the religion of migrants has been given considerable public attention, there is little evidence that the behavior of migrant-origin communities conflicts with that of the French. Given that French law prohibits questions on religious affiliation being asked in the census, one must rely on the few surveys and qualitative studies that have focused on the religious practices of migrant-origin populations. The conclusions of existing research can be summed up in three points: (1) a large-scale survey of the National Demographic Studies Institute (Tribalat, 1995) suggests that immigrants' children tend to adopt the ways of French natives after having been socialized in France and become 'securalized': attendance of religious services is low and religion is often limited to the private sphere (e.g. the family celebration of religious feasts); (2) the aforementioned survey and other studies reveal that, nevertheless, religion is part and parcel of the migrants' culture of origin and their attachment to certain traditions linked to religious practices (e.g. for Muslims, not eating pork or drinking alcohol, or fasting during Ramadan) is still strong, reflecting their dual cultural identity; and (3) for some youths of migrant-origin religion can be a refuge and they 're-discover' their religious heritage. Thus, although the overwhelming majority of migrant-origin people in France has assimilated the French secular approach to religion as a cultural and private practice, political debate has focused on the few that publicly claim their religious difference.

French institutions have been particularly slow at adapting to the presence of new religions, Islam in particular. The French situation stands in contrast with countries such as the Netherlands that officially acknowledged migrant religions such as Hinduism or Islam in the 1980s, yet resembles other cases such as Germany where authorities justify the lack of recognition of Islam by the absence of a head of the religious hierarchy. Yet, the inaction of the French state has created many problems for the Muslims who wanted to develop a French Islam rather than turn to North African and Gulf states governments for support.

During colonial times, in a 'top-down' approach, the government entertained relations with Muslim institutions such as the Paris Mosque (*Mosquée de Paris*) that it sponsored, without reflecting much on the link between such entities and religious followers. By the 1970s, the French government encouraged a more 'bottom–up' or spontaneous organization of the faith. For instance, fearing that Arab factory workers would join Communist unions, a ministerial guideline sent to public companies such as Renault suggested that factories make rooms available for prayers (Kepel, 1987). The central state left the resolution of practical problems such as ritual slaughtering to local politics. For as long as they could, French authorities, in particular the Ministry of Interior that is responsible for State–Church relations, ignored migrant religious demands. In this period of status quo, a so-called 'basement Islam' developed, as communities tried to organize with few resources except those from Muslim nations. Concomitantly, some young migrants from Muslim countries living in derelict city projects 'returned' to Islam as a means of affirming their identity. Thus, retrospectively, the French state's inaction and ignorance of religious questions in the 1980s now appear as a missed opportunity to organize a 'French Islam', in brief to help Muslims on French soil develop the infrastructure to practise their faith in their country of residence and to adapt laws to accommodate them (in the army, in schools, prisons, hospitals, cemeteries and other institutions that are affected by French regulations, yet where clerics may be needed).

Since the late 1980s, various initiatives have sought to help organize the Muslim faith to create an interlocutor for French authorities to address religious issues. While there has been a law separating Church and State since 1905, there has also been a corporatist system of intermediation between the Ministry of Interior and recognized faiths: Catholics, Protestants and Jews. Finding an agreement between the various components of French Islam turned out to be arduous. The three main Muslim federations that compete and fight for influence have had to cooperate while they represent different traditions and outlook, receive support from different countries and cater for different religious demands.

In 1999, the Socialist government set up a consultation process with the federations, meeting imams from five large independent mosques and experts. After three years of negotiations they came to an agreement in February 2003 that Right-wing Minister Sarkozy took credit for. The National Muslim Council (*Conseil National des Musulmans de France*) and regional councils made up of nominated personalities and elected members took office in the spring of 2003. This event marked the recognition of the presence of Islam in France and, in the words of the Interior Minister, the 'normalization' of its relations with the French state. The Minister also declared that the issues that the Council would have to address 'were at the heart of the question of integration and of the national identity of the France of 2003' (interview in *Libération*, 21 February 2003). The issues that the Council had to address were numerous from the insufficient number of prayer halls and mosques to the provision of *halal* meat in school canteens, and the wearing of 'le voile' or the headscarf (see Sophie Duchesne's chapter).

The lesson to be drawn from the long-awaited birth of an official body representing Islam in France is clear. For decades, governments have been reluctant for electoral and ideological reasons to address issues that stemmed from the presence of migrants. Yet, procrastinating can worsen a situation and make it harder to find a solution or broker a compromise. Waiting too long to recognize Islam or to remedy the socio-economic problems of certain migrant minorities makes it more difficult today to ensure their equal participation in the French polity and society.

Conclusion

French initiatives since 2000 conform to developments at EU level. Since the Amsterdam Treaty came into force in 1999, anti-discrimination on the basis of race and ethnic origin and immigration and asylum policy have become competences of the European Union (EU). Still, the French way of framing policy problems and policy solutions has its own specificities, reflecting domestic electoral constraints as well as the legacy of past political crises and hard-won compromises on national identity and 'Republican principles'.

France today faces the challenges and dilemmas experienced by many multicultural societies. While millions of immigrants have found a place in French society since the Second World War, some are in the process of becoming an 'underclass', living in excluded unsafe urban pockets rife with unemployment. While governments have tried to enact policies to improve the situation, their attitude towards migrants is at best ambiguous:

- A strict migration control policy and discourses that denounce illegal migration continue to make the presence of immigrants in France illegitimate.
- The political integration of migrants is a failure: too few are integrated in political parties, too few vote. A reform that would grant local voting rights to non-EU foreigners has been postponed *sine die*.

Anti-discrimination policy still has to be fully implemented. A Muslim Council of Faith was set up, yet the 2003 veil affair has again isolated Muslims as different from other citizens. Mainstream political parties seem ill-at-ease in their statements on immigration and the National Front still gathers a significant portion of the vote. Yet political inaction does not seem a viable option lest certain groups become permanent 'ethnic minorities', a crying failure of the Republican ideal, *liberté, égalité, fraternité*.

A ten-year-old project may provide a different perspective on immigrants in France: in July 2004, the museum of the history of migration and migrant cultures was officially launched by the Prime Minister. Located in Paris in a building erected for a colonial exhibition, it aims to teach the wider public about the cultural and economic riches that generations of migrants have brought to France.

Chapter 11

Economic Policy and Policy-Making

JONAH LEVY

France has long embodied the possibilities for state-led or *dirigiste* economic development (Shonfield, 1965; Cohen, 1977; Katzenstein, 1978; Zysman, 1983; Hall, 1986). For decades, French planners aggressively manipulated an array of policy instruments – from trade protection, to sub-sidies, to cheap credit, to exemption from price controls – in an effort to accelerate the pace of economic modernization. French authorities channelled resources to privileged groups, favouring investment over consumption, industry over agriculture and big business over small. They also 'picked winners' both in specific sectors, such as coal and steel in the reconstruction era and nuclear power and telecommunications in the 1970s, and specific firms, the so-called 'national champions', multinational corporations anointed as France's standard-bearers in the battle for global economic leadership. When 'national champions' did not exist, French planners constructed them through a series of state-sponsored mergers; when 'national champions' lacked capital, the planners financed them through cheap capital and guaranteed state markets; and when 'national champions' were deficient in technology, state-run labs performed research for them, transferring cutting-edge solutions in computers, nuclear power, high-speed trains and digital telecommunications switches (Cohen and Bauer, 1985; Cohen, 1992).

Beginning in 1983, French policy took a new direction. Confronted with double-digit inflation, rising trade and budget deficits, stagnant investment and a currency crisis that threatened to push the French franc below the minimum exchange rate allowed by the European Monetary System (EMS), Socialist President François Mitterrand opted to reverse his government's voluntarist tack. A Leftist administration that had been elected just two years earlier on a campaign to intensify *dirigisme* began instead to dismantle it.

Two false narratives have dominated the discussion of where French economic and social policy has moved since the 1983 U-turn. The first is that French policy hasn't really moved that much – *plus ça change, et plus c'est la même chose*. Notwithstanding the appearance of change, state authorities continue to seek to steer the economy. The Raffarin government, for

170

example, rescued a bankrupt France Télécom in 2002 and Alstom, the maker of high-speed trains, in 2003. The Alstom bail-out was designed to prevent a takeover by a German rival, Siemens. In 2004, the government encouraged the merger of two French pharmaceutical companies, Aventis and Sanofi, to create a 'national champion', at a time when a Swiss company, Novartis, was prepared to pay a higher price for one of the companies. Actions such as these have led casual observers, notably in the business press, to argue that the state's *dirigiste* habits are alive and well: 'In spite of the claim by ... the French finance minister that it was no longer the role of government to intervene in the affairs of listed companies, the centre-right government has been far from passive and has shown in the past two years all the traditional interventionist appetites of previous right- and left-wing administrations' (*Financial Times*, 29 January 2004).

This portrait of enduring *dirigisme* exaggerates the capacities and interventionist proclivities of state authorities, however. The rescue of France Télécom took the form of a loan guarantee that was never needed, while intervention in the Aventis Sanofi merger was confined to moral suasion. Altstom received some subsidies, but the amounts are quite small in historical perspective, and aid to struggling, high-profile companies, who are deemed 'too big to fail', is not unknown in other countries. In the current climate of big budget deficits and austerity, French authorities have little money for struggling companies. Even if the state were flush with cash, aid to industry tends to run foul of EU competition policy, as vigorously enforced by the European Commission.

More fundamentally, the portrait of enduring *dirigisme* neglects the far-reaching reforms since 1985 that have stripped French authorities of much of their capacity to intervene in the economy. Contrary to Anglo-American stereotypes, French policy *has* changed dramatically. Twenty years after Mitterrand's U-turn, virtually nothing remains of the institutions and practices associated with the *dirigiste* model. Planning, sectoral industrial policies and ambitious *grands projets* have been abandoned; the vast majority of nationalized companies have been privatized; credit, price and capital controls have been lifted; restrictions on lay-offs and temporary and part-time employment have been eased; and a macro-economic orientation emphasizing inflationary growth coupled with large devaluations has given way to one of the lowest inflation rates in Europe and a strong franc, culminating in European Monetary Union (EMU). Today, France is a much more market-oriented political economy than it was in the early 1980s, with economic performance resting overridingly on the calculations of profit-seeking businesses, as opposed to the developmental strategies of state technocrats.

The second false narrative operates at the other end of the analytical spectrum, arguing that European integration and globalization have marginalized the French state. The 1983 U-turn was triggered by the decision to remain within the European Monetary System. European integration triumphed over French statism. In 1995, history repeated itself at an accelerated pace. Less than six months after being elected president on a campaign pledge of expanded state intervention to reduce unemployment and heal France's 'social fracture', Jacques Chirac reversed course, announcing that qualifying for European Monetary Union (EMU) had become France's top priority, even if this meant austerity in the short run. The clear lesson, then, is that European integration and globalization leave no room for France's free-spending, statist ways.

The problem with the globalization narrative is that the eclipse of the *dirigiste* model since 1983 has not been synonymous with the eclipse of the French state. In the 1980s, policies of economic liberalization were accompanied by a substantial expansion of welfare and labour-market measures in order to protect French workers from the harshest effects of the move to the market and to undercut union resistance. These measures were expensive, and state spending increased as a share of GDP, despite the winding down of costly industrial policy instruments. Thus, rather than simply or solely retreating, the French state evolved. The *dirigiste* state morphed into what I call the 'social anesthesia state', its central mission to pacify and demobilize the potential victims and opponents of economic liberalization, thereby permitting the French economy to reorganize on a more market-rational basis.

This chapter analyses the post-1983 redeployment of the French state the evolution of French economic and social policy from the *dirigiste* state to the social anesthesia state. It also examines recent efforts to reform the social anesthesia state, notably under the Raffarin government. The first section traces the elimination of the key features of the *dirigiste* model following the 1983 U-turn. The next section describes the social anesthesia measures that accompanied this movement, and then a section assesses the strengths and weaknesses of the social anesthesia state and the difficulties of reform. The economic policy of the Raffarin government is next examined, while the conclusion presents the current debates within the right over the future direction of economic policy.

Dismantling *dirigisme*

The 1983 U-turn touched off a range of reforms that struck at the core of the *dirigiste* model (Cohen, 1989; Hall, 1990; Schmidt, 1997; Levy, 1999; 2000). These changes, inaugurated cautiously by the Socialists from 1983 to 1986, were amplified when the Right returned to power under a neoliberal banner from 1986 to 1988, and were confirmed and completed by subsequent governments on both sides of the political spectrum. Four sets of changes figured most prominently.

The first change concerned macro-economic policy. For much of the postwar period, French authorities stimulated the economy through a combination of deficit spending and lax monetary policy, with much of the money flowing to industry (Zysman, 1983; Hall, 1986; Loriaux, 1991). The effects of the resulting inflation on competitiveness were negated by periodic 'aggressive devaluations' that not only compensated for price differentials with France's trading partners, but also conferred a temporary advantage on French producers, albeit at the expense of worker purchasing power.

The Socialists broke with this strategy in 1983. Under the so-called *franc fort* policy, the French franc was informally anchored to the Deutschmark. Since devaluations were no longer an option (let alone 'aggressive devaluations'), France would gain the edge through 'competitive disinflation', that is by running a rate of inflation lower than that of its trading partners. Towards this end, Keynesianism demand stimulus gave way to austerity budgets, wage indexation was abandoned and, most importantly, monetary policy was tightened, with real interest rates ranging from 5 per cent to 8 per cent for over a decade (Fitoussi, 1995). Since the early 1990s, the French inflation rate has been among the lowest in Western Europe, while the balance of trade, after nearly twenty years in the red, has registered steady surpluses.

The second set of reforms pertained to France's public enterprises. In 1982, the left nationalized 12 leading industrial conglomerates and 38 banks. When combined with the Liberation-era nationalizations carried out by General de Gaulle, this latest programme, costing €7.2 billion, placed 13 of France's 20 largest firms and virtually the entire banking sector in state hands (Stoffaës, 1984). Public enterprises received mammoth subsidies, but were pressured to expand employment and invest in areas deemed strategic (if not profitable) by the government.

The 1983 U-turn brought a fundamental shift in the government's relationship to the public enterprises. Nationalized companies were released from their planning targets and instructed to focus instead on profitability. While slashing capital grants and subsidies, the Left offered no resistance when public enterprises closed factories and withdrew from strategic sectors. This shift in public-sector management set the stage for the Right to launch a campaign of privatizations upon its return to power in 1986. Before the privatization process was interrupted by the 1987 stock market crash, 13 financial and industrial groups had been sold off, netting €12.8 billion to the French treasury (Zerah, 1993, p. 183). Since 1993, a second round of privatizations has been conducted by governments of both the Right and the Left, reducing the once-vast holdings of the French state to little more than energy production, public transportation and some weapons manufacturers.

The third major policy shift after 1983 was the abandonment of state efforts to steer private industry. The guiding spirit of this change was that firms would receive less government assistance, but would be subject to fewer restrictions, so that they could raise the necessary resources by their own means (Hall, 1990). The hefty budgets for bail-outs of loss-making companies, sectoral industrial policy programmes, high-tech *grands projets* and subsidized loans quickly dried up, triggering a wave of bankruptcies. As a counterpoint, however, French business gained a number of new freedoms. The deregulation of financial markets, initiated in 1985, enabled firms to raise funds by issuing equity, reducing their dependence on state-allocated credit. The removal of price controls in 1986 allowed companies to reap the full benefits of successful competitive strategies. The elimination of capital controls in the late 1980s facilitated the expansion of production abroad and gave managers an 'exit' option if domestic conditions were not to their liking. Taken together, these and other reforms helped boost corporate profitability from 9.8 per cent of value added in 1982 to 17.3 per cent in 1989 (Faugère and Voisin, 1994: 32).

The revival of corporate profits was also fuelled by a fourth set of developments, the reform of France's system of industrial relations (Groux and Mouriaux, 1990; Howell, 1992a, 1992b; Labbé and Croisat, 1992). State authorities de-indexed wages and lifted a number of restrictions limiting managerial prerogatives, most significantly the administrative authorization for lay-offs (the requirement that lay-offs of ten or more employees for economic reasons receive the approval of an inspector from the ministry of labour). They also expanded the scope of workplace bargaining. In a context of high unemployment and weak and divided trade unions, French employers were able to use this new bargaining arena to introduce labour-market flexibility largely on their terms. Studies of initial firm-level deals revealed that most accorded no compensation to employees in return for acceptance of greater flexibility and that up to one third of these agreements actually violated French labour law. Not surprisingly, much of capital's gain in the post-1983 period would come at labour's expense. From 1982 to 1989, the share of value added received by capital increased from 24.0 per cent to 31.7 per cent, surpassing the levels of the early 1970s (Faugère and Voisin, 1994: 28–9).

The reforms since 1983 have left no *dirigiste* stone unturned. Looking across the wealthy democracies, one would be hard-pressed to find any country that moved so far away from its postwar economic strategy as the France of François Mitterrand and Jacques Chirac. Certainly, compared to other statist political economies such as Japan and Korea, France moved earlier and more aggressively in a market direction. If the break with *dirigisme* eliminated a number of interventionist policies, however, it also created pressures for new kinds of state intervention.

The expansion of social and labour market policy

Social and labour market policy played a critical role in France's move away from *dirigisme*. In a logic first articulated by Karl Polanyi, the extension of market forces was softened, made politically acceptable through the expansion of social protections for those most affected by liberalization (Polanyi, 1944). On the one hand, beginning in 1983, state authorities made a market, imposing liberalization from above. Austerity, privatization, deregulation and labour-market flexibility all heightened the vulnerability of French workers. On the other hand, successive governments, especially those on the Left, expanded the welfare state in a number of ways so as to cushion the blow to the working class and, equally importantly, to undercut the possibilities for union mobilization (Daley, 1996; Levy, 1999).

State intervention centred initially on early retirement, a strategy designed to square the circle of 'job loss without unemployment' (Daley, 1996). French authorities recognized the need for companies to be able to restructure in order to restore profitability and competitiveness, but such restructuring would not come at the expense of the workforce. Rather, government programmes would permit employees over the age of 55 – or, in some cases, 50 – to retire at close to full pension.

The expansion of early retirement to accommodate and humanize restructuring began under the Giscard presidency. Between 1974 and 1980, the number of early retirees more than tripled from 59,000 to 190,400 (DARES, 1996: 100). The Left tripled the figure again to over 700,000 workers in 1984. Such measures were expensive, costing as much as €150,000 per retiree, but they were assumed to be temporary. Officials expected that once French firms restructured and the economy recovered, job creation would begin anew, and early retirement programmes could be wound down. Employment creation has remained sluggish, however, and the number of participants in early-retirement programmes has held relatively steady, ranging from 450,000 to 600,000 since the mid-1980s. The effects of early retirement on the French labour market are striking. Today, fewer than one worker in three is still employed at age 60, and France's labour-force participation rate for men aged 55 to 64 is among the lowest in Western Europe, at just over 40 per cent (Scharpf and Schmidt, 2000: 350).

Labour-market policies were deployed not only to facilitate the movement away from *dirigisme*, but also to palliate the perceived limits or failings of economic liberalization. The restoration of corporate profitability and competitiveness in the mid-1980s did not bring about an appreciable reduction in unemployment. Consequently, beginning with the Socialist government of Michel Rocard in 1988, French authorities adopted a much more interventionist approach to labour markets. The Rocard government expanded active labour-market policies, notably training programmes, public internships and subsidies for hard-to-place youths and the long-term unemployed.

In the mid-1990s, centre-Right governments focused on the reduction of labour costs, particularly at the low end of the wage spectrum, where a relatively generous minimum wage (€1,150 per month) and heavy social security charges (roughly 50 per cent of wages) are said to discourage job creation. In 1994, Gaullist Prime Minister Edouard Balladur attempted to create a sub-minimum wage for youths 20 per cent below the legal minimum, before retreating in a hailstorm of protest. Subsidies and tax breaks for low-wage recruitment proved less controversial. Under Balladur, employers hiring low-wage workers were exempted from family allowance contributions, while a programme inaugurated in 1995 by Balladur's Gaullist successor Alain Juppé provided subsidies of €750 to €2,200 for jobs paying less than 1.3 times the minimum wage.

The centre-left government of Lionel Jospin added two further labour-market initiatives during its tenure from 1997 to 2002. The first was a youth employment programme, the (*Programme Emploi Jeunes*: PEJ), which occupied some 350,000 young people. The PEJ (*Programme Emploi Jeunes*) was targeted at youths with no significant work experience. In contrast to previous state-sponsored, make-work projects, the PEJ provided full-time employment for an extended period (five years). The government hoped that this extended tenure would enable participants to acquire the skills and experience necessary to secure permanent employment once the subsidies ran out. Under the highly generous terms of the PEJ, the state paid 80 per cent of the minimum wage and all social security contributions, leaving only 20 per cent of the minimum wage to the charge of the employer. Employers in the private sector were barred from participating, however. Fearful that private companies would substitute subsidized hiring of for existing personnel, the government restricted the PEJ to non-profit and public organizations. The PEJ was expensive, costing some €5.3 billion, although some of the money was recovered from other youth employment programmes that were terminated.

The second high-profile measure by the Jospin government was the reduction of the working week from 39 hours to 35 hours. Although conservative critics and the national employer association denounced the reform as a job-killer that would force companies to lay off workers as a result of higher labour costs, the government took a number of measures to assuage business concerns. The reform was phased in over a five-year period, giving employers time to adjust and to extract wage concessions from employees as the price for shorter working hours. Employers were also allowed to introduce flexibility into work schedules, which can now vary considerably from week to week. Finally, the government tendered significant subsidies to companies that signed collective bargaining agreements reducing work time. The subsidies are greatest at the bottom of the pay scale (€3,275 per year for a minimum-wage hire), declining gradually to €610 for jobs paying more than 1.7 times the minimum wage. The cost of the reform is estimated at €16.77 billion, although, again, part of the money is being shifted from other programmes, notably the Balladur and Juppé governments' subsidies for low-wage hire.

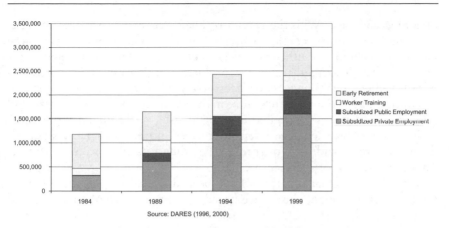

Source: DARES (1996, 2000)

Figure 11.1 *Number of French workers in public labour market programmes*

Looking at labour-market policy globally, Figure 11.1 reveals that the number of French workers enrolled in some kind of public labour-market programme has expanded two-and-one-half-fold in the post-*dirigiste* period – rising from slightly under 1.2 million in 1984, at the height of industrial restructuring, to nearly 3 million in 1999, where it has remained stable since (DARES, 1996; DARES, December 2000). Figure 11.1 also suggests that French labour-market expenditures have become more 'active' over the years, encouraging recipients to work ('active'), rather than to withdraw from the labour market ('passive'). Whereas the number of employees in passive early retirement programmes declined slightly from just over 700,000 in 1984 to less than 600,000 in 1999, subsidized jobs in the private sector expanded from 320,000 to 1.6 million, subsidized jobs in the public sector from 8,000 to 509,000, and positions in training programmes from 143,000 to 298,000. This total is in addition to the 2 million French workers who are formally unemployed. Aggregate spending on labour-market policy has shown a similar increase, expanding from slightly over 2 per cent of GDP in the mid-1980s to 3.2 per cent of GDP in 1999. Today, France spends as much as on labour-market intervention as Sweden, the Mecca of active labour-market policy.

The persistence of mass unemployment has led French authorities to innovate in the area of welfare policy as well as labour-market policy. France's Bismarckian welfare state was constructed on the basis of social insurance, as opposed to social assistance (Palier, 1999). In other words, benefits are tendered, not as a matter of right, to all citizens (social assistance), but in return for contributions, primarily payroll taxes, previously paid to the social security system (social insurance). Prior to the 1970s, the distinction between social insurance and social assistance was of little practical significance, since conditions of full employment enabled virtually all workers and their families to meet the requirements for obtaining coverage. With the spread of unemployment, part-time employment and temporary employment, however, French workers are often unable to accumulate sufficient social security contributions to qualify for insurance benefits. Aggravating the problem, surging rates of divorce and out-of-wedlock births have made it less likely that women and children will be covered under the insurance of a 'male breadwinner'. Thus, a large and growing segment of the population – the long-term unemployed, part-time and temporary workers, the intermittently employed, and many single or divorced parents and their offspring – has found itself unprotected by the traditional system of social insurance.

A number of social initiatives have been designed to plug the holes in France's Bismarckian, insurance-based system. In 1988, the Rocard government established a national social safety net or guaranteed income, the *Revenu Minimum d'Insertion* (RMI), for all adults over the age of 25. The RMI replaced a patchwork of local and targeted social assistance programmes that had left large segments of the population uncovered, notably the long-term unemployed and persons suffering from psychological problems, alcoholism and/or chemical dependency. In many instances, the RMI has functioned as a basic income support for adults who have exhausted or failed to qualify for unemployment insurance. Benefits are available on a means-tested basis to all citizens and long-term residents over the age of 25. The RMI provides a monthly allowance of €420 along with the promise of support services to help 'insert' (the 'I' in 'RMI') recipients back into society and, in some cases, into a job. Claimants are also eligible for housing allowances and free health insurance. Although the 'insertion' dimension of the RMI remains underdeveloped, the programme does provide non-negligible financial assistance to some 1 million of France's neediest citizens, at an annual cost of €3.8 billion.

The Jospin government launched the *Couverture Maladie Universelle* (CMU) in 2000, largely to provide supplementary health insurance for citizens not covered by employers. The CMU makes healthcare available free of charge to low-income groups. It originated with a pledge by the Juppé government in 1995 to extend public health insurance to the 200,000 French citizens (0.3 per cent of the population) who lacked such coverage. The Jospin government honoured Juppé's pledge, but also addressed the far greater problem of access among those who actually possess health insurance. France's public health insurance reimburses just 75 per cent of the costs of medical treatment on average (Join-Lambert and Bolot-Gittler et al., 1997). Although 85 per cent of the population reduces co-payments by subscribing to a supplementary insurance, for the remaining 15 per cent, low reimbursement rates tended to place all but emergency medical treatment out of reach. The CMU greatly attenuated this problem by providing free supplementary health insurance on a means-tested basis to an estimated 5 million people at a cost of some €1.5 billion annually.

Alongside these new social commitments, French authorities expanded spending in traditional areas. The two largest welfare programmes, pensions and healthcare, both experienced significant growth in the 1980s and 1990s. France's pay-as-you-go pension system is among the most generous in the world, and spending increased from 7.7 per cent of GDP in 1981 to 9.8 per cent in 2000 (Ministry of Finance, 2001: Statistical Annex, Table VII.2). French healthcare spending grew from 7.4 per cent of GDP in 1980 to 9.6 per cent in 1998, as France passed Austria, Belgium, Denmark, Holland and Sweden to become the number two spender in the EU, behind Germany (OECD, 2000, Table A7). The French healthcare system is not without problems, but thanks in part to this increased commitment of resources, the French system was rated the planet's best by the World Health Organization. Between the old activities and the new, total social spending in France rose from 21.3 per cent of GDP in 1980 to 26.5 per cent in 1990 to 29.5 per cent in 1998 (OECD, 2002), making France the biggest welfare state outside Scandinavia.

France's break with *dirigisme* in the 1980s provided a dual impetus to state intervention. The promise of liberalization induced authorities to commit vast resources to the transition process, to the alleviation of social pain and political resistance, in the expectation that a more flexible labour market would quickly generate enough jobs to make such costly transitional measures unnecessary (or, at least, much less necessary). The disappointments of liberalization, the continuing high levels of unemployment not only made it impossible to wind down supposedly transitional early retirement measures, but drove new spending in the form of active labour-market programmes and social assistance programmes. In short, 'de-*dirigisation*' and state expansion were two sides of the same (very expensive) coin.

The social anesthesia state and the challenge of reform

The social anesthesia strategy has brought significant benefits to the French economy. Whereas the *dirigiste* state sought to steer the market, the social anesthesia state has underwritten market-led, privately determined adjustment strategies. By protecting French workers from the worst effects of job loss, the state has allowed employers to reorganize their companies, closing unprofitable factories and down-sizing plants as necessary. In the 1980s, French industry rationalized, returned to profitability and drew down its heavy debt. France has enjoyed a steady trade surplus since 1992, as French firms have met European and global competition with great success.

Another benefit of the social anesthesia mission is that it enabled French authorities to disengage from dysfunctional *dirigiste* industrial policies. Here, a comparative perspective is revealing. In Japan, despite over a decade of economic stagnation and the discrediting of state guidance in the eyes of the population, government authorities have been able to implement only limited, partial liberalizing reforms, at best. Part of the reason is a reluctance of state authorities to cede traditional powers. In addition, the Japanese political system, with its weak governing coalitions, is ill-suited to the task of enacting sweeping, controversial reforms like liberalization packages. But perhaps of greatest importance is the fact that Japan lacks a French-style social safety net (Miura, 2002a, 2002b). Japanese authorities are spending vast amounts propping up debt-laden banks which are propping up, in turn, debt-laden companies because were those banks and their customers to shut down, millions of Japanese workers would lose their jobs and Japan has no social safety net to take care of them. Japanese state spending has increased even more than French spending, but without the corresponding liberation from expensive and dysfunctional industrial policies.

The social anesthesia strategy, as the label suggests, has offered social as well as economic benefits. French companies have been able to reorganize, much like their American or British counterparts, but worker living standards have been protected. In other words, the costs of industrial adjustment were socialized to the collectivity, rather than concentrated on those who lost their jobs. French authorities have also been attentive to new social needs, establishing programmes like the RMI and CMU to address emerging gaps in the social insurance system. In short, the social anesthesia state has moved France towards the market, while offering relatively humane treatment to the victims of industrial restructuring and economic liberalization.

If the social anesthesia strategy helped solve the problems of de-*dirigisation* and industrial restructuring, it has left other problems festering. From a social perspective, social anesthesia is a far cry from social integration. A minimum income of €420 per month may be acceptable as a stop-gap, but not as a way of life. In the long run, the RMI is no substitute for social integration through a steady job, for upward social mobility. Many of the supposed beneficiaries of social anesthesia policies harbour great bitterness towards a government that offers them meagre allowances and a succession of dead-end internships and substandard part-time or temporary jobs. This dissatisfaction probably cost Lionel Jospin the presidency in 2002, as Leftist voters flocked to three different Trotskyist parties, preventing Jospin from qualifying for the run-off election with President Chirac. This dissatisfaction has also helped fuel the rise of the xenophobic, racist National Front of Jean-Marie Le Pen, which has become the number one party among both blue-collar workers and the unemployed.

But it is on the economic front that French policy has come under heaviest criticism. The social anesthesia state is largely passive; it pays people not to work. If this represents an improvement over bailing out uncompetitive companies in order to prevent lay-offs, one can imagine better uses for the money. Once again, a comparative perspective is revealing. Social democratic countries like Sweden spend as much as or even more than France on social programmes, but the social democratic approach is centred around the so-called 'work line', the notion that every adult should be employed (Titmuss, 1987; Esping-Andersen, 1990; Huber and Stephens, 2001). As a result, passive measures tend to be limited, with much of the spending concentrated on 'active' measures that facilitate employment, such as education and training, relocation assistance and low-cost public childcare. Under the 'active' or 'social investment' model there is an economic pay-off beyond simply keeping displaced workers from protesting and blocking lay-offs. France's social anesthesia strategy offers few such benefits, few if any gains in human capital and employment. In recent years, the trend across Europe has been to 'activate' labour-market expenditures, to encourage and coerce the non-employed to take jobs, while expanding the financial rewards from employment. Critics charge that France's social anesthesia state is sorely in need of such a reorientation.

A second problem is that the social anesthesia state is very expensive. Social anesthesia measures have persisted far longer than initially expected. Many initiatives, such as generous early retirement programmes, were conceived of as temporary. Workers would be pensioned off, companies would restructure, then job creation would resume anew and early retirement programmes could be wound down. Instead of winding down, however, social anesthesia programmes have been preserved. What is more, new initiatives – such as a guaranteed minimum income – have been added as mass unemployment has claimed new victims. Finally, the social anesthesia state has become something of a magnet as every aggrieved party in French society – from displaced workers, to uncompetitive farmers, to overworked truckers – turns to the government for relief. In an extreme example, workers in a factory slated for shutdown occupied the factory and threatened to dump toxic chemicals into the river unless the state (not the company) dispatched a labour official to negotiate a better severance package! From a fiscal standpoint, the multiplication of social anesthesia measures has more than offset the savings from de-*dirigisation*. Despite the winding down of expensive industrial policy measures, state spending has increased since the early 1980s, approaching 55 per cent of GDP. While one can certainly sympathize with the effort to protect the poor and vulnerable, the cost of these programmes has pushed the French state to the limits of its taxing capacity.

Related to its passive orientation and high cost, the social anesthesia state is widely blamed for pushing up unemployment. Despite the proliferation of early-retirement and make-work programmes, the official unemployment rate has remained in the range of 10 per cent for over a decade. France's minimum wage is fairly generous (approximately €1150 per month), and social security charges can add as much as 50 per cent to the wage bill. Critics charge that this combination of high statutory wages and payroll taxes is pricing French workers out of the labour market. Moreover, fairly generous benefits can discourage job search by offering a reasonably attractive alternative to paid employment, particularly part-time jobs. In order to generate low-skill, low-productivity jobs in sufficient number to bring down unemployment, it is argued, France must loosen its social protections (Minc, 1994).

Despite broad agreement on the need to reorganize and curtail government spending, reform has proven exceptionally difficult. Three sets of obstacles have impeded reformers. The first is the nature of the reform. Whereas in the 1970s and 1980s, governments were often trading one benefit for another – plant closings in return for early retirement, fewer industrial policy subsidies in return for greater managerial autonomy – since the early 1990s, cash-strapped governments have had little to offer in the way of side-payments. Yet zero-sum reforms, when claimants are asked to give up benefits with only the vague promise of a healthier economy or stronger pension system in return, are the most politically difficult to undertake.

The second obstacle concerns the history of liberalizing reform. The experience of de-*dirigisation* has led many in France to feel that they have already been subjected to retrenchment – and have little to show for it. Since 1983, French citizens have reluctantly accepted a series of painful liberalizing measures. Each time, they were told that the reforms in question would relaunch growth and bring down unemployment: if French inflation were held below that of Germany or Italy, then French workers would get the jobs that were going to German and Italian workers; if the state spent less on uncompetitive firms, then fast-growing start-ups would arise to take their place; if wages gave way to profits, then investment and jobs would follow; if French employers were given the right to fire, then they would be more inclined to hire. The reforms were implemented one after the other, yet economic growth remains anaemic, and mass unemployment persists. Given these disappointments, the idea that what is needed is another turn of the neoliberal screw, welfare retrenchment on top of *dirigiste* retrenchment, does not elicit great popular enthusiasm.

The third obstacle stems from the actors of reform. French governments over the past ten years have rarely operated from a position of strength. One problem is that they have tended to be isolated. In many European countries, controversial reforms – whether to reduce budget deficits, pare social spending or overhaul labour markets – have been conducted either by broad coalitions, encompassing parties of both the Left and Right, or else through tripartite negotiations among the state, employers and unions. By widening the participants, governments have been able to spread blame for unpopular decisions and limit resistance. In France, by contrast, governments have almost always acted alone: the logic of bipolarization has trumped that of *union sacrée*, while negotiations with the social partners have been an afterthought at most.

French governments have tended to be vulnerable as well as isolated. Incumbent prime ministers have lost seven consecutive national elections since 1981, meaning that governments have often been unpopular and fearful of defeat at the polls. They have also had relatively short time horizons, due to the frequency of elections. Prime Minister Balladur assumed office in 1993, but was reluctant to take unpopular measures or face down protestors, since he was running for president in 1995. Prime Minister Juppé, fearful that austerity measures needed to qualify for EMU might cost the Right dearly in legislative elections scheduled for 1998, persuaded President Chirac to hold the elections early – only to have the Right lose. In theory, Juppé's successor, the Socialist Lionel Jospin, did not have to worry about legislative or presidential elections for the next five years. But in a situation of cohabitation with Chirac, Jospin knew that if his popularity slid, the president might call new parliamentary elections to turn the Left out of office. Jospin's reformist ambitions were further constrained by the need to placate his coalition Green and especially Communist partners, lest he lose his parliamentary majority.

The combination of anxious, change-resistant voters and fragile, isolated governments has made social and economic reform an extraordinarily difficult, politically parlous undertaking. Of course, some changes have been made. Early in his term, Prime Minister Balladur was able to significantly reduce the generosity of the pension system for private-sector employees. The Juppé and Jospin governments were also able to bring French budget deficits down to the level necessary to qualify for European Monetary Union (EMU). Still, significant reforms have been the exception, rather than the rule. In some cases, governments have launched reforms, usually with minimal consultation with the concerned parties, only to withdraw them in the face of protest strikes and street demonstrations. The ill-fated Juppé social security package of 1995, which was met with strikes that shut down public transportation for six weeks, was emblematic of this dynamic. The pattern of reform proposal, protest and retraction has applied to all manner of initiatives, from minimum wages, to education, to privatization – under governments of Left and Right alike. In other cases, reforms have been talked about and studied to death, but never actually initiated. The Jospin government commissioned multiple blue-ribbon panels on pension and healthcare reform, but in the run-up to the presidential election and fearful of criticism on his Left, Jospin opted not to move forward.

The Chirac–Raffarin government: limited liberalism

If reforming France's social anesthesia state is an incredibly difficult undertaking, the new government that emerged out of the 2002 elections possessed two advantages lacked by its predecessors. The first was a long time horizon. The fact that both presidential and parliamentary elections were held in 2002, with the Right winning both, meant that the government had a free hand for the next five years. Under these circumstances, reformers could consider enacting painful, unpopular reforms early in the term, in the hope that the benefits of these reforms would kick in before the next national election.

The other favourable circumstance was the emergence of a reform process, the so-called *refondation sociale*, involving the employer association, the *Mouvement des Entreprises de France* (MEDEF), formerly the CNPF, and the unions. The *refondation sociale* was launched by MEDEF in 2000 in response to what the employers and sympathetic trade unions, notably the CFDT, saw as excessive intervention and high-handed behaviour by the French state. The employers were particularly upset about Jospin's determination to impose the 35-hour working week via legislation, rather than relying on voluntary agreements. The social partners were also angered when the government attempted to drain funds from the unemployment insurance programme to help finance the 35-hour working week, arguing that the creation of jobs resulting from a shorter working week would reduce unemployment insurance pay-outs. MEDEF did not accept this argument, but more importantly, technically, the unemployment insurance programme is run by the employers and unions alone, so that the government had no legal basis for taking the money. Thus, the *refondation sociale* was created in a climate of anger and resistance to an interventionist Leftist government.

Concretely, the *refondation sociale* sought to overhaul the French system of social protection and industrial relations on the basis of bilateral agreements negotiated by the employers and the trade unions. The initial agenda encompassed nine areas of reform, including unemployment, healthcare, pensions, collective bargaining, workplace health and safety, and employee training. MEDEF portrayed the *refondation sociale* as an effort to narrow the scope of the state, denouncing the alleged interventionist excesses of the Jospin government in the harshest terms. MEDEF also negotiated very aggressively, challenging central components of France's system of social protection, and threatening to denounce collective agreements if the unions did not sign on to its proposals. That said, the *refondation sociale* yielded several significant reforms that provided benefits to both employers and workers. A reform of the unemployment insurance system created the *plan d'aide au retour à l'emploi* (PARE), which requires the unemployed to search for work and accept reasonable job offers under pain of losing their benefits; in return, eligibility conditions for unemployment insurance were loosened, expanding coverage, and benefits were made more generous. A 'common declaration on the channels and means of collective bargaining' established the principle that collective agreements, to be valid, must be signed (or not opposed) by unions representing a majority of workers, while offering employers expanded opportunities to bargain at the

workplace level. Another agreement increased payroll taxes to fund supplementary pensions in return for a commitment by the unions to support
a future reform of the entire pension system (basic and supplementary
alike) that would not raise employer contributions. Most recently, a deal
on worker training mandated increased employer spending on training
and created a right for workers to receive at least 20 hours per year of
training along with the possibility for workers to initiate that training; in
return, employers can require that some of the training take place outside
working hours.

When the Right returned to power in 2002, two channels of reform were
available. One was the political channel, the front-loading of controversial,
painful measures in the initial period in office, with the hope that all would
be forgiven by the 2007 elections. The other was the corporatist channel,
represented by the *refondation sociale* and pursued with considerable
success in other European countries, including those without strong union
movements, such as Holland, Spain, Portugal, Ireland and Italy (Rhodes,
2001). The *refondation sociale* held a critical advantage of moving the
state away from the front lines of reform, allowing the government to
shift blame to (or, at least, share blame with) the social partners. In the
end, though, the government opted to privilege the political channel of
reform. To some degree, MEDEF forced the government's hand: with a
sympathetic conservative government in place, the French employer association rediscovered the virtues of legislation, as opposed to collective
bargaining. Negotiations with the unions were allowed to lapse for over a
year, and the spiritual father and main actor of the *refondation sociale*
within MEDEF, Denis Kessler, was stripped of his responsibilities for
negotiating, before opting to leave the organization to head a reinsurance
company. At the same time, MEDEF was pushing on an open door, as the
government, anxious to demonstrate its capacity to reform the social
anesthesia state and get France moving again, was not inclined to wait for
the social partners to do its bidding.

The Raffarin government has been remarkably active in its first two
years, enacting a series of high-profile reforms. The main goals of these
reforms have been to make labour markets more flexible and encourage
hiring, curb social spending and reduce taxes. Five reforms have figured
most prominently.

The first important action of the Raffarin government was to loosen the
rules surrounding the 35-hour working week. The government stopped
short of repealing the 35-hour legislation, as MEDEF urged, but introduced
several provisions that facilitate longer working hours. Payment of overtime for the 36th through the 39th hour worked was reduced from 50 per
cent to 25 per cent in firms with more than 20 workers and from 25 per cent
to 10 per cent in the smallest businesses. In addition, the number of overtime hours that an employee can work without receiving the approval of a
labour inspector or negotiating an agreement with employee representatives

was raised from 130 hours per year to 180 hours. The reform means that employers can return to 39 hours per week, without negotiating with the unions, by paying (reduced) overtime rates for the four extra hours. In December 2004, Raffarin announced further measures to encourage longer working hours. Chief among these are: an increase in the annual ceiling on overtime hours from 180 to 220; the possibility for employees to receive overtime pay, as opposed to time off, in exchange for putting in extra hours; and an extension of the special status enjoyed by small firms for three more years, until the end of 2008.

The second significant reform was in the area of pensions. The Fillon Law of 21 August 2003 will gradually raise the required number of years for a full pension from 37.5 years in the public sector and 40 years in the private sector to 42 years for all workers in 2020. Civil servants' pensions were also made less generous by indexing them to prices, instead of wages, and by extending the period for the calculation of the reference wage. A further innovation of the Fillon Law was to create a system of voluntary private pension funds, the *Plan d'Epargne Retraite Populaire* (PERP), supported by tax breaks. The Fillon reform encountered considerable hostility, with unions mobilizing several million protestors in a series of demonstrations. Yet the government held true, making minor concessions – notably, the possibility for workers who began their careers between the ages of 14 and 16 to retire early – in order to gain the support of the CFDT.

The third important change is in healthcare. The reform by Minister of Health Philippe Douste-Blazy in July 2004 seeks to both reduce the mammoth deficit in the public health insurance system (€12.9 billion in 2003) and streamline treatment. The legislation imposed €5 billion in new fees: most controversially, a one-euro co-payment for doctor's visits. Co-payments have long existed for hospital stays, which the Douste-Blazy reform raised from €13 to €18 per day. The reform seeks to bring down spending by streamlining services and encouraging the substitution of generic drugs for brand-name drugs. It will also establish a computerized medical file for each patient, in the hope of avoiding repeated tests or lost information as the patient moves through the medical system. Finally, the Douste-Blazy law will require French patients to choose a primary care physician, ending the practice of 'medical nomadism' under which patients could self-refer to multiple doctors, including specialists, on their own initiative.

The fourth important shift is in the area of youth employment. The Raffarin government has repeatedly denounced the so-called 'social treatment of employment', notably placing unemployed youths in government make-work projects that are costly and rarely lead to permanent hire. For the Right, the symbol of such ill-advised public internships was the Jospin government's five-year *emplois jeunes*. The Raffarin government has introduced three modifications. The first is to allow the *emplois jeunes* to lapse after their five-year term expires. The second is to replace the *emplois jeunes* with a smaller programme, the *contrat jeunes en enterprises*, which seeks to place unskilled youths in jobs in the private sector. Employers hiring youths in this programme are exempt from social security charges for three years, but the contract must be permanent (*contrat à durée indéterminée*), offering the workers protection against dismissal once the subsidies run out. Partly for this reason, private-sector take-up has been below expectations. The third initiative, reflected in the *emplois-jeunes*, is to encourage job creation primarily through employer subsidies and tax breaks rather than public employment. Towards this end, the government extended the subsidies for low-wage hire that the Jospin government had conditioned on moving to a 35-hour working week to all companies. As a result, employer subsidies for companies paying less than 1.7 times the SMIC now total €15 billion annually.

The fifth significant area of reform is in fiscal policy. Tax cuts are central to the agenda of the Raffarin government. Raffarin's stated aim, echoing a MEDEF theme, is to bring French taxation down to the European average by 2007. More concretely, during the 2002 presidential campaign, Chirac pledged to reduce income taxes by 30 per cent. Despite ballooning budget deficits, the government has cut income taxes three times by a total of 10 per cent. That said, the 30 per cent target is in jeopardy as no new tax cuts are planned for 2005. The other area of aggressive tax-cutting has been in the encouragement of new recruitment. In addition to the tax cuts for low-wage workers and unskilled youths noted above, the government has offered €1.5 billion to hotel and restaurant owners and doubled the tax write-off for household employees from €2,450 in 2002 to €5,000 in 2004. The government has also completed a Socialist initiative, launched in 1999, to phase out the wage component of the local corporate income tax (*taxe professionnelle*) and expanded the Socialists' *prime pour l'emploi*, a kind of negative income tax benefiting low-wage workers.

The Raffarin government's tax cuts have not been accompanied by significant spending cuts. When combined with a sluggish economy, the effect has been to push state finances deeply in the red. The budget deficit reached 4.1 per cent of GDP in 2003, well above the 3 per cent ceiling mandated by the EMU Stability Pact. Public debt has also breached the ceiling, rising to 63.7 per cent of GDP at the end of 2003. President Chirac's reply to the critiques of the European Commission was that 'France has other priorities', meaning tax cuts, and that he refused to implement an austerity programme that might dampen demand and strangle economic growth. Because other EMU members, notably Germany, had also exceeded the deficit limits of the Stability Pact, the Commission was unable to impose sanctions on France. Chirac indicated initially that France would not reduce its deficit below 3 per cent of GDP before 2007 and then, only if economic growth accelerated. More recently, the government has shown some willingness to speed up the process of deficit reduction, notably by deferring income tax cuts that had been planned for 2005.

The strategy of privileging the political channel of reform over the corporatist reform has yielded some significant changes in French economic, social and labour-market policy. At the same time, it has left the government vulnerable to two sets of charges. The first relates to equity. The policies of the Chirac–Raffarin tandem speak with a distinct upper-class accent, concentrating favours on employers and high-income groups, while delivering austerity and eroding protections to the more vulnerable. If employer subsidies could be justified on the basis of job creation, the same is not true of reductions in the income tax. Moreover, the income tax is paid by only one-half of the French population, meaning that the lower half derived no benefit whatsoever.

The reforms of the welfare state also appear one-sided. The pension reform forces employees to work significantly more years for a smaller pension, yet leaves employer contributions essentially unchanged. The healthcare reform increases co-payments and limits the choice of physicians, while again sparing employers from tax hikes. The reform also spares doctors and pharmaceutical companies from cuts; indeed, one of the first actions of the Raffarin government in June 2002 was to increase public payments to general practitioners by 12 per cent. Finally, in the labour market, French workers who made numerous concessions as part of the negotiations to shorten the working week – wage restraint, a quasi-annualization of working hours, fewer breaks, a less predictable work schedule – now face the risk of being forced to return to 39 hours without recovering any of the previous concessions. In a similar vein, the careful balancing of rights and duties in the PARE was unhinged first by deficits in the unemployment insurance system that forced the unions to accept tighter eligibility conditions and a shorter indemnity period in return for increased employer payroll contributions, then by a government reform that sought to reduce the receipt of minimum unemployment benefits (*allocation de solidarité spécifique*: ASS) from three years to two.

The government's perceived pro-business, pro-wealthy bias has played an important role in its falling popularity and successive electoral defeats (regional, cantonal and European Parliamentary elections of 2004). In a recent opinion poll, 61 per cent of the French public favoured policies that are 'more social,' whereas only 21 per cent supported policies that are 'more liberal'. Resentment and insecurity have also fuelled protests. In January 2004, when 300,000 so-called *recalculés* lost their unemployment benefits as a result of the ASS reform, the government confronted a series of demonstrations and lawsuits, prompting it to repeal the reform.

The Chirac–Raffarin tandem has come under fire for failing to address some of the excesses associated with globalization and heightened employer leverage. To be fair, this concern was also present under the Jospin government. In 1999, the Michelin tyre company provoked a public furore by announcing lay-offs not to save the company from ruin – indeed, Michelin's profits were increasing at the time – but simply to improve competitiveness and profitability. Such behaviour, which was quickly dubbed *licenciements boursiers* (shareholder lay-offs), shocked a French public accustomed to viewing lay-offs as a measure of last resort rather than a means of improving the company's bottom line. Shock turned to anger when Prime Minister Jospin, asked what he planned to do about the Michelin affair, replied that in a market economy one should not expect the state to regulate everything. Jospin later attempted to redeem himself to the Leftist faithful and to assuage the anger of his Communist coalition partner by passing a law that slightly restricted lay-offs (commonly referred to as the 'Michelin amendment'). Such restrictions have not prevented other companies from engaging in similar practices, including Marks & Spencer and the Danone food group, a French conglomerate that had long enjoyed a reputation for progressive labour relations. Many on the Left never forgave Jospin for his callous statement, and his words no doubt cost him dearly in the 2002 presidential election.

The Raffarin government has appeared, if anything, even less inclined to check employer misdeeds, however egregious. In January 2003, President Chirac coined the phrase *patrons voyous* (hoodlum employers) to describe foreign-owned companies, operating beyond the reach of French law, who engage in unconscionable social and environmental practices. In the case that prompted Chirac's remarks, the owners of an oil tanker failed to take the necessary safety precautions, leading to a massive oil spill that devastated the coast of Brittany. Other highly publicized incidents of *patrons voyous* included a firm that removed all of its factory equipment during the Christmas holiday, leaving its employees without a job or a social plan, and a Swiss metalworking company that liquidated its French subsidiary without warning, leaving behind over 800 unemployed workers and a heavily polluted industrial site. Although the government has denounced the *patrons voyous* in the strongest terms, it has seemed powerless to prevent such actions, reinforcing a widespread belief in France that globalization has gone too far. Further inflaming public sentiment, in the summer of 2004, a series of French and foreign enterprises (Bosch electronics, Doux poultry, SEB kitchen products) renounced collective agreements that had reduced the working week to 35 hours. The companies forced their workers to accept longer hours and reduced pay by threatening to 'delocalize' production to countries with lower labour costs.

Economists have shown time and again that France benefits enormously from international exchange. Very few outward investments are motivated by the lure of lower taxes or wages, and a foreign presence is often a precondition for developing capacity in France. Still, incidents such as Bosch, Doux, SEB and the *patrons voyous* have reinforced a long-standing scepticism among the French public about globalization – and a growing anger towards politicians who fail to protect them from its perceived excesses.

The Chirac–Raffarin government is vulnerable on efficiency as well as equity grounds. By opting to move quickly and to privilege the political channel of reform over the corporatist channel, the government has been compelled to limits its ambitions. Lacking partners with whom to share the blame for painful or unpopular reforms, the government is wary of going too far and triggering mass protests. As a result, its reforms tend to fall well short of what is needed – inadequate, stop-gap, even symbolic, as opposed to comprehensive.

The pension reform is a clear example of a stop-gap measure. According to official estimates, the reform will cover only one third of the expected shortfall in 2040, and even this performance is contingent on a return to full employment (4.5 per cent unemployment) by 2010. The government has already announced its intention to revisit pension reform in 2008.

Other reforms leave problems half-resolved. The government has cut income and corporate taxes, but not spending. As a result, the budget deficit and public debt have risen to dangerous levels, jeopardizing the tax cuts to date. The government reformed the 35-hour working week, but did not repeal it, for fear of protests. While in theory the changes in the law permit employers to renegotiate working hours, few have exploited the opportunity, not wanting to open a new round of controversial negotiations and hoping that the government will eventually repeal the law altogether.

If most of the government's reforms offer partial solutions at best, the healthcare measures are largely an exercise in symbolic politics. The government claims that the reforms will raise €5 billion in revenues, while reducing spending by €10 billion, eliminating the deficit in the public health insurance programme by 2007. The sources of savings were never clearly spelled out, however, and the government steered clear of squeezing powerful doctors or pharmaceutical companies. It is not just the Leftist opposition that is dubious of promised savings; just before the healthcare legislation went to parliament, a note from the budget office of the Ministry of Finance estimated the savings at less than one-half the official figure. One week later, the National Health Insurance Council (CNAM) estimated the savings at only €5 billion, while noting that the secular trend in healthcare spending is an increase of €3 billion annually.

The Chirac–Raffarin government's strategy of limited liberalism through political channels, as opposed to more far-reaching reform through corporatist channels, has brought changes, for sure, but also risks. It is not entirely cynical to say that the government has introduced enough change, and done so in a sufficiently high-handed and regressive manner, to alienate large swathes of the French electorate, endangering its political future; yet it has not introduced enough change to resolve the economic problems that motivated reform in the first place. This uncomfortable positioning, along with personal rivalries within the governing majority, has opened a fundamental debate about the future direction of French economic policy.

Conclusion: the debate over French economic policy

The governing majority is increasingly divided between supporters of President Chirac and backers of his outspoken and famously ambitious UMP rival Nicolas Sarkozy. Sarkozy was Minister of the Interior from 2002 to March 2004, then Finance Minister until December 2004, when he left the government (at Chirac's insistence) to head up the UMP. Personal ambitions are at the heart of the conflict. Sarkozy makes no secret of his desire to become president in 2007, while Chirac wants to preserve the option of running again or, barring that, to choose his successor. The two men have developed an open dislike of each other, which can be traced to Sarkozy's support for Balladur in the 1995 presidential election (an unforgivable 'betrayal' in Chirac's eyes), and which provides entertaining fodder for the French press. Yet beneath the prickly personalities and ambitions, there is also a growing divide over the direction of economic policy.

Chirac's strategy has been to front load controversial, liberalizing reforms early in the mandate. At one point, he might have believed that these reforms would legitimate themselves by strengthening the French economy, or else that the general, worldwide recovery from the post-9/11 recession would raise his standing.

On the heels of the disastrous regional elections in March 2004, Chirac proclaimed a 'social turn' in government policy. Having implemented liberalizing reforms designed to strengthen the economy, it is now time to address social suffering. The reconstituted Raffarin government appointed Jean-Louis Borloo to head the Ministry of Employment, Labour, and Social Cohesion, a 'superministry', with five cabinet-level officials. In July 2004, Borloo presented a five-year, €13-billion 'social cohesion plan', the most notable feature of which is a return to the kinds of public internships and 'social treatment of employment' measures that Prime Minister Raffarin had so often denounced. Chirac has also announced the intention to increase state investment in education, training, innovation and research – all favoured programmes of the voters. The president has been far less clear on how he plans to pay for these measures, while reining in France's sizeable budget deficit.

The Chirac strategy, then, is to enact a pause in the programme of limited liberalization. His reasoning is that the government has implemented enough controversial, liberalizing reforms to insulate it against charges of inertia or ineffectiveness. The French economy is showing signs of recovery, with the growth forecasts for 2004 recently raised from 1.7 per cent to 2.3 per cent. If the recovery continues and unemployment falls, the Right will be in a strong position come the 2007 elections. In the meantime, new social measures and public investments will address the concerns over social justice and the necessary place of the state. France has had enough liberalizing reform for one term in office.

Chirac's conservative rival Nicolas Sarkozy by contrast is identified with advocates of intensified neoliberalism. This orientation can be traced in part to Sarkozy's former position as Minister of Finance, but it also corresponds to his convictions. Sarkozy is very close to the MEDEF both ideologically and by virtue of the fact that his older brother is a high-level figure in the movement. From the Sarkozy–MEDEF perspective, the problem of recent reforms is that they have not gone far enough. The government needs to fix the economy once and for all, through bold reforms, rather than half-measures.

In May 2004, Sarkozy reopened the debate over the 35-hour working week, stating that the reform was a mistake and should be modified. An able politician, he quickly added that the lengthening of the working week should be accompanied by an increase in pay. Chirac has also criticised the 35-hour working week, but argues that any changes should be negotiated through collective bargaining, rather than imposed by legislation. In addition to reforming the 35-hour legislation, the neoliberal wing calls for the repeal of the Jospin government's *loi de modernisation sociale*, which slightly increased the costs and the consultation requirements of economic lay-offs. Finally, Sarkozy has clashed repeatedly with Chirac over budgetary policy. Whereas Chirac has identified a multitude of priority public investments, Sarkozy declares that 'everything cannot be a priority'. Sarkozy challenged the president directly on defence spending and used his power to shrink the size of Borloo's social cohesion plan. Sarkozy has also pushed the government to move toward compliance with the Stability Pact, which is a much lower priority for Chirac.

Sarkozy is supported by two key constituencies of the Right, the employer association and the UMP. The President of MEDEF Ernest-Antoine Seillère has long urged the government to take advantage of its solid parliamentary majority to implement far-reaching neoliberal reforms, notably rolling back the 35-hour working week, facilitating economic lay-offs and reducing tax levels to the European average. In August 2004, Seillère moved from expressions of impatience to open criticism of the government, declaring that the administration 'has done nothing for business'. Two months later, when the government watered down a bill to liberalize lay-offs in response to union pressures, Seillère denounced 'little maneuvers leading to immobilism' and observed that 'economic stupidity (la bêtise économique) will not build a future for the country'. By contrast, Seillère has been effusive in his praise for Sarkozy, whom he describes as 'the Zidane of the economy', and the two men *tutoi* each other in public.

The UMP parliamentary group has also pushed the government to move in a neoliberal direction. In particular, parliamentarians have been lobbying for a reform of a wealth tax, the *Impôt de Solidarité sur la Fortune* (ISF). They argue that this tax encourages capital flight and because it is not indexed to inflation, it now reaches into the pockets of less affluent citizens. President Chirac strongly opposes any reform of ISF. Chirac believes that his repeal of the precursor to the ISF in 1986, which was widely unpopular, cost him the 1988 presidential election. Moreover, cutting the taxes of the super-rich is at odds with the 'social turn' that Chirac proclaimed following the regional elections. Prime Minister Raffarin, acting on Chirac's behalf, has regularly issued declarations that 'the reform of the ISF is not a priority of the government'. Still, as part of the 2005 budget package, Chirac and Raffarin were forced to accept two changes to the ISF: an indexing of the tax brackets to inflation and the possibility of deducting up to €10,000 invested in innovative small businesses (an idea put forward by Sarkozy). With the movement of Sarkozy from the Ministry of Finance to the helm of the UMP in November 2004, parliamentary pressures for additional liberalizing reforms can be expected to only intensify.

The position of the neoliberal wing of the Right, represented by Sarkozy, is that half-measures are not enough. More far-reaching neoliberal reforms of labour markets and public spending are needed to relaunch growth. In May 2004, Sarkozy established a commission under the former leader of the IMF Michel Camdessus to study the 'brakes on economic growth' in France. The Camdessus Report, issued in October, presented a clear neoliberal diagnosis (Camdessus, 2004). French growth has fallen off dramatically compared to the US and Britain. This decline (*décrochage*) is due to two factors: (1) a 'deficit of employment', stemming from shorter working hours and lower rates of employment, especially among the younger and older segments of the working-age population; (2) the 'excessive level and low effectiveness' of government spending. To turn the French economy around, the Camdessus Report recommends weakening restrictions on lay-offs, eliminating the distinction between fixed-term and permanent labour contracts, moderating annual increases in the minimum wage, encouraging part-time employment and cutting government spending by replacing only one-half of all retiring civil servants. Sarkozy and MEDEF have both praised the Camdessus Report, which is widely seen as an economic blueprint for Sarkozy.

Although Sarkozy is associated with neoliberal ideas, he is no Mrs Thatcher. In the spring of 2004, Sarkozy organized the rescue of Alstom, the failing manufacturer of high-speed TGV trains, effectively nationalizing the company in the process and preventing a takeover by the German multinational, Siemens. Moreover, Sarkozy's embrace of neoliberal ideas, particularly on the 35-hour working week, is carefully calculated to appeal to French employers and the UMP rank-and-file. Whereas Chirac is worried about the next national election and winning back moderate and low-income voters, Sarkozy has focused on winning the presidency of the UMP in November 2004, so his constituency has been the conservative mainstream and French employers. What will happen to Sarkozy's neoliberal leanings when he must reach out beyond the core conservative electorate is an open question. Nothwithstanding these electoral and personal considerations, the battle between Chirac and Sarkozy also attests to the enduring uncertainty about how to address the social anesthesia legacies of the *dirigiste* state. For Chirac, much of the work has been accomplished; for Sarkozy, it has only just begun.

Chapter 12

Education and Educational Governance

ALISTAIR COLE

Education is permanently near the top of the political agenda in France. It provides fertile terrain for the expression of competing ideological visions and contradictory social forces. It presents policy-makers with persistent resource dilemmas and presents difficult organizational challenges. In France, as elsewhere, investment in education and training has been one of the principal responses of governments to the rise of global economic forces. While governments have pushed the idea that countries need a highly trained workforce, there has also been a growing demand for educational provision from society. As a result of these converging forces, there has been a democratization of education in France during the past two decades. The numbers of pupils attending upper secondary schools (*lycées*) has grown strongly since 1984, when the then Education Minister J.-P. Chevènement announced the target that 80 per cent of an age cohort class should sit the *baccalauréat*. There has been a spillover effect on expansion in higher education. The past two decades have witnessed the emergence of a system of mass higher education in France, with 50 per cent of an age cohort now involved in post-secondary education or training.

This rapid expansion is, in most respects, a success story, but it has created its own set of problems. Expansion has brought in its wake fears that qualifications are worthless, and resentment that education does not always lead to employment. Expansion has also created new social actors, in the form of students and school pupils, whose capacity for collective action has surprised governments. The rewards to be derived from delivering education services are potentially great, but so are the hazards, in a context where educational demand appears insatiable. As a microcosm of society, schools (and to a lesser extent universities) are the site for the expression of many deeply ingrained social problems: problems of violence, of race relations, of economic deprivation, of diversity are played out in educational settings. In terms of logistics, the policy challenges of educational expansion are daunting. The growth of educational services has required more schools and universities, better equipment, more focused career advice. Provision of such varied services has mobilized new actors, such as local and regional

195

authorities, business organizations and voluntary associations. The need for good interorganizational collaboration has emerged as an important feature of the new educational governance in France.

Finally, education has a particular ideological resonance in France. No other policy arena is so redolent of the French Republican tradition. The founding fathers of the Third Republic (1870–1940) viewed schools as the means to integrate young citizens into the universal, lay and modern values of French Republicanism. A national education system was valued as a means of disseminating Republican ideals and subordinating France's provinces to an enlightened central state. The spread of national education through the nineteenth and twentieth centuries gradually broke down older regional barriers and inculcated a well-defined sense of Frenchness, not least through imposing the use of French over minority languages and regional dialects. There remains a close linkage today between a national education system and a centralized conception of French citizenship.

These various themes – human capital, social dynamics, public policy, ideology – can legitimately be treated from a variety of angles. Consistent with the underlying approach adopted in *Developments in French Politics*, we focus mainly upon how the structures of educational governance (institutions, interests, ideas) have evolved to cope with these new challenges, rather than with educational issues *stricto sensu* (such as academic disciplines or teaching methods), though we refer to the latter where appropriate. We begin the chapter by revisiting some traditional conceptions of French education. We then consider the modernization of the Education Ministry, the impact of political decentralization in secondary education and the move towards creating more autonomous universities in the higher-education sector. In the penultimate section, we discuss several recent events highlighting the resistance to change from professional interests and the secular lobby. We conclude that the past two decades have witnessed the emergence of interesting new forms of educational governance in France. Changes are partial and contested, however, and powerful forces within the education professional and policy communities resist them.

Centralization and the French education system

Centralization, uniformity and a neocorporatist policy style are traditionally presented as the principal macro-characteristics of the French education system (Ambler, 1985; Archer, 1979; Deer, 2002; Duclaud-Williams, 1993). Mary Archer's classic study provided a particularly influential framework for contrasting centralized and decentralized educational systems. The Archer model set up France as the paradigm of centralization. In the centralized system, the central state is the leading element, and all interactions are centripetal. Small modifications at the centre are felt throughout the system. In this model, a highly regimented education ministry guarantees the centralized State model. As an organization with 1,300,000 employees in 2004, the French Education Ministry is one of the world's largest bureaucratic structures. From the centralist perspective, the weight of this bureaucratic leviathan and the strength of the vested interests therein, is a powerful force favouring centralization. In theory, the education minister sits at the apex of a hierarchical, regimented organization, which is coherently organized in its Parisian headquarters (107 Rue de Grenelle). The main divisions within the education ministry are each directly responsible to the minister, as are the general and administrative inspectorates. The central ministry – *la centrale* – has a powerful outreach to French regions and localities through its regional and departmental field services (the 26 Rectorates and the 96 Academic Inspections in metropolitan France). At the bottom of the chain are the school heads in the primary, lower secondary (*collège*) and upper secondary (*lycée*) schools, directly responsible to the education minister, as well as to their own governing boards. The Archer model explicitly expects lower levels to implement rules and regulations that are defined by the centre.

In the orthodox representation, the centralizing forces in French education are sustained by a powerful bureaucratic–professional coalition. The civil servants of the main divisions within the education ministry and the powerful teaching unions act as the gatekeepers of professionalization at a national level. Ambler (1985) identified three neocorporatist features of French educational management: a mass membership trade union movement (then the FEN, now the FSU); a centralized form of bargaining and access to central policy-makers; extensive delegated administrative powers. As civil servants themselves, schoolteachers are organized into powerful trade unions which co-manage issues of salaries, pay and promotions with education ministry officials. As their support is essential for individual teacher mobility, the trade unions have a captive constituency amongst schoolteachers. This bureaucratic–professional coalition has a strong normative attachment to centralization as the only means of preserving public service, equality of opportunity and national standards.

We note in these accounts a strong dose of path dependency: the origins of the system perform a determining role for its future evolution. The institutions, interests and ideas that underpin the management of French education converge in favour of a national, uniform, state-centric system. For the rest of this chapter we engage with this prevailing representation. The educational challenges we referred to in the introduction require innovative responses that make classifying French education in terms of centralization infinitely more difficult. We look first at the process of administrative reform within the education ministry itself.

Modernizing the ministry

Under relentless pressure to deliver better services, the Education ministry has adapted its structures and reformed its central administration. The ministry has been amongst the most innovative in experimenting with various new management techniques, such as management by objectives ('projets de services') and financial decentralization ('globalization'). It has contributed to the effort to modernize the public sector through adopting new procedures of evaluation and contractualization (Champagne *et al.*, 1993; Thélot, 1994; Toulemonde, 2003). Education ministers (especially Jospin and Allègre) and a small group of top officials (within the *cabinet,* the Schools [DESCO], and Evaluation [DEP] divisions) have driven this reform process, which has encountered resistance from other civil servants in the central ministry and the field services. Reforming the administration was a particular concern of Claude Allègre (1997–2000). As Allègre set out more explicitly than any other recent education minister to reform the education ministry, we will focus our attention here on the 1997–2000 period.

One of Allègre's first acts as Minister was to eliminate 8 (out of 19) central divisions. Old divisions with powerful bureaucratic identities, such as the *Direction des Ecoles* and the *Direction des Lycées et des Collèges* were abolished. In their place, the *Direction de l'Enseignement Scolaire* (DESCO) brought together in one division two bureaux with highly distinctive organizational cultures. Allègre also engaged in ambitious attempts to introduce more flexible labour practices, to decentralize staff movement and transfers and to devolve more responsibilities to lower echelons of the education ministry. Some lasting reforms were implemented under Allègre. Since 1999, for example, staff transfers within the regions have no longer been managed by Paris, but have taken place at the level of the Academies (the field service of the education ministry). This measure posed a real threat to the power base of the SNES, the main secondary teachers' union, since the union dominated the committee in the Rue de Grenelle that determined staff transfers. As Allègre discovered to his cost, the successful implementation of educational policy still depends upon the acquiescence of the teaching unions. Though Allègre 'won' on staff transfers, he lost on a raft of other issues that the teaching unions opposed (teaching methods, school governance, the decentralization of some technical staff). Reforms that threaten the core interests of the teaching profession encounter the determined and often effective opposition of the teaching unions.

The most innovative change has been that of contractualization. In the words of one top-ranking official interviewed in June 2004, 'contractualization has transformed the ministry; the really interesting ideas are those coming from the academies, not the centre'. Contractualization has its origins in the Savary law of 1984, the Jospin law of 1989 and more generally in the dynamic process unleashed by Rocard's modernization of the public service. In the sphere of education, the first contractual experiments were carried out in the higher education sector; we consider these briefly below. Contractualization within the education ministry itself (as opposed to 'contracts' signed between the central ministry and the universities) was a by-product of Allègre's (1997–2000) determination to modernize the education ministry. Allègre introduced two specific types of contract: those agreed between the ministry and the regional field services of the education ministry (*contrats d'académie*); and those – initially limited to four pilot regions – concluded between the academies and individual schools (*contrats d'établissement*). Contractualization survived the change of government in 2002 and the first round of contracts signed in 1999 were complete by 2004. From the perspective of central government, contracts have been accepted across the administration as a useful management tool, as a 'modern' technique of central steering. From the perspective of local and regional actors, however, contracts open up new opportunities for building territorial coalitions around specific policy objectives that go beyond the capacity of any individual institutional actor.

Public-sector 'contracts' in the field of education are consistent with the main traits of French-style governance. They are not legally enforceable contracts. They are more akin to mission statements, setting out aims, objectives and means to achieve objectives, rather than mutually binding pledges. Unlike the State–Region planning contracts, moreover, education contracts are concluded between different actors within the education ministry. The *contrats d'académie* do not extend to external partners such as elected Regions, or parents. I have discussed these contracts in detail elsewhere (Cole, 2001). These contractual procedures represented organizational innovation in the context of the education ministry. For the first time, the academies were called upon to define their own pluriannual objectives, to set out a method for achieving these and to allocate resources for implementing goals from increasingly decentralized ('global') budgets. Within the financial limits imposed by the ministry, the academies are free to make policy choices, and to adapt their provision to specific local or regional needs. An academic inspector can decide to finance maternity education, for example, at the expense of regional languages. In at least some academies, contractualization came to be seen as a tool for developing closer contacts with the regional councils and social partners, the cooperation of which is essential for effective policy-making in vocational education.

During the past two decades, the education ministry has also become embedded in a complex set of localized partnership agreements and contractual relationships that go beyond the narrow confines of education. The ministry is a stakeholder in various local and regional networks aimed at poverty alleviation and combating social exclusion. The education ministry is the largest financial contributor to the City Contract programmes, for example, which are multi-agency initiatives aimed at alleviating poverty and improving social inclusion. In 80 per cent of cases City Contracts contain a specific chapter dedicated to Education (van Zanten, 2004). The education ministry is also involved in Local Security Contracts in partnership with the local authorities and the police. Within the ministry itself, there has been a policy of priority assistance to unfavoured schools or schools likely to experience violence. Education Priority Zones created by the Socialist government of 1981–86, represent the oldest policy programme aimed at targeting additional resources (money, teachers) to schools in underprivileged areas, especially in rundown suburbs. Through its participation in these various programmes, the education ministry has become involved in matters of health policy, economic development, social policy or security. It has been an active player in broadly based partnerships formed to tackle some of the worst problems of urban deprivation. City Contracts and Educational Priority Zones represent a significant departure from the traditional terms of the education debate, centred upon citizenship, equal opportunities and meritocratic selection.

In part in response to contractualization and enhanced institutional autonomy, evaluation has begun to make timid inroads into French education (Fixari and Kletz, 1996). At the level of the schools, there has been an increasing use of institutional audits. Since 1995, the education ministry has published league tables of school performance, classifying schools both in relation to their absolute and 'value-added' performance. In the sphere of higher education, evaluation was first introduced in the Savary law of 1984, which set up a National Evaluation Committee (*Commission nationale d'évaluation*: CNE) for universities. Universities are evaluated both in relation to their environment (their local political, cultural and economic contexts) and with respect to particular disciplines, where university departments are beginning to be measured on a scale from 4 (excellent) to 1 (inadequate) (Deer, 2002).

By comparison with the UK, evaluation is soft, rather than hard. Bodies such as the CNE are advisory committees, not autonomous agencies with funding powers, such as the Higher Education Funding Councils or the Quality Assurance Agency for UK universities. There are no imposed performance indicators (of the Research Assessment Exercise type in the UK) and there is, as yet, no clear linkage between evaluating performance and the allocation of resources, in either secondary or higher education. Within the French context of institutional underdevelopment, however, evaluations are an important evolution. Contractualization and evaluation both encourage greater diversity in provision, at secondary (through vocational streams) and higher education levels. Senior civil servants are now less important for the steering of higher education. Homogeneity of process and output is no longer regarded as a cardinal virtue.

Political decentralization and the secondary education sector in France

The governance of education in France has been influenced in various manners by political decentralization. The policy-makers of the early 1980s believed that the quality of educational services could be improved through increased school autonomy, and the involvement of the meso-level local authorities (the 96 departmental and 22 regional councils) in educational planning. The familiar arguments of proximity, of adaptation to local needs and of local participation were raised in education as in other policy fields. The involvement of locally elected councils in planning infrastructure (buildings and equipment) and making educational forecasts would alleviate the burden on the overloaded central state. Local and regional authorities would contribute to financing the efforts of national education policies. The commitment made in 1984 that 80 per cent of an age cohort should sit the *baccalauréat* required a large-scale expansion in the number of *lycees*; the new regional authorities would finance this expansion. Educational reforms (in 1983, 1985, 1989 and 1999) also attempted to open up schools to their external environment, notably through the creation of school projects (*projets d'établissement*), new teaching methods (team and tutorial teaching) and the involvement of parents, local authorities and local businesses on the governing boards of schools.

Education now represents a major service-delivery function on behalf of Regions, and Departments. It is by far the largest item of budgetary expenditure for the 22 regional councils, and generally the second item (after social welfare) in the 96 departmental councils' budgets. By 2003, there had been a 250 per cent increase in expenditure by local and regional authorities on education since 1985 (*Le Monde*, 5 June 2003). The real logic of the educational decentralization reform was arguably to decentralize responsibility for major items of educational expenditure, without the state losing control over educational policy. The state retained control over the core policy choices: course curriculum, overall pedagogical content, and the recruitment and management of teachers. In the education decentralization laws of 1983 and 1985, local and regional authorities were given several narrowly defined functions: new building operations, extensions and renovations to existing buildings, the supply of equipment for schools, provision for the daily functioning of schools and the – contested – right to produce educational forecasts. Within these narrow limits, the regions have responsibility for the *lycées* (upper secondary schools) and the departmental councils for the *collèges* (lower secondary schools). The 36,500 communes administer maternity and primary schools, as before. Control over core functions (staff movement between academies, overall pedagogical orientation and the distribution of financial resources to the academies) remains determined at the central level. Decentralization 'has gone much further than anyone expected' (van Zanten, 2004), however, as local and regional authorities have intervened at all levels of education, from maternity schools to university.

If the Jospin government focused on administrative reforms within the education community, the Raffarin government (2002–) was primarily motivated by decentralization *per se*, with educational reforms a by-product of decentralization and budgetary rigour. There were three aspects to the Raffarin government's decentralization programme as it affected education. The Raffarin government proposed to transfer technical, social service and medical staff to the Regions and Departments: to increase the responsibilities of the Regions for training, and to enhance university autonomy.

The most straightforward measure ought to have been that of the transfer of technical and service workers from the centre to the Departments (for the lower secondary schools, the *collèges*) and to the Regions (for the upper secondary schools, the *lycées*). There was an obvious logic to this reform: Departments and Regions have been in charge of buildings and main-tenance since the 1980s, but the technical and service workers are still nationally controlled. Raffarin proposed in March 2003 to transfer these workers to local and regional authorities. Far more controversial was the transfer of the educational health, social service and orientation workers. Though they were attached to schools, or groups of schools, these profes-sionals had their own national corps and were fearful of the consequences of decentralization. Most experts believed that transferring these profes-sionals to the Departments and Regions would improve service delivery – but not those professionals involved. Faced with massive opposition from the professions concerned and from the teachers, the Raffarin government announced in June 2003 that it would postpone the transfer of these staff for one year: 2005, instead of 2004.

The second theme was that of youth and young adult training. This was relatively straightforward, as the Regions already have a strong presence in this area. The Regions are involved at various levels of the education and training supply chain. Schooling is obligatory until the age of 16 years, but the Regions claim an influence in school-level planning, as choices made at 14 years will have an influence on the training and apprenticeship pro-grammes that the Regions must organize from 16 years onwards. Since 1987, the Regions have had the sole regulatory authority over apprentice-ships, which they organize and fund. Since 1993, the Regions have been given the main responsibility for planning post-school 16 to 26-year-old training and are required to draft an overall plan (the PRDF: *Plan Régional du Développement et de la Formation des Jeunes*) to this effect (Berthet and Merle, 1999). The Regions also have various programmes designed to foster lifelong learning and continuing education and they have contributed massively to the University 2000 scheme (see below). In practice, the Regions exercise a good deal of direct and indirect influence, especially in the field of vocational education. The Regions control apprenticeships and regulate the provision of training programmes for the 16- to 26-year-olds. Their influence spills over into the management of upper secondary schools, especially the vocational schools (*lycées professionnelles*). The head of the education ministry regional field service, the Rector, would not dream of opening a new vocational school (or even a general *lycée*) unless she had guarantees from the regional council that the appropriate level of equipment would be provided. Likewise, no school would open a post-*baccalauréat* technical class without consulting with the Region and the professional branches. The Regions have contributed to expensive investments in the vocational schools and the technical streams within general schools.

The local and regional authorities have definitely made an impact, way beyond their contribution to the total proportion of educational expenditure. They have renovated school buildings, built new schools and modernized the equipment used within schools. Certain councils have been increasingly ambitious in relation to educational content and have funded programmes of intensive language training, have given small group teaching grants or funded additional teacher training (Dutercq, 2003). In a more indirect manner, there is a regional political space, wherein elected Regions and state field service officials interact with regional lobbies such as the employers federation (MEDEF and its constituent elements), firms, chambers of commerce, trade unions and associations. This regional policy community has an influence on all decisions affecting vocational education and training. The smooth functioning of the system necessitates the cooperation of the State, the Regions and – increasingly – the professional branches (Cole, 2001). Regional leadership already exists *de facto* in many regions, but the fate of the 2003–4 reforms demonstrated that there remained much resistance to formalizing this.

We can also observe the emergence of territorial policy communities in the domain of higher education, the third of the major reforms announced by the Raffarin government that we now consider.

The university sector in France

There have been massive changes in the way French universities are run since 1985, as well as in relation to their position within society. Three changes in particular are worthy of note: the emergence of a system of mass higher education; the embedding of universities within their local and regional environments; and the development of more autonomous universities.

There has been a rapid university expansion since the early 1980s. Between 1980 and 1995, universities had to absorb an increase of 82 per cent in their student numbers (Musselin, 2003). French governments have used similar arguments in favour of developing the sector to those in the UK. Global economic competition and the need for a highly trained work-force have justified an important investment in human capital. From the early 1980s, French governments recognized that education was essential to allow France to compete in a post-industrial economy (where unskilled jobs would structurally decline). Expansion in high education would also allow the government to divert attention from a high youth unemployment rate. If, in the secondary sector, France has experienced a generalization of its vocational sector, the reverse is true in the higher education sector. Most expansion has occurred in the technical and vocational streams of uni-versity, and in private business schools (notably those run by the chambers of commerce). The technical *grandes écoles* remained relatively untouched by the democratization of the university sector. They remain highly elitist, meritocratic institutions that have been commented upon exhaustively elsewhere (see Howarth and Varouxakis, 2003).

The May 1968 events had a lasting importance in shaping ideas about the acceptable boundaries in French higher education. They created zones of non-decision-making, areas where no government would willingly venture. May 1968 embedded the belief that higher education is a public service open to everybody who has passed the *baccalauréat*. Formal selection is virtually taboo at the level of university entrance (though it is rife in the higher education system as a whole). When governments have attempted to introduce overt selection, they have faced powerful collective mobiliza-tion by students, as in the case of the failed Devaquet bill in 1986. The rise of the student movement as a social actor has been a corollary of the expansion of the university sector. Governments have been extremely cautious in their dealings with students. There have been repeated bursts of student anger – in 1986, 1993, 1995 and 2003 for example. Students have shown a remarkable capacity for collective action and for influencing educational policy. The demands articulated by student unions reinforce centralized forms of political action and the centralized structure of edu-cational decision-making.

As with schools, universities have also learnt the importance of positive engagement with their surrounding environments. Musselin (2003) argues there is a long tradition of universities engaging with their environment. After the 1982 decentralization reforms, there was renewed interest in the universities on behalf of the local authorities. Local authorities actively sought the implementation of branch campuses as a sign of vitality of their locality. Studies demonstrated that local university campuses were an important factor for economic development – firms were more likely to invest if there was a trained local labour supply. The University 2000 plan, launched by Jospin in the early 1990s, formally brought the local and regional authorities into the loop. Universities are now routinely included in the State–Region plans (Baraizé, 1996). For their part, local and regional authorities have seen the domain of research and development as one where they can make a difference. They have contributed to research budgets and sought to orient the direction of research.

The most significant governance change since 1985 has been the emergence of more autonomous universities. University level management has traditionally been weakly developed in France, because functions such as estates, finance and personnel remain with the centre. Since 1968, however, universities have slowly become more autonomous actors. The Faure law of 1968 gave universities a measure of freedom to organize their teaching activities. Moreover, by granting them the status of Public Corporations (*Etablissements Publics Scientifiques et Culturels*), it recognized them as institutions in their own right. The next turning point was 1989, with the implementation of the 1984 Savary law, which introduced four-yearly contracts between central government and the universities. Contractualization has had a great impact. It set in motion two parallel processes: it forced universities to define their projects, but it also constrained the central administration to reform itself. The central administration has become less organized on the traditional basis of academic disciplines, and more responsive to institutions in their localities. Even more than in the secondary sector, the ministry has had to develop tools of evaluation to measure the performance of individual institutions.

Universities have, by and large, played the game of contractualization. In their Strategic Plans (*projet d'établissement*), universities state their future priorities and detail the resources needed to achieve their goals. In return, the centre makes a number of financial commitments. Through contractualization, each university has had to define its own specificity, a major shift in the French cultural context. In terms of outputs, universities have been able to adapt the courses they offer within the framework of national degrees. The early contracts actually produced more teaching posts, though the sums involved in contractualization are small. There are a number of difficulties with contracts. It is easier to produce the *projets d'établissement* than to implement them. As with the academic contracts considered above, the State refuses to give iron financial guarantees. Budgets are annual affairs; pluri-annual planning is renowned for being discarded by annual budgets. Finally, the legal basis of these contracts is shady: as the universities are public corporations, the state is entering into a contract with itself.

The Raffarin government (2002–) came to office committed to enhancing decentralization, granting universities more autonomy and to reforming the 1989 Education Act. We considered decentralization above and at the time of writing the Green Paper for the promised new Education Act had not yet been published. The Ferry bill on university reform was presented in outline form to the unions on 9 May 2003. Several weeks later, the bill had already been postponed, the delay announced publicly by one of President Chirac's advisers. What follows is, thus, a summary of a bill that might never see the light of day. There were three main aspects to the proposals: to strengthen university autonomy, to encourage collaboration between institutions and to strengthen links with end-users. The Ferry proposals would invest universities with a real measure of financial autonomy, significantly lacking even under the Savary law. Until now, universities have had very limited financial autonomy, because they depend upon central government for most of their finance. Expenditure must follow strict budgetary headings. The main innovation is to introduce 'global' budgets, allowing universities to vire between budgetary headings and thereby giving them much greater flexibility. The functioning of universities would also be made more flexible. University presidents would be able to appoint their senior management teams without having to seek approval from the university representative committees. Universities would also be able to create or close departments without having to seek the approval of the ministry. The Ferry proposals also contained measures to facilitate the merging of smaller universities, to enhance cooperation with local and regional authorities and the business world and to embed evaluation as the counterpart of autonomy.

University autonomy is certainly limited by the standards of the 'Anglo-Saxon' countries. Universities do not possess all of the elements that would enable autonomy. They are not in control of their buildings, their staff or their administrative personnel, all of which are national. University presidents are still accountable to the central ministry. In spite of all of this, the emergence of universities as distinctive and variegated institutions is one of the most important features of French education in the past two decades.

In France, there has traditionally been little knowledge of other systems. Until the mid-1990s, intra-EU cooperation was limited to the exchange of students under ERASMUS schemes. The Europeanization of higher education has gathered pace rapidly under the 'Bologna process'. In 1998, on the initiative of French Education Minister Allègre, the education ministers of the four largest EU countries – the UK, Germany, France and Italy – committed themselves 'to harmonise the architecture of European higher education' (Musselin, 2003). French governments have been in the forefront of moves towards European harmonization, imposing the '3-5-8' (licence-mastère-doctorat) reforms on an initially reluctant higher education establishment. These moves have benefited from a cross-partisan political consensus, though there are various sources of resistance within universities (from students and certain academic disciplines). A number of French universities will move to the 3-5-8 cycle in 2004, with most others following in 2005. There have also been moves to create a European research space: notably through the European Commission's Framework programmes. Europeanization is another variable likely to increase the autonomy of universities within their national environment.

Resisting change in defence of public service and secularity

The existence of a centralized, uniform and secular state education system forms a powerful symbol of French Republican culture. Republican discourse has traditionally focused on the notion of equality, rather than equity (which recognizes diversity and initial inequality). In France, the polity, profession and students have all favoured an approach based on equality (Deer, 2002). This set of beliefs is essential to grasp, in order to understand why so much of the educational policy community appears to resist change in general and oppose decentralization in particular.

Elsewhere, I identified the struggle for control of the educational policy agenda in France between rival modernizing and traditionalist coalitions (Cole, 2001). While the modernizing coalition was willing to embrace innovations in educational practice, the traditionalist coalition equated any innovation with an attack on the public service ethos of education. This traditional viewpoint was strongest among the majority of secondary school teachers, most teaching unions (especially the SNES and UNSA) and traditionally minded inspectors. It had strong political support from within the Socialist Party (PS). These actors were profoundly sceptical about change. They adopted a traditional view of the role of the teacher as a transmitter of knowledge and of the academic disciplines (rather than institutions) as the basic organizing units in education. Above all, this group feared school autonomy and local influence, both of which are detrimental to an idealized vision of uniformity within the education system.

In 2003–4, teachers were particularly mobilized against the proposed decentralization reforms. In truth, there was no demand for decentralization from the academic or teaching professions. Decentralization was an option being pushed by international benchmarking organizations such as the OECD, but not one widely accepted by the educational community in France. The latter preferred to operate within the context of an understood national framework. The teachers unions and the Left strongly opposed the proposed transfer to the Regions and Departments of the 110,000 ancillary workers. From March to June 2003, there was a series of one-day strikes that mobilized 40 per cent–50 per cent of teachers and technical staff. By May 2003, the teaching unions were losing control of their grassroots to strike committees ('coordinations'), a recurrent phenomenon in social movements in France since the late 1980s. Most teachers opposed ideas of autonomy, decentralization and the invention of new managerial practices for they estimated that they threatened their professional status and standing.

Prime Minister Raffarin initially attempted to define education primarily in terms of decentralization and budgetary retrenchment, rather than substantive educational issues. He was eventually forced to backtrack, to launch a 'great debate' on education and to promise a new Education Act in 2005. The fate of Raffarin's first Education Minister Luc Ferry highlighted the difficulties of surviving in the education hotseat. Before becoming minister, Ferry had been president of the National Curriculum Council (*Conseil National des Programmes*) for 10 years and he came to office in April 2002 with a high capital of sympathy. By May 2003, he had been marginalized, with education being taken over directly by Raffarin and Nicolas Sarkozy the energetic Interior Minister. In June 2003, Sarkozy and Raffarin (not Ferry) announced that the decentralization of the ancillary staff would be postponed until 2005. Eventually, President Chirac had to reassure a sceptical electorate in his 14th July address, when he publicly reaffirmed that education was a governmental priority. Though the teachers did not get everything they wanted, this latest episode was testament to the ability of social movements and the inevitable contradictions of the sector to wear down education ministers. Ferry finally lost his job in the government reshuffle of April 2004.

Following the year-long findings of the Commission chaired by expert Claude Thélot, in November 2004 Education Minister François Fillon announced the measures that would form the substance of a new Educational Act (*loi d'orientation*), to succeed the 1989 Jospin law (*Le Monde*, 19 November 2004). The new Education Act, announced for early 2005, was due to be implemented from 2006. The government claimed that the new law would continue the process of democratization undertaken for the past century, consistent with the Haby law of 1975, which created lower secondary schools, and the Jospin law of 1989 which democratized secondary and, by extension, higher education. The proposed Fillon law reaffirmed the previous commitment that 80 per cent of an age cohort should sit the *baccalauréat* and that 100 per cent should leave school with some sort of qualification. For the first time, the law envisaged 50 per cent of an age cohort obtaining a higher education diploma.

As announced by the minister, the education bill was focused much more on issues of pedagogy than those of educational governance. The law emphasized the importance of all pupils mastering core skills in French, maths, information technology, citizenship and a foreign language (not necessarily English). The law announced a number of significant changes in the operation of the *baccaleauréat*, with a timid introduction of continuous assessment and a reduction in the number of core subjects assessed by examination only. In terms of educational governance, our principal concern in this chapter, the main provision of the proposed Fillon law was to strengthen the role and the classroom authority of teachers, who would now be given sole authority to decide whether failing pupils had to repeat a year (previously parents were associated with this decision). Against the advice of the minister, the law would create a High Council for the School (*Haut Conseil de l'école*) on the model of the High Council for the Audiovisual sector (*Conseil Supérieur de l'Audiovisuel*: CSA) as an independent agency charged with developing school programmes, a theme consistent with management reforms in this and other chapters (see Le Galès in this volume).

We have insisted in this chapter on the difficulties of developing educational policies acceptable to all. Perhaps unsurprisingly, the proposals immediately raised objections from both the main teaching unions and as well as leading parents associations. Teachers resented the new obligation to replace absent colleagues for up to three hours a week. Parents resented the new stipulation that only teachers could henceforth determine whether pupils should repeat a year. *Plus ça change ...*

To conclude this chapter, we consider two recent case studies that both throw light upon the powerful capacity for defensive mobilization by the teaching profession and the well-organized lay lobby. The first case concerns the teaching of regional languages, the second that of wearing ostentatious religious symbols at school.

The case of regional languages is chiefly interesting for how it revealed the existence of a powerful coalition resisting any changes that transgress the canon of secularity (*laicité*). On 29 April 2001, Jospin's second Education Minister Jack Lang signed an agreement with Andrew Lincoln, President of the DIWAN association of Breton-medium schools. Under the terms of the agreement, the 29 DIWAN schools (and their 2,300 pupils) would enter the public education service, an offer that was open to other language education movements (representing Basque, Corsican, Occitan, Catalan, Creole and Alsatien). This was radical, especially for a Socialist minister. For the most part, these schools already enjoyed 'contracted-in' status, rather similar to the denominational (mainly Catholic) schools. Becoming part of the public education service would give the schools much greater financial security. In return, they would be expected to teach as much French as other schools in the state sector. For opponents to the agreement within DIWAN, the schools would lose their specificity, as this provision would reduce the amount of time available for Breton.

Lang referred openly to the languages of France as a source of richness for the nation, a part of France's patrimony that must be preserved. The details of the Lang plan need not concern us here. The incident is principally interesting for demonstrating the depth of opposition it provoked. Opposition to the DIWAN agreement came from movements generally associated with the Left. The teaching unions were mainly against, as were the lay pressure groups (especially the National Committee for Lay Action [CNAL], powerful amongst teachers) and the main parents' association, the FNPE. In bringing its action, the CNAL complained that the agreement 'went against the principle of equality that underpins the Republic'. The education ministry itself was clearly divided between a sympathetic minister, on the one hand, and a reluctant top administration on the other. In November 2001, the Council of State advised against implementing the ministerial decree; in 2002 the Constitutional Council declared the agreement to be unconstitutional, on account of the 'immersive' teaching method whereby the language of instruction would be Breton, not French.

The DIWAN episode elucidated other interesting dynamics about micro-level educational decision-making in France. Had the agreement become law, the mayors of small communes within Brittany would have been faced with a major dilemma. The building and maintenance of state maternal and primary schools lies within the policy province of the communes, the smallest unit of local government in Europe. The mayors of small communes with existing DIWAN primary schools expressed unease about the prospect of taking over control of buildings and equipment once the 2001 decree had come into force. In some cases, supporting the DIWAN primary school might have led to closure of a longer-established state school. The prospect of closures also strengthened the national trade union federations in their opposition to the agreement, as well as the lay parents–teachers associations. Opposition to the agreement was firmly grounded in the orthodox Republican notion that equality precluded the acceptance of diversity within the state education service (as opposed to the 'contracted-in' private sector). Opposition also included the defence of established positions and trade union interests.

The second, more recent, case concerns the 2004 law that forbids pupils from wearing 'ostentatious' religious symbols in school (the veil, the kippa, the cross). The law on *laicité* is considered in more detail by Sophie Duchesne's chapter in this volume, as its consequences go well beyond the domain of education. From the perspective of the Republican lay lobby pushing for this reform, clear rules must be implemented to solve the contradictions of a multicultural society. During the repeated 'headscarf' affairs since 1989, many schoolteachers championed the Jacobin notion of the one and indivisible Republic and the concept of secularity. The principle of secularity is one traditionally espoused by the Left, dating back to the Third Republic when, as a result of the laws of 1881 and 1882, national unity in France was cemented by a system of secular primary schools. According to the partisans of this vision of society, the Muslim girls wearing the veil at school were negating Republican values since they were visibly differentiating themselves from other pupils and in so doing drawing attention to their religion. The secular school should permit no distinctive sign indicating the religious denomination of the pupil. Instead the defenders of the secular vision argued that Islam and indeed any religion should be practised in private, and that preferably Muslims should be persuaded to endorse secular values.

The cases of DIWAN and the 2004 law on *laicité* both illustrate, in rather different ways, the continuing pertinence of traditional secular frames of reference within the public education service, beliefs that shape a distinctive construction of reality and that impose boundaries on acceptable reforms.

Conclusion

The French state remains the principal player in French education policy-making. Even in its decentralized version at the level of the academies, the education ministry is a vast bureaucratic structure that controls far more resources than any other. Habits of centralized thinking remain very strong. National education traditions underpin values, norms and rules, as well as remaining deeply embedded in the consciousness and the behaviour of the actors. As we observed with the example of the teachers, deeply embedded ideas (of public service or academic integrity) and interests (teachers as a social movement) have combined to limit the development of schools and universities as more autonomous institutions.

At the same time, in education as elsewhere, the past two decades have seen the emergence of new forms of steering at a distance. The diminishing capacity of the central State as an educational policy actor has contributed both to internal changes within the education ministry and to the greater opening up of the education system to its external environment. The distinct practices of contractualization (within the education ministry, with the universities, between State and Region, within localities) and decentralization are powerful symbols of this. Rather than insisting upon uniform solutions across the national territory, contractualization and decentralization have encouraged local and regional differentiation, and the adaptability of educational systems to their overarching environments. The introduction of measures of positive discrimination in the Education Priority Zones (ZEPs) or the City Contracts goes in the same direction. There is much more than unites France with its European neighbours in this process than that which sets it apart from them. There have been common pressures across developed nations to improve economic performance by investing in human capital. There have been common efforts to develop more vocationally relevant forms of education, while raising general educational standards. The close linkage between education and economic performance operated by policy-makers has driven the move to mass secondary and higher education in France as elsewhere. Even if educational policy communities remain inward-looking, the direction of change has been for the gradual opening up of educational institutions to their external environment. The recent Europeanization of French higher education suggests that this process will continue.

Chapter 13

Gendering the Fifth Republic

AMY MAZUR

A new model for gender equality politics may be emerging on the French political scene. It incorporates a feminist approach to policy and politics. Here, government action is designed to tackle the deep-seated social causes of inequality between men and women and to change established gender roles that have served as obstacles in providing women with at least the same opportunities, if not the same results as men. A slow transition to the new model has become increasingly evident since 2000 in the context of a set of conditions that have put into question the prevalence of gender-biased Republican attitudes and the resulting resistance of key policy elites to feminist actor demands. This chapter first presents the legacy of the past – the over 250-year-old gender-biased universal model. It then turns to an analysis of the context for new beginnings in gender politics in France; or at least a shift in the direction. A shift that may very well be weathering the return of the Right to power in 2002. The third section assesses the degree to which the new model is concretely driving recent state action, adopted under governments of both the Left and the Right, that explicitly aims to strike down gender-hierarchies and promotes women's status, right or conditions; in other words feminist policy. At the centre of this discussion, is a perennial issue for feminist policy formation: to what degree are formal policy statements actually implemented in authoritative policy that closes the gap between men's and women's status and rights? In others words, when do feminist policies go beyond 'symbolic politics' (Edelman 1985)?

The legacy of the past: gender-biased universalism

A gender-biased universal approach to sex equality issues has been inextricably linked to the emergence and consolidation of the Republic and the welfare state. This approach contains two quite contradictory aspects: gender-blind universalism and gender-biased attitudes about women's and men's roles. The 'equality principle', since the Revolution of 1789, has emphasized pure equality between individuals and not groups, unless class interests are concerned, where equal treatment is accentuated over equal opportunity. From this deeply embedded standpoint in political culture and the operating principles of mainstream political actors both inside and outside the state, the identification of citizens in terms of specific group affiliation undermines the core principle of equality. This rejection of articulating policy and rights in terms of group interests is part of the well-established Jacobin suspicion of 'special interests'. The insistence on universalism makes it difficult formally to target women as a group when there is the need to assess how women's and men's different situations lead to inequality.

In contrast to the sacrosanct principle of universal equality, social policy has tended to promote notions of women's and men's roles that define women as primary family caretakers who combine part-time work with family obligations, and hence need to be protected, and men as full-time workers with few family obligations. In this view, women are seen as potential mothers and a reserve pool of labour and men as full professional and public participants. As a result, France's well-known family policy since the turn of the last century has sought to protect motherhood and boost the birthrate rather than to help men and women reconcile family and work obligations. With some of the most generous paid family leave anywhere and mandatory school for three-year-olds ('*école maternelle*'), the French system provides more flexibility to working mothers, but not working fathers, than most Western democracies. Driven by the same natalist logic, family allowances, called maternal salaries up to the late 1970s, have been provided since the Second World War essentially to pay mothers not to work – the more children the higher the allowance. While the women's rights ministers in the Socialist governments in the 1980s recognized the gender-biased nature of family allowances, Socialist family ministers instituted and increased a new child-rearing allowance given to couples with children, when one of the parents did not work. Both Left-wing and Right-wing governments have since maintained and/or increased the child-rearing allowance for additional children. Only a fraction of these allowances have been used by men – 8 per cent in 2002. Governments have consistently provided day-care allowances for home-care rather than developing low-cost day-care centres that would better serve lower-income families and help poorer women move up the economic ladder.

Similarly, French policy since the end of the nineteenth century has sought to protect women from the vicissitudes (*sic*) of work in order to protect their child-bearing capabilities. This protectionist approach was formally ended with the adoption of a 2000 law that lifted the century-old ban on women working at night as a result of a 1999 European Court of Justice proceeding and long-term opposition to protectionism by organized feminism. Until recently, efforts to push for authoritative policies that challenge these gender-biased assumptions and/or gender public policy discussions have tended to be undermined by a double standard of, on the one hand, holding up the value of pure equality without difference, and on the other, of promoting policies that are constructed on and perpetuate traditional differences in men's and women's roles.

Explaining the shift in 2000: the social and political context

Key developments in the social and political context provided an unprecedented set of conditions in the late 1990s to challenge dominant Republican norms on gender-equality issues and compel policy-makers to change their approach to feminist policy issues.

Persistent sex-based inequities and changing public opinion

Forty years following the explosion of new women's movements onto the political scene in the 1960s and the seismic shifts in gender relations triggered during that period, significant gaps in men's and women's status persist. The year 2000 is an important tipping point given the way in which persistent sex-based inequities are increasingly taken into account by feminist policy experts, the media and by public opinion. Feminist experts have used statistics on men's and women's status to draw attention to sex-based discrimination and inequities since the mid-1960s. Since the 1980s, the national statistics office, in collaboration with state-based women's policy offices, has published a regular series of aggregate statistics comparing men's and women's status (for example, INSEE, 2004). In the late 1990s, in response to the feminist demand for more accurate instruments for evaluating sex-based discrimination at the individual level, femocrats – the bureaucrats who work women's policy agencies – and gender equity experts initiated and developed sophisticated analytical instruments to be used by official policy actors to measure the complex causes of gender-based inequities.

In terms of economic status, while women with and without children have been entering the workforce in increasing numbers each year since the 1970s and the number of men has slightly decreased, women are still well behind their male counterparts, with very slow progress towards narrowing the gap. Much of the difference stems from the high rate of women in part-time jobs. In 2002, over 80 per cent of all part-time jobs were held by women. Thirty per cent of working women were in part-time work and 5 per cent of working men in 2002; in 1982 18 per cent of women worked part-time (*Services des Droits des Femmes*, 2004). Another indicator of stagnation is the persistent 20 per cent wage gap between men and women since 1980. A 2002 INSEE study, widely reported on in the media, produced the 'surprising' result that women's salary situation has actually worsened since the 1970s while men's has improved (*La Croix* 1, August 2002). Women's and men's unemployment rates have become more similar, but there is still a sex-gap of 2.2 per cent for all age groups and 4.6 per cent for 15–24-year-olds (*Service des Droits des Femmes*, 2004, p. 12). Occupational segregation remains the norm; women work much more frequently than men in sectors/levels with lower salaries. In 2004, 30 per cent of women held managerial posts in the private sector, while 55 per cent of all women were trained to be managers (*Le Monde*, 9 March 2004). The feminization of poverty has been increasing since the mid-1990s as well. A two-tiered employment system appears to be a permanent fixture in which sex gaps are narrowing in higher income groups and widening for lower groups (Laufer, 2003). The division of labour in the home has not appeared significantly to change either. In 1999, women spent twice as much time as men on domestic chores; only slightly less than in 1986 (INSEE, 2004: p. 119).

The poor record of sex equality is even more pronounced in politics. The percentage of women in the National Assembly went from 2 to 12 per cent after 1958, in City Councils from 2 to 22 per cent from 1971 to 1995, from 3 to 10 per cent in departmental councils after 1971, and from 2 to 11 per cent of all mayors after 1971 (Pinochon and Derville, 2003). In 1977, 12.5 per cent of the ministers in the Barre government were women, in the first Raffarin government from 2002–4, 26 per cent were women, with an all-time high of women ministers under the second Jospin government (1999–2002) at 33 per cent. The percentage of women in upper civil service positions went from 4.5 per cent in 1983 to 16.5 per cent in 2003 (*ibid.*: p. 55).

Recent public opinion polls indicate that the French are critical of the slow progress in gender equality and that criticism has been growing more acute in recent years. In 2004, 69 per cent of men and women said that there was much more to be done to improve gender equality (*Sofres/ Pélerin* February 2004), while 72 per cent state that the top priority for improving equality was to make men's and women's salaries and qualifications identical. A 2003 poll of men and women shows that 60 per cent of women and 50 per cent of men perceive that women suffer more than men from discrimination at work (*Cergors/Sofres* 2004 *www.tns-sofres.com*). Sixty-six per cent of women and 63 per cent of men expressed their desire to have a woman mayor (*CSA/Lunes* cited in *Le Monde*, 12 January 2001). The major weekly women's magazine, *Elle*, has conducted a series of polls of women since 1980. In 1980, 27 per cent of women stated that domestic tasks were constraining, in 2000 42 per cent of women gave the same answer (consulted at *www.tns-sofres.com*) In 1980, 54 per cent of women polled ranked the necessity to increase the family budget as the most important reason for women to work. In 2000 56 per cent ranked the necessity to earn a living as the most important reason. On the question of whether women's situation was worse than men's, there was little change from 1974 to 2000. On the issue of salaries, 79 per cent in 1974 said that women's situation was worse, compared to 83 per cent in 2000 on the same answer. Only 17 per cent of women polled in 2000 indicated that they thought women's representation had improved since the 1980s. In addition to the criticism, recent polls indicate that dominant gender roles may be in flux. In a 2001 poll, 52 per cent of men expressed the view that they would like to be able to take parental leave of 15 days or more and 60 per cent of women were in favour of daddy leave (*ibid.*).

Renewal of the feminist movement in the late 1990s

Another important contextual factor is the emergence of an issue-based and organized feminist movement, based for the most part outside the orbit of the political parties and trade unions of the Left. Overcoming the deep divisions over strategy and coalition-building and a propensity for anti-system stances in the 1970s, broad-based coalitions of feminist groups, called *collectifs* or *coordinations*, have mobilized around issue-specific campaigns to support specific policy reforms. With some organization after the 1995 strikes, the bulk of the activities gathered momentum in the late 1990s and has continued at the same pace up through 2004. The more prominent groups include: *Mix-Cité, Ni Putes-Ni Soumise, Les Sciences Potiches, Clasches, Féminin-Masculin, Chiennes-de-Garde; Coalition des Associations pour les Droit de l'Avortement et de la Contraception (CADAC), Collectif National des Droits des Femmes (CNDF); Demain la Parité; Association des Violence Faites contre les femmes au Travail (AVFT),Voix d'Elles, Marie-pas Claire*, and *Nanas Beurs*. The Internet has been an important tool for mobilization; all groups have their own website.

Issues of class and race have been an integral part of this revival. For instance, Ni Putes-Ni Soumise – (neither whores, nor submissive (s)), was created in 2002 by young, first-generation French women of sub-Saharan and North African descent, from the poor suburban ghettos of Paris. They used the brutal death of a 17-year-old woman, found burnt to death in a dumpster by her boyfriend for disobeying Islamic law, as a symbol for their political activities, which focus on sexism and violence against young women living in the ghetto. The group held major national meetings and organized several nationwide rallies, attracting over 40,000 people. New feminist scholarly and movement-oriented journals serve as crucial public platforms for the development and dissemination of women's movement positions and policy recommendations in the issue-specific campaigns. The National Association of Feminist Studies (ANEF) brings together gender experts and is also an important venue for women's movement activities inside and outside academia.

Women's commissions in the Left-wing trade unions and political parties, important and effective linkages between feminist actors and party and union leadership in the late 1970s and 1980s, have had less of a presence in the feminist renewal. More recently, representatives tend to make public appearances and lend formal support only when asked to by women's groups. The commissions do not try to convince often reluctant leaders to support feminist issues either. The women's commission in the Socialist party, one of the more important feminist conduits between party and state, has been strikingly absent from recent feminist activities. The fading Communist party and the Greens take vocal positions on women's rights issues, but have few direct links to specific feminist groups. The increasing weakness of the trade unions also undermines the influence of the once active women's commission.

Women's policy agencies: an increasing institutionalized presence in the state

State-based agencies that promote gender equality and the people who work for them – femocrats – have been important players in feminist politics since the mid-1960s. Since the first study group on women's employment was established in 1965, there has been a plethora of different structures at national and sub-national levels. Since 1974, when the centre–Right government created the first Deputy Minister of Women's Condition to the current Deputy Minister of Parity and Equal Employment under the Right-wing Raffarin government, there has been a ministerial portfolio dedicated to women's rights issues for 23 out of the 30 years, under governments both of the Left and Right. Since 1978, regional and departmental field offices have operated under the authority of first the ministerial office and, beginning in the early 1980s, under a central women's rights service, the *Services des Droits des Femmes*. An extensive network of women's rights information centres, funded by the women's rights administration, has developed throughout the country as well. In 2000, women's policy agencies employed over 500 people, a small portion of which had full-time civil servant status jobs. Since the early 1980s, the women's policy offices have provided crucial financing to women's groups and feminist academics and have worked closely with certain groups, depending on the politics of the government in power.

There are currently seven commissions under the aegis of the women's rights ministries and administration. Commissions typically include representatives from organized business and labour, experts and pertinent women's groups. Under some governments, but not all, feminist group representatives have been asked to participate. The commissions have different statutes and degrees of permanence and are usually created by the prime minister or president as a response to specific pressing policy issues. Their principal role is study and recommendation. Governments have often used the commissions to stall on taking concrete action over controversial issues. The Women's Rights Minister has the authority to call these commission, into session and often chooses not to do so. None of the commissions has any enforcement authority or permanent staff to evaluate policy.

From 1993 to 1997, under Right-wing governments, the budget of the Women's Rights Service was reduced and the ministerial post removed. In the first year of the Socialist government in 1997, under Lionel Jospin, this trend was continued. In 1998, following direct feminist pressure and in response to rising public awareness about gender-equality issues, Jospin named a Deputy Minister of Women's Rights and Job Training, placed under the authority of the Ministry of Social Affairs and restored the budget. Several of the moribund commissions were reconstituted and the new minister created a Parliamentary Commissions on Women's Rights in the Senate and the National Assembly in 1999. A delegation of women's rights was also established in 2000 in the Economic and Social Council.

With the defeat of the Socialists in 2002, a ministerial office was not included in the initial government. In June, after one of the more powerful feminist groups, the CNDF, made a public call for a ministry of women's rights, the ministry was restored and upgraded to a Delegate Minister of Parity and Equal Employment. In the most recent reshuffle in 2004, the ministry became a full-fledged Ministry: a status unequalled since the heyday of women's policy offices under the Socialists in the mid-1980s. Many feminist observers are dubious about the extent to which the new ministry is dedicated to sustaining the women's rights administration and actively pursuing feminist polices, given the poor record of many Right-wing governments on women's rights issues. It appears that the Minister may be looking to down-size both the central and territorial women's rights administration. Feminist campaigns in 2003–04 to protect the stature of the Service may make it more difficult for this down-sizing to occur and the new Minister Nicole Ameline may need the Service given the extensive feminist activities her Ministry has announced in the Equality Charter presented to the public in 2004.

Beyond the nation-state: the EU, the UN and the 'boomerang effect'

Since the early 1970s, the European Union has put into place an active policy that targets primarily equal employment in paid work. French feminists contributed to the formulation of the EU equality directives and used them to persuade French policy-makers to adopt equality policies in France. Up until recently, the EU dynamics contributed in part to a symbolic imperative (Mazur, 1995b). The 1997 Treaty of Amsterdam introduced a generalized approach to gender inequalities, 'gender mainstreaming', that is intended to compel governments to treat gender-equality issues systematically across all sectors of policy. First introduced via the UN women's policy conferences in the early 1990s, mainstreaming has become a central focus of EU gender equality policy since 1997 through financial incentives and soft law. Feminist activists, femocrats and policy experts throughout Europe support efforts to implement gender mainstreaming as long as it is used as a tool to promote gender equality and not as a strategy to dilute or eliminate feminist policies.

United Nations feminist activities since 1995 have also become an important rallying point for feminist activities in France, as in other countries and across countries through new transnational feminist mobilization. Through its worldwide women's policy conferences and the ratification process of the Convention for the Elimination of Discrimination Against Women (CEDAW), the UN actively pursues developing feminist networks worldwide, at all levels of government, to promote women's rights and gender equality policy. The 1995 Women's Conference in Beijing was the culmination of an emerging transnational feminist movement and an indication of the saliency of global feminism. The governments of many countries, including France, took seriously the process of preparing a formal report for the conference – a society-wide consultation was held in 1994, coordinated by women's policy agencies. The success and salience of the 1995 UN process led to a follow-up called Beijing-plus-5: providing a second opportunity for feminists to place pressure on governments and governments to evaluate the progress in gender equality. A second more comprehensive consultation of women's groups throughout France was made, this time under the coordination of the Deputy Minister of Women's Rights, which gave the process more legitimacy than in 1995. A worldwide march for women in the context of the Beijing-plus-five conference was organized in 2000. The French part of the march attracted 10,000 people in Paris alone (*Le Monde*, 6 February 2000). Both the EU and the UN therefore were important sites for the 'boomerang effect' (Keck and Sikkink, 1998) in the late 1990s, where local, sub-national and national-level feminists in state and society have used and contributed to feminist policy efforts elaborated beyond the nation-state to place pressure on their governments and, in doing so, have successfully contributed to the development of more authoritative policy and strengthened their own organizational influence.

Does the Left in power matter?

Keen observers of feminist politics in France and other countries often argue that Left-wing governments are more supportive of gender equality than their Right-wing counterparts. Comparative studies show increasingly that Left-wing governments are not as feminist-friendly as this conventional wisdom asserts. This appears to be the case in France as well. It is clear that many feminist-friendly polices were adopted under Left-wing governments in the 1980s, early 1990s and that women's policy agencies have benefited from strong support under Socialist governments. It is important to note, however, that many of the earlier feminist reforms that made the first step to improve women's rights were adopted under Right-wing governments, before the Socialists came to power. Moreover, the extensive women's policy machinery found in France today was put into place under centre-Right governments under President Giscard's leadership. Likewise, some of the most ineffective equal employment reforms were adopted and implemented under the PS's watch and governments of the Right and the Left have both supported policies that have made it difficult for women to advance on the same footing as their male counterparts. Socialist governments too have downgraded the women's policy machineries and have been resistant to feminist calls for policy change, particularly from 1988–1993, when organized feminism was at a low point.

In the current period, both the Jospin and Raffarin governments were initially reluctant to appoint ministers of women's rights in their initial governments; both responded to feminist criticism to do so. As the next section shows, while many feminist reforms were adopted under the Left-wing Joplin majority, the Raffarin government appears to be continuing the new approach in feminist reforms. Thus, more than a shift to a Left-wing governing majority by itself, the across-the-board feminist policy reforms from 2000–4 may be more a result of the changing context that this second section has mapped out; a context that makes it difficult for policy-makers in governments of both the Right and the Left to ignore demons for more authoritative feminist policy.

New beginnings: symbolic politics as usual or a new approach to feminist policy?

Although not an exhaustive analysis of all feminist policies, recent developments are examined in several key areas to assess the degree to which a shift away from the gender-biased universal approach to gender policy may have been occurring since 2000.

Reproductive rights: law of 4 July, 2001

Legalized definitively in 1979, French abortion law can be viewed as one of the most pathetic laws on abortion in Europe. Abortion on demand was provided if the woman was in a 'state of distress' up to 10 weeks into the pregnancy, well below the European norm. Minors were required to have parental permission, doctors could refuse to provide abortions and counselling was required prior to the procedure. The restrictions of the law and the resistance of the health administration to put adequate funds into abortion services had led to a crisis in women's reproductive rights by the late 1990s. Fewer and fewer services in hospitals provided abortion and women were forced to leave the country to get abortions. Since the Socialist government in 1982, under the pressure of the Women's Rights Ministry, had allocated state funds to cover two thirds of the cost of abortions, government policy had been silent on abortion and contraceptive issues.

In 1999, with increasing pressure from a well-supported CADAC (with its 150 member groups) the Jospin government, through Minister of Social Affairs Martine Aubry, initiated a new campaign for reproductive rights, issued a report on abortion provision and promised to reform abortion and contraceptive rights.

Taking two years to be adopted, due to opposition from the medical establishment and a comparatively moderate pro-life movement – by the time the law was presented to parliament Minister Aubry had removed her support of the reform – the 2001 law responded to many of the demands of the feminist campaign: the extension of the period for legal abortion to 12 weeks and up to 14 weeks in cases of emergency; ensuring that abortions would be provided in public hospitals where doctors refused to perform them; removal of the requirement for parental permission; elimination of required counselling; reduction of penalties for abortions after 12 weeks; and legalization of sterilization. The law also legally connected contra-ception and abortion rights for the first time; a consistent feminist demand for over thirty years.

While on one hand press reports and feminist observers drew attention to the slow implementation of the new policies, to resistance of doctors in public hospitals, and to low levels of public funding for the new abortion services, on the other, the formal obligations of the new law engaged public officials in the health administration to comply. Furthermore, in the Right-wing government's Equality Charter, 11 out of 30 detailed measures on women's health targeted implementation, including informing women of the new rights in low-income areas and the DOM-TOM and reorganizing hospital administration to better accommodate the expanded services. The Upper Council on Sexual Information, Regulation of Births and Family Education, with the participation of 51 groups, including the CADAC and the feminist Family Planning Association, brought women's groups into the process of overseeing the implementation of the new law. Although the CADAC, according to one source, was asked to leave the Upper Council in 2002 and the Minister of Health publicly discussed the rights of the unborn fetus as patient, it appears, at least through the work of the Parity Ministry, that the feminist intent of the law may be respected.

Equal employment – Génisson Law of 9 May 2001

Since the first equal employment laws were adopted in the 1970s up to the adoption of the 2001 law, a clear symbolic imperative has operated in this second area of feminist policy. The 1983 Roudy law put into place a voluntaristic process of asking management and trade unions in the firm to report annually on women's and men's status in order to develop equality plans for the firm to bring women up to speed with their male counterparts. With no penalties given to the actors for non-compliance, no authority given to the Commission established by the law to monitor the new process, no real interest on the part of trade unions and management to pursue the new programmes, and virtually no powerful feminist groups coming forward to promote the programmes, equal employment policy was publicly recognized a failure. One paper called the equality contracts a 'fiasco'.

The Socialist government's 1999 announcement of a new law was met with the usual suspicious feminist criticisms and lack of enthusiasm by even its proponents. There was little fanfare for the 2001 law, even though it had been the direct by-product of an intense consultation with the social partners and feminist policy actors in 1999 by Socialist deputy Catherine Génisson, who presented the law. Only the CGT's equality commission took a public stand on the issue at a conference which the union sponsored on women's employment. The law made the annual report-equality contract a legal obligation, subject to fines, provided more details about the specific indicators to be used in comparing men's and women's status in the firm, and, for the first time, included provisions for equality measures in the civil service.

With implementation orders put into place in Autumn 2001, the few actors interested in the law were highly sceptical of any significant change in the symbolic imperative. The Socialist government created a new committee to study the low presence of women in the civil service and launched a campaign to promote the revised equality measures. The Deputy Minister of Women's Rights was the lead office neither on proposing the law to parliament nor in its implementation, due in part to the lack of support the parent Minister Martine Aubry gave to feminist positions in general. In addition to withdrawing support from the abortion reform, Aubry had opposed including any feminist positions in the reforms on the 35-hour working week. As a result, the permanent Council created to oversee equal employment, under orders from the Aubry Ministry, was not called into session. To date, no fines have been given for non-compliance. Nonetheless, since the victory of the Right in 2002, several developments indicate that social partners may be engaging in the reformed measures.

Five major firms signed equality agreements and made promises to take concrete steps to address the thorny problem of salaries. President Chirac hosted the CEOs of the firms in February 2004 to applaud the agreements, present the firms as examples and to discuss a broader agreement to be signed by private sectors on employment equality. Chirac is the first president actively to promote the detailed process of equality. Equality experts indicate that these plans are sound and represent a new desire on the part of business leaders to become involved with equality. Reflecting this new interest, the major employer's union initiated a general equal employment agreement signed by all trade unions except for the FO. In contrast to the virtual absence of organized feminism in the implementation of the equality programmes prior to 2001, firm-based networks of women, such as Inter-elles, began to appear to take advantage of the equality measures.

The Minister of Parity has a major focus on equal employment, given the inclusion of the concept of *égalité professionnelle* in its title and given that one third of the actions in the Equality Charter are centred on the different aspects of equal employment policy. Reflecting the Right-wing's hands-off approach to business, Ameline is focusing the ministry's attention on educating business leaders and developing a new equality 'label' for firms to adopt. Whether the new support for equality efforts on the part of firms, organized labour and management, and the president's office breaks the symbolic imperative of this policy area remains to be seen. As one feminist expert asserted, whereas managers clearly understand the importance of women in the workforce and support the idea of gender equality, they are unwilling to establish specific indicators and targets to achieve equality in the firm. With a government that appears reluctant to enforce the new penalties for non-compliance, the equality stalemate that has become the industry norm may not be so easy to end.

Reconciliation: 2001 paternity Leave

Breaking with the gender-biased nature of past family policy, policy actors involved with family policy appear more to favour pursuing policies that provide real choices for working mothers and fathers to fairly reconcile home and work duties. Numerous conferences organized by the state-based offices responsible for family issues are well attended and have included a significant component on reconciliation. More than organized feminism, it has been individual feminist experts and femocrats that have made strong arguments for including reconciliation issues in family policy. For instance, Dominique Méda, a graduate of the *grande écoles* and *chargée de mission* in a feminist policy unit in the ministry of education, has become the guru of reconciliation policy; her numerous books on the topic are widely read (e.g. Méda, 1999). The reform that reduced the working week in 1999 to 35 hours was seen by many feminist advocates as an opportunity to formalize a government stance that promoted sharing work and family obligations between men and women. The society-wide discussion on the laws barely mentioned gender issues and the final law gave no specific directions for making sure that working week reduction would not further marginalize women. Nonetheless, feminists are still hopeful that the reduction of the working week will give men the opportunity to spend more time to share in family responsibilities.

In 1999, the Prime Minister's newly created Council of Economic Analysis issued a report that asserted that women workers were a key to economic growth and that family policy needed to be more feminist. In 2001, the Socialist government sponsored the first government effort to promote paternity leave. A budget law provided pay for working fathers to leave their jobs for up to 11 days after the birth of their child. In 2002–3 50 per cent of new fathers took advantage of the leave. Unlike previous women's policy ministers under Right-wing governments who tended to emphasize maternity over employment for women, Minister Ameline's Equality Contract stresses the importance of a gender-balanced work–family relationship in improving women's status and outlines a set of actions that are in line with past feminist demands for reconciliation policy, e.g. better day-care, more financial support for paternity leave, and financial help to working mothers in lower-income categories.

Parity: 1999 constitutional amendment and 2000 law

A broad-based and well-supported movement that engaged the full range of women's and feminist actors, non-feminist groups and leading women political figures first appeared in the early 1990s. One of the major successes of the movement was the development and popular support given to the idea of parity, a homegrown French concept that resonated with French culture, as opposed to other gender equality concepts imported from other countries, like quotas, positive action and mainstreaming. Based on difference between the sexes, parity came to represent a more gendered and softer version of equality that aimed to achieve equal representation of men and women in elected office and all decision-making positions.

Up until the late 1990s, the issue of women's low representation was a focal point of neither the women's movement nor of government attention. A 1982 law stipulating a 25 per cent quota of women on municipal lists was nullified by the Constitutional Council. Responding to persistent low levels of women in political office, the lack of government policy on the issue and empowered by increased international attention on gender balance in politics, the highly popular parity movement placed parity reform on the agenda of first the Gaullist government in the 1995 and then the Socialist government in 1998. In 1998, the Socialist government presented to parliament a proposal to amend the Constitution and soon after a bill proposal to implement the constitutional principle. The parity movement's success did not continue in determining the content and the implementation of the new reforms, in large part due to the disagreements in the movement itself about how to put the quite abstract principle of parity into action. By 1999, the movement had mostly disappeared.

The two constitutional provisions were diluted due to fierce opposition in parliament, primarily in the Senate – 'The law favors the equal access of women and men to political mandates and functions' and 'Political parties contribute to the implementation of this principle.' The word parity is not mentioned, the notion of guaranteeing gender equality was replaced by the more tentative 'favouring', and the political parties, rather than government, were given formal responsibility over implementation. Despite the limits, the inclusion of the gender equality principle in the body of the Constitution, and not just in the preamble from the Fourth Republic, marks an important departure from gender-blind approaches to women's rights.

Adopted with less opposition, due to the compromises made in the constitutional revisions, the 2000 law reflects what many feminists have seen as a partial commitment to parity.

The political parties, already with poor track-records, are given the major responsibility of promoting women in elected office, through the candidature process and not the outcome of elections. For elections run on list systems – European, municipal and regional – parties are required to submit alternating lists of men and women. Cantonal elections and elections in cities under 3500 are not covered. There are no stipulations about the heads of lists or of determining the composition of the powerful collective municipal councils that pool several cities' resources. For National Assembly elections, financial incentives are applied; state subsidies to each party are reduced proportionately to the gap in male and female candidates nationwide.

The immediate results of the reforms have been mixed, reflecting the reluctance of the mostly male party leadership to redistribute candidacies from long-time male party loyalists to female newcomers. For the legislative elections, all of the political parties took a reduction in state subsidies. The Socialist party, for example, refused to put forward more than the 30 per cent female candidates; an outcome that was partially due to the lack of influence of the party's women's commission. In 2002, as a result, the percentage of women in the National Assembly only went from 11 to 12 per cent. After the 2002 municipal elections, 47.5 per cent of city councillors in cities over 3,500 were women, with only 6.9 per cent of mayors. In March 2004, women on regional councils went from 27.5 per cent to 47.6 per cent. One female regional president was elected. The importance of parity laws is even more clear in light of the results of the 2004 cantonal elections, where 10.9 per cent of cantonal councillors were women. The executive boards of town collectives still comprise 90 per cent men, however and only 5.7 per cent have female presidents.

Clearly there has been some real progress for women as a result of the parity reform but the inherent limits of the reform compromise the degree to which women gain access to a highly male-dominated political hierarchy. Parties have proven to be resistant to placing female newcomers into positions of power that serve as gateways to top elected and appointed offices at the national level. It is important to note that it has only been three years since the radical concept that puts into question the established balance of power within political parties has been put into place. In this perspective, the regional and municipal election results may be an indicator of the possibility for real change. In addition, the Right-wing government has continued to take action on parity; a 2003 law addresses some of the gaps and the Ameline ministry, named the Ministry of Parity, has announced specific measures, including better tracking of women in elected office and providing funds to cover child-care expenses for elected officials. These policy initiatives are in deep contrast to the stalling tactics of the

Right-wing government to demands for parity reform under Prime Minister Juppé and President Chirac.

Sexuality and violence: 2000 report on sexual violence and law of 16 November 2002

Underpinned by what many feminist observers identify as Latin, southern European macho attitudes, public responses to sexual violence issues like rape, battery of women, and sexual harassment have been less pronounced than other areas of feminist policy. In the late 1990s, feminist groups increasingly turned their attention to public expressions of sexism against women in the media and politics. Since its creation in 1999, the group *Chiennes-de-garde* pursued a highly public campaign, ranging from denouncing Marc Blondel's (head of the trade union FO) sexist remarks against a female minister to organizing a demonstration against a sexist window display at the Galéries Lafayette in Paris. Up until the late 1990s, public sexism was an important feminist issue, but groups had been unable to persuade public authorities to take action. For example, a 1985 anti-sexist law aimed at regulating sexist images in the media was withdrawn by the Socialist government due to extreme opposition from the advertising industry.

In addition to difficult-to-verify and often stereotypical notions of macho sexism, the puritan influence present in many other countries that gives a certain legitimacy to regulating pornography, sexual harassment, prostitution and sexual violence more generally is not present in France. Sexual relations between colleagues are quite the norm in France – for example a recent essay competition for young business people was on 'les aventures amoureuses au travail' (romantic exploits at work). Anti-sexual harassment laws have often been seen to threaten individual freedoms: described by members of parliament and the mainstream press as an American invasion of 'repressive Puritanism' into private sexual relations. Many in France were perplexed by the Thomas-Hill sexual harassment affair in the USA.

Since the early 1990s, feminist activists have asserted that sexual harassment against women at work is a real problem that needed to be addressed. The *Association des Violences Faites contre les Femmes au Travail* (AVFT), created in 1989, became a major force in the campaign for the 1992 anti-sexual harassment law and has continued to be an important player in helping victims of sexual harassment. Reflecting the lack of support for expansive laws, the 1992 law sanctioned only direct harassment of lower-level employees by their bosses, and not hostile environment harassment. The word harassment was not mentioned in the law. Litigation has remained limited due to the reluctance of women to come forward and a certain assumption in the criminal justice system that sexual harassment is not a serious problem. The code-law legal system in France also makes high-price lawsuits virtually impossible.

Up until 2002, the issue of sexual harassment in universities was seldom mentioned. In that year renowned demographer Hervé Lebras was accused of sexual harassment by his doctoral student. The campaign was highly publicized by a new feminist student group: Clasches. Nearly 1,600 students signed a petition identifying sexual harassment in the university as a problem and the group was received by a Ministry of Education official. A debate raged in the press about whether the claim against Lebras was legitimate and whether the group was identifying a real problem. In 2002, a law on moral harassment included an amendment that made hostile environment harassment illegal. The article drew little public attention during its discussion. To be sure, the rising awareness about sexual harassment in universities and the new feminist mobilization has drawn increased attention to the issue; there has been no clear policy response to this unveiled problem, nor does there appear to be a clear consensus that sexual harassment is a serious enough problem for public authorities to take definitive action.

The issue of sexual violence has not been as contested in France, but systematic recognition of the problem and reforms have been just as slow in coming. Up until 2000, issues of sexual violence were rarely discussed in the media or major public fora. Only a small network of feminist groups and underfunded battered women's shelters received limited support from the already meagre and over-taxed budgets of the women's policy agencies. Women's ministers of the Left and the Right have made violence against women an important issue and pursued policies commensurate with their lack of power in the ministerial hierarchy, such as sensitizing administrative actors about violence issues and informing women about ways of dealing with domestic violence.

In 2000, the *Service des Droits des Femmes*, and not the minister itself, commissioned the first systematic national study of sexual violence against women in France, the *National Inquiry into Violence against Women* (*Enquête Nationale sur les Violences Envers les femmes en France*: ENVEFF). The findings of the study released in late 2000 shocked the public, showing that women in couples were the most victimized and that the highest incidence of violence was found in middle-class couples. One out of every ten women had been victims of violence by their partners or spouses, an estimated 48,000 women were raped in 1999; in one third of the cases, by their partners or spouse. With the damning results of the report, domestic violence was given unprecedented public attention. International Violence Against Women Day was officially commemorated for the first time in France in November 2002. Several high-profile cases of women being murdered by their partners in 2003 and the broad-based efforts of the new feminist group *Ni Putes-Ni Soumise* in the same year made the issue even more prominent. In an article in the Right-wing daily newspaper, *Le Figaro*, the Parity Minister stated that violence against women in couples was 'organized barbary', made a call for increased efforts to address domestic violence against women, and lent her support to a bill proposal on divorce that would make it legal for spouses to evict a violent partner from the home. Significant measures were also included in the Equality Charter, including a new zero-tolerance campaign called zéro-violence. A recent public outcry about the rate of women murdered by their partners – 30 in the summer of 2004 – and the lack of police response indicates that there is still much to be done in seriously addressing domestic violence (*Libération*, 9 September 2004).

EU gender mainstreaming: the *Jaunes Budgetaires* (2002) and the Equality Charter (2004)

In the late 1990s, gender mainstreaming became a major instrument for feminists within the state to reduce gender equalities. In interviews with femocrats in the PACA region in 2000, all pointed to the promise of gender mainstreaming for their own work, which has become by necessity trans-versal. Femocrat mainstreaming efforts are also legitimated by subsidies from the European Social Fund allocated to Regions that have put main-streaming measures into place. Since 1999, different parts of the women's rights administration and femocrats in other ministries have held con-ferences and workshops on gender mainstreaming to educate public officials about the new concept. Despite the concept being an English term and linked to feminist forces outside France, gender mainstreaming has become a watchword for most state feminist texts since the Péry Ministry. It resonates with the consensus in the feminist community that gender-based inequities need to be addressed in all areas.

The Socialist Péry ministry instituted a new budget instrument in 2000, *les jaunes budgétaires,* that reports on all equality measures and specific budget measures taken by the ministry in the public accounting process of the government each year. The Ameline ministry's Charter for Equality – a 280-page document that outlines detailed government plans, by sector and ministry – is another indicator of the extent to which gender main-streaming is becoming a permanent part of the politico-administrative system. For the most part the measures reflect the work of the women's rights administration through its sectoral committees and hence to a certain degree the positions of feminist groups and experts that are partners with the women's policy agencies. Over three hundred representatives of non-feminist groups, ministries and agencies signed the final charter, as a symbol of their engagement with the mainstreaming document. Minister Ameline presented the Charter to the public in March 2004 as the government's response to 'gender mainstreaming'. The use of the English term rather the French translation is an important break with the past.

Both mainstreaming documents can be downloaded from the Minister's homepage. Given the propensity for symbolic politics in feminist policy in France, these texts alone do not indicate that the government and the social partners will actually take concrete action on all measures. The sheer magnitude and scope of the charter implies an extraordinary effort that probably is unreasonable to expect. More importantly, the two main-streaming documents indicate a new public accountability and transpar-ency on principles of gender equality, on the part of the government and various social actors, by providing publicly accessible instruments to assess the promises and actions of the government.

Conclusion

Right-wing and Left-wing governments have responded to feminist demands for more authoritative gender-equality policies in a wide range of policy issues. The symbolic reform imperative seems to be in the process of being broken as more substantive feminist policies are adopted and followed up with real administrative clout. Whether real change in the behaviour of powerful players, like the healthcare and employment administrations, business leaders, trade unions and the political parties in following up these policies remains to be seen. What is certain is that feminist actors in society and an increasingly institutionalized women's policy administration have capitalized on supportive public opinion and extra-national cues to gain new leverage for compelling recalcitrant elites to accept a new model for gender equality that will narrow the status gap between men and women; a model that no longer defines gender-role change and the advancement of women's rights and status as a threat to the republic, but rather as a necessity and even an asset to the development of an effective and healthy democracy that is part of the global community. With the year 2000 as a key triggering point, the emerging gendered republic may very well be part and parcel of the larger process of globalization. It suggests a positive aspect of globaliza-tion, providing an opportunity for democracies to be more inclusive of gender issues and interests. In the final analysis, while the gender-biased Republican model may still be quite operative in French politics and the changes in gender dynamics proposed by the new policies difficult to bring about, political and social forces appear to be in the process of realigning to make previously marginalized feminist demands and interests an integral part of the political dynamics of the Fifth Republic. Therefore it is the process of their development, just as much as the future impact of these new feminist policies, that is harbinger of a new, more democratic political system in France.

Chapter 14

Identities, Nationalism, Citizenship and Republican Ideology

SOPHIE DUCHESNE

Citizenship and national identities are central elements of political systems. They account for the political link, for the relationship between the citizens as well as between citizens and rulers. Citizenship is often analysed through the notions of rights and obligations (Walzer, 1989). As Jean Leca pointed out, these rights and obligations are not only a matter of status or of legal rules (Leca, 1983). They also encompass a set of values or moral qualities as well as a series of social roles. The relationship between rules, values and roles is not straightforward. Civic values and the distinction between citizens' and private roles are part of the political culture of a country. The legal regulation of membership, rights and obligations is also supposed to reflect this political culture, but it may be influenced by external sources of constraint, such as supranational integration.

Moreover, a political culture is not an homogeneous set of values shared by all members of a political community. It is an evolving but persistent configuration of competing ideologies inherited from the main political struggles that the national community has gone through. The notion of national identity is embedded in the political culture. In the fullest sense of the term, a national identity is a complex pattern of meanings and values related to the group whose borders are defined by the state's capacity to intervene. Any change in the regulation of the group may be interpreted as a consequence as well as a cause of some change in national identity.

In the French case, political culture and national identity have long been described as very specific, in terms of Republican ideology. Indeed, the notion of *République*, a key notion of Republican ideology, is a rather odd one. The Republican political community is basically conceived as a neutral sphere, where all citizens are considered equal, regardless of any difference such as gender, religious affiliation, ethnic and/or geographical origins, cultural preferences. This abstract concept is a product of the Revolution.

In seeking to break with the *Ancien Régime*, the French invented a universalistic model of citizenship, in which there is no *corps intermédiaire* (any intermediary body) between the citizen and his/her fellow, between him/her and the nation. This was achieved through the destruction of local and territorial representation and allegiance (Rosanvallon, 1990), and by not recognizing dependent people as citizens (Rosanvallon, 1992). Accordingly, in the public sphere, the citizens are supposed to express their opinion and act in accordance with a general will. This general will is embodied in and implemented by the State, which leads them on the way to progress. In particular, the State is responsible for the schools where citizens will be educated in order to become competent, rise above their private interests and get involved in the French Republican community. Anybody can enter the political community, as long as they accept giving up their distinctive identities. By default, being born and raised on the soil of France is acknowledged as a sufficient condition to become a citizen. The French nation, considered as a common inheritance, gives its substance, colours and taste to this abstract political community. (Nicolet, 1982)

Despite an apparent coherence, the French concept of the citizen and the nation combines different traditions and has given rise to different facets of nationalism (Hazareesingh, 1994). Famous French discourses about the nation, from Renan to De Gaulle, are the result of a compromise between competing ideologies, mainly the Catholic and the Republican ones, which have struggled for domination for more than a century in French political culture. Before the Revolution, France was a completely Catholic country, Catholicism referring not only to religious belief, but also very much to a Church, to a supranational hierarchical source of power. France was well known as the 'eldest daughter of the Church'. By the Revolution, the fight against Catholicism had at least two very different objectives: first that of ensuring pluralism of religion, in the sense of giving some space and recognition for others, especially Jews and Protestants, to practise their faith; second, granting freedom of conscience, the liberation of the minds of French people from any religious power (Baudérot, 2000). The fight against the Catholic Church and the attempt to eradicate the Catholic Church's domination is a very long story (Rémond, 1985), with lots of twists and turns, from the civil constitution of the clergy in 1790 to the separation of Church and State in 1905, via the Concordat from 1801. The education system, particularly primary and then secondary schools, provided the main battlefield (Déloye, 1994). Because in the early years of the Third Republic, the education system was completely dominated by the Catholic Church, the Republican government considered that the Republic could not be established without the setting up of a system of public, free, compulsory and lay primary schooling, where all citizens would be educated, taught Republican values and be free from any kind of domination of their thoughts. Indeed *Laïcité*, whose direct translation 'laicity' does not make much sense, is not a plain equivalent for secularism. More than referring to the temporal dimension of life, by contrast with a spiritual or religious dimension of it, it refers to the independence of the temporal from the religious. Throughout this chapter we will use the French noun, rather than its English-language equivalent.

The current and familiar figure of the French citizen is the product of this long battle between, mainly, Republicans and Catholics. Despite the efforts of pre-eminent intellectuals to give this concept of French citizenship a rational and consistent shape (Schnapper, 1994), French citizens have actually inherited mixed beliefs about who they are and what their nation should be. Being a combination of meanings and values from different ideologies is not specific to the French national identity, nor does it mean that it is particularly fragile. But this special mixture of Republicanism and Catholicism (plus other minor influences) gave rise to a tension between the desire for universalism and a need for a distinctive identity that is particularly acute in the French case. People do feel at the same time members of a distinctive united community and universal individuals responsible for humanity. They often feel themselves to be uneasy about fulfilling the contradictory requirements of these different ways of feeling about oneself (Duchesne, 1997). This results in a significant difficulty in understanding pluralism, a tendency to confuse equality and uniformity and to suspect any claim to difference of being a step towards communitarianism – and hence towards the breaking of the national cohesion.

Thus, contrary to what it may appear from political discourse, where the myth of republican citizenship (Cole, 1998) is strongly and regularly reasserted, it is really the mix of Republican and Catholic traditions and the resulting tensions that are specific to French national identity. How does such a complex balance between originally antagonistic concepts of membership of the political community react to the rapid transformation of the French political system caused by the growing mobility of people, the increasing interdependence of governments, the supranational integration of political communities, the fast expansion of worldwide communication systems and mass culture – in short, all the processes encompassed by the notion of globalization? The question is too difficult to be answered as such. Instead, this chapter will deal with four questions, related to nature of the political community, that have been subject to a change of regulation in the last decade. For each of them, we will try to assess if these changes seem to indicate a corresponding change in the configuration of French representations of citizenship. We will first consider the nationality laws which, in the French system where citizenship and nationality are almost equivalent, play an important role in the definition of the political community. Secondly, we will examine the decision on parity and discuss how far there has been a change in traditional French blindness to differences in the sphere of gender. Then we will turn to European integration and the multi-level democracy France seems to be becoming. We will observe that, if something is changing here, this is less the very nature of the national identity than the uneasiness of French people with the pluralism of power. Lastly, we will have a longer discussion of the headscarf affair. The ferocity of this debate, that has lasted for a decade now, does not make sense unless we understand the centrality of *laicité* at school as a symbol of the battles between Republicans and Catholics that lie at the core of French political culture.

The return of the *jus soli*

In 1993, in a context of strong political controversy, a law on French nationality was adopted introducing a further requirement for people to become French, the so-called 'declaration of will'. This rule was first suggested in 1986 by the Chirac government: a young person born in France of foreign parents would not automatically be French on becoming 18 but would have to express his or her will to become French. This proposal gave rise to a hotly contested debate. The government reconsidered and gave a special committee, chaired by Marceau Long, the task of examining possible ways to reform the legislation on nationality. By this time, the system had become quite complicated. The committee interviewed many people and wrote a report entitled 'Being French today and tomorrow' (*Commission de la Nationalité*, 1988). With the re-election of François Mitterrand and the forming of the Rocard government, nothing happened. But when the Right came back to power in 1993, they made their intention of legislating on immigration very clear. Charles Pasqua, the Interior Minister, gave his name to a law on the conditions of entering and living in France for foreigners and Pierre Méhaignerie, the Justice Minister, gave his to the reform of nationality laws. This proposal was officially inspired by the Marceau Long report, which was quite consensual. Most people declaring themselves as Republican first found that the 'declaration of will' suited the Republican idea of the nation, as famously expressed in Renan's 1982 conference, 'What is a nation?' (Renan, 1991). But in 1993 the law was explicitly meant to satisfy the Right-wing electorate, whose expectations on the matter had been raised by the influence of the FN. The Left parties made the commitment to change the laws as soon as they came back into power. Indeed, the reform of the Méhaignerie laws was mentioned by Lionel Jospin in his investiture declaration in 1997. The new socialist government asked Patrick Weil, a sympathetic political scientist, to establish another report explicitly on the application of *jus soli* (*Le Monde*, 1 August 1997). A preliminary analysis of the consequences of the application of the 'declaration of will' showed that the young people did not reject it at all, as it had sometimes been argued. On the contrary: in 1994, 33,255 young people became French after having expressed their will to do so, and 30,526 in 1995, in comparison with a mean of 23,000 of 18 year-olds who automatically became French in previous years (the increase being a mechanical result of the change in the range of age, from 16 to 21 years, provided by the law). A closer scrutiny revealed some problems, especially in the examination of rejected cases. There were differences in the treatment of applications according to the location, gender and geographical origin of the young people. Moreover, it appeared that some young people were not really aware of the fact that they had to express their will, and others, especially young women, could even be prevented by their family from applying. Nevertheless, the assessment was not all negative.

Elisabeth Guigou, the new Justice Minister, presented a reform plan while Jean-Pierre Chevènement, Minister of the Interior, introduced a new law on immigration. The debate was fierce amongst the Left, as the government did not choose to reintroduce an 'integral' *jus soli*, which would have meant that a child of foreign parents born in France is French from his/her birth. Nor did they decide to return to the former arrangement, where the parents could apply on behalf of children under 18. In the first proposal, the *jus soli* was to apply only at 18. The opposition was fierce within the Right-wing parties, too. They had the majority in Senate, and even voted for an amendment providing for a referendum on the subject. Finally, the following measures were introduced. A young person born in France of foreign parents is French when he/she is 18, if he/she has lived in France for five years in total since the age of 11. He/she can anticipate the recognition by the State of his/her quality of Frenchness and express his/her will to become French from the age of 13 (with his/her parents' consent between 13 and 16). Or he/she can turn it down from six months before being 18 and for one year afterwards.

Should this return of the *jus soli* be interpreted as a new episode in Brubaker's point, namely the way in which nationality laws epitomize a given concept of the nation? In an often quoted book, based on a French–German comparison, Brubaker argued that the *jus soli* embodies a civic notion of the nation, open to newcomers, while *jus sanguinis* characterizes an idea of the nation based on ethnicity (Brubaker, 1992). This demonstration has been contested recently (Weil, 2002). First, *jus soli* cannot be considered as a French Republican feature: it has been part of French law since only 1889. After the Revolution, French legislators chose the *jus sanguinis* as a way of breaking the allegiance to the *Ancien Régime* that used to be implemented through the *jus soli*. Moreover, the idea that nationality laws epitomize one country's idea of the nation is debatable. According to Weil, *jus soli* is not the mark of civic nations but the rules adopted by countries that have come to consider themselves as countries of immigration. Nowadays, in the European Union, far from diverging from one another according to contrasting ideas of the nation, nationality laws tend to converge according to a common experience of massive postwar immigration (Hansen and Weil, 2001).

This demonstration contradicts most beliefs expressed in France in the last decade, where *jus soli* is generally considered as a Republican principle. It is symptomatic that a Right-wing government, even in its attempt to satisfy the Far-Right-wing electorate, has not even tried to suppress the *jus soli*. The declaration of will has been interpreted by their opponents as reintroducing a sort of requirement of allegiance for children of foreign origin. Moreover, it has been considered at odds with the principle of equality. During the Third Republic, Republicans fought against Catholics to impose the idea of the citizen as a person who has been educated according to certain values and principles. The second generation that was required to declare the will to become French has been socialized in French schools and hence educated as French citizens. The national identity which in contemporary France encompasses *jus soli* as one of its devices is not a set of consensual beliefs. The French obsession with nationality laws (Favell, 2001) accounts for the persistent questioning amongst French people about the very nature of their political community.

The law on parity: a breach in French universalism

Voting became really universal – meaning for men and women – in France after the Second World War. Forty years later, French women were a tiny minority in all elected Assemblies – less than 10 per cent in the National Assembly until 1997, amongst the smallest proportion in the EU. Indeed, universalism has long stood in the way of French feminists. First, because the feminist movement itself has been fiercely divided, between supporters of the recognition of differences between men and women as a fundamental characteristic of human nature, and promoters of pure equality between them. Then secondly because the Left-wing parties, which in other countries have been the best allies of feminist claims, were in France the more universalist, and hence the more likely to reject any demand for specific treatment for women (Duchen, 1986). The disconnection between gender differences and inequality of women claimed by Anglo-Saxon feminists (Young, 1990) is far from achieved amongst French intellectual women. Thirdly, for a very long time, public opinion itself resisted the idea of treating men and women differently, because of the strength of universalism in French political culture. The notion of affirmative action has never won support in this context. The idea of giving any advantage to anyone because of what he/she is, even with the argument that because of what he/she is, his/her opportunities in life are lessened, is very difficult to justify for a French audience. Affirmative action definitively bears a notion of unfairness that is made obvious by its (not very accurate) translation as 'discrimination positive' (literally positive discrimination) (Calvès, 1999). In 1982, the National Assembly, that had recently acquired a Socialist majority, adopted a proposal of law that prohibited any list for city council elections with 75 per cent or more candidates of the same gender. The Constitutional Council interpreted even this very light formulation as introducing a quota of reserved places for women. The requirement for equality is set out in article 6 of the French Declaration of the Rights of Man and Citizen of 1789: 'All citizens being equal before it [the law], are equally admissible to all public offices, positions, and employments, according to their capacity, and *without other distinction than that of virtues and talents.*' The Declaration of the Rights of Man and Citizen being part of the Constitution, the project was declared unconstitutional.

As a consequence of this defeat, the claim to a better representation of women in the political sphere has been reformulated differently, as the so-called *parité* (parity). Instead of quotas or any kind of affirmative action, feminist supporters of the recognition of gender difference have done their best to change the debate. Within a decade of mobilization, and with the support or even the encouragement of the Council of Europe, they have succeeded in framing the claim of equal representation through the quest for more democracy. Instead of focusing on the quest for equality, they have argued that women would act differently from men if they had power, and denounced the very low proportion of women in ruling positions as a consequence of a deliberate attitude of male politicians (Mossuz-Lavau, 1998). A high point of the parity movement was the publication in the newspaper *Le Monde* of a 'Manifesto of the 577 for parity democracy' (*Manifeste des 577 pour une démocratie paritaire* – 577 being the number of seats in the National Assembly) signed by 289 women and 288 men, belonging to Left and Right parties. Parity did not win the support of all the feminist movement; for a hint on the persistent reluctance of some of them, contrast for instance (Pisier, 2001) and (Baudino, 2003).

But parity won greater support outside feminist circles and became one of the issues at stake for the 1995 presidential campaign. In October 1995, the new Right-wing government set up an a committee to observe the evolution of parity between men and women (*Observatoire de la parité entre les hommes et les femmes*), which played an important role both in documenting the gap between men and women in ruling positions and as a resource, an arena for the supporters of parity. Alain Juppé did not respond very positively to the propositions made in the report that the *Observatoire* published in December 1996. But the dissolution of the National Assembly in spring 1997 resulted in a change of majority. Lionel Jospin, the new Left-wing Prime Minister, committed his government to this reform and decided to revise the constitution accordingly. The revision was meant to prevent any further rejection of parity laws by the Constitutional Council. It also had a high symbolic value. In Republican ideology, the Constitution epito-mizes both the social contract (it sets the fundamental rules according to the people's choice) and the revolutionary spirit; the Constitution may be changed as the course of history may be changed, but not easily, and only for major purposes. It is symptomatic of a period of doubt about French citizenship that the Constitution has been revised twelve times since 1992 (while it was changed only five times between 1948 and 1992). Two amendments were adopted in July 1999 by the National Assembly and the Senate. A paragraph was added in article 3 dealing with sovereignty: 'the law favours the equal access of women and men to political mandates and functions' while article 4 now states that the political parties contribute to the implementation of this principle. These changes were far below the parity movement's expectations. So was the law adopted in June 2000. Basically, equal numbers of male and female candidates are required only for elections fought under proportional representation: European elections and regional and municipal elections. There are some restrictions, the most important being for the municipal elections in cities with less than 3,500 inhabitants where the electoral system is not proportionally representative. Senatorial elections are subject to specific rules. No rule applies for the presidential election. As for the National Assembly, there are only financial incentives: half of the subsidy for a party may be reduced if parity between males and female candidates is not respected.

Even opponents of parity cannot deny that the constitutional change and the 2000 law constitute a success for the feminist movement. The equality of representation of men and women is now recognized as desirable, even if parity itself is far from being imposed. In many areas, as Amy Mazur shows in the preceding chapter of this book dedicated to women's issues, the European Union has been quite effective at gendering the French legal and social system. But the French tendency to confuse uniformity and equality persists at the core of the belief system, the political level.

Is France turning into a multi-level democracy?

The learning of abstract citizenship was made possible by the building of the nation, whose warmth and strength made up, in the long term, both for the wrench from distinctive identities and the holding of civic duties (Nora, 1992). Looking today in depth into the imagination of French citizens, you can see how the power of the nation is exchanged against the complete helplessness of the atomistic individual citizen. The identification with their nation is made reality by a feeling of common possession, of collective inheritance of the soil of France. It is fuelled by the memories of the dead, of the ancestors who fought, together or against each other, to make the country what it is now (Duchesne, 1997). The nation is imagined as embodying a common will, in a way which rules out any kind of plurality. Renan's well-known phrase, the nation as 'daily plebiscite', is a good example of the way anonymity is given distinctive identity in the imagination of a will inherited from ancestors. This gives the nation an exclusiveness in the affections and solidarities of the citizens, which reflects the centralization of the French political system and the lack of pluralism, of checks and balances, in the distribution of power. This exclusiveness was challenged in only a few Regions, Brittany, the Basque Country and Corsica, where the Region competes against the nation for these affections. Yet in the last decade, the French political system has been challenged from below and above, by decentralization, by the Europeanization of the State and, more generally speaking, by the impact of globalization (see the Le Galès, Levy and Smith chapters in this book) Does this redistribution of power affect the national focus of French citizens' identification? Has multi-level governance altered French citizens' allegiances? Is France slowly beginning to turn into a multi-level democracy? (Schild, 2001)

As a first remark, let us state that national pride, the most common measure of national identification, has not decreased in the last ten years. On the contrary: in France as in most European countries, the proportion of people who declare themselves proud of their country has tended to increase, the French being below the European mean (less than 40 per cent of respondents saying that they are very proud). Obviously, survey questions are poor measures of in-depth feelings of identity. Many social scientists prefer other methods of inferring attitudes – in-depth qualitative interviews or social practice. The regular decrease of turnout in general elections, and especially in the first ballot of the 2002 presidential election, could, for instance, be interpreted as a contradictory indicator of a weakened national identification.

What about Europe then? Should the low level of turnout for the June 2004 European election (42 per cent) be seen as an indicator of a persistent difficulty for French people in accepting the European level as legitimate? For a long time, attitudes towards Europe have been considered in France, as in most European countries, as mere opinions, as attitudes towards a remote object, superficial, something that could not properly be analysed as an identity (Duchesne and Frognier, 1994). After the ratification of the Maastricht Treaty, many observers expected the continuation of European integration and the institutionalization of a European citizenship to result in the growth of more deeply grounded feelings towards Europe – mainly negative feelings because of the strength of the potentially competing national identification (Mayer, 1996).

Actually, general attitudes towards the EU continue to be largely positive. In a recent survey, the French Electoral Panel 2002, hardly 5 per cent of the interviewees considered that France belonging to the EU was a bad thing. And this, even though most of them answered at the same time that they fear that the European Union will result in a deterioration of the social welfare system and an increase in immigration. Interestingly, positive attitudes towards the EU are so widespread that it makes more sense to search for an explanation of the resistance to Europe than of acceptance (Belot and Cautrès, 2004). This is confirmed by the way French people have easily become accustomed to the euro, even if, like all other people in the euro zone, they have complained about the increase in prices that was hidden by the change of currency. All fears that people might be unable to cope with the new range of values or that they would feel deprived of some part of their identity have quickly vanished.

An explanation for this general acceptance of Europe without a corresponding weakening of national identification could run as follows. Instead of giving rise to a competing identification, attitudes about Europe seem to have easily fitted into a pattern of identifications based on the national level. The identification with one's nation is a process of building one's abstract loyalty. Rather than introducing a new kind of commitment between citizens and their polity, Europe seems to be one step further in this process that Inglehart has described as a cognitive mobilization (Inglehart, 1977). When French people imagine the work in progress that is the European Union, most of them figure it out as the replication, at another time and on a different scale, of the process of nation-building that France has gone through before. That is, a process of homogenization. Hence they basically do not experience European belonging as a threat to French allegiance, as long as their politicians do not present it in that way. In France – and contrary to what happens in the British Isles – national and European are less competitive than cumulative. Instead of being a handicap for the development of European identification, strong national feelings open the way in a process of growing abstraction of the political community (Duchesne and Frognier, 2002). But the nature of the link between the citizen and the polity remains the same: he/she becomes part of the quest for a European general will, something very different from the kind of relationship you would expect in a multi-level democracy.

What about the regional level? The new regional assemblies and executives have long been in search of legitimacy and tried to get any possible evidence for it. For two decades now, the *Observatoire Interrégional du Politique*, a public survey institute funded by the Regions, has carried out large opinion polls and looked for any sign of increasing identification of the French with their Regions, with little success. The desire for greater proximity between citizens and their rulers seems to clash with a fear that more competences given to the Regions would result in the disengagement of the State. The 2004 regional elections came as a surprise: first, because of the (relatively) low level of abstention: more than 62 per cent voted, which contrasts with the persistent decline of turnout since 1986, secondly, because of the results: in all mainland Regions but one the opposition won the majority. This has been widely interpreted as a negative verdict from the voters against the government. It is always very risky to attribute a will to the electorate; similar votes may have very different motives and most voters find it difficult to really explain their choice anyway. However, another interpretation of the dramatic victory of Left-wing parties is the growing capacity of French people to accept or favour some sharing of power. This could be compared with the different experiences of *cohabitation* (these situations where the French president is in political opposition with the majority of the National Assembly), originally analysed by French observers as consequences of irrational electoral behaviour, but subsequently found to be appreciated by public opinion. As well as a sanction against the government, the 2004 regional elections could then be seen as a consequence of a growing acceptance of institutional pluralism, something that is supposed to be rather alien to French political culture (Safran, 2002).

This is a vexed question, but matters of identification are complicated ones and it is difficult to give evidence to support one argument against another. The point here is that the strength and abstraction of the French national community makes the development of European identification easier. It appears as a 'natural' extension of the process of homogenization that former French regions went through in the nineteenth century. But this kind of identification is not the kind of relationship between a citizen and the polity that would be expected in a system of multi-level governance, where there is no supposition of a general will behind the complexity of the decision-making process. Nevertheless, some other elements indicate that French people are slowly becoming accustomed to some kind of pluralism of power. This may be a sign of a deeper change in French citizenship.

Laicité at school: the return of the repressed

'Something disturbing is happening in France. It started with a seemingly innocuous debate about Muslim schoolgirls' headscarves, yet it got transmogrified into a veritable Kulturkampf about the nature of public space in the French Republic' (*Herald Tribune*, 5 February 2005) How come France made such a fuss over ten Muslim schoolgirls a year refusing to get rid of their headscarves? This is what most countries, especially Britain and the United States, have wondered about France in the last couple of years. Indeed, when looking at the facts, it is difficult to understand why French people have been so fiercely committed in the headscarf affair. Let us briefly recall what happened.

In 1989, three Muslim schoolgirls were expelled from their school because they refused to give up their headscarves when asked to by the teachers, who considered that this was an offence to school neutrality in religious matters. Their parents went to appeal and finally Lionel Jospin referred to the Council of State. The decision was that expressing one's belief through any piece of clothing was no breach of *laicité* as long as it was not meant to convert others to one's religion and did not affect teaching. For five years, similar cases occurred, calling into question what should be considered as proselytism and more precisely, if a headscarf, what kind of headscarf should be considered as such. In 1994, Minister of Education François Bayrou published a circular and ordered schools to forbid any form of religious ostentation. The controversy gradually developed. According to Luc Ferry, Minister of Education between 2002 and 2004, there were about 1,500 girls wearing headscarves at school, of whom about a hundred went to mediation, which failed to resolve matters in about ten cases.

In 2002, in Lyon, teachers went on strike because the local education authority refused to punish two schoolgirls who were wearing a bandana at school by way of a headscarf. The debate became intense. A first manifesto in favour of a law on *laicité* at school was signed by about two thousand intellectuals. Jean-Louis Debré, chair of the National Assembly, set up a parliamentary mission 'to think about religious signs at school'. Jacques Chirac then asked Bernard Stasi, ombudsman of the Republic, to chair a committee of 20 experts to reflect upon the contemporary meaning of *laicité*. While the parliamentary mission kept the focus on *laicité* at school, the wider scope of investigation of the Stasi committee, whose hearings got a large audience, contributed to an impression of creeping islamicization of French society. The expulsion from their school, in Aubervilliers, of two sisters, Alma and Lila, got widely publicized. By this time, Jacques Chirac had let it be known that he would address the nation in December, when the conclusions of the Stasi Committee would be published, and make a decision then.

The discussion was lively and quite confused. Every group, every political or religious affiliation was divided between those for and those against a law prohibiting the headscarf. Differences of opinion were highlighted, sometimes in inconsistent combinations. At the forefront was obviously a variable tolerance of foreigners; 9/11, as well as more than two decades of FN's campaigning, carried great weight in the debate. A second important line of differentiation was the belief (or not) in the persistent efficiency of the Republican integration model: are French schools still capable of making citizens? Since the mid-1980s, civic education has been reintroduced in primary schools, and the curriculum constantly refined and strengthened by every government, Left or Right. In 1999 'civic, legal and social education' was set up in secondary schools as well. The concept of citizenship taught at school is quite traditional and meant to be squarely in the Republican tradition: a citizen should be independent of his/her distinctive affiliations and commit him/herself into the public sphere in rising above his/her private interests. In a social context of cultural diversity and relative values, civic education claims the existence of common values, shared by all French citizens and embodied in the Republic. A third and very confusing aspect of the debate was from the women's liberation point of view. For French feminists, the headscarf was an obvious sign of women's alienation. Shortly before Chirac's decision, the magazine *Elle* circulated a petition asking the president to adopt a law against the headscarf considered 'a visible symbol of the submission of women in places where the State has to be the guarantor of a strict equality between genders' (*Elle*, 9 December 2003). In polls, opinion was favourable to a law: 55 per cent in October, 53 per cent in November, 57 per cent in December, according to the survey institute CSA.

The report of the Stasi Committee was made public on 11 October 2003. It strongly reaffirmed *laicité* as a principle of French public service, arguing that it should be implemented by public servants and respected by users. At the same time, it emphasized the necessity for more respect for religious diversity in France. It suggested the adoption of a law on *laicité* including articles in school prohibiting clothes and signs of religious or political affiliation. Large crosses, the veil and the kippa should be considered as such. It also suggested a couple of measures to encourage respect for religious diversity, including turning the two religious festivals Yom Kippur and Aid-el-Kebir into bank holidays. This latter point gave rise to fierce opposition in the media.

A week later, Jacques Chirac declared himself in favour of a law prohibiting overt religious signs at school. In a passionate speech recalling the history and principles of the French Republic, he endorsed most of the conclusions of the Stasi Committee, apart from the point concerning new bank holidays. President Chirac placed special emphasis on the need for neutrality in schools. Indeed, instead of a broad and all-encompassing law on *laicité*, the government prepared and presented on 7 January 2004 a bill with only three articles, preceded by a long statement of motivation. Basically, the bill prohibited ostentatious religious symbols at school. These symbols were defined as the wearing of pendants or items of clothing whose religious affiliation was immediately obvious. Whereas the previous rules were ambivalent, the law now imposes upon schools the responsibility for prohibiting headscarves and other ostentatious religious symbols.

The debate around the adoption of the law was complicated, and the parties were divided over it. Quite a few demonstrations occurred. But the government pushed it through fast. By 3 March 2004, the law had been adopted without major change by the two Assemblies and by mid-May, the implementation circular had been adopted by the High Council of Education. The law came into force in September, in a tense atmosphere as two French journalists were taken hostage in Iraq, their kidnappers demanding that the government cancel the law. Nevertheless, the law seemed to be generally accepted as no incident occurred when the children went back to school.

What does this all mean? Why did so many people mobilize for a law that really concerns a couple of schoolgirls? Obviously, because the principles at stake were felt to be of major importance. *Laicité* and school happen to be two of the most emblematic points of tension and conflict in the French pattern of ideologies. We have seen how French people invented *laicité* because of the complete domination of the Catholic Church in the Kingdom of France. After a century of battle between Republicans and Catholics in and about schools, the so-called neutrality of the French education system remains a very sensitive aspect of French national identity. Two decades ago, the then new Socialist government dramatically failed to reform public financial support to Catholic private schools. Today, *laicité* is at stake in the headscarf affair. It reactivated important features of the French pattern of ideologies: the recurrent implication of Catholic domination over French society, the difficulty in understanding pluralism and the infinite quest for concrete, flesh-and-blood individualism. Public opinion reacts massively when such questions are at stake while French intellectuals keep trying to assert French distinctive identity in universalistic terms – indeed quite a challenge (Jennings, 2000). Two enemies are pointed at in this quest: (selfish) individualism and communitarianism.

Two elements were particularly confusing in the headscarf affair. First, the way the question of *laicité*, which had been developed because of the domination of the Catholic Church, was raised again and applied without change to a minority religion. This practice indeed allowed people to suspect that a persistence of Catholic domination over French society was hidden behind the alleged defence of State neutrality. Jacques Chirac recently spoke of 'our Jewish or Muslim countrymen, or most simply sometimes French people' in terms reminiscent of an unfortunate declaration of Raymond Barre, former Premier Minister, after an anti-Semitic attack in the Rue des Rosiers in Paris (Jacques Chirac, televised interview, 14 July 2004). This manifests the tendency to mix up French people with people from non-Jewish and non-Muslim religions. This obviously gives foreign observers good reasons for suspecting that the law against the headscarf is mainly inspired by xenophobia. It is much more complicated than that.

Another element that has to be taken into account is the reluctance of French people to think that religious belief may be a matter of choice. Again, because of the long-term domination of the Catholic Church in French society, religious practice is considered a conventional behaviour, a way people conform to authority. The statistical relationship between church attendance and conservative political orientation has long been interpreted as a confirmation of religious alienation (Michelat and Simon, 1977) and of the implausibility of freedom of choice in religious matters (Donégani, 1993). And yet, sociologists demonstrated early on that the decision made by French schoolgirls to wear the headscarf was mostly their own (Gaspard and Khosrokhavar, 1995). At best, people could believe that young Muslim girls could find in the headscarf a way to gain some freedom and, for instance, to get family permission to go to university (Venel, 1999). The incredulous comments on Alma and Lila's case was a good example of that. The two schoolgirls have a Jewish atheist father and a mother who is Kabylian Catholic. They were expelled from school because they refused to renounce their headscarf. The press could hardly believe that this was anything other than a teenage fancy manipulated by an activist father (Levy and Levy, 2004). The way the report of the Stasi Committee interpreted the wearing of the headscarf as a sign of 'serious worsening of the situation of young women' is consistent with the general belief that nobody could ever choose to do such a thing of their own will. Again, French national identity is the result of an unfinished rebellion against Catholic domination that left little space for a recognition of religious beliefs as a personal choice.

Conclusion

Far from being a consensual and homogeneous ideology, French national identity is underpinned by tensions and ambivalences hidden by a recurrent and loud claim to the Republican tradition. Recent developments have shaken up the fragile balance that seemed to have been found after the Second World War. Massive immigration, women's liberation, European integration, globalization: the last decade has been full of major changes in French political citizenship. Most of them are not specific to France. But the strong tension in French political culture between an atomistic and abstract concept of the individual citizen and a cohesive and distinctive national identity seemed to leave only a limited space for change. The difficult adaptation of French citizenship to globalization became manifestly apparent on 21 April 2002. The four case studies presented in this chapter give an insight into the difficulty of adapting the French pattern of ideologies. The resistance is all the more strong when the change concerns the core of the Republican tradition, established as a compromise: the openness and universalism of the political community, the existence of a general will and the role of schools in the making of the citizens. Change is going on despite this resistance and a different compromise will emerge from the inside the old Republican outfit.

Further Reading

Chapter 1   The Shifting Politics of the Fifth Republic

For generations of students, the study of modern and contemporary France has been a vibrant and exciting subject. The interested reader can explore the general themes raised in this chapter in a wide variety of sources. *Developments in French Politics 3* is the successor text to Guyomarch, Machin, Hall and Hayward (2001), which remains a valuable reference. There are a number of good undergraduate texts, including Cole (2005), Stevens (2004), Howarth and Varouxakis (2003) and Elgie (2003). Vincent Wright's classic text has been revised and expanded by Knapp (Knapp and Wright, 2001). William Safran (1999) remains very readable and relevant. In French, Bernstein (1999) is stimulating on Republicanism and Wieviorka (1997) on Identity.

Chapter 2   Parties and Organizations

Much of the literature on political parties is in French. Chiche, Haegel, and Tiberj (2002) and Chiche, Haegel and Tiberj (2004) explore in depth the theme of partisan fragmentation. Dolez and Laurent (2000) and Haegel (2002) provide good recent accounts of developments on the French Right; Sauger (2004) on the recomposition of the centre. Lefebvre (2004) is good on the municipal roots of French socialism; Mischi (2003) on the PCF. The theme of intra-party democracy and party conferences is well developed in Faucher-King and Treille (2003). The special issue of the *Revue française de science politique* (2001) on party activists is a valuable contribution. Tiberj (2004) provides a good critique of the rational voter. On general overviews on the development of party systems, see Dalton, McAllister and Wattenberg (2002), and Mair and van Biezen (2001). In English, Evans (2003) and Knapp (2004) both provide very good general overviews.

Chapter 3   Electorates, New Cleavages and Social Structures

There is a very rich literature in the field, referred to throughout the chapter. The classic references on the importance of social class and religion as determinants of voting behaviour are Capdevielle (1981) and Michelat and Simon (1977). Boy and Mayer (2000) give a more recent overview. On the role of social class, Clark, Lipset and Rempel (1993) and Hout, Brooks and Manza (1993) provide differing

245

viewpoints. On the role of political space and the structure of political competition, Evans (2003) is the best recent collection in English. Grunberg and Schweisguth (1997) provide a powerful statement on the 'tripolarization' of political competition in France. On specific parties, Mayer (2002) provides a sustained study of the FN electorate; Rey (2004) on the changing bases of the left-wing electorate. The 2002 elections are dealt with best by Cautrès and Mayer (2004).

Chapter 4   Associational Life in Contemporary France

For an attempt to apply the pluralist framework developed in the United States by Arthur Bentley and David Truman to France, see the (flawed) classic by Meynaud (1962). A more recent treatment that reaches some similar conclusions is that of Frank Wilson (1987). Relations between interest groups and political parties are covered in Appleton (2001). A good overview of the universe of social movements in contemporary France can be found in Xavier Crettiez and Isabelle Sommier (2002). Thorough treatments in English include Duyvendak (1995) and Appleton (2000). The classic essay on the evolution of relations between social movements, civil society and state institutions remains that of Tilly (1986).

Chapter 5   The Political Executive

All textbooks provide details of the executive in France, including 'cohabitation'. An overview about the different ways in which the executive can operate can be found in Elgie and Griggs (2000, chap. 2). In English by far and way the most informative book is now Hayward and Wright (2002). A more chronological account of presidential politics is provided by Bell (2000). A similar style is adopted by Thody (1998). In French, the classic text is the second part of Duverger (1978). A more recent general text is Wahl and Quermonne (1995). A critical view of France's presidential system is provided by Duhamel (2002).

Chapter 6   Prometheus (Re-)Bound? The Fifth Republic and Checks on Executive Power

On the constitutional council, the classic studies are those of Stone (1992) and Avril and Gicquel (1998). Good accounts of the Council of State are those of Robineau and Truchet (1994) and Stirn (1994). On the French judiciary, Bernard (1998) gives a general account; van Ruymbeke (1996) provides first-hand evidence on the role of the investigating magistrates. On parliament, Camby and Servent (2004) are up-to-date and concise. Critical accounts of the Fifth Republic are those of Donégani and Sadoun (1998) and Duhamel (1999). Cole (1993) is the classic account of the presidential party. Knapp (2004) gives a detailed overview of French parties and the party system. Wolfreys (2001) provides a lively account of political corruption.

There are good special issues of the journal *Pouvoirs* on themes covered by this chapter: no. 64, 1993 on 'Le parlement'; no. 91, 1999 on 'La cohabitation'; no. 92, 2000 on 'La responsabilité des gouvernants'; and no. 99, 2001, on 'La nouvelle Ve République'. We also dispose of excellent summaries of the development of public opinion in the form of the annual SOFRES, *L'état de l'opinion* series. All dates from 1987 to 2004 are valuable. Teinturier (2004) gives a very good overview of the general theme of the French and politics.

Chapter 7   The Europeanization of the French State

There is an imposing literature on the various dimensions covered by this chapter. Smith (2004) provides an overview of the government of the EU. Radaelli (2001) offers a cogent summary of the concepts, methods and the challenge of empirical research in the EU. On the policy issue-areas covered by this chapter, the reader is invited to consult Dumez and Jeunemaître (1993) on competition policy; Fouilleux (2003) on the Common Agricultural Policy; Guiraudon (2003) on immigration and justice and home affairs; Rivaud (2001) and Sandholtz (1998) on telecommunications; Irondelle (2002) on external security and defence; and Bigo (1996) on European police collaboration. General overviews of French public policy are provided by Jobert (1994) and Muller (1998)

Chapter 8   Reshaping the State? Administrative and Decentralization Reforms

There is a large literature on the related themes of the reform of the state and decentralization. On the reform of the state, the best recent accounts are those of Bezès (2001) and Bezès (2004). On local public policy-making in France in general, Balme, Faure and Mabileau (1999) is a useful work. Borraz and Le Galès (2004) provides a more detailed development of the themes raised in this chapter. Trends towards city governance are well covered by Baraize and Négrier (2001). Cole and John (2001) is an innovative comparative study in English. On the state field services, Duran and Theonig (1996) is the key reference, as is that of Gaudin (1999) on contractualization. On local finance, Gilbert and Thoenig (1999) is a key text. Local political leadership is well covered in the book by Sorbets and Smith (2003).

Chapter 9   Foreign and Defence Policy: Constraints and Continuity

The interested reader is guided towards the following sources for more information on the issues raised by this chapter: Bozo (1997) provides a very good overview on French foreign policy since 1945. Gregory (2000) is a rigorous exposition of French defence policy at the beginning of the new millennium. Howorth and Menon (Howorth 1997) place the French case in comparative context. Keiger (2001) offers a comprehensive overview of France and the world since 1870. Keiger and

Alexander (1999) is a shorter, historically based account. A special issue of the journal *Relations Internationales et Stratégiques* in 1997 (no. 25) deals with the foreign policy of the first two years of the Chirac presidency.

Chapter 10　Immigration Politics and Policies

Immigration figures are published annually by the OECD. Immigration policy is discussed in Hollifield (2005). Integration policy is analysed in Favell (2001) and Kastoryano (2002). For a history of immigration in France, see Noiriel (1996). On the history of French Islam, see Kepel (1987). In French, books on postwar immigration policy include Weil (1991), Guiraudon (2000) and Viet (1998). The High Council for Integration publishes annual reports on immigration-related policy issues (see, for example, HCI, 1993; 1998).

Chapter 11　Economic Policy and Policy-Making

Good analyses of the postwar statist approach to economic development can be found in Shonfield (1965), Zysman (1983), Hall (1986), and Cohen and Bauer (1985). The crisis and transformation of the *dirigiste* model are covered in Cohen (1989), Levy (1999) and Schmidt (1996). Sympathetic treatments of the economic policies of the Jospin government include Pisani-Ferry (2001) and, on the new economy, Trumbull (2004). The contours and evolution of French social policy are described in Join-Lambert and Bolot-Gittler *et al.* (1997) and Palier (2002). An account of the *refondation sociale* is provided by Adam (2002). For a balanced analysis of globalization in France, see Gordon and Meunier (2001). More alarmist interpretations of globalization and France's economic situation include Forrester (1996) and Bavarez (2003). Minc (1994) and Camdessus (2004) offer a neoliberal diagnosis and prescriptions for France's economic difficulties. Finally, the conseil d'analyse économique, attached to the prime minister's office, has commissioned over fifty studies of current economic issues, which are generally of very high quality. The reports are published by *La Documentation Française* and can also be downloaded at either *www.ladocumentationfrancaise.fr* or *www.cae.gouv.fr*.

Chapter 12　Education and Educational Governance

Most of the relevant literature on this subject is in French. Van Zanten (2004) provides the best recent summary of education in France. It is rich, yet succinct. Toulemonde (2003) is a very useful edited collection. Musselin (2003) is good on higher education. In English, Howarth and Varouxakis (2003) is a good introduction, Duclaud-Williams (1993) is theoretically and empirically vigorous. Ambler (1985) and Archer (1979) are classic readings for the interested student. Corbett and Moon (1996) provides a very thorough treatment of the Mitterrand presidency. Deer (2002) is good on higher education.

Chapter 13   Gendering the Fifth Republic

For recent gender equality statistics go to *http://www.social.gouv.fr/femmes/* and see the series on 'femmes en chiffres' published by INSEE since the early 1980s. The most recent edition is INSEE (2004). A plethora of recent studies too numerous to cite here treat the issue of women's political representation. Pinochon and Derville (2004) uses the most prominent of these sources to present comprehensive data on women in all public offices under the Fifth Republic and to examine systematically the determinants of women's low presence in political life. For more information on the evolution of gender and politics issues across a wide range of issues under the Fifth Republic, Allwood and Kursheed (2004); Bard, Baudelot and Mossuz-Lavau (2004); and Jenson and Sineau (1995) are all useful. For recent work on the women's movement see Picq (1993) and Mazur (forthcoming and 1995b) and on the women's policy agencies see Mazur (1995a). For analyses of equal employment and reconciliation policies see Mazur (1995b); Laufer (2003); Heinen (2004); Reuter and Mazur (2003); on parity see Baudino (2003); on sexuality and violence see Ferrand (2004) and on sexual harassment see Saguy (2003). The Bibliothèque Marguerite Durand in Paris is entirely devoted to feminist issues and is an excellent resource for all related issues.

Chapter 14   Identities, Nationalism, Citizenship and Republican Ideology

There is a very rich literature in the field of identities, nationalism, citizenship and Republican ideology. Baudérot (2000) is a concise history of *laïcité*. Baudino (2003) is an excellent overview of the debate on parity. The question of education and citizenship is best dealt with in Déloye (1994). On identity, Duchesne and Frognier (2002) and Schild (2001) present rather different approaches. On immigration and integration, Favell (2001) and Hansen and Weil (2001) are rich accounts. On headscarves, Gaspard and Khosrokhavar (1995) is a key reference. On the French nation, the classic reference is that of Renan (1991), to which we would add Weil (2002).

Bibliography

Adam, G. (2002). *La refondation sociale à réinventer*. Paris: Editions Liaison.

Alland, A. (1994) *Crisis and Commitment: The History of a French Social Movement*. Yverdon: Gordon and Breach.

Allwood, G. and Kursheed, W. (2004) *Politics in France*. London and New York: Routledge.

Ambler, J. (1985) 'Neo-Corporatism and the Politics of French Education', *West European Politics,* vol. 8(3).

Anderson J. (1990) 'Sceptical Reflections on a Europe of the Regions: Britain, Germany and the European Regional Development Fund', *Journal of Public Policy*, vol. 10(4).

Andolfatto, D., Greffet, F. and Olivier, L. (eds) (2001) *Les partis politiques: Quelles perspectives?* Paris: L'Harmattan.

Appleton, A. (2001) 'France: Party–Group Relations in the Shadow of the State', in C. Thomas (ed.), *Political Parties and Interest Groups: Shaping Democratic Governance*. Boulder, CO: Lynne Rienner Publishers.

Appleton, A. (2000) 'The New Social Movement Phenomenon', in R. Elgie (ed.), *The Changing French Political System*. London: Frank Cass.

Archer, M. S. (1979) *Social Origins of Educational Systems*. London: Sage.

Avril, P. and Gicquel, J. (1998), *Le Conseil constitutionnel*. Paris: Montchrestien.

Baguenard, J. (1996) *Le Sénat*. Paris: Presses Universitaires de France.

Balme, R., Faure, A. and Mabileau, A. (1999) *Politiques locales et transformations de l'action publique locale en Europe*. Paris: Presses de Sciences Po.

Baraizé, F. (1996) 'L'entrée de l'enseignement supérieur dans les contrats de plan Etat-régions: La mise en réseau de la décision universitaire', in J. P. Gaudin (ed.), *La négociation des politiques contractuelles*. Paris: l'Harmattan.

Baraize, F. and Négrier, E. (eds) (2001) *L'invention politique de l'agglomération*. Paris: L'Harmattan.

Bard, C., Baudelot, C. and Mossuz-Lavau, J. (eds) (2004) *Quand les femmes s'en mêlent*. Paris: Editions de la Martinière.

Bartolini, S. (1984) 'Institutional Constraints and Party Competition in the French Party System', *West European Politics*, vol. 7(4).

Baudérot, J. (2000) *Histoire de la laïcité française*. Paris, PUF.

Baudino, C. (2003) 'Parity Reform in France: Promises and Pitfalls', *Review of Policy Research*, vol. 20(3).

Bavarez, N. (2003) *La France qui tombe*. Paris: Perrin.

Bell, D. S. (2000) *Presidential Power in Fifth Republic France*. London: Berg.

Belot, C. and Cautrès, B. (2004) 'L'Europe, invisible mais omniprésente', in B. Cautrès and N. Mayer (eds), *Le nouveau désordre électoral: Les leçons du 21 avril*. Paris: Presses de Sciences Po.

Berger, S. (2001) 'Trade and Identity: The Coming Protectionism?', in G. Flynn (ed.), *Remaking the Hexagon: The New France in the New Europe*. Boulder, CO: Westview Press.

Bernard, C. (1998) *La justice entre soumission et émancipation*. Paris: Le Monde/ Marabout.

Berstein, S. (ed.) (1999) *Les Cultures politiques en France*. Paris: Seuil.

Berthet , T. and Merle, V. (1999) *Les Régions et la formation professionnelle*. Paris: LGDJ.

Bezès, P. (2004) 'Concurrence ministérielle et différenciation, la fabrique de la réforme de l'Etat en France dans les années 1990', in F. Dreyfus and J.-M. Eymeri (eds), *Pour une sociologie politique de l'administration*. Paris: Economica.

Bezès, P. (2001) 'Defensive and Offensive Approaches to Adminstrative Reforms in France (1989–1997): The Leadership Strategy of French Prime Ministers', *Governance*, vol. 14(1).

Bigo, D. (1996) *Polices en réseaux*. Paris: Presses de Sciences Po.

Boëldieu, J. and Catherine B. (2000) 'Recensement de la population 1999. La proportion d'immigrés est stable depuis 25 ans'. *INSEE première, no.* 748, Paris: INSEE.

Borraz, O. and Le Galès, P. (2004) 'Local Government in France: Inter-communal Revolution and New Forms of Governance', in B. Denters and L. Rose (eds), *Comparing Local Governance: Trends and Developments*. Basingstoke: Palgrave.

Boy, D., Platone, F., Rey, H., Subileau, F. and Ysmal, C. (2003) *C'était la gauche plurielle*. Paris: Presses de Sciences Po.

Boy, D. and Mayer N. (2000) 'Cleavage Voting and Issue Voting in France', in M. Lewis Beck (ed.), *How France Votes*. New York: Chatham House.

Bozo, F. (1997) *La politique étrangère de la France depuis 1945*. Paris: La Découverte.

Brénac, E. (1994) 'De l'Etat producteur à l'Etat régulateur, des cheminements différenciés: L'exemple des télécommunications en France, en Allemagne et en Grande Bretagne', in B. Jobert (ed.), *Le tournant néo-libéral*. Paris: l'Harmattan.

Brubaker, R. (1992) *Citizenship and Nationhood in France and Germany*. Cambridge, MA: Harvard University Press.

Buchet de Neuilly, Y. (2001) 'Les cheminements chaotiques de la politique étrangère européenne'. Unpublished Ph.D Dissertation, University of Paris I.

Calvès, G. (1999) 'Les politiques de discrimination positive', *Problèmes politiques et sociaux*, no. 822.

Calvès G. (2002) 'Il n'y a pas de race ici': le modèle français a l'épreuve de l'intégration européenne'. *Critique Internationale* no. 17.

Camby, J.-P. and Servent, P. (2004) *Le travail parlementaire sous la Cinquième République*. Paris: Montchrestien.

Camdessus, M. (2004) *Le sursaut: Vers une nouvelle croissance pour la France*. Paris: La Documentation Française.

Capdevielle, J. (1981) *France de gauche, vote à droite*. Paris: Presses de la FNSP.

Cautrès, B. and Mayer, N. (eds) (2004) *Le nouveau désordre électoral: Les leçons du 21 avril 2002*. Paris: Presses de Sciences Po.

Champagne, P., Cottereau, Y., Dallemagne, G. and Malan, T. (1993) 'Le processus de modernisation dans l'administration de l'Education Nationale', *Politiques et Management Public*, vol. 11(1).

Charon, J.-M. and Furet, C. (2000), *Un secret si bien violé: la loi, le juge et le journaliste*. Paris: Seuil.

Chiche, J., Haegel, F. and Tiberj, V. (2004) 'Erosion et mobilités partisanes', in B. Cautrès and N. Mayer (eds), *Le nouveau désordre électoral*. Paris: Presses de Sciences Po.

Chiche, J., Haegel, F. and Tiberj, V. (2002) 'La fragmentation partisane', in G. Grunberg, N. Mayer and P. Sniderman (eds), *La démocratie à l'épreuve*. Paris: Presses de Sciences Po.

Clark, T., Lipset, S. and Rempel, M. (1993) 'The Declining Political Significance of Social Class', *International Sociology*, vol. 8(3).

Clift, B. (2003) *French Socialism in a Global Era*. London: Continuum.

CNCDH (Commission nationale consultative des Droits de l'Homme) (2004) *La lutte contre le racisme et la xenophobie: rapport d'activité 2003*. Paris: La Documentation française.

Cohen, E. (1992) *Le Colbertisme 'high tech': Economie des Telecom et du Grand Projet*. Paris: Hachette.

Cohen, E. (1989) *L'Etat brancardier: Politiques du déclin industriel (1974–1984)*. Paris: Calmann-Lévy.

Cohen, E. and Bauer, M. (1985) *Les grandes manoeuvres industrielles*. Paris: Belfond.

Cohen, S. (1977) *Modern Capitalist Planning: The French Model*. Berkeley, CA: University of California Press.

Cole, A. (1998, 2005) *French Politics and Society*. London: Prentice-Hall.

Cole, A. (2001) 'The New Governance of French Education', *Public Administration*, vol. 79(3).

Cole, A. (1993) 'The Presidential Party and the Fifth Republic', *West European Politics*, vol. 16(2).

Cole, A. and John, P. (2001) *Local Governance in England and France*. London: Routledge.

Collectif pour les Droits des Femmes (2003) *De nouveaux défis pour le féminisme: Forum du Collectif pour les Droits des Femmes, 9–10 mar 2002*. Pantin, Le Temps des Cerises.

Commission de la nationalité (1998) *Être Français aujourd'hui et demain*. Paris: La Documentation française.

Constantinho, P. and Dony, M. (1995) *Le droit communautaire*. Paris: Armand Colin.

Converse, P. (1966) 'The Concept of a Normal Vote', in A. Campbell *et al.* (eds), *Elections and the Political Order*. New York: John Wiley.

Corbett, A. and Moon, J. (eds) (1996) *Education Policy in France Under Mitterrand*. London: Routledge.

Costa, J.-P. (1993) *Le Conseil d'Etat dans la société contemporaine*. Paris: Économica.

Crettiez, X. and Sommier, I. (eds) (2002) *La France Rebelle: Tous les foyers, mouvements et acteurs de la contestation*. Paris: Michalon.

Daley, A. (1996) *Steel, State, and Labor: Mobilization and Adjustment in France*. Pittsburgh, PA: University of Pittsburgh Press.

Dalton, R., McAllister, I. and Wattenberg, M. (2002) 'Political Parties and their Publics', in K. Luther and F. Muller-Rommel (eds), *Political Parties in the New Europe: Political and Analytical Challenge*. Oxford: Oxford University Press.

Dalton, R., Flanagan, S. and Beck, P. (1984) *Electoral Change in Advanced Industrial Democracies: Realignment or Dealignment?* Princeton: Princeton University Press.

DARES (December 2000) *La politique de l'emploi en 1999*. Paris: Direction de l'Animation de la Recherche, des Etudes et des Statistiques.

DARES (1996) *40 ans de politique de l'emploi*. Paris: Direction de l'Animation de la Recherche, des Etudes et des Statistiques.

Deer, C. (2002) *Higher Education in England and France since the 1980s*. Oxford: Symposium Books.

Déloye, Y. (1994) *Ecole et citoyenneté*. Paris: Presses de la FNSP.

Dolez, B. and Laurent, A. (2000) 'Quand les militants du RPR élisent leur président (20 novembre–4 décembre 1999)', *Revue française de science politique*, vol. 50(1).

Donégani, J.-M. (1993) *La liberté de choisir: Pluralisme religieux et pluralisme politique dans le catholicisme français contemporain*. Paris: Presses de la FNSP.

Donégani, J.-M. and Sadoun, M. (1998) *La Ve République: Naissance et mort*. Paris: Calmann-Lévy.

Dreyfus, F. (ed.) (2000) *Nouveaux partis, nouveaux enjeux*. Paris: Presses de la Sorbonne.

Duchen, C. (1986) *Feminism in France: From May '68 to Mitterrand*. London: Routledge.

Duchesne, S. (1997) *Citoyenneté à la française*. Paris: Presses de Sciences Po.

Duchesne, S. and Frognier, A.-P. (2002) 'Sur les Dynamiques sociologiques et politiques de l'identification à l'Europe', *Revue Française de Science Politique*, vol. 52(4).

Duchesne, S. and Frognier, A.-P. (1994) 'Is there a European Identity?', in O. Niedermayer and R. Sinnott (eds), *Public Opinion and the International Governance*. Oxford: Oxford University Press.

Duclaud-Williams, R. (1993) 'The Governance of Education in Britain and France', in J. Kooiman (ed.), *Modern Governance*. London: Sage.

Duhamel, O. (2002) *Vive la VIe République*. Paris: Seuil.

Duhamel, O. (1999), *Le pouvoir politique en France*. Paris: Seuil.

Duhamel, O. and Grunberg, G. (2001) 'Système de partis et Vèmes Républiques', *Commentaire*, vol. 24(95).

Duhamel, O. and Méchet, P. (1996) 'Une grève d'opinion', in SOFRES, *L'état de l'opinion*. Paris: Seuil.

Dumez, H. and Jeunemaitre, A. (1993) 'Les Privatisations en France, 1986–1992' in Wright, V. (ed.) *Les Privatisations en Europe*, Actes Sud, Paris.

Dumont, L. (1991) *L'idéologie allemande: France-Allemagne et retour*. Paris: Gallimard.

Duran, P. and Thoenig, J.-C. (1996) 'L'Etat et la gestion publique territoriale', *Revue Française de Science Politique*, vol. 44(4).

Dutercq. Y. (2003) 'La Politique française de décentralisation en éducation: bilan et perspectives', *Regards sur l'Actualité*, no. 293.

Duverger, M. (1978) *Echec au roi*. Paris: Albin Michel.

Duyvendak, J.-W. (1995) *The Power of Politics: New Social Movements in France*. Boulder, CO: Westview.

Dyson, K. (1980) *The State Tradition in Western Europe*. Oxford: Martin Robertson.

Edelman, M. (1985) *The Symbolic Uses of Politics*. Urbana: University of Illinois Press.

Elgie, R. and Griggs, S. (2000) *Debates in French Politics*. London: Routledge.

Espinasse. M.-T. and Laporte. C. (1999) *Des contrats d'agglomération aux contrats locaux pour l'accueil et l'intégration. Notes et Documents 44*. Paris: Direction de la Population et des Migrations.

Esping-Andersen, G. (1990) *The Three Worlds of Welfare Capitalism*. Princeton: Princeton University Press.

Evans, J. (2004a) 'Ideology and Party Identification: A Normalisation of French Voting Anchors?', in M. Lewis-Beck (ed.), *The French Voter: Before and After the 2002 Elections*. Basingstoke: Palgrave.

Evans, J. (2004b) *Voters and Voting: an Introduction*. London: Sage.

Evans, J. (ed.) (2003) *The French Party System*. Manchester: Manchester University Press.

Evans, J. (2000) 'Le vote gaucholepéniste: Le masque extrême d'une dynamique normale', *Revue Française de Science Politique*, vol. 50(1).

Evans, G. (1999) 'Conclusion', in G. Evans (ed.), *The End of Class Politics?* Oxford: Oxford University Press.

Eymeri, J.-M. (2002) 'Définir "la position de la France" dans l'Union européenne: La médiation interministerielle des généralistes du SGCI', in O. Nay and A. Smith (eds), *Le gouvernement du compromis: Courtiers et généralistes dans l'action politique*. Paris: Economica.

Fanachi, P. (1995) *La justice administrative*. Paris: Presses Universitaires de France.

Fassin, D. (2002) 'L'invention française de la discrimination'. *Revue française de science politique* 52(4).

Faucher-King, F. and Treille, E. (2003) 'Managing Intra-party Democracy: Comparing the French Socialist and British Labour Conferences', *French Politics*, vol. 1(1).

Faugère, J.-P. and Voisin, C. (1994) *Le système financier français: Crises et mutations*. Luçon: Nathan.

Faure A. (ed.) (1997) *Territoires et subsidiarité*. Paris: l'Harmattan.

Faure, A. and Smith, A. (1998) 'Que changent les politiques communautaires?', *Pouvoirs Locaux*, no. 40.

Favell, A. (2001) *Philosophies of Integration: Immigration and the Idea of Citizenship in France and Britain*. Basingstoke: Palgrave.

Favier, P. and Martin-Rolland, M. (1990, 1991, 1996, 1999) *La Décennie Mitterrand*. Paris: Seuil, 4 vols: I: *Les ruptures*, 1990; II: *Les épreuves*, 1991; III: *Les défis*, 1996; IV: *Les déchirements*, 1999.

Favoreu, L. and Philip, L. (2003) *Les grandes décisions du Conseil constitutionnel*, 8th edn. Paris: Sirey.

Ferrand, M. (2004) 'L'Etat, les lois du sexe et le genre', in C. Bard, C. Baudelot and J. Mossuz-Lavau (eds), *Quand les femmes s'en mêlent*.

Fitoussi, J.-P. (1995). *Le débat interdit: Monnaie, Europe, pauvreté*. Paris: Arléa.

Fixari, D. and Kletz, F. (1996) 'Pilotage d'établissement scolaire: auto-évaluation et évaluation', *Politiques et Management Public*, vol. 14(2).

Forrester, V. (1996) *L'horreur économique*. Paris: Fayard.

Fouilleux, E. (2003) *Idées, institutions et dynamiques du changement de politique publique: Les transformations de la politique agricole commune*. Paris: l'Harmattan.

Fouilleux, E., de Maillard, J. and Smith, A. (2002) 'Council Working Groups: Their Role in the Production of European Problems and Policies', in G. Schaefer (ed.), *Committees in EU Governance*, report to the European Commission.

Franklin, M., Mackie, T. and Valen, H. (1992) *Electoral Change: Response to Evolving Social and Attitudinal Structures in Western Countries*. Cambridge: Cambridge University Press.

Frears, J. (1990) 'The French Parliament: Loyal Workhorse, Poor Watchdog', *West European Politics*, vol. 13(3).

Gaspard, F. and Khosrokhavar, F. (1995) *Le foulard et la république*. Paris: La Découverte.

Gaudin, J.-P. (1999) *Gouverner par contrat: L'action publique en question*. Paris: Presses de Sciences Po.

Geddes, A. and Guiraudon. V. (2004) 'The Emergence of a European Union Policy Paradigm amidst Contrasting National Models: Britain, France and EU Anti-Discrimination Policy', *West European Politics* 27(2).

Gilbert, G. and Thoenig, J.-C. (1999) 'Les cofinancements publics – des pratiques aux rationalités', *Revue d'Economie Financière*, no. 1.

Glaude, M. and Borrel, C. (2002) 'Immigrés et marché du travail: regard statistique', in Commissariat Général du Plan, *Immigration, marché du travail, intégration. Rapport du séminaire présidé par François Héran*. Paris: la Documentation française.

Gordon, P. (1996) *Relations Internationales et Stratégiques*, no. 22.

Gordon, P. (1996) 'A travers les colloques', *Relations Internationales et Stratégiques*, no. 22, p. 168.

Gordon, P. and Meunier, S. (2001) *The French Challenge: Adapting to Globalization*. Washington, DC: Brookings Institution.

Gregory, S. (2000) *French Defence Policy into the Twenty-First Century*. Basingstoke: Palgrave.

Groux, G. and Mouriaux, R. (1990) *Le cas français: Les syndicats européens à l'épreuve*. In G. Bibes and R. Mouriaux. Paris: Press de la FNSP: 49–68.

Grunberg, G. and Schweisguth, E. (1997) 'Vers une tripartition de l'espace politique', in D. Boy and N. Mayer (eds), *L'électeur a ses raisons*. Paris: Presses de Sciences Po.

Guiraudon. V. (2000) *Les politiques d'immigration d'immigration en Europe*. Paris: L'Harmattan.

Guiraudon, V. (2003) 'The Constitution of a European Immigration Policy Domain: a Political Sociology Approach', *Journal of European Public Policy*, vol. 10(2).

Guyomarch, A. (2000) 'The Europeanization of Policy-Making', in A. Guyomarch, H. Machin, P. Hall and J. Hayward (eds), *Developments in French Politics 2*. London: Palgrave.

Haegel, F. (2004) 'The Transformation of the French Right: Institutional Imperatives and Organizational Changes', *French Politics*, vol. 2(3).

Haegel, F. (2002) 'Faire l'union: La refondation des partis de droite après les élections de 2002', *Revue française de science politique*, vol. 52(5–6).

Hall, P. (1990) 'The State and the Market', in P. Hall, J. Hayward and H. Machin (eds), *Developments in French Politics*. London: Macmillan, pp. 171–87.

Hall, P. (1986) *Governing the Economy: The Politics of State Intervention in Britain and France*. New York: Oxford University Press.

Hansen, R. and Weil, P. (2001) *Towards a European Nationality: Citizenship, Immigration and Nationality Law in the EU*. Basingstoke: Palgrave.

Hayward, J. and Wright, V. (2002) *Governing from the Centre: Core Executive Coordination in France*. Oxford: Oxford University Press.

Hazareesingh, S. (1994) *Political Traditions in Modern France*. Oxford: Oxford University Press.

HCI (Haut Conseil à l'Intégration) (1993) *L'intégration à la française*. Paris: La Documentation française.

HCI (Haut Conseil à l'Intégration) (1998) *Lutte contre les discriminations: faire respecter les principes d'egalité.* Rapport au Premier ministre. Paris: La Documentation française.

HCI (Haut Conseil à l'Intégration) (2004) *Le contrat et l'intégration. Rapport au Premier ministre.* Paris: la Documentation française.

Heinen, J. (2004) 'Genre et politiques familiales', in Bard, Baudelot and Mossuz-Lavau, *Quand les femmes s'en mêlent.*

Hollifield, J. (2005) *Immigration and the Nation-State: Searching for a National Model is under contract.* New York: Routledge.

Hout, M., Brooks, C. and Manza, J. (1993) 'The Persistence of Classes in Post-industrial Societies', *International Sociology,* vol. 8(3).

Howarth , D. and Varouxakis, G. (2003) *Contemporary France: An Introduction to French Politics and Society.* London: Edward Arnold.

Howell, C. (1992a) 'The Dilemmas of Post-Fordism: Socialists, Flexibility, and Labor Market Deregulation in France', *Politics & Society,* vol. 20(1).

Howell, C. (1992b). *Regulating Labor: The State and Industrial Relations Reform in Postwar France.* Princeton: Princeton University Press.

Howorth, J. (1997) 'France', in J. Howorth and A. Menon, *The European Union and National Defence Policy.* London: Routledge.

Huber, E. and Stephens, J. (2001) *Development and Crisis of the Welfare State: Parties and Policies in Global Markets.* Chicago: University of Chicago Press.

Ignazi, P. (1992) 'The Silent Counter-Revolution: Hypotheses on the Emergence of Extreme Right-Wing Parties in Western Europe', *European Journal of Political Research,* vol. 22(1).

Ikenberry, J. (2003) 'Conclusion', in J. Ikenberry and J. Hall (eds), *The Nation State in Question,* Princeton: Princeton University Press.

Inglehart, R. (1977) *The Silent Revolution: Changing Values and Political Styles among Western Publics.* Princeton: Princeton University Press.

INSEE (2004) *Femmes et hommes: Regards sur la parité.* Paris: INSEE.

IPSOS (2002) *Sondage sortie d'urnes* (Exit Poll survey by phone on election day). 21 April 2002. Paris: IPSOS.

Irondelle, B. (2002) 'Europeanization without European Union? French Military Reforms, 1991–1996', *Journal of European Public Policy,* vol. 10(2).

Jacquet, S. and Woll, C. (eds) (2004) *Les usages de l'Europe: Acteurs et transformations européennes.* Paris: l'Harmattan.

Jennings, J. (2000) 'Citizenship, Republicanism and Multiculturalism in Contemporary France', *British Journal of Political Science,* vol. 30, (1).

Jenson, J. and Sineau, M. (1995) *Mitterrand et les françaises: un rendez-vous manqué.* Paris: Presses de la FNSP.

Joana, J. and Smith, A. (2004) 'Changing French Military Procurement Policy'. Paper presented at the congress of the British Political Science Association, Lincoln, April.

Joana, J. and Smith, A. (2002) *Les commissaires européens: Technocrates, diplomates ou politiques?* Paris: Presses de Sciences Po.

Jobert, B. (ed.) (1994) *Le tournant néo-libéral.* Paris: l'Harmattan.

Join-Lambert, M.-T. and Bolot-Gittler, A. (1997) *Politiques sociales.* Paris: Presses de la FNSP.

Kastoryano. R. (2002) *Negotiating Identities: States and Immigrants in France and Germany.* Princeton: Princeton University Press.

Katzenstein, P. (ed.) (1978) *Between Power and Plenty: Foreign Economic Policies of Advanced Industrial States*. Madison: University of Wisconsin Press.

Keck, M. E. and Sikkink, K. (1998) *Activists Beyond Borders*. Ithaca: Cornell University Press.

Keiger, J. F. V. (2001) *France and the World Since 1870*. Oxford: Oxford University Press.

Keiger, J. F. V. and Alexander, M. S. (1999) 'Defending France: Foreign Policy and the Quest for Security, 1850s-1990s', in M. S. Alexander (ed.), *French History since Napoleon*. London: Arnold.

Kepel, G. (1987) *Les banlieues de l'Islam*. Paris: Seuil.

Kimmel, A. (1991) *L'Assemblée Nationale sous la Cinquième République*. Paris: Presses de la FNSP.

Kitschelt, H. with McGann, A. (1995) *The Radical Right in Western Europe: A Comparative Analysis*. Ann Arbor: University of Michigan Press.

Knapp, A. (2004) *Parties and the Party System in France: A Disconnected Democracy*. Basingstoke: Palgrave.

Labbé, D. and Croisat, M. (1992) *La fin des syndicats?* Paris: L'Harmattan.

Laufer, J. (2003) 'Equal Employment Policy in France: Symbolic Support and a Mixed Record', *Review of Policy Research* vol. 20(3).

Lavabre, M.-C. and Platone, F. (2003) *Que reste-t-il du PCF?* Paris: Autrement.

Lebon, A. (2003). *Migrations et nationalité en France en 2001*. Paris: La Documentation française.

Leca, J. (1983) 'Questions sur la citoyenneté', *Projet*, no. 171-2.

Lefebvre, R. (2004) 'Le socialisme français soluble dans l'institution municipale', *Revue française de science politique*, vol. 54(2).

Le Lidec, P. (2001) *Les maires dans la République. L'associaiton des maires de France, élément constitutif des régimes politiques depuis 1907*. PhD thesis, University of Paris 1

Le Pape, Y. and Smith, A. (1999) 'Regionalizations and Agricultures: Rhône-Alpes and Pays de la Loire Compared', *Regional and Federal Studies*, vol. 9(2).

Lequesne, C. (1993) *Paris-Bruxelles*. Paris: Presses de la FNSP.

Levy, J. (2000) 'France: Directing Adjustment?', in F. Scharpf and V. Schmidt (eds), *Welfare and Work in the Open Economy: Diverse Responses to Common Challenges*. Oxford: Oxford University Press.

Levy, J. (1999) *Tocqueville's Revenge: State, Society, and Economy in Contemporary France*. Cambridge: Harvard University Press.

Levy, A. and Levy, L. (2004) *Des filles comme les autres: Au-delà du foulard*. Paris: La Découverte.

Lewis, J. (1998) 'Is the 'Hard-Bargaining' Image of the Council Misleading? The COREPER and the Local Elections Directive', *Journal of Common Market Studies*, vol. 36(4).

Lewis-Beck, M. and Nadeau, R. (2003) 'Dual Governance and Economic Voting: France and the United States', in Michael S. Lewis-Beck (ed.), *The French Voter. Before and After the 2002 Elections*. London: Palgrave.

Lijphart, A. (1978) 'Religious v Linguistic v Class Voting: The "Crucial Experiment" of Comparing Belgium, Canada, South Africa and Switzerland', *American Political Science Review*, vol. 73(2).

Lipset, S. and Rokkan, S. (eds) (1967) *Party Systems and Voter Alignment: Cross-National Perspectives*. New York: the Free Press.

Loriaux, M. (1991) *France after Hegemony: International Change and Financial Reform*. Ithaca: Cornell University Press.

Lorrain, D. (1991) 'De l'Administration républicaine au gouvernement urbain', *Socologie du Travail*, vol. 4.

Lorrain, D. (2000) 'Le gouvernement municipal en France un modèle d'intégration en recomposition'. *Pôle Sud*, no. 13.

Mair, P. and van Biezen, I. (2001) 'Party Membership in Twenty European Democracies', *Party Politics* vol. 7(1).

Majone, G. (1995) *La communauté européenne, un Etat régulateur*. Paris: Montchrétien.

Manza, J. and Brooks C. (1999) *Social Cleavages and Political Change: Voter Alignments and US Party Coalitions*. Oxford and New York: Oxford University Press.

Maus, D. (1996) *Le parlement sous la Ve République*. Paris: Presses Universitaires de France.

Mayer, N. (2002) *Ces Français qui votent Le Pen*. Paris: Flammarion.

Mayer, N. (1996) 'La fierté d'être Français, de l'indépendance algérienne à Maastricht', *L'année sociologique*, vol. 46(1).

Mayer, N. (1986) *La boutique contre la gauche*. Paris: Presses de Sciences Po.

Mazur, Amy G. (1995a) 'Strong State and Symbolic Reform in France: le Ministère des Droits de la Femme'. In D. McBride and A. Mazur (eds), *Comparative State Feminism*. Thousand Oaks, CA: Sage.

Mazur, A. (1995b) *Gender Bias and the State: Symbolic Reform at Work in Fifth Republic France*. Pittsburgh: University of Pittsburgh Press.

Méda, D. (1999) *Qu'est-ce que la richesse?* Paris: Flammarion.

Menon, A. (2001) ' L'administration française à Bruxelles', *Revue française de science politique*, vol. 51(5).

Menon, A. (2002) 'Playing with Fire: The European Union's Defence Policy', *Politique européenne*, no. 8.

Meynaud, J. (1962) *Les groupes de pression en France*. Paris: Librairie Armand Colin.

Michelat, G. and Simon, M. (2004) *Les Ouvriers et la politique: Permanence, ruptures, réalignements*. Paris: Presses de Sciences Po.

Michelat, G. and Simon, M. (1977a) *Classe, religion et comportement politique*. Paris: Presses de la FNSP.

Michelat, G. and Simon, M. (1977b), 'Religion, Class, and Politics', *Comparative Politics*, vol. 10(1).

Minc, A. (1994). *La France de l'an 2000*. Paris: La Documentation Française.

Ministry of Finance (2001) *Projet de loi de finances pour 2002*. Paris: Ministry of the Economy, Finance, and Industry.

Mischi, J. (2003) 'La recomposition identitaire du PCF', *Communisme*, no. 72–3.

Miura, M. (2002a). 'From Welfare through Work to Lean Work: The Politics of Labor Market Reform in Japan' Unpublished PhD Dissertation, Department of Political Science, University of California Berkeley.

Miura, M. (2002b). *Playing without a Net: Employment Maintenance Policy and the Underdevelopment of the Social Safety Net*. Annual Meeting of the American Political Science Association, Boston, MA, 29 August–1 September 2002.

Mossuz-Lavau, J. (1998) *Femmes/hommes. Pour la parité*. Paris: Presses de Sciences Po.

Muller, P. (1998) *Les politiques publiques*. Paris: PUF.

Muller, P. (1984) *Le technocrate et le paysan*. Paris: Economie et humanisme.

Musselin, C. (2003) 'L'Evolution des universités depuis vingt ans', *Regards sur l'Actualité*, no. 293.

Nicolet, C. (1982) *L'idée républicaine en France, 1789–1924 : essai d'histoire critique*. Paris: Gallimard.

Nora, P. (ed.) (1984–1992) *Les lieux de Mémoire* (vol. I, *La République*, vol. II, *La nation*, vol. III, *Les France*). Paris: Gallimard.

Noiriel, G. (1996) *The French Melting Pot Immigration, Citizenship and National Identity*. Minneapolis: University of Minnesota Press.

OECD (2003) *Trends in International Migration 2003*. Paris: OECD.

OECD (2002) *OECD Statistics Database: Total Social Expenditures*, URL: *http://oecdnt.ingenta.com*.

OECD (2000) *OECD Health Data*. Paris.

Olivier, L. (2003) 'Ambiguïté de la démocratisation partisane en France (PS, RPR, UMP)', *Revue française de science politique*, vol. 53(5).

Palier, B. (2002) *Gouverner la Sécurité Sociale*. Paris: Presses de la FNSP.

Palier, B. (1999) 'Réformer la sécurité sociale: Les interventions gouvernementales en matière de protection sociale depuis 1945, la France en perspective comparative', unpublished paper Institut d'Etudes Politiques de Paris.

Perrineau, P. (ed.) (2001) *Les croisés de la société fermée*. La Tour d'Aigues: Les Editions de l'Aube.

Perrineau, P. (1997) *Le Symptôme Le Pen: Radiographie des électeurs du Front national*. Paris: Fayard.

Picq, F. (1993) *Libération des femmes: les années- mouvement*. Paris: Seuil.

Pinochon, S. and Derville, G. (2003) *Les femmes en politiques*. Grenoble: Presses Universitaires de Grenoble.

Pinson, G. and Vion, A. (2000) 'L'internationalisation des villes comme objet d'expertise', *Pôle Sud*, no. 13.

Pisani-Ferry, J. (2001) *La bonne aventure: Le plein emploi, le marché, et la gauche*. Paris: La Découverte.

Pisier, E. (2001) 'Parité', in P. Perrineau and D. Reynié (eds), *Le Dictionnaire du vote*. Paris: PUF.

Pollitt, C. and Bouckaert, G. (2000) *Public Management Reform: A Comparative Analysis*. Oxford: Oxford University Press.

Polanyi, K. (1944) *The Great Transformation*. Boston, MA: Beacon.

Pouvoirs, no. 64, 1993, 'Le parlement'; no. 91, 1999, 'La cohabitation'; no. 92, 2000, 'La responsabilité des gouvernants'; no. 99, 2001, 'La nouvelle Ve République'.

Prudhomme-Leblanc, C. (2002) *Un ministère français face à l'Europe*. Paris: l'Harmattan.

Radaelli, C. (2001) 'The Domestic Impact of European Union Public Policy: Notes on Concepts, Methods and the Challenge of Empirical Research', *Politique européenne*, no. 5.

Raffarin, J.-P. (2003) *Discours lors du vingtième anniversaire de la marche pour l'égalité. 03-12-2003*. Paris: Site du premier ministre, http:/www.premier-ministre.gouv.fr.

Raffarin, J.-P. (2002) *Pour une nouvelle gouvernance*. Paris: Archipel.

Rassat, M.-L.(1996), *La justice en France*. Paris: PUF.

Rémond, R. (1985) *L'anticléricalisme en France de 1815 à nos jours*. Bruxelles: Complexe.

Renan, E. (1991) *Qu'est-ce qu'une nation? et autres essais politiques*. Paris: Presses Pocket.

Reuter, S. and Mazur, A. (2003) 'Paradoxes of Gender-biased Universalism in the Dynamics of French Equality Discourse', in U. Liebert (ed.), *Europeanisation and Gender Equality: Reframing Public Policy in EU Member States*. Bruxelles: Peter Lang.

Revue de Droit Public, (1998) 'Les 40 ans de la Ve République'. Special issue, May–June.

Revue française de science politique (2001) 'Les carrières militantes'. Special issue, vol. 51, no. 1–2.

Rey, H. (2004) *La Gauche et les classes populaires: Histoire et actualité d'une mésentente*. Paris: Presses de Sciences Po.

Rhodes, M. (2001) 'The Political Economy of Social Pacts: "Competitive Corporatism" and European Welfare Reform', in P. Pierson (ed.), *The New Politics of the Welfare State*. Oxford: Oxford University Press.

Rivaud, P. (2001) 'Leadership et gouvernance communautaire: la Commission européenne et l'idée de service universel des télécommunications (1987–98)', Unpublished Ph.D thesis, Institut d'Etudes Politiques, Paris.

Robineau, Y. and Truchet, D. (1994), *Le Conseil d'Etat*. Paris: PUF.

Rosanvallon, P. (1992) *Le Sacre du citoyen. Histoire du suffrage universel en France*. Paris: Gallimard.

Rosanvallon, P. (1990) *L'Etat en France de 1789 à nos jours*. Paris: Le Seuil.

Rouban, L. (1998) *La fin des technocrates*. Paris: Presses de Sciences Po.

Rozenberg, O. (2004) 'Du non-usage de l'Europe par les parlementaires nationaux : la ratification des traités européens à l'Assemblée nationale', in S. Jacquet and C. Woll (eds), *Les usages de l'Europe: Acteurs et transformations européennes*. Paris: l'Harmattan.

Safran, W. (2002) ' Pluralism and Multiculturalism in France: Post-Jacobin Transformation', *Political Science Quarterly*, vol. 118(3).

Saguy, A. C. (2003) *What is Sexual Harassment? From Capitol Hill to the Sorbonne*. Berkeley: University of California Press.

Sandholtz, W. (1998) 'The Emergence of a Supranational Telecommunications Regime', in W. Sandholtz and A. Stone Sweet (eds), *European Integration and Supranational Governance*. Oxford: Oxford University Press.

Sartori, G. (1976) *Parties and Party Systems*. Cambridge: Cambridge University Press.

Sauger, N. (2004) 'Entre survie, impasse et renouveau : des difficultés persistances du centrisme français', *Revue Française de science politique*, vol. 54(4).

Scharpf, F. and Schmidt, V. (eds) (2000) *Welfare and Work in the Open Economy: From Vulnerability to Competitiveness*. Oxford: Oxford University Press.

Schild, J. (2001) ' National versus European Identities? French and German in the European Multi-Level System', *Journal of Common Market Studies*, vol. 39(2).

Schmidt, V. (1997) 'Economic Policy, Political Discourse, and Democracy in France', *French Politics and Society*, vol. 15(2).

Schmidt, V. (1996) *From State to Market? The Transformation of French Business and Government*. New York: Cambridge University Press.

Schnapper, D. (1994) *La Communauté des citoyens: Sur l'idée moderne de nation.* Paris: Gallimard.

Schrameck, O. (2001) *Matignon Rive Gauche 1997–2001.* Paris: Seuil.

Services des droits des femmes (2004) 'Chiffre Clés: L'égalité entre les femmes et les hommes'. Downloaded from *http://www.social.gouv.fr/femmes/*

Servolin C. (1989) *L'agriculture moderne.* Paris: Seuil.

Shonfield, A. (1965) *Modern Capitalism: The Changing Balance of Public and Private Power.* Oxford: Oxford University Press.

Sicard, A. (1995) 'L'impact du droit communautaire de l'environnement en France'. Unpublished PhD thesis: University of Nantes.

Silberman, R. (2002) 'Les enfants d'immigres sur le marché du travail: les mécanismes d'une discrimination sélective', in Commissariat Général du Plan, *Immigration, marché du travail, intégration. Rapport du séminaire présidé par François Héran.* Paris la Documentation française.

Sineau, M. (2004) 'Les paradoxes du *gender gap* à la française', in B. Cautrès and N. Mayer (eds), *Le nouveau désordre électoral. Les leçons du 21 avril 2002.* Paris: Presses de Sciences Po.

Smith, A. (2004) *Le gouvernement de l'Union européenne: Une sociologie politique.* Paris: LGDJ.

Smith, A. (1995) *L'Europe au miroir du local: Les fonds structurels et les zones rurales en France, en Espagne et au Royaume Uni.* Paris: L'Harmattan.

Smith, M. (1998) 'Rules, Transgovernmentalism and the Expansion of European Political Cooperation', in W. Sandholtz and A. Stone Sweet (eds), *European Integration and Supranational Governance.* Oxford: Oxford University Press.

SOFRES (1987–2004) *L'état de l'opinion.* Paris: Seuil.

Sorbets, C. and Smith, A. (2003) *Le leadership politique et le territoire: les cadres d'analyse en débat.* Rennes: Presses Universitaires de Rennes.

Soysal, Y. (2002) 'Locating Europe', *European Society.* vol. 4(3).

Stirn, B. (1994) *Le Conseil d'État: son rôle, sa jurisprudence.* Paris: Hachette.

Stoffaës, C. (1984) *Politique industrielle.* Paris: Les Cours de Droit.

Stevens, A. (2004) *The Government and Politics of France.* London: Palgrave (3rd edition).

Stone, A. (1992) *The Birth of Judicial Politics in France: The Constitutional Council in Comparative Perspective.* Oxford: Oxford University Press.

Suleiman, E. (1974) *Power, Politics and Bureaucracy in France: The Administrative Elite.* Princeton: Princeton University Press.

Tarrow, S. (1994) *Power in Movement: Social Movements and Contentious Politics.* Cambridge: Cambridge University Press.

Teinturier, B. (2004) 'Les Français et la politique: entre désenchantement et colère', SOFRES, *L'état de l'opinion.* Paris: Seuil.

Thatcher, M. (2001) 'The Commission and National Governments as Partners: EC Regulatory Expansion in Telecommunications 1979–2000', *Journal of European Public Policy*, vol. 8(4).

Thélot, C. (1994) 'L'évaluation du système éducatif français', *Revue Française de Pédagogie*, no. 107.

Thody, P. (1998) *The Fifth French Republic: Presidents, Politics and Personalities.* London: Routledge.

Tiberj, V. (2004) 'Compétence et repérages politiques en France et aux Etats-Unis: une contribution au modèle de l'électeur raisonnant', *Revue française de science politique*, vol. 54(2).

Tilly, C. (1986) *The Contentious French: Four Centuries of Popular Struggle*. Cambridge: Harvard University Press.

Titmuss, R. (1987) 'Welfare State and Welfare Society', in B. Abel-Smith and K. Titmuss. *The Philosophy of Welfare: Selected Writings of Richard Titmuss*. London: Allen & Unwin.

Toulemonde, B. (ed.) (2003) *Le système éducatif en France*. Paris: Documentation Française.

Traïni, C. (2003) *Les braconniers de la République*. Paris: PUF.

Tribalat, M. (1995) *Faire France. Enquête sur les immigrés et leurs enfants*. Paris: La Découverte.

Trumbull, G. (2004). *Silicon and the State: French Innovation Policy in the Internet Age*. Washington, DC: Brookings Institution.

Uggla, F. (2003) 'Global Demands and National Opportunities: ATTAC in France and Sweden', unpublished manuscript.

Van Ruymbeke, R. (1996) *Le juge d'instruction*. Paris: PUF.

Van Zanten, A. (2004) *Les Politiques de l'Education*. Paris: PUF.

Venel, N. (1999) *Musulmanes Françaises: Des pratiquantes voilées à l'Université*. Paris: L'Harmattan.

Verrier, B. (1999) 'Chronique d'une rupture de "Socialisme et République" au "Mouvement des citoyens"', *Politix*, no. 45.

Viet, V. (1998) *La France immigrée. Construction d'une politique 1914–1997*. Paris: Fayard.

Wahl, N., and Quermonne, J.-L. (1995) *La France présidentielle. L'influence du suffrage universel sur la vie politique*. Paris: Presses de Sciences Po.

Walzer, M. (1989) 'Citizenship', in T. Ball, J. Farr and R. L. Hanson, *Political Innovation and Conceptual Change*. Cambridge: Cambridge University Press.

Waters, S. (1998) 'New Social Movement Politics in France: The Rise of Civic Forms of Mobilization', *West European Politics*, vol. 21(3).

Weil, P. (1991) *La France et ses étrangers. L'Aventure d'une politique de l'immigration, 1938–1991*. Paris: Calmann-Lévy.

Weil, P. (2002) *Qu'est-ce qu'un Français? Histoire de la nationalité française depuis la Révolution*. Paris: Grasset.

Whiteside, K. (2003) 'French Regulatory Republicanism and the Risks of Genetically Engineered Crops', *French Politics*, vol. 1(1).

Wieviorka, M. (ed.) (1997) *Une société fragmentée? Le multiculturalisme en debat*. Paris: La Découverte.

Williams, P. M. (1964) *Crisis and Compromise: Politics in the French Fourth Republic*. London: Longman.

Williams, P. (1969) *The French Parliament, 1958–1967*. London: George Allen & Unwin.

Wilson, F. (1987) *Interest-Group Politics in France*. New York: Cambridge University Press.

Wolfreys, J. (2001) 'Shoes, Lies and Videotape: Corruption and the French State', *Modern and Contemporary France*, vol. 9(4).

Young, I. M. (1990) *Justice and The Politics and Difference*. Princeton: Princeton University Press.

Zerah, D. (1993) *Le système financier français: Dix ans de mutations*. Paris: La Documentation Française.

Zappi, S. (2003) 'Immigration: le virage à droite'. *Le Monde*, 29 April.

Zysman, J. (1983) *Governments, Markets, and Growth: Financial Systems and the Politics of Industrial Change*. Ithaca: Cornell University Press.

Index